*The Julian Jaynes Collection*

# THE
# JULIAN JAYNES
# COLLECTION

Edited by

Marcel Kuijsten

Julian Jaynes Society

First Julian Jaynes Society Softcover Edition 2018

Library of Congress Cataloging-in-Publication Data

Kuijsten, Marcel
The Julian Jaynes Collection
Includes index with bibliographical references.
1. Consciousness. 2. Consciousness—History. 3. Psychology.
ISBN: 978-0-9790744-2-4 (hardcover)
ISBN: 978-0-9790744-4-8 (softcover)
Library of Congress Control Number: 2011938615


Cover design by Marcel Kuijsten

Cover photograph of Julian Jaynes taken by Roger Ressmeyer on September 29, 1981. © Roger Ressmeyer / CORBIS

Brain scan showing right and left temporal lobe activation during auditory hallucinations from Renaud Jardri, D. Pins, C. Delmaire, J-L. Goeb, and P. Thomas, "Activation of Bilateral Auditory Cortex During Verbal Hallucinations in A Child with Schizophrenia," *Molecular Psychology*, 2007, Vol. 12, 319. © 2007 Nature Publishing Group. Reprinted with permission.

Julian Jaynes Society
Henderson, NV
julianjaynes.org

Printed in the United States of America

# CONTENTS

## PART III
*Interviews*

## PART IV
*Discussion*

*The Julian Jaynes Collection*

# Introduction

## Marcel Kuijsten

IN JANUARY OF 1977, Julian Jaynes released to the world his book *The Origin of Consciousness in the Breakdown of the Bicameral Mind*. It was the culmination of decades of thinking and research and proposed a radical new theory on the origin of the modern mind. Integrating psychology, neurology, anthropology, ancient history, and linguistics, Jaynes argues that subjective consciousness is a learned process based on metaphorical language and, in historical terms, a relatively recent development.

Prior to the development of consciousness, Jaynes argues that humans could communicate, learn, organize, and problem-solve, but did so without introspection. The brain used language to convey experience from the right hemisphere to the left hemisphere in the form of verbal commands, which directed non-habitual behavior and were triggered by the stress of decision-making. Jaynes called this earlier mentality the bicameral mind. Today we see vestiges of the bicameral mind in a wide range of phenomena such as the command hallucinations of schizophrenia patients, the loss of personal authorization in hypnosis, "possession" and poetic frenzy, the imaginary companions of children, and the nostalgic quest of modern religions for the lost voices of the gods.

Calling into question conventional views of human history, Jaynes's theory is initially shocking to many readers. Yet this should not be surprising, as nearly all new ideas that do not simply build on previous theories are initially met with skepticism, and theories that deal with "the big questions" — such as the origin of consciousness and religion — provoke even greater resistance. As the biologist William Ian Beveridge notes in *The Art of Scientific Investigation*, "The human mind likes a strange idea as little as the body likes a strange protein, and resists it with a similar energy." The tendency toward rejection of the unfamiliar is widespread, even among academics, who are often thought to be more rational or impartial.[1] The progress of science requires agnosticism toward new ideas rather than an unthinking or irrational skepticism. As pointed out by the cognitive neuroscientist Michael Persinger in *Reflections on the Dawn of Consciousness*, "reflexive rejection of novel concepts is the antithesis of discovery."

Another obstacle to the acceptance of new ideas is the general propensity to quickly form a strong opinion based on limited information. This is even more problematic in light of the fact that once an opinion is formed, even if based on the flimsiest of evidence, we tend to seek information that confirms that opinion and avoid information that contradicts it. Known in psychology as the confirmation bias, this tendency leads to group polarization. When a person is asked the reasons why they hold an opinion on a subject that does not involve their day-to-day experience, they often cannot say. Similarly, those who reject Jaynes's theory, when pressed, often can't articulate their reasons, or state reasons based on misconceptions. We have the illusion that we reach all of our opinions through conscious deliberation, yet opinions are often formed outside of our awareness.

The process of unconscious opinion formation is well described by the French-Swiss psychoanalyst Charles Baudouin in his 1921 book *Suggestion and Autosuggestion*:

> You hear an opinion stated; you are well aware that it is nothing more than opinion; you have your reserves when you accept it; you intend to look into the matter more closely, to reason about it. At this stage you think about the judgments that have been formulated, without believing them in the strict sense of the term. What you have in your mind are not complete judgments, for belief is an integral part of judgment, and here belief is lacking. All that you have is what we may call the "schema" of a judgment, the idea of a judgment (or of that series of judgments which constitutes an opinion).

> Time passes, and you no longer think about verification. You even forget the original source of your idea. But one day you are called upon to decide the question, and you discover that your mind is made up; you hold the very opinion which you heard expressed formerly, although you have never had any proof. The ordinary newspaper reader, the man-in-the-street, is continually circulating these "hear-says," without professing any credence in them. Nevertheless, the newspaper reader's opinions are based on falsehoods he reads in his favorite paper. He does not realize it, but such is the fact. The grain planted in him when he

---

1. See Milton Rokeach, *The Open and Closed Mind* (New York: Basic Books, 1960).

read, has germinated in the subconscious. He has made up his mind, and he believes that his opinion is established upon reason.

Given the pervasiveness of an emotionally-based hostility toward the unfamiliar, coupled with the tendency to unconsciously form strong opinions based on limited information, we must learn to withhold judgment on new ideas until they can be properly evaluated. Having no opinion on a subject one is unfamiliar with should be encouraged, rather than feeling socially pressured to offer an opinion on everything. In addition, personal biases and the evidence for long-held beliefs must be critically examined — a process few seriously engage in despite being advocated as far back as 1620 by Francis Bacon in his influential *Novum Organum Scientiarum* (New Instrument of Science).

The unconscious adoption of the prevailing views that consciousness evolved biologically over millions of years and plays a role in all aspects of our mentality often results in hostility to ideas that challenge those views. But for many of those who remain open-minded, carefully consider all of the corroborating evidence, and weigh the evidence against any existing biases, Jaynes's theory demonstrates remarkable explanatory power. Those who come to fully appreciate the tremendous significance of the theory often regard Julian Jaynes as one of the most important and original thinkers of the twentieth century.

## WIDE-RANGING INFLUENCE

In the decades since it was first published, Jaynes's theory has had a large and wide-ranging influence. *The Origin of Consciousness in the Breakdown of the Bicameral Mind* has been translated into Italian, Spanish, German, French, and, most recently, Persian. Although still considered controversial, as of this writing Jaynes's theory has been cited in over 9,000 books and articles.[2] The vast majority of these references are positive. Jaynes's theory has been influential to many scholars, including philosophers such as Daniel Dennett, psychologists such as Endel Tulving, Antonio Damasio, and David Foulkes, psychiatrists such as Timothy Crow, and science writers such as Tor Nørretranders and Charles Hampden-Turner. My previous book, *Reflections on the Dawn of Consciousness*, contains discussion of Jaynes's theory by scholars from a variety of academic disci-

---

2. See books.google.com. A partial list of scholars who have written on Jaynes's theory is available on the Julian Jaynes Society website at julianjaynes.org.

plines. Another book discussing Jaynes's theory, *Il Nostro Inquilino Segreto: Psicologia e Psicoterapia della Coscienza* (Our Secret Tenant: Psychology and Psychotherapy of Consciousness), was recently published in Italy.

Jaynes was frequently invited to speak on his theory to both academic and general audiences in the U.S. and abroad, often giving a dozen or more lectures per year. Jaynes's theory has been the subject of conferences at McMaster University in 1983 and Harvard University in 1988. More recently, the Julian Jaynes Conference on Consciousness was organized by Professor Scott Greer at the University of Prince Edward Island in 2006 and 2008. In addition, Jaynes's theory was the subject of a speaker session at the Toward A Science of Consciousness conference in 2008.

The impact of Jaynes's book in the late 1970s helped to stimulate a renewed interest in consciousness. Although a popular topic in the late nineteenth and early twentieth centuries, for the next 50 years the strong influence of behaviorism largely discouraged investigations of consciousness. Since the publication of Jaynes's book, renewed interest in consciousness has grown steadily. More recently, the availability of new brain imaging technologies has helped continue this trend and created opportunities for consciousness research that were not previously possible.

The modern interest in auditory hallucinations among normal, non-psychotic people can be traced directly to Julian Jaynes. The association of auditory hallucinations with mental illness — rather than spiritual communication or divine revelation — goes back to Plato, but the idea did not take hold until the Enlightenment. Since then, the subject of hallucinations in normal, non-psychotic people has been studied only sporadically. One of the first studies was done in 1881 by Sir Francis Galton. In a lecture to the Royal Institution on the "Visions of Sane Persons," Galton reported that "the visionary tendency is much more common among sane people than is generally expected" and noted that the tendency toward hallucination starts in childhood and is subsequently repressed in those societies where it is discouraged.[3]

Despite Galton's intriguing findings, only a handful of other studies on this subject were undertaken in the century that followed, until the release of Jaynes's book rekindled the interest in hallucinations in normal people. Inspired by Jaynes, in 1983 psychologist Thomas Posey and then graduate student Mary Losch published a study on hallucinations in the normal population, reporting that roughly 70 percent of those sampled had

---

3. Francis Galton, *Memories of My Life* (London: Methuen & Co., 1908).

experienced a brief hallucination at some time.[4] Also inspired by Jaynes, in 1985, clinical psychologist John Hamilton published a study of auditory hallucinations in a group of non-verbal quadriplegics.[5] A great number of studies followed, and the idea that normal everyday people occasionally hear voices became a popular topic. This has led to international support groups for normal, non-hospitalized people who experience auditory hallucinations and several recent books on the subject, including *Hearing Voices: A Common Human Experience* (2008) by the Australian counselor John Watkins and a series of books by the Dutch psychiatrist and professor Marius Romme and Dr. Sandra Escher.[6]

Jaynes's theory has also influenced ideas about the underlying neurology of auditory hallucinations. Psychiatrists such as Henry Nasrallah in the United States, Timothy Crow in the United Kingdom, and Iris Sommer in the Netherlands, who all reference Jaynes, have proposed right temporal lobe language explanations for auditory hallucinations similar to Jaynes's.[7]

Jaynes's theory has also had an influence on popular culture, inspiring books by several well-known fiction writers. Philip K. Dick corresponded with Jaynes about his own auditory hallucinations and incorporated ideas from Jaynes's theory into his novel *A Scanner Darkly*, which was later made into a movie. More recently, science fiction authors Neal Stephenson and Robert Sawyer have each incorporated ideas from Jaynes's theory into several of their popular novels. Jaynes's theory also influenced Philip Pullman's popular *His Dark Materials* trilogy (of which the first book, *The Golden Compass*, was made into a movie), in which each of the human characters has a *daemon*, or animal companion, that serves a guiding function similar to a bicameral voice.[8]

---

4. Thomas B. Posey and Mary E. Losch, "Auditory Hallucinations of Hearing Voices in 375 Normal Subjects," *Imagination, Cognition, and Personality*, 1983, *3*, 99-113.

5. John Hamilton, "Auditory Hallucinations in Nonverbal Quadriplegics," *Psychiatry*, 1985, *48*, 4. Reprinted in M. Kuijsten (ed.), *Reflections on the Dawn of Consciousness* (Julian Jaynes Society, 2006).

6. See Marius Romme and Sandra Escher, *Accepting Voices* (1993), *Making Sense of Voices* (2000), *Living with Voices* (2009), and *Children Hearing Voices* (2010).

7. Henry Nasrallah, "The Unintegrated Right Cerebral Hemispheric Consciousness As Alien Intruder," *Comprehensive Psychiatry*, 1985, *26*, 3, 273–282; Timothy Crow, "Is Schizophrenia the Price that Homo Sapiens Pays for Language?" *Schizophrenia Research*, 1997, *28*, 127–141; Kelly Diederen and Iris E.C. Sommer, "Auditory Verbal Hallucinations and Language Lateralization," in I.E.C. Sommer and R.S. Kahn (eds.) *Language Lateralization and Psychosis* (Cambridge University Press, 2009).

8. Pullman also refers to Jaynes's theory in a column he wrote for Penguin Books, "Philip Pullman Celebrates the Penguin Epics," calling it a "crazy and yet tantalizingly rich idea."

## IMPLICATIONS OF JAYNES'S THEORY

Jaynes's theory provides a richer, more accurate understanding of human history, and more specifically, the development of the modern mind in history. Without Jaynes's theory, many phenomena — ranging from oracles, divination, monumental mortuary architecture such as the pyramids in Egypt, and even the origin of religion — remain either poorly understood or a complete mystery. Entire fields of study have yet to be reexamined through the lens of Jaynes's theory.

But Jaynes's theory also has practical implications for modern life. It provides insights into the human tendency to seek guidance from external authorities as evidenced in everything from cult behavior to authoritarian religious and political movements. Jaynes provides a neurological model for auditory hallucinations that psychiatrists and neuroscientists have now validated with brain imaging technology. The confirmation that auditory hallucinations originate in the right temporal lobe should lead to more effective treatments for those with severe hallucinations, both through pharmaceuticals and as well as emerging alternative therapies such as transcranial magnetic stimulation and neurofeedback. The application of Jaynes's theory thus has the potential to positively impact the lives of millions of people worldwide who suffer from hallucinations of a persistence and severity so as to warrant medical intervention.

The theory has other applications as well. The idea that consciousness is not biologically innate but rather is learned in childhood and taught to each successive generation has practical implications for child development. Jaynes emphasizes the important role of parents in the development of consciousness in children. And while many theorists' definitions of consciousness are nebulous at best, Jaynes's detailed description of the different features of consciousness could potentially lead to new programs that might better develop different aspects of consciousness in children. These include increased concentration, spatialization of time, memory development, critical thinking skills, and impulse control through the expansion of the gap between stimulus and response. Although not directly related to Jaynes's theory, potential strategies that are worth investigating can be found in Dr. Mel Levine's *A Mind at a Time*.[9]

The discovery that subjective consciousness is a learned process and a recent development in human history — and not genetically evolved — also raises questions about the future development of consciousness. As

---

9. Melvin Levine, *A Mind at a Time* (New York: Simon & Schuster, 2002).

you will see in the Discussion section, the direction of the future development of consciousness was one of the most frequent questions raised after Jaynes's lectures, and many areas remain to be explored. For example, will the growing ubiquity of technology have a positive or a detrimental effect on consciousness? What methods can be used to better train consciousness even in adulthood? Using hypnosis or other methods such as neurofeedback, to what degree can one gain greater control over unconscious and habitual influences on thought and behavior? Given the dramatic changes to consciousness that have taken place over the past 3,000 years, in what unanticipated ways will consciousness develop several thousand years from now? I hope to explore these topics in a future publication.

## Status of the Theory

A significant percentage of those who reject Jaynes's theory tend to fall into one of two groups. The first group consists of those who have not read or briefly skimmed Jaynes's book and misunderstood his definition of consciousness or what he means by the bicameral mind. Their rejection of the notion of consciousness as a relatively recent development historically often results from confusing their own usually broad definition of consciousness (often conflating it with learning and sense perception) with Jaynes's narrower, more precise definition. Jaynes argues persuasively that we can react to our environment, learn, and solve problems, all without subjective consciousness or introspection.

The second group consists of those who may understand Jaynes's theory but are heavily invested in an alternate definition of consciousness, for example that consciousness involves all sense perception. Defined in this way, consciousness becomes indistinguishable from sense perception and, by this definition, all animal life (and, as Jaynes, points out, even white blood cells, which react to their environment) would have to be considered conscious. In an attempt to address this problem, different "levels" or "types" (e.g., Ned Block's *access* vs. *phenomenal*) of consciousness are proposed, usually with vague definitions. Others subscribe to a form of neo-dualism (the idea that the mind is composed of a nonphysical substance and is separate from the body) known as panpsychism, arguing that consciousness is somehow a basic property of the universe. Still others bury the problem in quantum physics. These more mystical views of consciousness are particularly non-evidence based and, at least in some cases, seem to stem from the desire to incorporate deep-seated beliefs in an afterlife or the survival of consciousness after bodily death.

While those that fall in the second group are unlikely to be persuaded, I think those in the first group can be, as misconceptions are clarified and additional evidence for Jaynes's theory is presented. As discussed in *Reflections on the Dawn of Consciousness*, new research over the three decades since the publication of Jaynes's book provides a great deal of additional support for Jaynes's theory.[10] For sake of clarity, Jaynes's theory can be divided into four hypotheses: that consciousness is based on metaphorical language; dating of the development of consciousness to roughly 1200 B.C. in areas such as Greece, Egypt, and Mesopotamia; that prior to the development of consciousness humans operated under a different mentality called the bicameral mind; and the neurological model for the bicameral mind. While space precludes an exhaustive review, I will briefly touch on some of the new evidence for each of these hypotheses here.

*Hypothesis One: Consciousness Based on Language*

The debate over the importance of language for consciousness has a long history and has seen renewed interest in recent years. While many theorists continue to assume that infants are born conscious (confusing consciousness with sense perception), the work of child psychologist Philip Zelazo strongly supports Jaynes's argument that consciousness develops in children over time through the acquisition of language. Building on the work of the early twentieth century Russian psychologists Lev Vygotsky and Alexander Luria and the Swiss psychologist Jean Piaget, Zelazo and his colleagues propose a model for the development of consciousness in children that highlights the importance of the interaction between thought and language.[11] Zelazo describes "four major age-related increases" in consciousness in children and corresponding increases in children's ability to spatialize time. Zelazo's fourth stage, *reflective consciousness*, corresponds roughly to Jaynes's definition of consciousness, whereas Zelazo's first stage, *minimal consciousness*, describes what Jaynes would term reactivity or basic sense perception.

---

10. Marcel Kuijsten (ed.), *Reflections on the Dawn of Consciousness* (Julian Jaynes Society, 2006).

11. Philip D. Zelazo, Helena Hong Gao, and Rebecca Todd, "The Development of Consciousness," in P. Zelazo, M. Moscovitch, and E. Thompson (eds.), *The Cambridge Handbook of Consciousness* (Cambridge: Cambridge University Press, 2007).

Child psychologist and dream expert David Foulkes's research also supports Jaynes's idea that consciousness develops in children over time. Foulkes describes how the development of consciousness in children can be observed both in normal waking behavior as well as in the content of their dreams. Based on his extensive research with children, Foulkes challenges the popular assumption that dreaming is "a given" in human experience, noting that children's dreams go through distinct developmental stages. Sounding very reminiscent of Jaynes (see Chapter 20 of this volume), Foulkes states: "I hypothesize that dreaming is simply the operation of consciousness in sleep ... that consciousness develops, and that it does so more slowly and later than is generally believed."[12]

Consciousness theorists such as Daniel Dennett and Peter Carruthers also argue that children do not develop subjective consciousness until they acquire language. Dennett notes that "acquiring a human language ... is a necessary precondition for consciousness ... It would follow that non-human animals and pre-linguistic children, although they can be sensitive, alert, responsive to pain and suffering, and cognitively competent in many remarkable ways — including ways that exceed normal adult human competence — are not really conscious (in this strong sense)."[13] In *Language, Thought, and Consciousness* (1998), Peter Carruthers develops a similar argument, stating "...language is not just a very important, but nevertheless peripheral, channel of communication. It is, rather, constitutive of many of our central processes of thinking and reasoning, particularly those that are conscious."

Further support for the necessity of language for consciousness comes from cases of children with delayed language acquisition. Helen Keller, who went blind and deaf at the age of 19 months after an illness and only began to acquire language around the age of 7, offers rare insights into the experience of non-linguistic mentality. When she began to learn sign language, she felt as though she "thought" and "desired" with her fingers, stating that: "If I had made a man, I should certainly have put the brain and soul in his fingertips." On her life before acquiring language, Keller observes:

> Before my teacher came to me, I did not know that I am. I lived in a world that was a no-world... I had neither will nor intellect. I was

12. David Foulkes, *Children's Dreaming and the Development of Consciousness* (Cambridge: Harvard University Press, 2002).
13. John Brockman (ed.), *What We Believe But Cannot Prove* (New York: Harper Perennial, 2006).

carried along to objects and acts by a certain blind natural impetus.
... I never viewed anything beforehand or chose it. ... My inner life,
then, was a blank without past, present, or future, without hope or
anticipation, without wonder or joy or faith... Since I had no power of
thought, I did not compare one mental state with another... When I
learned the meaning of "I" and "me" and found that I was something, I
began to think. Then consciousness first existed for me.[14]

Cases of children raised in isolation and without language — such as
Kaspar Hauser[15] in nineteenth century Nuremberg and the more recent
case of Genie[16] in the United States — provide further clues concerning
the necessity of language for consciousness. With the exception of Genie,
however, most of these cases unfortunately are not studied by those with a
deep interest in the relationship of consciousness and language.

Evidence of the importance of language for consciousness also comes
from research on tribal groups. While the study of differing aspects in
consciousness between modern and preliterate societies is not the focus of
most anthropologists, important differences have been noted. For example, the Pirahã tribe of the Brazilian Amazon's language does not contain
words for numbers larger than two, referring to larger quantities simply
as "many." A study by Columbia University psychologist Peter Gordon
found that without the precise language for numbers larger than two, the
Pirahã were unable to reliably discriminate between four or five objects.[17]
University of Portsmouth Psychology of Language professor Chris Sinha
and his colleagues describe the lack of the modern concept of time among
the Amondawa, also of the Amazon. According to Sinha, "An abstract
term for *time* does not exist in Amondawa."[18] This has been noted in other
groups as well, such as the Nuer of East Africa. Jaynes views the ability
to spatialize time as one of the primary features of consciousness. This
new evidence for the idea that lacking words for certain concepts can
inhibit the understanding of those concepts (often referred to as linguistic
determinism) provides additional support for Jaynes's ideas on the role of
language in the development subjective consciousness.

14. Helen Keller, *The World I Live In* (New York: The Century Company, 1908).

15. Catherine Lucy Wilhelmina Powlett Cleveland (Duchess of), *The True Story of Kaspar Hauser* (London: Macmillan and Co., 1893).

16. Susan Curtiss, *Genie: A Psycholinguistic Study of a Modern-Day "Wild Child"* (Boston: Academic Press, 1977).

17. Peter Gordon, "Numerical Cognition Without Words," *Science*, 2004, *306*, 496–499.

18. Chris Sinha, et al., "When Time is Not Space: The Social and Linguistic Construction of Time Intervals in An Amazonian Culture," *Language and Cognition*, 2011, *3*, 1. See also note 3 on page 291.

Psychologists such as John Limber,[19] Henry Schlinger,[20] and Joseph Church[21] also discuss the importance of language acquisition for the development of consciousness, while Steven Pinker[22] and others describe the essential role of metaphor. While this necessarily brief overview barely scratches the surface of this complex subject, it nonetheless should demonstrate that many of today's leading thinkers are in general agreement with Jaynes on this aspect of his theory. Although each theorist's ideas differ from one another and from Jaynes in some respects, taken together, their work adds persuasive new evidence for Jaynes's first hypothesis that subjective consciousness is based on language and is learned in childhood.

*Hypothesis Two: Dating the Development of Consciousness*

Jaynes's second hypothesis, dating the development of consciousness to roughly 1200 B.C. in Greece, is also supported by a variety of new research. Based on a meticulous analysis of Chinese linguistics and rituals, the sinologist Michael Carr documents the transition from bicamerality to consciousness in early China during the same time period that Jaynes documents it in Greece.[23] Whether this happened independently or through diffusion remains unclear, but the observation of this transition in another civilization adds another very important piece to the puzzle.

Additional evidence for a recent date for the development of consciousness comes from the work of the British psychologist Nicholas Humphrey. Cave paintings have in some cases been suggested as evidence of modern consciousness, which would place the date for the development of consciousness much earlier. This notion was seriously called into question by Humphrey, who reports the case of a three-year-old autistic child without language who demonstrated remarkably similar artistic ability.[24] The subject of cave art will be discussed further in Chapter 11.

---

19. John Limber, "Language and Consciousness," in Marcel Kuijsten (ed.), *Reflections on the Dawn of Consciousness* (Henderson, NV: Julian Jaynes Society, 2006).

20. Henry Schlinger, "Consciousness Is Nothing But A Word," *Skeptic*, 2008, *13*, 4.

21. Joseph Church, *Language and the Discovery of Reality* (New York: Random House, 1961).

22. Steven Pinker, *The Stuff of Thought: Language as a Window into Human Nature* (New York: Viking Press, 2007).

23. Michael Carr, "The *Shi* 'Corpse/Personator' Ceremony in Early China," in Marcel Kuijsten (ed.), *Reflections on the Dawn of Consciousness* (Henderson, NV: Julian Jaynes Society, 2006).

24. Nicholas Humphrey, "Cave Art, Autism, and the Evolution of the Human Mind," *Cambridge Archaeological Journal*, 1998, *8*, 2.

Intriguing new evidence for Jaynes's dating of the development of consciousness also comes from the study of dreams. The common assumption that dreams have been consistent throughout recorded history is incorrect: the first recorded dreams show a stark contrast when compared with modern dreams. In modern conscious dreams, we see ourselves acting out events in other places and from various perspectives. By contrast, the earliest recorded dreams completely lack these features. Jaynes labels these bicameral dreams, as they typically consist of the dreamer having the feeling of being asleep in bed and then being visited by a god or spirit who issues a warning or command.

An example of a bicameral dream is Agamemnon's dream in the beginning of Book II of the *Iliad*. In this dream Agamemnon is visited by Onieros, who appears in his dream as Nestor (one of the generals of the army) and tells him to start the Trojan War. This is not an isolated example — the ancient literature "is full of these 'godsent' dreams in which a single dream-figure presents itself, as in Homer, to the sleeper, and gives him prophecy, advice, or warning."[25]

Bicameral dreams have also been documented in preliterate societies, and, as previously mentioned, children's dreams seem to go through similar developmental stages. Dreams in bicameral cultures lack consciousness — an analog 'I' narratizing in a mind-space — and mimic the waking experience of receiving behavioral commands from gods. In contrast, the dreams of conscious individuals reflect conscious narratization during sleep. If consciousness developed far back in our evolutionary past, we would expect dreams to remain unchanged both throughout recorded history and throughout an individual's development. Instead, the content of dreams change as consciousness develops. Thus dreams provide another method to gauge the level of consciousness in a given culture or individual.[26]

New evidence from the study of early Chinese rituals and linguistics, the cave art style drawings of an autistic child without language, and the study of dreams all provide stimulating new evidence for Jaynes's dating of the development of consciousness. Much more research remains to be done, such as the in-depth study of other early civilizations from the perspective of Jaynes's theory, in such cases where evidence is available.

---

25. E.R. Dodds, *The Greeks and the Irrational* (Berkeley: University of California Press, 1951/2004).

26. See Chapter 20 of this volume as well as William Vernon Harris, *Dreams and Experience in Classical Antiquity* (Cambridge: Harvard University Press, 2009).

*Hypothesis Three: The Bicameral Mind*

Jaynes's third hypothesis — that prior to consciousness non-habitual human behavior was guided by auditory hallucinations — is initially perhaps the most shocking, yet a great deal of new evidence supports this hypothesis as well. The occurrence of auditory hallucinations in a wide variety of non-clinical populations such as children (in imaginary companions), university students, individuals in isolation or under stress, and the elderly has now been well documented in dozens of studies.[27] The subject of imaginary companions in children has seen a particular (and long overdue) increase in interest among child psychologists over the past decade.

In the seventies and eighties, much of the research on imaginary companions (then referred to as imaginary playmates) was done by the husband and wife team of Yale psychology professor Jerome Singer and Yale research scientist Dorothy Singer. The Singers felt Jaynes's theory was compatible with their research on imaginary companions, and describe the theory in one of their books.[28] Imaginary companions are now a more popular topic for research. The British clinical psychologist David Pearson and his colleagues conduct research in this area and reach the same conclusion as Jaynes: the phenomenon involves actual hallucinations and not just imagination.[29] Many other researchers and clinicians now agree.[30] Over the years, estimates of the number of children that experience imaginary companions has ranged from 30 percent to as high as 65 percent. In a large study of 1,800 children, Pearson and his colleagues found that 46 percent experienced imaginary companions.[31] These numbers are startling considering mainstream psychology's failure to offer a persuasive explanation of the phenomenon.

Further evidence for the bicameral mind comes from research on the content of hallucinations in patients labeled as schizophrenic. Rather than

27. Marcel Kuijsten, "Consciousness, Hallucinations and the Bicameral Mind: Three Decades of New Research," in M. Kuijsten (ed.), *Reflections on the Dawn of Consciousness* (Julian Jaynes Society, 2006).

28. Dorothy G. Singer and Jerome L. Singer, *The House of Make-Believe: Children's Play and the Developing Imagination* (Cambridge: Harvard University Press, 1992). In the book, the Singers also comment "… we do not believe [Jaynes's] thesis should be ignored or dismissed out of hand. We once invited Jaynes to a dinner party along with Yale scholars of ancient Sumerian, Hebrew, Egyptian, and Greek, and they were quite impressed with his technical knowledge of the texts they study."

29. David Pearson, Andrea Burrow, Christina FitzGerald, Kate Green, et al., "Auditory Hallucinations in Normal Child Populations," *Personality and Individual Differences*, 2001, *31*, 3.

30. See for example, Kanwar Ajit S. Sidhu and T.O. Dickey III, "Hallucinations in Children: Diagnostic and Treatment Strategies," *Current Psychiatry*, 2010, *9*, 10.

31. David Pearson, H. Rouse, S. Doswell, C. Ainsworth, O. Dawson, K. Simms, et al., "Prevalence of Imaginary Companions in a Normal Child Population," *Child*, 2001, *27*, 1.

being simply random in nature (as is often presumed), new research shows hallucinated voices frequently command or direct behavior.[32] Known as "command hallucinations," this finding, now documented in numerous studies, is precisely what Jaynes's bicameral mind hypothesis would predict.

Studies of preliterate societies past and present clearly describe what can be termed vestiges of bicamerality and thus provide additional evidence for Jaynes's third hypothesis. Many people are not aware of this data, as an atmosphere of excessive political correctness for a long time suppressed widespread discussion of psychological differences between pre-literate and literate societies. Jaynes wrote a chapter on vestiges of bicamerality in tribes, but due to space constraints it was not included in *The Origin,* and his second volume unfortunately never materialized.

If one reads accounts of preliterate tribes from the late nineteenth and early twentieth centuries, they are rich with descriptions of vestiges of bicamerality, including frequent auditory hallucinations, visions, idolatry, and seeking guidance from gods, spirits, and dead ancestors. The French anthropologist Lucien Lévy-Bruhl's *Primitive Mentality* (1923) and *How Natives Think* (1926) were books Jaynes used for research on this subject, and both describe vestiges of bicamerality in preliterate societies worldwide.

For example, in *Primitive Mentality*, Lévy-Bruhl quotes a missionary who, describing the voices and visions of the Ten'a of Alaska, states "with these undesirable denizens of the spirit-world ... the Ten'a may be said to have an almost continual intercourse. They hold themselves liable to see or hear them at any time." Lévy-Bruhl also provides a description among tribes of the slow fading away of the hallucinated voice after someone dies. This same phenomenon is described by Jaynes in the double burials of many early cultures and by Michael Carr among the early Chinese.[33] Lévy-Bruhl notes:

> In short ... the dead are alive, at least for a certain time; they are living beings of a different kind from ourselves, beings in whom certain participations are ruptured or at least impaired, but who only by slow degrees cease to belong to their social group. To understand the primitives' mentality, we must first of all rid our minds of our own idea

---

32. For a recent example, see Nicky Reynolds and Peter Scragg, "Compliance with Command Hallucinations," *The Journal of Forensic Psychiatry and Psychology*, 2010, *21*, 1.

33. Michael Carr, "The *Shi* 'Corpse/Personator' Ceremony in Early China," in Marcel Kuijsten (ed.), *Reflections on the Dawn of Consciousness* (Henderson, NV: Julian Jaynes Society, 2006).

of death and the dead, and try to replace it by that which dominates their collective representations.

Elsewhere he describes further vestiges of bicamerality:

> Speaking of a Bantu tribe, a careful observer tells us "It is of the utmost importance for students of the sociology of these people to try and realize the reality and closeness of the influence of the ancestral spirits upon the daily life of the native, and unless an ethnologist has been in daily contact with the people, and striven to understand their point of view, it is difficult for the weight of this to be felt to a full extent."

Jaynes describes in great detail the evidence for hallucinations in ancient civilizations. Descriptions of hallucinations in preliterate societies therefore demonstrate a remarkable, previously unexamined parallel between the inhabitants of ancient civilizations and many recent preliterate societies. A further parallel is the inability to spatialize time (as was noted in some tribes in the previous section), as evidence suggests the Greeks did not develop a fully modern concept of time and history until as late as 500 B.C.[34]

Another intriguing area of evidence for Jaynes's bicameral mind hypothesis comes from individuals who have had the connection between their brain hemispheres severed as a last resort treatment for otherwise intractable epileptic seizures, often referred to as "split-brain patients." While Jaynes discusses this evidence, a great deal more has been written on this subject since the late seventies, and the additional research and discussion of split-brain patients offers significant support for Jaynes's bicameral mind hypothesis.

All of the principle investigators of split-brain patients maintain that the severing of the corpus callosum results in multiple "selves" or "spheres of consciousness," one per hemisphere. Roger Sperry, who won the Nobel Prize for his split-brain research, states: "Everything we have seen so far indicates that the surgery has left each of these people with two separate minds, that is, with two separate spheres of consciousness."[35] Elsewhere, Sperry notes that "both the left and right hemisphere may be conscious simultaneously in different, even in mutually conflicting, mental experiences that run along in parallel."[36] While some commentators disagree

---

34. Chester Starr, *Awakening of the Greek Historical Spirit* (New York: Alfred A. Knopf, 1968).

35. Roger Sperry, *Problems Outstanding in the Evolution of Brain Function (James Arthur Lecture on the Evolution of the Human Brain)* (New York: The American Museum of Natural History, 1964).

36. Roger Sperry, "Lateral Specialization in the Surgically Separated Hemispheres," in F.O. Schmitt

with these conclusions, Sperry notes "we have not been able to see any real justification in our test findings for denying consciousness to the disconnected mute hemisphere."[37]

Two of Sperry's colleagues — Michael Gazzaniga, a psychologist, and Joseph Bogen, a neurosurgeon, who both studied split-brain patients for decades — also argue that the split-brain procedure results in distinct "selves" in each hemisphere. Bogen comments that "the data are consistent with the interpretation that disconnection of the hemispheres splits not only the brain but also the psychic properties of the brain."[38] Gazzaniga notes that after the split-brain procedure, "common normal conscious unity is disrupted, leaving the split-brain patient with two minds"[39] and "both hemispheres can be viewed as conscious."[40]

It is important to note that the above researchers use the term consciousness more broadly than Jaynes. The disconnected right hemisphere seems to demonstrate some aspects of Jaynesian consciousness, while not demonstrating others — most notably an analog 'I' narratizing in a mindspace. Split-brain patients have no awareness of the ideas communicated to or the judgments made by their right hemisphere. Their sense of self is associated with their left or language-dominant hemisphere. The implications of the association of subjective consciousness with the language-dominant hemisphere in split-brain patients remain largely unexplored. Most of the abilities of the disconnected right hemisphere — its ability to perceive, learn, respond, and show preferences — Jaynes argues can be accomplished without subjective consciousness. The important point for Jaynes's bicameral mind hypothesis is that in the split-brain condition, the two hemispheres are able to function independently of one another at a high level. As Sperry notes, the right hemisphere "perceives, thinks, learns, and remembers, all at a very human level."

In a series of articles, the philosophy professor Roland Puccetti also argues that the split-brain procedure indeed results in "two minds," rather than just two disconnected brain hemispheres. Puccetti goes on to question whether the right-hemisphere "mind" emerges as a result of the

and F.G. Worden (eds.), *The Neurosciences: Third Study Program* (Cambridge, MA: MIT Press, 1973).

37. Roger Sperry, "Consciousness, Personal Identity, and the Divided Brain," in D. Frank Benson and Eran Zaidel (eds.), *The Dual Brain* (New York: The Guilford Press, 1985).

38. Joseph E. Bogen, "The Other Side of the Brain: An Appositional Mind," in Robert Ornstein (ed.), *The Nature of Human Consciousness: A Book of Readings* (New York: W. H. Freeman, 1973).

39. Michael Gazzaniga, "One Brain — Two Minds?," *American Scientist*, 1972, 60.

40. Michael Gazzaniga, "The Split Brain Revisited," *Scientific American*, 2002; see also Michael Gazzaniga, "The Split Brain in Man," *Scientific American*, 1967, 217.

split-brain procedure or if it is there all along, but in normal circumstances remains undetectable,[41] and Bogen makes a similar argument for a certain degree of mental duality in the intact brain.[42]

Further support comes from individuals with only one brain hemisphere. As far back as 1844, the English physician Arthur Ladbroke Wigan described cases of individuals who lived normal lives despite having only one hemisphere. Wigan first became interested in the degree to which the brain hemispheres could function independently when he witnessed an autopsy in which, when the man's skull was cut open, he was shocked to see that one of the hemispheres "was entirely gone," even though the patient "had conversed rationally and even written verses within a few days of his death."[43]

Since the 1980s, hemispherectomies (the removal of a brain hemisphere) in very young children have been successfully performed as a last resort for cases of severe epilepsy. The neuroscientist Antonio Battro reports the case of a boy named Nico who had his entire right hemisphere removed at the age of three due to severe epileptic seizures. Battro notes that Nico's musical abilities, motor capabilities, and attention span have all developed normally despite the fact that many researchers have determined that these functions are mediated by the right hemisphere.[44] The case of Nico, as well as other cases of hemispherectomy, suggest that one hemisphere in isolation can act as a complete brain, and give rise to a normal "mind."

The knowledge that the brain hemispheres can act both independently (in the case of split-brain patients) and in isolation (in the case of hemispherectomy patients), should facilitate increased understanding of Jaynes's bicameral mind hypothesis. The independent function of the disconnected hemispheres in split-brain patients provides a modern example of how the brain hemispheres could have operated in a less integrated manner in the past than they do today, with the right hemisphere issuing direction in the form of verbal commands across the corpus callosum to the left hemisphere. Similarly, cases of hemispherectomy, which demonstrate that one hemisphere is enough for one mind, make it easier to

41. Roland Puccetti, "Two Brains, Two Minds? Wigan's Theory of Mental Duality," *The British Journal for the Philosophy of Science*, 1989, *40*, 2.

42. Joseph E. Bogen, "Mental Duality in the Anatomically Intact Cerebrum," *Presidential Address to the Los Angeles Society of Neurology and Psychiatry*, January 19, 1983.

43. A.L. Wigan, *The Duality of Mind* (London: Longman, Brown, Green, and Longmans, 1844).

44. Antonio Battro, *Half a Brain is Enough: The Story of Nico* (Cambridge University Press, 2000).

conceive that two hemispheres, under conditions of less integration, could result in the bicameral mind as described by Jaynes.

Finally, research on brain plasticity over the past three decades has forced neuroscientists to rethink the long-held view that the brain is inflexible and largely fixed at birth. A large number of recent studies now show that new neurons are created throughout life (neurogenesis) and that significant changes to brain function can take place without major physiological changes to brain structure (neuroplasticity).[45] Hemispherectomy patients such as Nico demonstrate that brain function can change much more dramatically in an individual than was previously believed — in Nico's case the left hemisphere taking over some of the functions of the missing right hemisphere. The research on neuroplasticity supports Jaynes's contention that the integration of the hemispheres in the transition from bicamerality to consciousness was driven primarily by cultural changes, and that these changes could affect brain function over a relatively short time period — rather than being dependent on genetically-based biological changes to brain structure over much longer periods.

Thus, a wide range of new evidence from a variety of sources converges to provide a compelling case for the bicameral mind hypothesis. This includes the frequency of auditory hallucinations in the general population, imaginary companions in children, command hallucinations in those labeled as schizophrenic, vestiges of bicamerality in preliterate tribes, studies of split-brain and hemispherectomy patients, and new research on neuroplasticity. Without Jaynes's theory, it is difficult to make sense of the facts that large numbers of normal people occasionally experience hallucinations, a large percentage of children experience imaginary companions, and the hallucinations of those labeled schizophrenic often command behavior. No viable alternate explanations for these phenomena have been proposed.

*Hypothesis Four: Jaynes's Neurological Model*

The first neuroimaging study providing evidence for Jaynes's neurological model by showing auditory hallucinations are based on an interaction of the right and left temporal lobes appeared in 1999.[46] Since then,

---

45. Christopher A. Shaw and Jill C. McEachern (eds.), *Toward A Theory of Neuroplasticity* (Philadelphia, PA: Taylor and Francis, 2001).
46. Belinda R. Lennox, S. Bert, G. Park, Peter B. Jones, and Peter G. Morris, "Spatial and Temporal Mapping of Neural Activity Associated with Auditory Hallucinations," *Lancet*, 1999, *22*, 615–621.

this finding has been confirmed by numerous other studies.[47] The brain scan on the cover, from a recent article in *Molecular Psychiatry* by the French psychiatrist Renaud Jardri and his colleagues titled "Activation of Bilateral Auditory Cortex during Verbal Hallucinations in a Child with Schizophrenia," shows this right and left temporal lobe interaction.

Over the course of the past thirty years, Jaynes's neurological model for the bicameral mind — the idea that auditory hallucinations are generated by the right hemisphere language areas and perceived by the left hemisphere language areas — has gone from being for the most part ignored (and, at least in one case, dismissed as "too simplistic" — when supportive evidence existed even at the time),[48] to now being considered the most widely accepted explanation for the neurological underpinnings of auditory hallucinations. For example, in a recent illustrated book on the brain geared toward the general public, the authors note that "during auditory hallucinations, fMRI scans show activity mainly in right-hemisphere language areas, rather than in the left-hemisphere language areas typically active in speech production. This may explain why ... the patient mistakenly attributes them to an external source."[49] Unfortunately, the authors do not credit Jaynes for first proposing these ideas three decades before their widespread acceptance.

In summary, a great deal of new evidence from a wide variety of sources supports each of Jaynes's four main hypotheses. These new findings build on the substantial evidence Jaynes details for his theory in *The Origin of Consciousness in the Breakdown of the Bicameral Mind* and in this volume. In the more than three decades since the publication of his book, nothing significant has been found that contradicts Jaynes's ideas. Although the first three hypotheses remain controversial, Jaynes's fourth hypothesis — his neurological model for the bicameral mind — has now been confirmed by more than a decade of brain imaging studies. Although Jaynes is not always acknowledged for being the first to propose a right hemisphere language area locus for auditory hallucinations, this hypothesis has now reached the level of general scientific acceptance.

---

47. See Marcel Kuijsten, "Consciousness, Hallucinations, and the Bicameral Mind," in M. Kuijsten (ed.), *Reflections on the Dawn of Consciousness* (Henderson, NV: Julian Jaynes Society, 2006).

48. See comments by doctors Ghazi Asaad and Bruce Shapiro in H. Steven Moffic, "What About the Bicameral Mind?" *American Journal of Psychiatry*, 1987, *144*, 696.

49. Rita Carter, et al., *The Human Brain: An Illustrated Guide to Its Structure, Function, and Disorders* (London: Dorling Kindersley, 2009).

## THE CONSEQUENCES OF CONSCIOUSNESS

Julian Jaynes promised a second book titled *The Consequences of Consciousness*. Unfortunately, this widely anticipated book never materialized. We now know that the book was never completed. However, based on the discussion contained in the present volume, along with the Afterword to the 1990 and later editions of *The Origin of Consciousness in the Breakdown of the Bicameral Mind*, we have a good idea of what Jaynes would have included.

Jaynes would have discussed the impact of consciousness on emotions. With the development of consciousness, affect becomes emotion, shame becomes guilt, fear becomes anxiety, anger becomes hatred, and affiliation becomes love. Also, mating becomes modern sexual behavior, as the development of consciousness for the first time provided humans with the ability to engage in sexual fantasy. Jaynes covers this subject in Chapters 12, 14, and 16 as well as in the Interviews and Discussion sections.

Jaynes would likely have also discussed the development of consciousness in children. Jaynes argues that children develop consciousness between the ages of four and six through the acquisition of language and training by parents. Jaynes discusses this in the interviews in Chapters 25, 26, and 27, as well as in the Discussion section.

He would have also included his writings on the difference between conscious dreams and bicameral dreams. Some of his ideas on dreams can be found in Chapter 20 as well as in the Discussion section. Jaynes would likely have also included his writings on vestiges of bicamerality in preliterate societies. Some of his thoughts on this topic can be found in the Discussion section. He might have also written on the nature and development of the self (see Chapter 14), the discovery of the concept of time in ancient history (see Chapter 14), and the development of autobiographical memory (see chapters 12, 14, and 16).

## WHAT'S INCLUDED IN THE BOOK

Included in this volume are the majority of articles published by Jaynes along with both published and previously unpublished lectures, interviews, and question and answer sessions. Not included in the book are early scientific articles by Jaynes on animal behavior that would generally not be of interest to those outside of the field of ethology. Also not included are four articles that were included in my previous book, *Reflections on the Dawn of Consciousness*. These are "Verbal Hallucinations and Preconscious Mentality," "The Ghost of a Flea: Visions of William Blake," "The Meaning of King Tut," and "Dragons of the Shang Dynasty."

The first section provides the reader with biographical information on Julian Jaynes. The next section, Articles and Lectures, consists of articles and lectures by Jaynes ordered chronologically. In reading them in the order they are presented, one can see Jaynes's ideas as they develop over time. We first learn about psychology's struggle to break free from philosophy and become more like the physical sciences, and the negative impact this would have on the study of topics such as consciousness and hypnosis. His metaphors for the distinct methods of discovery between physics and psychology remain relevant to psychology and consciousness studies today.

In Jaynes's memorial to the psychologist Edwin Boring, we learn not only about Boring but also about the history of psychology and about Jaynes himself. It also contains a foreshadowing of Jaynes's later writing on consciousness as well as his characteristic bits of wisdom ("A man to others is like a many-sided mirror…"). Next Jaynes discusses more specifically the importance of understanding the history of psychology, so that one might understand the impact of various trends on how the field developed, and stresses the importance of learning the history of any subject one tries to understand, rather than only studying it from a modern perspective. In "The Problem of Animate Motion in the Seventeenth Century," Jaynes suggests that to a large extent the modern scientific disciplines are structured out of seventeenth century divisions of the problem of motion. We learn more about the history of science, the important role of metaphor in the process of scientific discovery, and the roots of Descartes's dualism.

The remaining articles and lectures discuss various aspects of Jaynes's ideas about the origin of consciousness, the evolution of language, the bicameral mind, and the many implications of his theory. In two previously unpublished lectures, Jaynes extends his theory to dreams and discusses his ideas on the nature of the self. The remaining articles and lectures have been previously published in academic journals, but will be new to most readers of this volume. Previously difficult to obtain by those outside of academia, having these articles and lectures gathered in one volume ensures they will be much more widely read and referenced.

For the sake of completeness, some repetition was unavoidable, both in the lectures and discussion. However, given the number of misconceptions about Jaynes's theory, some degree of repetition is probably desirable. Those who wish to minimize repetition can read the longer explanation of Jaynes's theory in Chapter 19 and skip the shorter versions in Chapters 8 and 17. These shorter versions may be useful for instructors teaching courses on consciousness or others interested in more succinct explanations of Jaynes's theory.

In the last two sections, Interviews and Discussion, readers will find many of their questions about Jaynes's theory answered. In these sections Jaynes also delves into many interesting topics that are not covered in his book. It is hoped that these interviews and discussions will both deepen readers' understanding of Jaynes's theory as well as clear up many of the lingering misconceptions.

While aspects of Jaynes's theory remain controversial, it should be pointed out that no theory of consciousness is widely accepted. There is only the prevailing view that consciousness somehow evolved biologically and is thus found in prehistoric humans as well as some higher mammals. However, this view is based more on unchallenged assumptions than clearly defined evidence. Biologically-based views of consciousness ignore the well documented variability and malleability of consciousness in pre-linguistic children, preliterate societies, and in normal adults in trance states such as hypnosis. If they are to be taken seriously, it is incumbent upon critics of Jaynes's theory to offer persuasive alternate explanations for such things as imaginary companions, command hallucinations, and the frequency of hallucinations in both modern and tribal peoples. In the absence of viable alternatives, Jaynes's theory must be viewed as the best explanation for these phenomena.

The nature of consciousness will undoubtedly be debated for generations to come, and any major consensus in the short term is unlikely. Jaynes's ideas on consciousness remain not only highly relevant but indeed far ahead of much of the current thinking in the field. It is hoped that as new evidence for Jaynes's theory becomes more widely known, the theory will continue to gain the wider appreciation it merits.[50]

---

50. For a thorough understanding of Jaynes's theory, readers of this volume are encouraged to also read Julian Jaynes's original work, *The Origin of Consciousness in the Breakdown of the Bicameral Mind*, as well as *Reflections on the Dawn of Consciousness: Julian Jaynes's Bicameral Mind Theory Revisited*. To learn about upcoming events and to join the online discussion, please visit the Julian Jaynes Society website at julianjaynes.org.

# PART I

# Biography

# CHAPTER 1

# Julian Jaynes: 1920–1997

Byron A. Campbell
Sam Glucksberg
Marcia K. Johnson

JULIAN JAYNES WAS BORN IN WEST NEWTON, Massachusetts on February 27, 1920. After work at both Harvard and McGill Universities, he received his bachelor's degree in 1941 from McGill University. He earned his master's degree from Yale University in 1948. His doctoral degree from Yale University was not awarded until 1977, some 13 years after his arrival at Princeton University in 1964 — more on this later. Dr. Jaynes served as a reader in psychology at the University of Toronto from 1944 to 1960. While at Princeton, Dr. Jaynes served as Research Psychologist, then Lecturer with rank of Associate Professor, and finally as a visiting Lecturer and Senior Fellow until his retirement because of illness in 1995. From 1965–1969 he was master of Wilson College, the first undergraduate college at Princeton, and he was instrumental in the development of alternatives to selective eating clubs for upperclassmen and for women. On November 21, 1997, at the age of 77, Julian Jaynes died in Charlottetown, Prince Edward Island, Canada. He greatly loved Prince Edward Island, where he had spent summers since childhood at his family's summer home.

Jaynes's scientific career spanned almost five decades. His first published paper, "The Function of the Cerebral Cortex" with W.C. Stanley, was published in the *Psychological Review* in 1949. It was an influential paper relevant to the view that a primary function of the cortex was an inhibitory one. During his time at Yale Dr. Jaynes made major contributions to our

---

Memorial Resolution prepared by special committee, approved by unanimous vote at the meeting of the Princeton University Faculty on March 2, 1998.

understanding of imprinting, and became a leading expert on the interaction of learned and innate behavior. When he completed his graduate
work at Yale he declined to submit a dissertation. There are at least two
stories about this (and perhaps some truth to each): that he wanted to feel
free to pursue not only his scientific but also his literary and philosophical interests, and felt that he should not be burdened by the responsibility
of living up to a doctoral degree in experimental psychology from Yale
University. Another story is that he was asked for some revisions on his
dissertation and didn't agree with them. In any event, he then went to
England on one of his periodic long-term visits to pursue interests in
literature, theater, philosophy, and history. These interests would later bear
fruit in his scholarly career.

Jaynes returned from England in 1964 ready to resume his work in
experimental psychology. Fortunately for us, he recalled an open-ended
invitation made nearly a decade earlier from a classmate at Yale, Byron
Campbell, to join his research group at Princeton. While at Princeton,
Jaynes made important contributions to our understanding of how memory processes develop in infant mammals, and to the history of psychology. He was the founding chairman of Cheiron, the International Society
for the History of the Behavioral and Social Sciences, and served on the
editorial boards of important journals in this field. He stayed at Princeton
until his retirement in 1995, enjoying the relative freedom of his part time
lecturer position to follow his interests wherever they led. He cared about
the intellectual development of students and his courses on the History of
Psychology and on Consciousness were challenging and popular, drawing
students from many departments.

In 1977, in recognition of Jaynes's contributions, the faculty of the
Psychology Department at Yale took the extraordinary step of collating
a set of Jaynes's most influential and important papers, and submitted
the bound set as his doctoral dissertation. Jaynes was simply told that he
would be granted the doctoral degree whether he liked it or not. Jaynes
graciously accepted the invitation to accept it in person, so after an inter-
val of over two decades, was awarded the degree that he richly deserved.
Throughout his career, Jaynes would confound conventional wisdom with
his original, if not to say maverick ideas, and won acclaim and recognition
both within academic circles and without. He received honorary doctor-
ates from Rhode Island College in 1979 and from Elizabethtown College
in 1985.

The book for which Jaynes was best known was published in January 1977: *The Origin of Consciousness in the Breakdown of the Bicameral Mind*. It was a runner up for the National Book Award in 1978, and led to world-wide speaking and lecture invitations. In this book, Jaynes offers a number of provocative ideas about human consciousness: He argues that as recently as 2000 B.C., people did not make decisions, introspect or reminisce. Rather when faced with decisions, they, as did the characters in the *Iliad*, heard voices that they took to be gods directing their actions. Jaynes proposed these admonitions were stored in the right hemisphere and communicated to the left hemisphere. According to Jaynes, this bicameral mind contributed to social organization that worked under conditions of strong authority and consensus, but that broke down with the spread of writing, increases in population, and large migrations — conditions in which the voices no longer agreed. Jaynes proposed that modern consciousness arises from the power of language to create metaphors and analogies: consciousness as a "mind-space" — a *place* inside our heads in which an 'I' approaches problems, *sees* solutions, and creates a *narrative* out of events. This phenomenal location of consciousness is arbitrary — a learned, social construction. In a scholarly tour de force, he used literary, historical, philosophical, anthropological, psychological, and neurological evidence to argue for his bold and, to some, outrageous theory. The theory remains contentious today, but no one doubts its originality or its impact in fields as disparate as theology, cultural anthropology, and psychopathology. Neither can anyone doubt the theory's continued appeal: it is still being hotly debated in scholarly circles, as well as on the internet by a devoted group of passionately interested people.

We think that this is what would be most gratifying to Julian Jaynes: that he inspired lively debate across the spectrum of intellectual thought. Whether his theory of consciousness will prove right or wrong, he took on the problem of human consciousness and aroused intense interest in it. That this problem remains at the center of contemporary intellectual thought is a testament to Jaynes's qualities as an original and provocative thinker.

CHAPTER 2

# Humility as a Profession:
# A Memorial to Julian Jaynes

Brian J. McVeigh

IT HAS NOW BEEN TEN YEARS since the death of a professor who influenced me in so many ways. I can remember him sitting before me, savoring each sip of his beer in the Annex Restaurant and Cocktail Lounge across from Princeton University's main library. Though a graduate student, I signed up for this professor's PSYCH 319 ("Psychology of Consciousness") in the spring of 1987. About once a week he would invite me out to share a pitcher or two of beer at the Annex, at the time a favorite meeting place for Princeton graduate students and faculty. He always insisted on paying. With his disheveled raincoat that made him look like Lieutenant Detective Columbo, it was hard to believe that the professor, Julian Jaynes, was an *enfant terrible* of the psychology world. I found it flattering, exciting, and exhilarating to be asked to have drinks by a man who had ignited a nuclear bomb of a theory under the citadel built to house the academic disciplines.

His ideas were not about rearranging the furniture; they were about an intellectual earthquake that could reshape the architectonics far beyond any scholarly sanctuary. For a man who had decentered us further away from our divine heritage, his attitude was strikingly nonchalant. For a man who, like Galileo and Darwin, had knocked humankind down one more rung on the ladder to divinity, his disposition was disconcertingly matter of fact. For a man who had set out to show how the most cherished feature of our being — conscious interior experience — was culturally learned during a historical period that could be pinpointed rather than biologically innate, he seemed terribly unconcerned.

First published in *The Jaynesian*, Vol. 1, Issue 2. © 2007 Julian Jaynes Society.

Nevertheless, detached, dispassionate, or indifferent are not the adjectives I would choose to describe his stance toward his findings. This was a scholar's scholar who had devoted his life to solving the enigmas of conscious experience.

My mother had ordered me a copy of *The Origin of Consciousness in the Breakdown of the Bicameral Mind* when I was in high school. In the early 1980s I actually heard him speak at a small college in upstate New York. In his book Prof. Jaynes had discussed spirit possession, the topic I chose for my dissertation when I entered Princeton University. Frustrated by the lack of a comprehensive theory as to why possession was possible in the first place, I dusted off my copy of *The Origin* and made an appointment to visit Prof. Jaynes to discuss my research. His office, cluttered with papers and books, was inconveniently tucked away behind a classroom. After I introduced myself, he allowed me to do most of the talking. For someone with something so historically momentous to say, he was surprisingly modest, unassuming, and politely reticent. Indeed, if one word comes to mind that most accurately captures Julian Jaynes it would be humility.

As I got to know him during our weekly chats in the Annex we would discuss history, psychology, politics, and my research. But he never told me about his many years spent in England as a playwright and actor. It would not be until 2006 that I learned of his artistic achievements and actually saw some of them in his family summer home in Keppoch, Prince Edward Island. He also never told me about his three-year imprisonment (at the U.S. Penitentiary at Lewisburg, Pennsylvania) during World War II for fleeing from a Civilian Service work camp for conscientious objectors.

More than once Prof. Jaynes mentioned how much he admired what another scholar had said: "the willingness to be wrong." About a decade after his book appeared, he was still wondering how it might have been written differently. Maybe he had gotten some of the details wrong. Maybe the dating for the emergence of consciousness was off. Maybe the deception demonstrated by chimpanzees was more sophisticated than he thought. Maybe hypnosis did not have the significance he thought it had. "Oh well, these are issues that need to be cleared up," he would say with a wave of his hand. His attitude to his critics was understated disappointment rather than burning bitterness.

If humbleness is what I associate with Prof. Jaynes, arrogance is what comes to mind when I think of my days in Princeton University's Anthropology Department. When I was a graduate student, a narrow

alley separated Aaron Burr Hall and Green Hall. The former housed
the Anthropology Department, and the Psychology and Sociology
Departments were in the latter. In spite of their proximity there was very
little communication between them, and while Prof. Jaynes was always
eager to hear about the findings of anthropologists, my mentors and peers
in the Anthropology Department had very little interest in learning from
the other social sciences. In my department, graduate students discussed
Freud as if he had single-handedly founded the social sciences; Marx was
viewed as if he had useful relevance for what ailed whole swathes of the
globe; and there was still enthusiastic hope for the success of the Soviet
Union. Meanwhile, Julian Jaynes quietly pursued his research with an
open mind. He saw no need to dress up his scholarly findings in trendy
identity politics that seemed to motivate the research agendas of some in
my department.

While certain professors in my department pontificated, Prof. Jaynes
expressed his genuine humility by asking me, a lowly graduate student,
what I actually thought about an issue.

Jaynes did not publish volumes of jargon-filled, technical, or abstruse
writings. His goal was to explain, not to impress. We are fortunate that
*The Origin* is relatively short, highly readable, and even entertaining. This
is no small feat in today's world of academics, glutted as it is with unread-
able, long-winded, and pompous tomes. Whatever one may make of his
conclusions, even the casually interested reader has no excuse not to read
Julian Jaynes's book. It is a product of a man who stood in reverential awe
of that crown of both our social and natural development — the human
psyche. His ideas lead in so many potentially fascinating directions. It is in
a spirit of hope — and as I am certain Julian Jaynes would want it, humility — that we look forward to their future impact.

# CHAPTER 3

# Julian Jaynes: Portrait of the Psychologist as a Maverick Theorizer

## Sam Keen

PARTISANS OF JULIAN JAYNES'S THEORY claim it explains everything you always wanted to know about consciousness but couldn't find anybody to ask. To his detractors, Jaynes is a dilettante who ranges over many fields in which he lacks expertise, picking and choosing facts that can be woven into his woolly hypothesis. Some are calling him the Velikovsky of the psychological world. Velikovsky's theories, in *Worlds in Collision* and other works, are also wild and controversial, but some of his predictions have proved accurate, and he enjoys a certain amount of credibility among scientists.

Just who is Julian Jaynes, and why is he saying all these radial things about consciousness? He is something of a maverick among academic psychologists. Since 1964, he has been a member of the psychology department at Princeton, where he directs research and teaches courses in the history of psychology. It is not wholly inaccurate to see Jaynes as a monomaniac, but all that means is that he has pursued a single question with unusual passion.

His quest for the grail of consciousness began early. "As a child," he says, "I was fascinated by the inner world I alone could see, and I wondered what was the difference between seeing inwardly and outwardly." His search took him into philosophy and literature at Harvard and McGill universities. But he was dissatisfied with the imprecision of poetry and switched to psychology with the hope of finding an approach to consciousness that had the rigor and exactness of physics. At Yale, he did graduate studies in human physiology and animal behavior, with the naïve assumption that by isolating the relationship between the brain and

First published in *Psychology Today*, Vol. 11, 66–67. © 1977 Sussex Publishers, LLC. Reprinted with permission.

behavior he could capture the meaning of consciousness. But the more he studied the history of the efforts to understand consciousness, the more he became convinced that psychology was bad poetry masquerading as science. It was confused because it was based upon unexamined metaphors — consciousness as a blank slate, a computer, or a camera.

Although Jaynes remained at Yale as a student and research assistant for ten years, he finally left without completing the requirements for the Ph.D. He has remained critical of the apprenticeship system, in which students are indoctrinated into the prejudices of their professors and receive degrees for furthering unoriginal research. Until the recent publication of his book, Jaynes was best known at Princeton as the master of Wilson College, the home of the outcasts and individualists who do not fit into the system of "eating clubs." His publications range from "Neural Mediation of Mating in Male Cats: Effects of Unilateral and Bilateral Removal of the Neocortex" to "The Evolution of Language in the Late Pleistocene." But it was not until *The Origin* that Jaynes announced he had discovered the grail.

There is an important factor that separates Jaynes's audacious theory from tissue-thin speculations like Erich von Däniken's *Chariot's of the Gods* or claims that Noah's ark has been found on Mr. Ararat — evidence. Jaynes's conclusions are an affront to common sense (the pyramids built by unconscious men?), but so are most of the theories in modern physics. He has been careful to avoid the stigma of mere speculation by making his hypothesis testable. He begins with a definition of consciousness that is specific enough to allow us to see whether it is present in given situations. "I have purposely tried to make my hypothesis falsifiable," he says. "I keep climbing out on limbs. For instance, by dating the origin of consciousness at 1000 B.C., I leave myself open to evidence from archeology. If we found a cuneiform tablet from 3500 B.C. that said something like 'I, King of Lugush, now in the prime of my life, was in my childhood happy, and will until I die to devote myself to expanding my kingdom,' my theories would be seriously in question because this would show early evidence of planning and narrating which are functions of consciousness." The neurological model of the bicameral mind could be cast into doubt if we found that schizophrenic hallucinations did not have their source in the right temporal or parietal lobe.

After the first shock wears off, Jaynes's conclusions do not seem unlike those that have been knocking on the door of our awareness.

Anthropologists have been telling us that there is a radical difference between the mentality of pretechnological peoples and our own. Myths have always pictured a golden age before our age of anxiety when there was no alienation that characterized the difference between the sacred and the profane mind, between peoples who live only within the parentheses of history. What Jaynes has done is to give an exact description of the way in which three modes of human awareness — the bicameral premodern mind, consciousness, and schizophrenia — function. And he takes us on a Cook's tour of the history of civilization in search of evidence of the birth of consciousness.

Jaynes is unlikely to be right in every detail. We can depend on scholars of discrete disciplines to conduct postmortems on the anatomy of his errors. Most experts will miss the point — the delight and fruitfulness of the hypothesis. You will argue with Jaynes on every page, even as you become more conscious of what your own consciousness is and is not. He will stretch your mind. His ideas crawl into your right hemisphere and you will see new patterns and watch the dance of evidence creating a new vision. The man is a dilettante. He delights in playing with ideas. And real thought, like art, involves exaggeration: "The road of excess leads to the palace of wisdom" (Blake). Thinking, especially creative thinking (is there another kind?), involves overstepping the facts. Every metaphor is a mistake. It is, strictly speaking, as inaccurate to say, "My love is like a red, red rose," as to suggest that space is curved, or that quarks have charm. Mind, as Jaynes points out, is metaphor, and thinking is inseparable from poetry. Jaynes's bold theory, warts and all, stimulates the mind and invites it to consider the marvels within its own firmament. And, as Aristotle noted, the mind that can contemplate itself is nearly divine. As Jaynes's ideas run through my mind (at 3:48-mike pace), I begin to see clearly (20-20 vision) how interrelated (like father and son) metaphors and consciousness are. And an old poem, author unknown, keeps floating up from four fathoms deep:

> When the universe began,
> God, they say, created man.
>
> Conversely: dancing round the sod,
> Man, they say, created God.
>
> Watch your words or they may do
> Something of the same to you.

# PART II

## Articles and Lectures

# CHAPTER 4

# The Routes of Science

I WRITE THIS IN A SCORN of the unity of science. My impulse is a disturbed feeling that, as science folds back on itself and comes to be scientifically studied, it is being caricatured into a conformity which is nonsense, into a neglect of its variety which is psychotic, into a nagging and insistent attention to its cross-discipline similarities which are of trivial importance. And having just returned from a fortnight walking tour of a variety of countryside, reading at evening some volumes in the history of science, I want to venture an extravagant metaphor which brings out the differences as I see them between the two extremes of the scientific continuum.

Physics is like climbing a mountain: roped together by a common asceticism of mathematical method, the upward direction, through blizzard, mist, or searing sun, is always certain, though the paths are not. The problem of each new generation is easy: rope on, test the pitons, follow the leader, look out for better lay-backs and footholds to the heights. A source book in its history is a simple and inspiring matter; it is ledge to ledge upward. This clear? Well, no, even though physics text books try to structure our perception so. But the disorder is on the ledges, never in the direction.

Psychology is so different! Instead of the difficult simplicity of physics, psychology is full of an easy complexity. While physics gains in truth when most quantitative, psychology when most quantitative is of least scope, though the sweetness of elegance lingers over. And with its infinity of problems throughout the evolutionary scale, its Baroque experimental paradigms with which it attempts them, with its own criteria of excellence that change from one area to another, from one point of view to another, with its laws that are laws of themselves, and its embarrassed shiftiness from objective to subjective languages and back to describe its purposes and observations, it is less like a mountain than a huge entangled forest in full shining summer, so easy to walk through on certain levels, that

Article by Julian Jaynes first published in *American Scientist*, Vol. 54, Issue 1. © 1966 Sigma Xi, The American Research Society. Reprinted with permission.

anyone can and everyone does. The student's problem is a frantic one: he must shift for himself. It is directions he is looking for, not height. And the direction out of the forest is unknown, perhaps nonexistent, nor is it even certain that that is what he is meant to do. Multitudes cross each other's paths in opposite directions with generous confidence and happy chaos. The bright past and the dark present ring with diverging cries and discrepant echoes of "here is the way!" from one vale to another. Ear-plugs and blinders curiously replace boot cleats and pitons. If less invigorating than mountain climbing, it is, or should be, more fun for adventurists. And being closer to an altitude where most people live, psychology is ununited and unisolated with the necessity of difficult techniques in common, and so shows a remarkable variety of behavior corresponding to the variety of the terrain. In this forest, its history shouting with opinions clashing in the darkness of evidence, its tangled variety of paths, some overgrown with disuse, some broadened with fashion, and other weaving somewhere under the strange shrieks of religious and political vested interests hidden high in the foliage, in all this challenge of complexity and divergence, is it possible that psychology could or should pattern itself on physics? That a forest is like a mountain? Can all complexity be reduced to simplicity as in physics if we work hard enough?

What rubbish that it was once thought so! The time was not so distant when, following Mach's attempt to unify all science about "sensations," and the physicalism of the Vienna Circle, Carnap[1] could say "every sentence of psychology may be formulated in physical language," not evidently realizing that that itself is a sentence of psychology and so on in infinite regress, which, since physical language cannot be infinite, negates Carnap's position, at least to me. How much truer, for example, to say that every statement of physics must reduce to a statement in psychology since it is the behavior of an organism! But such illogicality (to which Whitehead and Russell's Theory of Types does not apply) was never apparent then, back in the days when something called *The Encyclopedia for the Unity of Science* was first appearing, bluebook by bluebook from Chicago. Science then was thought of as a thing, unconscious of the metaphor of thingness. It was thought meaningful to speak of one science as being where another science was at a particular time, as if all were traveling the same road, or of the normal development of a science, as if the various "sciences" were so many tadpoles waiting on Froghood, and something more than mere

---

1. Rudolf Carnap, "Psychology in Physical Language," reprinted in Alfred J. Ayer (ed.), *Logical Positivism* (Glencoe, Ill.: Free Press, 1959).

academic conveniences. And even today, there are still individual scientists so timorous of their status as to think of it as a cult, a cult united by a mystique called "the scientific method," a cult that has nothing in common with ordinary rational activities, a kind of pure virginal objectivity that has to guard its beauty against the wrinkled advances of religion, art, or ethics like a Susanna among her peeping Elders. How long gone such notions!

And where was psychology in all this? Anxiously toadeating with the positivists. Weaned too quickly from philosophy, psychology mewled around for other dependencies. Accused of being not really a science, it nervously sprang to conform. It purified its journals into an objective aridity. It sophisticated itself above all other sciences in statistical and design techniques. It wrapped itself in cunning lingos that hid its softer parts from critical view. It followed Bridgman into operationism. It wandered the Gothic wonders of Hull's crumbing theorems or reduced into Skinnery descriptivism. I doubt if all that valiant nonsense could have taken place had it not been that the aggressive anti-intellectualism of naïve behaviorism was frightening psychologists away from the marshes and bogs of the forest where perhaps its greatest adventure lie, and onto its drier, more barren knolls where the mountain of physics is most easily seen.

But that is history now, though I hope I've stepped on a few viable toes in the last paragraphs; I was stamping in the hope that I was. Rarely since World War II have there been similar attempts to confine the activities of psychologists into any particular laws or paradigms or methods. Although not always within academic departments of psychology, there has been a tremendous rise in various types of observation of both men and animals, in controlled and uncontrolled environments, with hosts of new variables both in and outside the organism, and observations where the very idea of a variable is eschewed, descriptive theories that do not pretend, though they may say something real of what lies behind the phenomena they are summarizing. While physics lends itself to the metaphorical verb "breakthrough," perhaps psychology's correlative verb is "breakout," as a previous attempt to throw an envelope around some aspect of research is suddenly seen to be a subjective barrier that is part of the psychodynamics of the scientist himself, and with the succession of generations gives way to the larger visions. Certainly, there is a sense now of an explosive expansion of vision in all fields of psychology, with more and more of the forest visible at each glance, vistas that would be strange and frightening to the battle-scarred veterans of a previous era, the Hunters and the Lashleys hunting and lashing (why not?) their half-imaginary opponents over the wastelands of behaviorism. Be it immediately said here that it is not behaviorism I object to, but behaviorism alone. Or anything that waves off whole areas as unimportant because they conflict with theory, any refusal to welcome whole-heartedly the multi-pathed nature of the endeavor. My point is that the history, philosophy, and sociology of one science should not be modeled on that of another, that there is no such thing as normal scientific progress, no one pattern of scientific activity, no one criterion of excellence though there may be of aesthetic satisfaction, that there is no one "scientific" method, and no one way of scientific history.

I erect this discussion of the unique divergent complexity of psychology as a background against which to consider some problems in the history of science and to praise a cluster of excellent new books in the history of psychology which represent these problems. As I have written elsewhere, there are three possible modes or cause-sets of intellectual history: *ethnographic*, or science as generated by culture and epoch; *biographic*, or science as generated by the lives and aspirations of scientists; and *doxographic*, or science as generated by previous science. Ideal scientific histories are mixtures of all three in which it is part of the historian's integrity to estimate in each new step which of the three cause-sets were most important. In any of the three there are two methods of composition or types, *representative* history, or writing history as it really was, making one's work representative of the time one is talking about, and *parapposite* history, which I have coined from *para* = near + *apposite* to mean history conceived as a dialogue of the present with the past. We do not attempt in parapposite history ever to resurrect archaic problems or the blind alleys of science, only to record its successes as they throw light on the problems of current interest.

Here again, we find a difference between sciences as to the applicability of this distinction. Representativeness and parappositeness coalesce in the history of physics. Physics is too theoretically simple to have many great errors and too technically difficult to invite them. Such errors as it does have are not blind alleys as they tend to be in psychology, but ledges on the upward climb. The Rutherford atom is not so much an error as a first approximation to Bohr, and so on. It is ledge to ledge, as in the succession (what a noble one) of Newton, Euler, Lagrange, Hamilton, etc. And that part of the thought of a particular age which is relevant to physics is also representative of its time. But in psychology, where every man, woman, and child is his own busy laboratory — theories of other people and animals being a necessity to ordinary life — representativeness is a much more difficult affair. Much of what a previous epoch was thinking in psychology may be quite irrelevant to current problems. These considerations suggest a law that might be stated: The narrower the topic, the more nearly parappositeness equals representativeness. In the rest of this essay, I am using these distinctions to ask questions of recent books in the history of psychology whose answers demonstrate a unique complexity unlike any other science.

The first point about all of the current work in the history of psychology is that none of it is or tries to be either representative or parapposite the history of psychology as a whole. It is not even representative of the major ideas through time. If the material of these and most other books in the field is plotted against the age from which it comes, the most apparent characteristics of the resulting graph is the inevitable J-shaped dip through the long Medieval period. While the Greek heritage is usually given some representation, the huge Christian confusion of psychology and ethics, so important in cultural history, is carefully avoided. Nor should the dip in the Middle Ages be as deep as it is if a work is to be representative of history. It is, of course, quite true that, after the Roman defilement of its Greek sources and the huge oppressiveness thrown over science by the victory of Augustine's ideas after the fall of Rome in 410, there is nothing of intellectual originality in science written until ninth century Basra. But some thought was going on which a representative history would have to represent. And the Renaissance, particularly in psychology, occurred long before any of these books give an indication. I am referring particularly to that resplendent meeting of Arabic, Greek, Christian, and Hebrew ideas that coalesced so brightly in Islamic Spain just after 1000 A.D. The sixteenth century, that thrilling crescendo of adventure and exploration, the century that practically invented the idea of nature and so began modern biology, the century that had so much to show and so little to say, is never mentioned. And through later periods, books differ widely, some being more representative of some things than others, but none representative of the history of psychology as a whole.

Nor could any of the recent work be considered parapposite to modern psychology as a whole. Older histories, particularly when psychology was cramped up into psychophysics, could attempt parapposite history. But so broad is the spectrum of interest and endeavor, so free its viewpoint and methodology, that a parapposite history of modern psychology as a whole is unfeasible. How crisscrossing the paths are! How lesser trails are grown over with disuse! How some can never now be traced, while others may be reblazed and made clear by some new discoverer who makes it all parapposite to some new relevance! How many new ones are starting now that will go we know not where! If the history of a divergent and less sequentially dependent science like psychology is to be coherent, it must abandon all wish that it feel or look like the mountain climbing of physics. Its task must be the disentangling of confused paths. The more these paths are restricted to single topics, the more representative and parapposite history can coalesce into something sound and with meaning. All of the books mentioned here have used this approach, and examined together they mark a significant and abrupt change in the way psychologists look at their own history.

Let us first take the masterful new *Source Book in the History of Psychology* by Herrnstein and Boring.[2] There have been two previous sourcebooks, a mentalistic one by Rand in 1912, and a much more valuable and parapposite one by Dennis in 1942. But both stagger about like drunks through a single reeling chronology that is oblivious to any meaningful succession of steps. And this is where Herrnstein and Boring do something different. They map a certain part of the forest into fifteen separate tracks going in usually different directions, the beginnings and endings in time varying haphazardly with the path — as certainly they should. And this they do very successfully. The ground-swells under these paths are usually doxographically indicated in succinct introductions. Half of the paths are safely over next to the mountain of physics in what is chummily called, since Fechner, psychophysics. I say "safely" because these problems in sensation and perception are precisely those which yield to a ledge to ledge metaphor most easily. These are the paths of sensory specification and measurement, of size, distance, and space perception, and three in psycho-neurology: cerebral localization, isomophism, and the reflex. A few of the other paths, like Functionalism, I am not sure exist in the same way the authors do. And perhaps one of the paths should have been motivation, even though that subject is sometimes a little like the Emperor's clothes to me. But the four articles which comprise the path of comparative psychology of Romanes to Jennings made me gasp with their rightness. The paths on learning, association from Aristotle to Wundt and experimental studies

2. Richard J. Herrnstein and Edwin G. Boring (eds.), *A Source Book in the History of Psychology* (Cambridge: Harvard University Press, 1965).

from Ebbinghaus to Köhler, are impeccable composings. As a selection of the important ways winding over what these particular authors feel is the abiding terrain of psychology, this is an extremely welcome book. It should also be mentioned that almost 20 percent of the book is comprised of new translations which alone make this beautifully produced work a necessity for the serious bookshelf on the history of psychology.

This path-mapping type of history is also the plan of that superbly help-ful *Psychology in the Making*,[3] the histories of selected research problems that Postman has edited. There are two dangers when active researchers write up the histories of their subjects as they have in this book: a dependence on secondary and tertiary sources, not having the time or the lingual abilities to go straight to the source; and second, cliché historical general-izations that are best forgotten. Some of these twelve rich chapters suffer here and there from one or the other of these errors, making the work not always reliable in detail. But the virtues of having active researchers write history overwhelm these faults: the far greater understanding of the specific problems that is seldom grasped by the historian of science, the immensely sharper focus with which we are shown previous work, the sense and soundness and evidence-orientation that would otherwise be missing. The book sets a standard for histories of special subjects, and, like the Herrnstein and Boring, is successful precisely because parapposite and representative history coalesce with restriction of the topic.

The same realization that the history of psychology is an untangling of complexity seems to be the practical decision behind an admirable series of new books on selected fields of psychology now coming out under the general editorship of Kessen and Mandler. These are volumes on a much less ambitious scale than Herrnstein and Boring, though similar in that they are comprised of historical excerpts fitted together by commentary. It is perhaps illustrative of this freer way of looking at intellectual history that I am espousing, that they are on casually incognate topics, the three I have read being on a method, a concept, and a biological time-span, respectively. All three are utterly different in their purposes and virtues, demonstrating again that the history of science has no normality.

Miller's *Mathematics and Psychology*[4] will be daylight and release to those who, through bad education, have become darkened with anxiety at facing this swiftly developing field that is sometimes too careless with its assignations of significance to be followed by anybody but its initiates.

---

3. Leo Postman (ed.), *Psychology in the Making* (New York: Knopf, 1963).

4. George A. Miller, *Mathematics and Psychology* (New York: John Wiley and Sons, 1964).

Not that this book takes one very far. All its selections and textual material have been restrained to a level that — perhaps unfortunately — never peers beyond simple calculus, making its insights and clarities and structurings available to any intelligent reader. The tremendous service Miller does is to dissipate certain confusions which have clouded the field by distinguishing between five main uses of mathematics in psychology: *discursive* as in Herbert and Lewin; *normative* or theories of utility and risk taking where equations are deduced which usually maximize some efficiency value; *determinate functional*, or functional inferences of processes that are actually going on, usually after the pattern of early physical theory, from Fechner to Simon; *statistical functional*, dealing with sets of anything from judgments as in Thurstone to stimuli and responses as in recent stochastic models by Estes or Bush and Mosteller; and *structural* applications to various problems from intelligence in Spearman, through linguistics in Chomsky, to patterns of group structure in Festinger, Schachter, and Back. There is even some cybernetical frosting to this delicious multi-layered cake, although my kitchen metaphor is sickening next to the power and lucidity with which these selections have been made and text written. As history it is too recent to have much, only four of its twenty-seven selections being prior to 1900. But as history I miss Borelli, whom I regard as the founder of biophysics, and who incidentally got the Bernoullis interested in psychology, one of whom is represented with an excellent excerpt; and I disagree with Miller that Rashevsky is unexcerptable, having done so myself for an abortive handbook on the subject some years ago. But these are trivial. Every course in quantitative psychology should begin with this book.

The terrain that the Mandlers face in their *Thinking*[5] is so different! Whereas Miller faced a near absence of material in previous centuries, and further restricted himself by the mathematical level of his intended readers, the Mandlers have just the opposite. Everyone who ever lived has at some time thought about thinking, and their problem was somehow to cut away the luxurious overgrowth of the subject to obtain some clear path. This they have done by leaving other topics of thinking to other books and by structuring a point of view that can stand in modern problem-solving in a Gestalt manner, looking back around the corners of directed thinking and the problem of imageless thought straight back into the broad road of associationism all the way to Aristotle. It is thus constantly concerned

---

5. Jean M. Mandler and George Mandler, *Thinking: From Association to Gestalt* (New York: John Wiley and Sons, 1964).

with making discriminations within the problem, distinguishing it from contemporaneous others along the way with a well-written commentary that seems to have an uncanny grasp of the essentials. It is much more history than Miller's book, about half of the selections being prior to 1900. But it is even more than merely parapposite history. It is history as the texture of a problem where it is to be unraveled and pondered. It is a use of history unknown because unnecessary in physics. And their adventurous conclusion after these two battles of associationism that there is "a core problem still to be solved, some grand design that will unlock the mysteries of the nature of thought," coming at the end of a work so carefully wrought, sounds like a bugle call that will rally new battalions into the fields. It contains new translations by the authors from G. E. Müller, Oswald Külpe, and a particularly welcome one from Otto Selz that the Mandlers have discovered, at least for me. But how regrettable that they did not retranslate Aristotle, since they have been misled by the foul rendering of Hammond into a distortion of Greek thought. The very first line of their first excerpt, for example, has Aristotle saying that the mind thinks its ideas in the forms of images. This should read that thinking thinks the forms in the images, a more difficult and quite different notion.

While Miller's book is a disentangling of recent beginnings, and the Mandlers' is the discovery and putting in order of one, Kessen's *The Child*[6] treats the forest of history in yet another way. It demonstrates how a fan of paths in the eighteenth and nineteenth centuries, from Locke, Rousseau, and Pestalozzi on theoretical levels to the Earl of Shaftesbury's righteous lashings in Parliament of English child-hirers, climb up through the sloping highroad of evolutionary theory, only to diverge in the twentieth century into the grand designs of Freud and Piaget on the one hand and into the different views on development and diversity on the other, as in Binet, Gesell, and Watson. Because of the author's purpose, his erudition, and the amenability of his subject, this is most historically satisfying. Psychology, when it turns full face to human behavior, is scarcely extricable from the proliferating vines and ivies of values and aspirations. Nor should it be, the good of man being not always the good of science and always, always far outweighing it. The scientific history of such confrontations, particularly in the study of the child, must recognize the common texture that it has with cultural values as both change through time. Kessen, because of his subject, is refreshingly aware of this and is the most ethnographic of these

6, William Kessen, *The Child* (New York: John Wiley and Sons, 1965).

authors. His commentary constantly paints in the chiaroscuro of thought and prejudice against which the child is being viewed. His appreciation of Hall ("no descendents — only heirs"), for example, is unforgettable. A few of his judgments perhaps need qualification, and both he and Herrnstein and Boring are quite wrong in thinking that comparative psychology was a completely Darwinian affair; it was founded, at least in name, by anti-Darwinian sentiments in France. But these cavils aside, this is a fascinating book that will be a delight to readers far beyond collegiate walls.

All these works, then, illustrate my theme that sciences are different. They do not have a common pattern of growth. Not even the parts of psychology grow alike nor contain cognate materials. In at last shaking free from physicalist structures and confined aims anxiously patterned on physics, psychology should free its sense of history from the historical pattern of physics as well. And the new recognitions of these books, their vigorous avowal of variety, of the need for separating new paths as in Miller, or pruning out unrecognized ones as in the Mandlers, or describing a diverging convergence as in Kessen, or of separating out diversely directed tracks through the forest as Herrnstein and Boring and the Postman book have done is my evidence that this is happening.

Science is one in the sense in which the forest and its hills and mountains are one. We are all on the same land. But the terrains differ. And the routes of science are various. Let us celebrate our variety.

# CHAPTER 5

# Edwin Garrigues Boring:
# 1886–1968

S OME MEN DOMINATE an area of their time by growing admiration on themselves. A few by the affection they instill. Others by power over positions and events. Still others by the genius of their work. Edwin G. Boring dominated his area by none of these. His quality was more complex, sprawling, elusive, intensely personal, without copy or example. It was a blend of deep personal yearnings to love and be loved, to be powerful yet right in the exercise of that power, to be famous yet beget fame in others, to achieve order and establish patterns of merit, and that with a merciless integrity whose fierceness appalled less disciplined men. In 1892, he was a small, unwanted, enuretic, excitable boy, forbidden playmates by insensitive parents, imprisoned upstairs with his feminine imaginary playmate "Mamie," who had a repeated paranoic fantasy of marching down into that matriarchal adult world and shouting "I have found you out!" Three quarters of a century later in 1966, he awoke one night in an absolute darkness, stumbled up out of bed onto some huge plain screaming for lights and for someone to answer him, when suddenly the place he had stumbled to became embathed in search lights and the whole scene turned into a carnival that somehow made him the center of attention, at which point he awoke again, realizing his previous awakening had been a dream, and that he was an old man lying on a hospital cot in Stillman Infirmary dying of a progressive unhealable breaking of his bones. Between these two events was one of the great careers in modern psychology.

*Youth and Early Research*

Born in Philadelphia over the drug store of his great grandfather on October 25, 1886, Boring grew up in a household of older sisters, a callous

Article by Julian Jaynes first published in the *Journal of the History of the Behavioral Sciences*, Vol. 5, Issue 2. © 1969 Wiley Periodicals, Inc. Reprinted with permission.

mother, maiden aunts, and grandmothers all dominated by Quaker faults and virtues. He was first educated at home by the women and then at a Quaker school. In 1904, he went to Cornell to continue a boyhood interest in magnetism and electricity into the study of electrical engineering. Graduating four years later with his M.E., he worked for the Bethlehem Steel Company in Bethlehem, Pennsylvania, during which time he developed an interest in teaching science and physical geography in the Moravian parochial school. With the idea of continuing this more suitable occupation, he returned to Cornell in 1909 to study physical geography, electing as an addition the laboratory course in experimental psychology given by Madison Bentley.[1]

It was Bentley who first encouraged Boring to enter psychology in general, and comparative psychology in particular. And it was as a comparative psychologist that Boring began his research career. His first research demonstrated visual contrast effects in planaria and was the first behavioral study of this species so popular in comparative psychology since.[2]

A complicated maze study was begun about the same time. Lloyd Morgan's program of reasoning by analogy from our own introspection to what the consciousness of animals might be on the basis of similarity of response patterns (what Romanes had earlier called ejective knowledge) had long been (and still is) unrealized by research. Again with Bentley's encouragement, Boring began a maze study along these lines. Human subjects would learn a maze, introspective reports being taken on almost a continuous basis. These reports would then be analyzed for principles and hypotheses which, in the second half of the study, would be tested in rats learning the same maze pattern. So would the minds of men and rats be compared.

The first half of this study was completed even to the point of tying pierced flour sacks on the backs of the subjects (who included Bentley, Dallenbach, and Lucy Day).[3] They were then blindfolded and asked to trace out the maze pattern on the green lawn in front of Morrill Hall — which they did after a fashion. The study was never completed partly

---

1. Boring's own autobiographical writing is remarkable in its candor and fullness, and gives these facts more amply. See particularly his *Psychologist At Large* (New York: Basic Books, 1961) which is an expansion of his chapter in *A History of Psychology in Autobiography*, Vol. IV (Worcester: Clark University Press, 1952).

2. "Note on the Negative Reaction under Light-Adaptation in the Planarian," *Journal of Animal Behavior*, 1912, *2*, 229–248.

3. Edwin G. Boring and Lucy M. Day. "The Use of the Maze in Comparative Psychology," *Psychological Bulletin*, 1912, *9*, 60–61.

because Boring fell in love with the third named subject above. They were married a year or so later, beginning a partnership in which both husband and wife addressed each other as thee and thou throughout a marriage of great mutual devotion.

Another reason the study was not completed was his growing interest in other fields. While still a graduate student, he conducted his now classical four year long experiment on protopathic and epicritic sensibility during nerve-regeneration after cutting one of his own nerves in his arm.[4] At the same time he was doing a fascinating and pioneering study of learning in schizophrenics.[5] He found that they could readily learn simple tasks, but had difficulties where speed was a criterion and showed a lack of normal transfer from one problem to another. The maze part of this study is extremely interesting; as in his earlier study, he found that the course of consciousness in learning a maze went from verbal, visual, and attitudinal cues to kinesthetic ones, and then became automatic. He also completed a study of fidelity of report using moving picture incidents.[6] And all this while he was partly earning his living by preaching in various country churches around Ithaca (he was always an agnostic), as well as working on his thesis topic given him by Titchener. This was his work on visceral sensibility. Using a stomach-tube technique, he found greater sensitivity in the esophagus and stomach to warmth, cold, and the pressures and pains of distension than had ever been guessed at before.[7]

But the major reason why Boring left comparative psychology as well as his other fields of interest was the slow acting but finally pervading influence of Titchener.

*The Influence of Titchener*

Boring had taken Titchener's great course in elementary psychology seven years earlier, but it was only in 1912 when Bentley went to Illinois that Titchener's influence became so deep. "What a man!", Boring later

---

4. "Cutaneous Sensation after Nerve-Division," *Quarterly Journal of Experimental Physiology and Cognate Medical Science*, 1916, *10*, 1–95.

5. "Introspection in Dementia Precox," *American Journal of Psychology*, 1913, *24*, 145–170. "Learning in Dementia Precox," *Psychological Monographs*, 1913, *15*, 2, iv + 101 pp.

6. "Capacity to Report Upon Moving Pictures as Conditioned by Sex and Age: A Contribution to the Psychology of Testimony," *Journal of Criminal Law and Criminology*, 1916, *6*, 820–834.

7. "The Sensations of the Alimentary Canal," *American Journal of Psychology*, 1915, *26*, 1–57. "The Thermal Sensitivity of the Stomach," *American Journal of Psychology*, 1915, *26*, 485–494.

exclaimed, "the nearest approach to genius of anyone with whom I have been closely associated."[8]

Whatever he was, there was no doubt that Titchener was a remarkable phenomenon. He dominated the Cornell department like a feudal lord, had his assistants brush off the magisterial robes in which this bourgeois Englishman with the careful mask of Oxonian diction and German pomp insisted on lecturing, dispensed advice on everything from mushrooms to hardwood floors, from Mohammedian coins to the length of one's honeymoon (he wrote to the Borings on their honeymoon the day they ought to be back at work and they obeyed). He was a paternalistic authoritarian who spoke always with the royal "we," and who never distinguished between his wisdom and his convictions and never hid either.

Titchener was the key influence in Boring's professional life, determining his writing style, his habitual way of thinking about psychology, his relationship to his colleagues, and his ideas of what was important both in science, in men, and in the world. The style of both Titchener and Boring is one of confidential clarity, a simple style with that tendency of simple styles toward oversimplification of complicated matters — a fault which both men shared. Like Titchener, Boring placed a huge emphasis on the German root of experimental psychology to the neglect of others. What and who Titchener thought was important, was equally important for Boring and, regardless of Boring's resilience in changing with the times through the twentieth century, they remained just as important throughout his life. During his last illness, Boring's conversation often wound itself back towards Titchener. Only a year past, he was contemplating writing a huge biography of Titchener using Catherine Drinker Bowen as a model, and like Titchener, Boring grew fat, uncompromisingly fat, though he blamed his ample beltline on cream prescribed for a supposed ulcer during the Clark controversy.

Yet few men could have been so different! And perhaps this explains some of the personal problems which beset Boring's career in middle life. Titchener was distant and outrageously pompous. Boring was warm and confidential — embarrassingly so to many. Titchener froze at self-revelation; once when a student went inquiring about him from an old porter at Oxford and later told Titchener, Titchener walked away in rebuking silence, an incident which perhaps still rankled ten years later when

---

8. For Boring's assessment of Titchener's stature in psychology, see his *A History of Experimental Psychology* (New York: Century, 1929), but also his more personal obituary of Titchener, "Edward Bradford Titchener," *American Journal of Psychology*, 1927, *38*, 489–506.

Titchener wrote the offending student (by then a prominent psychologist), "Do not communicate with me. If you must on departmental matters, go through Weld." In contrast, Boring, like the unwanted boy upstairs with his imaginary playmate, reveled in self-revelation, needed to tell his sorrows and triumphs to others, hid only what might hurt others about himself, found himself a fascinating psychodynamic problem of roomy proportions and welcomed others' interest in it. Titchener barricaded his beliefs against new directions. Boring welcomed them, welcomed Behaviorism when it came along, welcomed operationalism, and more recently in conversation with me welcomed mathematical psychology with the hope that it might "act the Lycurgus for psychology." Titchener never waited for or understood another's ideas. Boring was scrupulous in his respect for an alternative view. Titchener would not abide dissent. Boring encouraged it. Titchener had a sense of honor. Boring had a sense of duty, duty in which he found release. Titchener in his last decade hid from science indulging in irrelevant hobbies. Boring in his last decade was — as he always was — up to his ears in responsibilities and plans. And when illness barred him from them, it was hard. A year ago, he suddenly wept and then shouted angrily at me, "Oh to have died once! And cleanly and quickly! Instead of lingering on with all my responsibilities unfulfilled!"

Twice he told me how he once wished to compare himself (whom he considered to have ordinary intelligence) with Titchener (whom he considered to be a genius), and so in Titchener's presence tried to make a detailed comparison. He found no second to second difference, and no minute to minute difference, but over longer time durations, several, the chief one being that there was no wool gathering in Titchener. According to Boring, if an ordinary person lost his glasses, he would probably look in the same spot twice, while Titchener would only look once. Perhaps. Titchener died an old man at sixty. Boring at eighty-one died young.

## The Grand Trilogy of Histories

Boring's greatest contributions were in the history of psychology. They were contributions which became an influence on the very sense of what psychology was about, where it had come from, and where it was going. And so pervading and accepted has this influence become, that even if wrong, it is difficult now to unravel. Originally, this work was planned as a great trilogy of books. But after finishing the first volume in 1929, he had doubts about his ability to go further, and gave it the title of the trilogy, *A History of Experimental Psychology.*

Its title should have been *Men and Systems in Modern Psychology.* For that is precisely its emphasis. It appeared the same year as Gardner Murphy's *Historical Introduction to Modern Psychology.* Was the zeitgeist, that favorite concept of Boring's, operating in that coincidence? At any rate, both books leaned heavily on secondary sources, Murphy's on such works as Merz's *History of European Thought in the Nineteenth Century,* and Boring's on Titchener's lectures, emphasis, and selectivity. Murphy's book is a more complete free-flowing critical discussion of trends; Boring's a more didactic person-focused journey through the rise of scientific psychology much as Titchener himself would have written it. Indeed, when Titchener died in 1927 mid-way along in the book, Boring felt as relieved as must have John Stuart Mill when his dominating father died. And thereafter the book moved to its final shape with a more Boringian breadth.

It is, as he said himself, a spindle-shaped history stressing the psychology of the half-century from 1860 to 1910, and psychology mostly as Wundt (who is on the frontispiece) and therefore of course Titchener (to whom the book is dedicated) would have defined it. In competition with Murphy's book, it easily won out, becoming as it still is, the basic text for courses in the history of psychology in the world over. This popularity is partly because of the authoritativeness of its tone, the scholarship of its references, and the warm personality of its author that shines through.

Men and authority mattered to Boring, and his history is concerned in selecting what is important rather than what is true, and this slightly hedged criterion accounts for some of its readability and interest. Its neglects are the neglects of Titchener, with an overriding and often unjust emphasis on German psychology with a map of German universities as a cover lining. It followed the Titchenerian habit of cutting off psychology from its contemporaneous sources in philosophy, biology, and general culture in a way that is not entirely acceptable to modern historiography of science. The work is thorough yet sometimes wrong, easy to read yet sometimes difficult to understand, always interesting but seldom profound.

Although he doubted his ability to go farther, he did complete the second volume, working on it between 1935 and 1942. This is his *Sensation and Perception in the History of Experimental Psychology,* which treats its material by topic and problem instead of by men and schools. It is a definitive, always useful and sometimes provocative discussion of experimental phenomena, space perception, smell and tactual sensibility, kinesthesis, internal sensations such as visceral, hunger, and thirst, and perceptions of time and motion. It is doubtful if anyone will ever again reach so much of the primary material in these areas. Certainly no one had when it came out, and consequently there was no one erudite enough to review the work. What an irony of scholarship that a book so snows its generation that it slips into permanence almost unnoticed!

And again he had doubts about his ability to complete the grand trilogy. There doubts, alas, won. The volume was to be on feeling, emotion, learning, memory, attention, affection, and thought in the history of experimental psychology. But the task would, of course, have been enormous even for Boring who always wanted to reach beyond his abilities. When the choice came between beginning his third volume or accepting the flattering sociability of beginning a new journal, *Contemporary Psychology*, there was no inner struggle. The trilogy was never completed.

### His Conversion to Physicalism

By his lonely childhood, his reflective nature, and his Titchenerian training, Boring was a dedicated introspectionist. He was a student of his own awareness, ever the identifier with others, trying to imagine what it would be like to be this person or that. Such experiencing fits tongue-and-groove with a regular dualistic position. Indeed, it was structured by definition into classical psychology, the study of experience as experienced by the subject. And this was exactly how Boring thought of his field at the beginning of his career.

But Boring was never a defier of the times. He needed approbation too much for that. And as American psychology was caught up in the great tide of objectivism in the 1920s with everyone running for the nearest monism, he went with the rush. In the late 1920s, he began a fundamental conversion towards a physicalist monism which to my knowledge of him was forced and not sincere. Historian as he was, he appreciated the fact that behaviorism was a more promising and vigorous program than the now pale and effete introspections of the Titchenerian sort. A new bustling generation had no patience with such absurdities as Titchener's "stimulus error," and Boring wished to be with the new generation. He felt he had proved it to himself. He remembered at this time his experience in 1922 when he had received a skull fracture in an automobile accident that had caused a retroactive and progressive amnesia. He had chatted with everyone but immediately had forgotten what he had said or that he had talked. A man is therefore never conscious in the sense of being immediately aware of his awareness. Awareness always involved memory. Introspection was really retrospection.

In 1932, he wrote his position paper on the subject entitled, "The Physiology of Consciousness,"[9] saying: "Dualism is dead. It ought to be buried. It cannot work for us anymore and we do not need it." This was followed the next year with his second published book, *The Physical Dimensions of Consciousness*. As its title implies, it is Boring's attempt to describe Titchener's attributes in physical terms, to squeeze down Titchener's dualism into a physical monism. Physicalism, the same thing as what was later called operationalism, insists that consciousness as an object of observation by science, reduces to the operations by which consciousness becomes known to scientists. A sensation, for instance, is not something in consciousness but a man reporting in words the difference between two hues, or a rat turning away from the light into the dark.

But this operationist logic was not clearly spelled out in the book, so that he called it his immature book. For myself, I don't think he was clear about it because I don't think he ever really believed it. His physicalism was forced and verbal. Statements such as that "introspection is a method for the observation of certain events in the brain" are catastrophic logic. And in its emphasis on dimensions of consciousness, it was very Titchenerian indeed. Perhaps because of this ambivalence, its public reception was ambivalent as well. At the same time that Geldard was praising it highly, Woodworth held up a copy to a visitor in his office, saying, "Silly little thing, isn't it?" Since it has just been re-published in paperback and since the tides of fashion are ebbing away from behaviorism, the work may be due for a reassessment more generous than that of its author.

That the book was a break with Titchener was not an idle matter for Boring. Perhaps Titchener, if he had lived, would also have gone with the times. In a late paper which I helped write, he tried to show that Titchener was really in at the beginning of behaviorism by assuming in the context theory of meaning that the context could be subconscious and the sensation really discrimination.

---

9. "The Physiology of Consciousness," *Science*, 1932, 75, 32–39.

*A Torrent of Papers*

The influence of Titchener led directly to the development of his histories. But the influence of Titchener, who was never a good research experimenter, also may have reduced his ambitions in that direction. At any rate, the fervor, originality, and catholicity in his personal research, so striking when he was a graduate student, was never again to be repeated. Only a few of the 176 papers, 202 editorials, 45 book reviews, and 82 other items over the next 50 years are on his own experimental research.[10] These few include several studies with students which show that size constancy holds in free binocular vision up to 200 feet and that it is reduced towards the proportionality of apparent size to retinal size by successively eliminating the cues to perceived distance.[11] Also several on the moon illusion. That the moon high in the sky looks smaller than at the horizon had always intrigued him. With an elaborate apparatus with mirrors at the end of long arms built on the roof of Emerson Hall, he showed that this is due to the elevation of the eye in the head and not to movement of the head, and that it depends on the use of the two eyes.[12] It was a discovery hailed by astronomers as taking the moon problem out of astronomy into psychology (though he had not solved the fundamental psycho-physiological problem of why apparent size is changed in this manner by movement of the eye).

But most of this huge stream of papers over this half century of maturity are on theoretical topics: defenses of physicalism, temporal perception and operationism, psycho-physical systems and isomorphic relations, and a few attempts to give the *coup de grace* to privacy of experience by conceiving of the organism as a series of communicating systems in which the action is in the afferent-efferent direction,[13] and discussions of every conceivable psychological topic.

---

10. A bibliography of his most important papers up to 1960 is published in the back of his *Psychologist at Large* (New York: Basic Books, 1961). Another volume of Boring's selected papers has been collected by Robert I. Watson and Donald T. Campbell under the title *History, Psychology, and Science: Selected Papers* (New York: Wiley, 1963).

11. (With D.W. Taylor) "Apparent Visual Size as a Function of Distance for Monocular Observers," *American Journal of Psychology*, 1942, *55*, 102–105.

12. (With D.W. Taylor) "Apparent Visual Size as a Function of Binocular Regard," *American Journal of Psychology*, 1942, *55*, 189–201. "The Moon Illusion," *American Journal of Physics*, 1943, *11*, 55–60.

13. "A Psychological Function is the Relation of Successive Differentiations of Events in the Organism," *Psychological Review*, 1937, *44*, 445–461.

*As an Editor*

It was never Boring's ambition to write an introductory text. There were too many and the writing took energy from research. But when Weld came to Boring and Langfeld with the idea of producing an authoritative text which they would only edit, getting others to do the actual writing, the possibility of achieving the perfect text where facts would be stressed (this is what Wundt-Titchener would have wished) was exciting. The reach of it was too tempting and Boring agreed. The first of the Boring, Langfeld, and Weld textbooks came out in 1935, the second in 1939, and the third in 1948. It should be stated that the authors of the different chapters were mercilessly edited, occasionally to their lasting displeasure. These texts were always factual, emphasizing sensation and perception slightly more than other texts, and, I think, made a grievous error in omitting anything controversial. This meant omitting a great deal of the excitement of modern psychology. But the texts did establish new standards at a time when they were needed and are often close to being handbooks of experimental psychology.

The 1950's were the happiest decade of his life. The small boy had really come downstairs; he had indeed found out the world, and the world had found him; and they liked each other. So that when he had the choice between completing his trio of histories (is not an unwritten book like an imaginary playmate?) and the social excitement and creative power of the editorship of a new journal of reviews, there was — as I have said — no contest. Since 1920, he had been one of the hard-working editors of *The American Journal of Psychology* (appointed to it by Titchener), and he brought to this new venture a tremendous know-how. So against the advice of some friends, *Contemporary Psychology* was begun.

What emerged was something more Boringian, more full of his own personality and wit, than anything he had done before. He plotted its course, style, makeup, and philosophy, and it surpassed even his own expectations. It was a journal of reviews that overnight changed reviewing from adjectival knifing to intelligent criticism, and woe to the reviewer that ever struck below the level of objectivity! But it is the spirit of the journal with its fresh little quotations, its encouragement of fun and intelligence, that has lifted CP into an overview into the on-going adventure of psychology as seen through its books that is currently invaluable. Boring's column, "CP Speaks," was full of articulate wisdom with its windows open on every side to everything that was going on. What he knew, he knew well and could tell to others with clarity of style unequalled by any other scientific writer of his time. And those qualities were why "CP Speaks" was read first by most of its subscribers. "We got away with that, didn't we?" he once mischievously purred to me about it. And when the APA board did not appoint him to another term as editor of his own journal, he was stung with astonishment and hurt.

## His Academic Career

As with any man of his persuasiveness and structuring dominance, the succession of professorships, administrative offices, committee chairmanships, and presidencies of psychological associations that Boring held have all gone to influence modern psychology in special ways. His teaching that began at Cornell, after several years as a psychologist with the Army in World War I, was continued at Clark where he tried to build up a satellite department to Titchener's at Cornell. He left Clark in 1922 over the issue of free speech (the President had stopped a Marxist in mid-lecture by pulling the main light switch, the incident resulting in what came to be called the Clark Controversy). He then went to what Titchener had always pronounced as "the strongest university in America."

Boring remained at Harvard for the rest of his life, rising through its ranks, guiding the severance of experimental psychology first from philosophy (which he regarded as his Titchenerian mission), and then from the sociotropic (a word coined by Boring) aspect of psychology which became the department of Social Relations. Some of these divisions, particularly the latter, may have been more personal than rational. At any rate the splintering of the department at Harvard was not a good thing, and the new William James building was in part an effort to put Humpty Dumpty back together again. But this would not work, not in a high-rise building whose fifteen floors divided its occupants into fifteen departments in effect. "Even with six elevators instead of three," he once complained to me, "we would still be separated, even with brass poles to slide down or moving staircases all the way; man was meant for the flat earth!"

As a teacher he was both good and bad. He was good in his simplification and clarity for introductory students, just as Titchener once was. He was bad in that the complexities and subtleties in philosophical margins of many psychological problems were not hinted at. Indeed, in all his work, Boring reached for simplicity and clarity and certainty exactly as had Titchener. He once criticized William James to me as of questionable greatness because — and he said this with a rising cadence of exasperation — "because he never *settled* anything!" Boring's course made it appear that things were settled.

Originally, this course was two years and 200 lectures long. Fifty years later it had shrunk to a half year of 28 lectures. He used the same demonstrations year in and year out until every class in ensuing years knew at precisely which point Professor Boring would suddenly produce a pistol from his desk drawer, squinny his eyes, and shoot it into the air to demonstrate the startle response — which even though expected still worked. Others remember him making all the Piderit faces with his wonderfully large features, his huge browed eyes, pursable white moustache, and generous mouth. But philosophy students remember how they were forced to take the course against their will (the James tradition), and had sat in sullen defiance in the back row, finding Boring boring and simple.

In 1960, the course was shrunk a little more into thirty-eight half-hour lectures which were put on video tape by Boston's Education TV channel and are therefore preserved. These were a splendid success in which Boring used no notes and no prompter but the usual demonstrations. For the most part he sat on the corner of a table talking enthusiastically in a paternal manner to the red lights on whatever camera was on the air, calling the lights in his imagination, Papa, Mama, and Johnnie. And this familiarity and paternalism, combined with his simplicity and certainty without simplification or dogmatism made them a tremendous success, resulting in some fan mail which pleased him exceedingly.

But this geniality, while it was impartial, was — shall I say — along a different avenue of attitudes than those he showed as a department chairman. For in administration he was more ruthless than Titchener. Once when a graduate student was a few days late with his thesis because his wife had been ill, Boring refused it on the grounds that this would not be fair to others in a similar predicament who had simply dropped out and not complained. The candidate never received his degree from Harvard. Such actions are hard to defend, and earned him at one time many detractors.

*His Despondency in Middle Age*

Boring thought of himself as an ambitious man driven to scientific productivity by the whip of his compulsions, who had to make it by persistence rather than genius. Even his photographs in middle age show a rigid sternness that was not present before and certainly not present in his later years. When such a man meets sub-standard work in others, he can deal with it summarily with no loss of sleep. But when he meets it in himself, what can he do?

Just after he finished *The Physical Dimensions of Consciousness*, the book that broke with Titchener, the book that was only half thought through, he plunged into a psychological crisis that left him sterile, troubled with autistic thinking. A part of this may have been his determined opposition to a Harvard appointment for Wolfgang Köhler which lost him several important friendships. So evident was his emotional distress that his friends urged psychoanalysis. He agreed. He chose an analyst that reminded him of Titchener, Hans Sachs, a pupil and friend of Freud's. With Sachs, he worked through many of his emotions. He wept. He threw things. At other times on the couch, he felt how much this was costing, had images of pennies scurrying by as costly seconds were lost without any progress in his therapy. And all through the analysis, he felt the inadequacy of psychoanalytic doctrine which seemed to him a loose and indeterminate mixture of voluntarism and determinism.

The analysis closed with failure.[14] He felt no different from the outmoded bundle of incompatibilities which he had always felt himself to be and was struggling to reach out of. He had expected to be changed from Saul to Paul, but nothing of the sort happened. And when his analyst went abroad, ending the analysis, he was distraught, unable to write or even read effectively. Even four years later, he had not regained the productivity that in vain he demanded of himself. And in his anguish, he turned more and more to the easier motivations and immediate feedbacks of administration and editing.

### His Attitude Toward Dissent

In his administrating and editing, his feeling about disagreements was very characteristic. Science, he felt, moved forward by dissent, and so he encouraged it, sometimes even surreptitiously, around him. He built the

---

14. Characteristically, he wrote this up in an article entitled, "Was this Analysis a Success?" answering his question in the negative. Also characteristically, he insisted that Sachs be given a chance for public rebuttal which he did, calling Boring's personality "a dignified and respectable house which has given comfort and shelter for a long time, even if it causes to its inhabitants a good deal of inconvenience." *Journal of Abnormal and Social Psychology*, 1940, *4*, 16.

Harvard department up partly on this basis. I remember him telling me with relish the reasons why he brought Skinner to Harvard, and how at his staff luncheons in the basement of Memorial Hall, Skinner habitually sat at one corner telling everybody what was wrong about everything. In such dissent, the role Boring sought was not that of peacemaker, but of referee.

A similar instance is in his interest in extrasensory perception as a phenomenon of history. One of his last pieces of work was an introduction to a new review of the evidence pro and con, and his last appearance on television was in a popular panel show on the subject. And these he did because he enjoyed playing a referee between intellectual alternatives in which his own distance from emotional conviction could be preserved.

But the dissent must never be emotional or subjective. Emotion is the friend of action but the enemy of wisdom, and it was wisdom he wished over and against a thoroughly emotional nature. He dreamed of a world of pure science and pure objectivity. "Would psychology could be just friends subjectively helping each other, and change all *ad hominems* to *ad verbums!*" was a familiar pivot in his conversation. He helped others to be themselves, and his occasional impatience was an impatience for them rather than with them. He never spoke ill of anyone, nor stooped to recrimination. In interpersonal dispute, he verbally withdrew into an objectivity that explained, rather than into a bitterness that blamed. And yet he was as prone to personal dislike as anyone. The difference was that he felt all such emotions should be kept out of speech and writing, and tried to believe behavioristically of himself that out of speech was out of mind — something which was not always true.

He encouraged dissent even from himself. He liked nothing better than a good clean intellectual hassle in which neither side was emotionally involved. And the dissenting notion was usually recognized by a cavernous grin and a "well!" When I insisted a recent paper of his had to be thoroughly reorganized and rewritten, there was not a trace of pride or defensiveness of sarcasm when he exclaimed with great geniality and glee, "Well! You are the first person to take me in tow since Titchener!" He seemed to enjoy like a child the reversal of roles. And in another context, he once exclaimed how he had always assumed everyone wants to be a leader when in fact most people want to be followers. Could he have been speaking of himself?

Only once did the dissent between us harden into opposed convictions. Boring wrote me that a paper of mine was autistic and self-indulgent, and that never in his entire career had he seen a paper so unworthy of being published. I replied that never in his entire career had he made such an error, that he did not understand the role of metaphor and conceit (in the Elizabethan sense) in the sub-structure of scientific theory and that what he was doing was resenting by dredging it up into the surface of words.

My defiance of his criticism contrasted with his accepting objectivity to mine. I regretted its sharpness because he backed down. He wasn't supposed to. And then he wrote me:

> I think this whole business is like a lump of tar on a hot day. It will change its form as time goes on, the sharp edges will disappear, the shape will be different, and yet there will be enough left of the original dichotomous discussion to form a background for our further thinking.

## "An Unproductive Manipulator of Other Men's Minds"

He lived on the creative edge of a good intelligence. When he wrote he had the feeling that his typewriter did the thinking for him. He spoke of his compulsions and giving over control of himself to them. Men of such subjective daring often have the fear of being foolish as well as the courage not to mind it if they are. Two years ago he wrote to me:

> Is not the last century's wisdom often today's foolishness? Was Kepler foolish about the inversion of the retinal image? Were the Greeks foolish about the objects shooting off eidola which were conducted to the sensorium for perception? A question that has always fascinated me has been this: how much of my present thinking is utter foolishness without my being in the least aware of it? Is not posterity going to see what a very great deal of it is?

Probably not. The capacity to let his typewriter think for him resulted not so much in profound theories that might to a later age prove foolish, as in sparkling discussion of topics in which lights and associations glanced from all sides, revealing the problem more than an answer.

At the time of his death, he was probably the most famous psychologist in the academic world. The popular press called him "Mr. Psychology." Articles and books were written about him. And as every famous and powerful man begets various attitudes and affects toward him, so Boring often smarted under overpraise or was sad at overblame. What many of his intimates missed was the true self-assessment so free of pride or ego-solace. Perhaps this was the result of his crisis in middle age. Even as he lay dying, when the impulse to wish one's life worth greater than it was must be strong, he doubted the value of his greatest works, his histories of psychology. And once when I had taken on a job of editing a series of books with him, he wrote:

> But I do not have a guilt-edged dubiety. Have I helped spoil you for psychology? Reduced you from a mother to a mid-wife? What's the male figure? From an Achilles to an Eisenhower? Have I helped make you more like me? An unproductive manipulator of other men's minds? I couldn't do it all. The zeitgeist. The American Ortgeist that ruined the Münsterberg that James discovered. So let this paragraph act as a bit of counter-balance.

### *"So This is This!"*

Wundt liked facts. Titchener liked facts. Boring liked facts. But in Boring, this worked out into a marriage, not just an affair. Facts were to be faced, not just found. And this made for a splendid old age, full of acceptance and mellow wisdom. Conversation with him in these years was personally delightful, hearty, and contoured easily around issues, changes in topic turning on his genially crying out as he spread his hands on his desk, "So this is this!" Translated, taking context and the invitational inflection into account, this apparent tautology meant that wishes do not alter facts, nor are facts to be brooded over once sorted into generalizations. This was a very deep trait in his character. Once when I described to him one of my own problems to which I was reacting with typical Peter Pan immaturity, he replied, "Well, think on these things. You are a big boy now and I am an octogenarian. I don't like it. You don't like it. Nevertheless, we must face reality."

The reality of death is difficult to face, if only because death is nothing rather than real. He wept, urgently wept — I should say blubbered like a child — when his first broken bone would not heal, denoting the graveward journey he was to undergo. But such spells would end with the familiar "Well, this is this," said with a hesitant difference, a downward inflection that saw death. He had watched his elder sister die lingeringly and painfully of the same illness several years before, and he knew every downhill step of the way. Face it, weep for it, and struggle through. With his typical self-exposure, he sent me a copy of his medical diagnosis of multiple myeloma with the handwritten marginal note, "Lots of pain, lots of lethargy, but still I keep things going." He buried his pain in an accumulation of decisions and responsibilities, editing an extensive new series of books covering all psychology, writing articles and prefaces and letters — magnificent letters — to friends and strangers by the hundreds. He might spend two days researching a ten page answer to some high school student who had seen his television series and had written him a question. And so he worked incessantly throughout his illness, speaking of its progress with a fierce courage, of its treatment and pain with a flat acceptance through which, occasionally and suddenly, would erupt huge wells of suffering and regret.

Six months ago, there was a remarkable arrest in his illness due to new medication. Although the pain in his bones was always there, the atmosphere in his study on Bowdoin Street at this time was one of hope and happy work in the midst of suffering. Pudgily seated in his Morris chair in a dressing gown and high sneakers, unable to rise, his poor bones pinned together by surgeons, ("I am almost a pin-up!", he laughed) he would raise up both arms in greeting, his eyes goggling with excitement, his huge mouth wide with pleasure and his large tongue flicking about it in excitement. And even though there was business to transact, the conversation would soon swerve over and go bouncing down more profoundly exciting topics, such as the nature of the unconscious assumptions in the problem of the universality of the Weber-Fechner function, or was parallelism really epiphenomenalism, or just what is the significance of the normal distribution curve, for what are the rules of its application? It applies to the weight of peas, the diameter of peas, but how about the volume which is not linearly related?

*"Tout comprendre, c'est tout pardonner."*

A man to others is like a many-sided mirror. Others see in him unrecognized snatches of themselves, as many different snatches as the viewpoints taken. A man is finally unknowable. But the more various the viewpoints through which we approach him, the fuller and richer, the unconscious inference and large hidden texture of assumption which constitutes one man's knowledge of another. This has been the rationale of my remembrance.

Edwin G. Boring, unlike the present writer, was a single spirited man, and that single spirit, around which he organized a furiously active life, was experimental psychology. He helped fashion it out of its nineteenth century heritage, helped structure it with two classical histories used throughout the world, helped fill in that structure with various theoretical and experimental work through half a century of working his eighty-hour week, and told others where to build other parts of the edifice in his role as chairman of the Harvard department and his many editorships. Knowing and being known by everyone, he moved through that structure with the ease of a foreman who realized he was not the architect, but who felt sincerely that without his integrity that building would not be as safe for posterity.

His faults were ordinary and obvious. But his virtues were so rare as to be wonderful in our time. In part, they were the virtues of Titchener; a definitiveness of utterance, absolute clarity even of clouded things, an implacable sense of fairness. But much more than Titchener. For with these went his huge cordiality to all, his abhorrence of pride so unlike Titchener, his childlike ebullience, and particularly his astonishing candor that could even embarrass as it flattered, a candor that would have appalled the ceremonious Titchener. And this was his most memorable distinction. For he represented the unfortunately disappearing idea that a psychologist enters his profession like a religious order, making himself a part of his own subject matter, and baring his soul to the cruelty of objectivity. It was both his creed and his *cri de coeur* out of his child-past that he turn himself inside out without shame or calculation. And so he did.

We are all subjects, one of another.

### By Way of Requiem

I last saw him on my way to give some lectures at an NSF Conference in the History of Psychology. I was told he would not recognize me. His bone marrow had almost ceased to function and the red blood cells obtained by transfusions could not prevent the starving of his cortex of oxygen. He spoke through his semi-coma as over an immense distance, as from behind an intolerable burden he could no longer carry, as he was already slipping down on the other side of the mystery of awareness that he had long studied. I said I wished him to get better. "Why not? Why not do what should be — see what happens?" His speech was thick, laborious, and slow. He writhed and grimaced with the pain.

"I am sorry you have broken your arm," I replied, horrified at my ineffectuality. His last break had been that of his right arm which had utterly incapacitated him.

"Oh, all right!" His voice rose and was firm. "Oh, all right. That's it, that's it. That's it ... that's all there is to do about it."

He then became confused and added, "The only thing to do is to fall off, to fall off backward and that way out." He then spoke unintelligibly for a few sentences and finally looked up and said slowly, "I'd like to go back to work."

I asked him would he like to go home.

"I have been home."

"Do you want to go back to William James?"

"No. Enough of that. Enough of that is good now."

"Are you unhappy here in the hospital?'

"I am not happy. I am not happy. I decided last week to give up the whole thing."

"Gave up? Did you decide just to give up?"

There was a long pause. He looked at me and took hold of my hand that was resting on the guard rail of his bed and throbbed it back and forth for the rest of my visit.

"Yes." He said it with pain and weariness. And then he added, "No, I need. I need to reach. Oh, I need to reach."

"To reach?"

"Yes, to reach. I need to reach!"


There is no stone and no grave.

Among unknown hedges and flowerbeds of Mount Auburn are his ashes strewn.

# CHAPTER 6

# The Study of the
# History of Psychology

W HY STUDY THE HISTORY OF PSYCHOLOGY? To most historians of
science the question is not very interesting. The answer is quite
obvious: the historical study of man's Promethean attempt to understand
himself on this planet is a fascinating adventure that needs no rationale.
It is the view from the mountain tops, the surveying of man's most profound problem against the huge panorama of his history, the place where
the grandeur is, where the findings, theories, changing importances, and
intellectual heroics of every age — including the present one — are woven
into exciting patterns. Why study the history of psychology? Because it
*is* psychology, all of it, and psychology cannot be studied seriously apart
from its history.

One way to see that is in the everyday nature of contemporary research.
Throughout his research, each scientist is actually an historian in his own
specialty. Every journal article he writes describing new results necessarily
begins with the immediate history of the problem. And it is only that context of history, of what has led up to that particular research, that can give
significance and meaning to new findings. And so it is with his specialty.
Its meaning, its significance within psychology, depends upon its relation
to the larger ongoing history of which it is a part.

This first answer to our question merely touches the surface, for if we
probe deeper we come upon more profound reasons which are not so
apparent. There is, for example, a kind of truth in the history of a science
which transcends the science itself. The history of a science as a kind of
metascience is rarely seen by the individual scientist confined to his own
specialty, for the very historical contexts that bestow significance on any
discovery or specialty reach back in time to prior contexts, which in turn
have been generated by still prior causation.

First published as the Introduction to Mary Henle, Julian Jaynes, and John J. Sullivan (eds.), *Historical Conceptions of Psychology*. © 1973 Springer Publishing Company. Reprinted with permission.

As we examine these matters, we are struck by a remarkable fact: the paths of these questions and contexts through time are not necessarily linear or logical. They diverge and come together, expanding and contracting, on the basis of many variables, only a few of which are what we generally think of reasoning out the world. The purpose of history is to discover and understand this historical structure which lies at the very foundation of the logical surface of science and to which all present discovery is relative. Why study the history of psychology? For itself alone.

Neither science nor the individuals who perform its rites of discovery are outside historical causation. Psychologists, in particular, are as deeply embedded in textures of personal and chance situational causation as the very subjects they study. We can see what to do only by seeing what has been done. We can discover in the present only what we have conjectured in the past. We can recognize in front of us only what past scientific perception has trained us to see. And just as an individual, on the basis of his past history, selects out of his environment a particular phenomenon to attend to and to label as important, so an entire science, utilizing instruments of perception, moves about through its problems and its vital aspects with the same dependence on its history. And just as an individual, to be free, must verbalize the past that has resulted in his present, so an entire science must remain in dialogue with its past and analyze its hidden biases and omissions if it is not to wither away into dried-up specialties and unfulfilling evasions. Why study the past of psychology? Because it is the only way to understand the present.

Most of what I have said so far pertains to all sciences. But there are reasons applicable to psychology alone, for current psychology is wedded to its history with much stronger ties than any other science. As a laboratory investigation, psychology is only a century old; as a body of insights, observations, and hypothesis, it is the oldest science in the world. Moreover, its history is not a musty attic of intellectual bric-a-brac and mildewed curiosa, as are often found in the history of chemistry or neurology, for example. It is instead a continuing discussion of the perennial and enduring problems of human and animal nature. It attempts the same questions again and again, even by the same routes. Current work on the nature-nurture problem, on emotion and intellect, on thought and language, on the problem of consciousness — all are simply the most recent voices in discussions which have been reverberating through history for more than two thousand years. Why study the history of psychology? It is relevant to present research, a fact that is not true of other sciences.

Another particular reason is the recently complicated and often bewildering growth of psychology. The oldest science in the world has suddenly expanded its factual content and the ranks of its scholars at a rate exceeding all other sciences. No other science, in no other century, has moved with such swiftness, confusion, and vigor. This is seen in the number of persons in professional societies, the expansion of academic departments and the demands upon them by students, the proliferation of specialist journals, the tumultuous diversity of research papers, the special jargons and schismatic methods, the huge conventions now too cumbersome to fulfill their original purposes, and the influence of psychology on the entire fabric of our times. What geology was to the early nineteenth century, biology to the late nineteenth century, and physics to the first half of the twentieth century, so psychology is very much the central major science of the latter half of the twentieth century. How did all this happen? The need for proper study of this phenomenal growth and its deep causes, rational and irrational, is obvious and urgent.

The urgency stems from the fragmentation by specialization that has accompanied this astonishing growth. Psychology has not only been expanding, it has also been separating. How can we understand it all? One problem has led to another, moving psychology to newer subsciences at an ever-increasing rate. And with each new field, thousands of research titles soon make their appearance. Psychology has diverged beyond the scope of any one specialist, shattering into brilliant fragments by its own progress and causing areas to lose touch with each other in their very successes. All about us, research pushes into research, often evading the larger questions with which it began.

As a result, psychology is at a critical stage in its development, and I would suggest that only its history can fit together all this divergence. The increasing multiplicity of psychology is not logical, but historical, like a jigsaw puzzle that cannot be fitted together in space, but only in time.

Why study the history of psychology? For all the reasons I have mentioned: to discover the historical structure under the logical surface of science, to understand the present, to be relevant to real questions, to liberate ourselves from the persuasions of fashions, to comprehend psychology as a whole, but also because it is the only way to understand a field of such divergence and conflicting emphases, which is at the same time the central science of our era.

# CHAPTER 7

# The Problem of Animate
# Motion in the Seventeenth Century

MOTION IS NOW so much the domain of physics that it is difficult for us to appreciate that this was not always so. Before the seventeenth century, motion was a far more awesome mystery. Shared by all objects, stars, ships, animals, and men — and, since Copernicus, the very earth itself — it seemed to hide the answer to everything. The Aristotelian writings had made motion or activity the distinctive property of living things, an idea that occurs naturally to children and primitive peoples of all centuries. Because they moved, the stars were thought by no less a scientist than Kepler to be animated. Motion perplexed Gilbert, who became convinced that magnets had souls because of their ability to move and to be moved. And Campanella in his Neapolitan prison, when he understood what Copernicus was saying, that the earth really moved, exclaimed, "Mundum esse animal, totum sentiens!"[1] In a world so sentient and alive, motion is everywhere. And one of the major intellectual developments of the seventeenth century gathered itself to this theme. I shall try to show in this essay that when this idea of animate motion is clarified, one result is the sorting out of the sciences by their subject matter as we know them today.

The background of this concern with motion is complex. In the Aristotelian heritage, motion was of three kinds: change in quantity, change in quality, and change in spatial locality. While the sixteenth century was beginning to use the word only in its third sense as we do today, the mysterious aura of its other two meanings hung about it like ghosts into the next century.

---

Article by Julian Jaynes first published in *The Journal of the History of Ideas*, Vol. 32, No. 2, and reprinted in Mary Henle, Julian Jaynes, and John J. Sullivan (eds.) *Historical Conceptions of Psychology.* © 1973 Springer Publishing Company. Reprinted with permission.
1. Tommaso Campanella, *De Sensu Rerum*, Book 1, Chapter 9.

There was a practical background as well. The sixteenth century, with its political upheavals and religious wars, had seen the beginning of engineering as a political, military, and mercantile necessity. The tricks of the trade were called machines, from the Latin *machina*, meaning a trick or device, ways of making physical objects animate to do work that otherwise men or beasts would have to do. There had, of course, been a long history of such tricks. In the earliest times, machines had been mostly for enjoyment, such as the "automata," originally some kind of dancing dolls moving externally by an elaborate hidden mechanism of strings, weights, and rollers. Such automata are used to illustrate the principles of animate motion in both the Aristotelian writings on the subject, particularly 701B of *De Motu Animalium*, and then in Galen who was copying him. Machines later came to be used for practical purposes and, instead of making dolls dance, were made to lift weights or pump water. Particularly in the Roman period, mechanical devices of all sorts were brought to bear on many practical problems. And a usually neglected part of the Renaissance was the reawakening of that Roman fascination with the possibilities of mechanical engineering. Its first text appeared at the end of the sixteenth century in Jacques Besson's *Théâtre des Instruments* (Paris, 1594). And Galileo himself, at about the same time, spoke of the kinds of problems that were arising in the shipbuilding yards at Venice, or in handling artillery, or in the pumping of water in mines, problems which Leonardo da Vinci had brushed with his vision a century earlier.

This tremendous increase in the number of different devices to obtain motion induced a curiosity about the ingenuity of God or nature, which could make animals or stars move. One of the great turning points in science was when man-made machines became the hypotheses or models of natural phenomena. As early as the fourteenth century, when clocks worked by wheels were still new, it was suggested that the stars were actually a piece of clockwork. While the Greeks had made the analogy that the automaton was like animal movement, some scientists in the seventeenth century, as we shall see — e.g., Descartes — were to insist that the two were identical. Motion, therefore, haunted by ancient meanings that made it seem more than it was, and pushed into central focus by the practical necessity of harnessing it to man's use, was a central problem of the century in a unique way.

The story begins when Fabricius ab Aquapendente (1537–1619) and Galileo (1564–1642) were rivals for the intellectual attention of Venice a few miles from Padua.[2] In 1610 Galileo emulated the older man Vesalian in fame-getting ways by holding his own public demonstration, not of ana-tomical dissections, but of his new thirty-power telescope with which he was soon to discover the moons of Jupiter, the rings of Saturn, and the cause of the shine of the Milky Way. But even at this time, Galileo was retreating from this data-collecting into reasoning about motion. The ensuing argu-ments between Galileans and Aristotelians created an atmosphere of dis-cussion about motion under the overhanging pillared galleries of Padua that involved the whole university. And the aging Fabricius, just before he was poisoned,[3] was swept up into this youthful intellectual *mêlée*, writing his last work on animate motion in 1618, *De Motu Locali Animalium*.

This work should be compared to its similarly titled inspirations, the two brief Aristotelian treatises on the same subject.[4] The latter are excit-ing patchwork, remarkable for discovering the problems rather than for solving anything. Coming from them to Fabricius' work is like emerg-ing from a teeming, disorderly, and exciting town into a neat meadow, a more coherent panorama of observations. Because species of the same class often exhibit different modes of motion or combinations of them, he organized his material according to the type of motion: creeping, fly-ing, swimming, walking in bipeds, and, finally, walking in quadrupeds and multipeds. These modes of locomotion are correlated with the nature of a particular ground, whether the habitat is level or hilly, wet, sandy, or grassy. Moreover, the variability of a particular terrain or habitat finds itself mirrored in the variability of the locomotions of the particular ani-mals living there. Not having the advantage of Galileo's *Della Scienza Mecanica*, which did not appear until 1634, Fabricius' mechanics of these motions only began what Borelli was to complete at the end of the cen-tury. But the work also contains much that is new: the first real description of the peristaltic movement, and attempt to derive all locomotions from two archetypes, walking with diagonal limbs in unison and leaping with opposite limbs in unison — an idea begun in the Aristotelian works,[5] and a fascinating section relating wing structure in birds and insects to their flight behavior. Whereas the Aristotelian writings everywhere assume

---

2. One student wrote home in 1549 that Padua was "an infinite resorte of all nations where all kynds of virtue maie there be learned." Clare Howard, *English Travelers of the Renaissance* (New York: John Lane, 1913, p. 53).

3. Cf. *Biographie Universelle*.

4. The *Peri Zoon Kineseos* and the *Peri Zoon Poreias* of the Aristotelian works. I refrain from ascribing them to Aristotle since they are obviously multi-authored and are collections of scraps from various sources from the fourth to second centuries B.C.

5. *Peri Zoon Poreias*, 705A.

that everything in nature has a function, Fabricius turns this into a principle of economy, that there is nothing extra in behavior. And instead of the Aristotelian principle that nature does what is best, Fabricius states that nature perpetuates what is best.[6] This change of verb is a giant step between ancient and modern biology. But in spite of these huge ideas that squeeze in among the detail of Fabricius' observation, the work as a whole is a failure and merely reopens the problem.

William Harvey (1578–1647) was Fabricius' best student, and most of his work can be considered an extension of Fabricius'. Recently, a new manuscript of Harvey's has been discovered.[7] Somewhere around 1627, while putting the final touches on his work on the motion of the blood, he began a notebook for his own work on the problem of animate motion, with Aristotle as "my General" and Fabricius as "my Guide." But either because of the ravages of the English civil war, or more probably because of Harvey's despair with the problem, only the notes have survived. They are a fascinating failure, altered and crossed out as Harvey's restless and unsatisfied thought frustrated and teased itself further and further into the unresponsive mysteries of behavior. He tried to refine Fabricius' classification of animal movement in terms of the means of propulsion, the kinds of movements involved, whether sequent, simultaneous or alternating, or the particular organs used. He pushes Fabricius' ecological determinism into generalizations that merely return us to Aristotelian loose ends which, for example, classify human gaits as to whether they resembled "a duck, a crane, a crow, Jew of Malta, ambling Turk,[8] servile trot, etc." The physiology is essentially Galenic in its resort to animal spirits, but breaks off into exasperated splurges of metaphor. The brain in particular is compared to a choirmaster, who performs behavior with an exquisite sense of rhythm and harmony. When the brain was removed — and here he cut off the head of a chicken and watched its behavior to prove it — behavior is disorderly, for muscles are like separate living creatures that have to be directed in harmony by the choirmaster of the brain. And from his metaphor, too, comes his emphasis on rhythm in muscular coordination, how each muscular

---

6. A relevant passage remarkably prescient of nineteenth-century biology is the following (my translation): "In truth, nature fulfills her aim by so bestowing behavioral movements and functions among animals that they preserve themselves through them; this consists in a preservation of the ablest in obtaining food, in continuing the species, and in avoiding injury" (*De Motu Locali Animalium secundum totum*, Padua, 1618, p. 8).

7. William Harvey, *De Motu Locali Animalium* (1627), ed. and trans. by G. Whitteridge (Cambridge University Press, 1959).

8. Perhaps indicating something about the flamboyance of acting style of the time, since these are obviously references to two characters from Marlowe's plays.

system has a subrhythm of tension and relaxation just as the beat of the heart has its systole and diastole. Such rhythms range from the very short period of the heart to such seasonal rhythms as when "frogs and swallows hide in winter and give forth no movements," showing that he had read the erroneous statement of Olaus Magnus in 1555 on the hibernation of swallows as an explanation of their seasonal appearance in Britain. The emphasis on rhythms is a huge thought, but with Cromwell battering the king's armies outside his windows (Harvey was a loyalist), it was scarcely a propitious time for a naturalistic investigation.

In fact, his very emphasis on order and harmony reflects the civil commotion all about him. Political struggles of his day become a model of learning. The muscles of the organism are compared to a commonwealth of persons[9] that must be governed by a set of laws, where no citizen is useless and where, once order is established, there is no more need of a separate monarch to preside over each several task. Cromwell had Charles I beheaded just at this time. Harvey meant that, in learning, we are conscious of each part of a total action, but that once the action is learned, "one thing follows another in its accustomed order," and no monarch of conscious control is necessary. Harvey's interest in learning was something new to science, though the subject had become fashionable in educational discussions at Padua when Harvey was there around 1600. He is an elementarist on one page, saying that learning proceeds from parts to wholes, from particular movements that "connect up and are commanded as one whole."[10] While on another, he astonishes us with a Gestalt pronouncement that "nature thinks of the works to be performed and not of the movement of the muscles."[11] But the book as a whole is a failure, and the deletions and lacunae in the manuscript demonstrate that these were Harvey's feelings as well.

The notebook ends with lists of metaphors that might generate some kind of truth. The choirmaster model is reiterated. Or the heart is compared to a general or king, the brain to a judge or sergeant-major, the nerves to leaders or magistrates, and the muscles to soldiers — all, be it noted, enclosed within the animal without relating to its environment. A new metaphor through which to "see" behavior was indeed needed before any further progress could be made. But it was not to be found in Harvey's beautiful and grand similes to music or architecture or government, so

---

9. An analogy made also in the Aristotelian *Peri Zoon Kineseos*, 730A30.

10. Harvey, p. 122.

11. *Ibid.*, p. 123.

complimentary to the reader, but in something much less inspiring, a hydraulic statue, and by someone far more insensitive: René Descartes.

In 1614, Descartes,[12] a maternally deprived eighteen-year-old student, suffered the first of several breakdowns and hid himself away in Saint-Germain for two years. The only recreation available at that then rural village near Paris was a visit to the royal gardens. They had recently been designed for the new Queen by her fountaineers, the Francini brothers, and consisted of a cascade of six enormous terraces cut into the steep bank of the Seine. Each terrace ended in a row of dark subterranean grottoes connected by stone vaulted corridors, and in these high gloomy echoing chambers, flickering with torch light on their sculptured ceilings and walls and often filled with eerie music from a hydraulic mechanical organ or mechanical singing birds, were the Francinis' masterpieces: complicated hydraulic statues that moved, danced, or even spoke.[13] Descartes had been a student at the King's Jesuit school at La Flèche and so, I presume, would have been allowed in. I am suggesting that these glistening, fizzing statues in their eerie torch-lit world became the surrogate friends of a brilliant intellect unable to cope with people. Descartes tells us himself[14] how he made them move without knowing it; how, on entering, he trod on hidden plates that, for example, when he approached a bathing Diana, caused her to hide her bronze allurements in bronze rose bushes, and when he tried to follow her, caused a stern Neptune to clank and hiss forward to intercept him, creaking his dripping trident puritanically over the delighted philosopher's head.

These images, perhaps aiding his recuperation with their paradigms of behavioral control, perhaps stayed at the very depth of Descartes' thinking. He seems to view the entire physical world as though it were modeled on the Francinis' work. It was nothing but a vast machine. Just as in the Queen's gardens, there was no spontaneity at any point. He loathed animism. He loved the statues. Later he named his only child, an illegitimate daughter, Francine, perhaps after their creator. All moved by fixed principles of extension and motion. He was even contemptuous of action at a distance, for this was nothing but animism, and of course found Kepler

---

12. I am here advancing a theory about Descartes. I have not been able to find more pertinent evidence than I have here cited, and I realize I am being more inferential than scholarly. Descartes nowhere (that I know of) refers to the Francini statues by name or actual place, or as to when in his life they so probably impressed him.

13. For further descriptions of these grottoes, see Paul Gruyer, *Saint-Germain* (Paris, 1922) and Georges Houdard, *Les Chateaux Royaux de Saint-Germain-en-Laye* (Saint-Germain, 1911–12). John Evelyn, the diarist, visited them in 1644 and described them as already beginning to decay.

14. Descartes, *L'homme*, ed. by Cousin (Paris, 1824), IV, p. 348.

unreasonable when the latter took the world for a single animal, a levia-
than that roared in caverns and breathed in ocean tides. Except for human
consciousness, there is only matter, dead matter, measurable and orderly
matter, matter that acts on other matter by pushing or pulling matter next
to it. And all goes on with the regularity, precision, and inevitability of a
smoothly running machine made of nothing but matter.

Sometime between the period of his breakdown and 1633, he wrote his
*L'Homme*, and then, in the winter of 1645–46, *Passions de l'âme*. Both may
have been haunted by these early experiences in his late teens. Particularly
in the former, he asks: What is the difference between the hydraulic statues and the people from whom he has fled, or between the bronze animals
in the Orpheus grotto and real animals?

As for animals, the answer seemed self-evident. There was no difference
whatever. Animals were mere water statues, not conscious, not really living
— machines without will or purpose or any feeling whatever. He dissected
them alive (anesthetics were far off in the nineteenth century), amused at
their cries and yelps since these were nothing but the hydraulic hisses and
vibrations of machines. Everything was the same. The hollow nerves and
cavities of the brain were the Francinis' pipes, full of animal liquids. He
called them spirits, and in some places referred to them as a subtle air, but
it is more correct to think he meant the cerebro-spinal fluids that were fil-
tered from the blood of the cerebral arteries. The muscles and tendons are
merely like the "various engines and springs" which moved the statues. The
nerve pipe fed into the muscle, and when the fluid came down, it billowed
the muscle out like a balloon, and so made the limb move.

Now the important thing about this conception is not its hydraulic neu-
rophysiology (though the hydraulic model is to return again and again in
modern psychology) but the treadle side of the business. Unlike Harvey's
metaphors, the model of the statue demands that animate behavior be
thought of in an environment that triggers these limb movements. The
objects affecting the sense organs themselves were the treadles which the
visitors stepped on, thus making the statues work. Descartes seems to have
two ideas of how this came about. In some passages, he has what I will call
with more correctness than taste the flush-toilet model. He thought he
had found in his dissections that there was a thread running through the
center of a nerve. So he considered that the sense organs contracted when
stimulated, pulling this thread which ran through the nervepipe all the way
up to the brain, which there pulled out a little valve allowing the animal

fluids to gush back down and billow out the muscle.[15] But this couldn't
explain very much, certainly not the variations in the intensity of muscular
movement. So in other passages he speaks of the transmission of sensation
to the brain being hydraulic as well, perhaps as a wave of pressure rising to
the brain and there — and this is extremely important — reflecting back,[16]
just as the water pressures were reflected in the joints of the Francinis' pipes,
a reflection of the fluids that returned them down other pipes to billow out
appropriate muscles. This is the beginning of the idea of the reflex.[17] The
Francini brothers from Florence had built more than they knew; they had
created the essential image behind modern psychology.

But Descartes' rapier-like attack on animism in animals stopped short
of himself and his own species. He couldn't quite say that he himself and
other non-bronze men are merely machines — as La Mettrie was to say
later. In fact, the big feature of his philosophical method in his *Discourse*
was its new starting point in self-consciousness. And for Descartes to conceive of one of these bronze spurting statues to introspect, perhaps to suddenly spout bronzily at him "*Cogito, ergo sum,*" was a rather disconcerting
thought. Never bothering to appreciate the problem he had initiated by
beginning with a mechanical model as his premise, he backed out of it by
calling his self-consciousness a thing, in the same sense that the statue was
a thing. There were two such things, mind and body. Instead of harmoniz-
ing the discrepancy of viewpoint by analyzing in a skeptical fashion his own
thought processes as he should, he simply asserted the discrepancy was in
nature rather than in his own thinking. Without a quiver of the plume in
his hat, he reified his own consciousness into a substance, perhaps even
like the mists that hung glistening in the air over the beautiful hydraulic
automatons in their irresponsible grottoes, an airy substance uncontrolled
by the pipes, springs, and water pressure; in fact, the soul — the soul that
has its own laws, is not dependent on the brain, and has innate structuring
and innate ideas prior to experience; the soul that is the misty origin of
volition and unbounded place of thought, that at least could be imagined
at death to rise, either steamy with sin or misty with innocence, to a heaven
situated somewhere above the engaging motions of Saint-Germain.

---

15. *Ibid.*
16. Article 38 of *Passions de l'âme.* The only passage where any reflex-like word appears in Descartes
is in this sense in Article 36, where he speaks of "les esprits réfléchis de l'image ainsi formée sur la
glande…"
17. The two important works on this history of the reflex are Franklin Fearing, *Reflex Action* (The Williams & Wilkins Company, 1930) and Georges Canguilhem, *La Formation du Concept de Réflexe aux
XVIIe et XVIIIe Siècles* (Paris: Presses Universitaires de France, 1955).

But even this mind, in Descartes' compulsively mechanical and materialistic thinking, had to be joined to the body, though there was no rational
necessity to do so. Recent Paduan anatomists had mentioned the pineal
gland, whose function is just becoming known today.[18] Since it is in the
center of the head, and is single rather than double, as most other parts
of bilaterally symmetrical animals, here was the great tiny bridge between
the two worlds where the whole mystery of creation was concentrated,
where thought meets extension and mastered it, and where extension
moves toward thought and is perceived. The soul or mind squeezed the
pineal gland this way and that, nudging the animal fluids in the human
brain into the pores or valves,

> and according as they enter or even only as they tend to enter more or
> less into this or that nerve, they have the power of changing the form of
> the muscle into which the nerve is inserted, and by this means making
> the limbs move.[19]

Animals, according to Descartes, had no pineal gland (even though it had
been first discovered in animals!), and thus no bridge to the other realm,
no thoughts. If they had any thoughts, they would say so and tell us about
them. Their silence condemns them into mere automation.

It was all so clear and simple that anyone could remember it and everyone did. Thought so novel, so attractive in its bold, clear images amidst the
remaining murk of scholasticism, and so flattering to the human species
(everything immortal this side of the pineal gland) could not but lift up the
attention of a century already impatient with ancient philosophy and longing
for a new one. Like magic, a prevaricating magic I might add, it swept all the
old insolubles and scholastic confusions out of sight and effort, and into the
mists of consciousness, leaving the visible world merely a catching clockwork
like the flickering grottoes hissing with hydraulic life at Saint-Germain.

It is important to appreciate the enormity of the reaction to Descartes
so that we realize the importance even of his mistakes. Brilliant and arro-
gant, he was just that bit beside the point on most of the psychological

18. The pineal gland was so named by Galen because in the ox brain he was studying, it was shaped
like a pine cone (Latin: *pinare* = pine cone). Vesalius in 1540, caught up in the Renaissance love of
metaphor, called the pineal gland the cerebral penis, a notion that may have at least stressed its importance to Descartes and given him the absurd supposition of its motility. See *Vesalius' First Public
Anatomy at Bologna 1540, An Eyewitness Report* by Baldasar Heseler, ed. by R. Eriksson (Uppsala &
Stockholm, 1959). Its true function is still obscure, but it is believed to be an evolutionary vestige of an
ancestral light-sensitive organ still present in some lizards. It probably is involved in regulating biological functions related to the amount of light. Its very high concentration of serotonin suggests that some
important new discoveries may soon be made here, particularly in regard to insanity.
19. Descartes, *L'homme*, p. 347.

problems he tackled so as to stir calm reflection into heated discussion. As to the problem of animate motion, the reaction to Descartes is in three phases: (1) the refutation of the localization of soul action in the pineal gland; (2) the refutation of his theory of nerve-muscle action and, with it, the long history of the doctrine of animal spirits; and (3) the continuation of his emphasis on animal motion being caused by stimuli.

Archaic for its own day, the errors of Descartes' physiology were pointed out one by one as they appeared. The year following the publication of *Traité de l'Homme*, Nicolas Steno (1638–1686), the young Danish theologian and physiologist, found himself "obliged to point out ... the vast difference between Descartes' imaginary machine, and the real machine of the human body";[20] he showed that the pineal gland existed in animals as well as in man (as had been know before), and in no case had the rich nerve supply which the Cartesian theory demanded. The drive wheel of Descartes' animal machine had been the brain, with its ventricles full of valves; but as had long been known, the brain was unnecessary to many animal movements. Redi noticed the movements of decapitated snakes. So did Boyle, who also went searching for the seat of the soul in snakes by removing one internal organ after another until his specimens even ...

> two or three days after the skin, the heart, and the entrails are separated from it are seen to move in a twining or wriggling manner, may appear to be manifestly sensible of punctures, being put into a fresh and vivid motion when it lay still before, upon the being pricked especially on the spine or marrow, with a pin or needle.[21]

And the chance finding that a decapitated tortoise moved three days afterward provoked an anonymous writer for the recently begun *Philosophical Transactions of the Royal Society* to exclaim that this was a "sore blow" to the Cartesians, "so the Disciples thereof are here endeavoring to heal the wound."

But if the Cartesian soul was not in these locations, perhaps it might be in the blood. Blood transfusions, following the technique of blood infusion developed by the architect Sir Christopher Wren, were begun by Richard Lower. Lower replaced the blood of a sheep with the blood of a calf, after

---

20. Nicolaus Steno, *Lecture on the Anatomy of the Brain* (1669), ed. by Gustav Scherz (Copenhagen: Nyt Nordisk Forlag, 1965). The great Bishop of Titopolis did not tackle the problem of animal motion himself, but he came to understand the nature of muscle better than anyone else of his century. He knew that if a muscle is cut up lengthwise by scissors in three or four bits, each bit may be made to contract, proving that the power of contraction lies in the muscular substance rather than in the whole muscle as a machine.

21. *Philosophical Trans. of the Royal Society* (1665–1667), p. 387.

which the sheep bounded away and reacted to a dog in a typical sheep-like fashion, proving that habits and instincts are not situated in the blood.[22] Descartes' idea that the soul had a particular location or isthmus in the body and Steno's immediate disproof had thus begun a quandary that was both futile and regressive, and would last well into the next century.

The second aspect of Descartes' physiology to be refuted was his concept of muscle action and, with it, a part of the long tradition of animal spirits. The importance of this refutation must be understood against the larger background of the rivalry between the two great medical theories of the seventeenth century, the Physiatric and the Chemiatric. The former, stressing physical therapies, surgery, and anatomy, was the chief trend of the century, and became even more prominent after the exciting success of Galileo's mechanics, Harvey's theory of circulation, and the many mechanical inventions of the time. But the older Chemiatric School, with its chemical and alchemical therapies and theories, was nevertheless still flourishing in the haunted heritage of that wondered, wandering cabalistic drunk, Paracelsus, particularly in Germany and Holland, where he had established it. Early in the seventeenth century, a new offshoot of the Chemiatrics appeared, calling themselves Rosicrucians, still a going concern today. From this time to our own, the Rosicrucians have kept alive the older mystiques about motion, referring to vital forces that pass through one body to another. Like Paracelsus, they wallowed in undulant metaphors, using them as explanations, as in the analogy of animate motion with magnetism that later grows into Mesmer's "animal magnetism" and thence into hypnosis.

In general, the Chemiatrics saw the thickening of muscle tissue in contraction as a swelling of the animal spirits similar to the swelling up of a liquid during fermentation. Van Helmont (1557–1644), their most respectable member, did so, although he buried the causative part of the problem of animate motion in spiritual occult agencies called "blasses," interacting with the body through the pylorus, which were little else than the archei of Paracelsus revived for a more critical age. The influence of this idea of muscle action went quite beyond the Chemiatric school itself. John Mayow (1645–1679), for example, perhaps because of Lower's experiment, thought the air rather than the blood was impregnated with a "certain, universal salt, of a nitro-saline nature, that is to say, with a vital, fiery and in the highest degree fermentative spirit"[23] whose particles are breathed in

22. *Ibid.*, pp. 353–358.
23. Mayow, *De Sal Nitro* (London, 1668), cited by Michael Foster, *Lectures on the History of Physiology*

and become the animal spirits that account for animate motion. This idea, like Rosicrucian doctrine, had also lasted into our own time, its most recent manifestation being the orgone theory of Wilhelm Reich.[24]

Descartes had simply taken over this idea of muscle action and crystallized the problem beautifully and wrongly with the simplicity of his vision. The animal spirits that had begun as a confused doctrine over a thousand years before in Alexandrian physiology had indeed come to this. If this could be disproved, if it could be shown that the muscle was not swelled up by liquid or airy animal spirits, the Chemiatrics had lost their most promising solution to the problem of animate motion and therefore much of their hold on seventeenth-century thought. And this is precisely what happened.

The famous experiment of Jan Swammerdam (1637–1680) was one of the most important of the century. What a brilliant simplicity it was! Dissecting out the gastronemius muscle of a frog with its attached nerve, he immersed it in water, pinched the nerve, and showed that there was no displacement of the water as the muscle contracted.[25] Nothing could therefore have been added to the muscle. Even the very demonstration of such an artificial irritation of the nerve-muscle preparation ruled out all notions of animal spirits being flushed down from the ventricles of the brain, as Descartes had arrogantly insisted. The experiment was definitive. The Chemiatric theory of animate motion was never a serious scientific trend again.

The more agreeable side of Descartes' influence on the problem of animal motion is not in physiology. It is the idea that animate motion is to be understood by correlating it with physical stimuli which occasion it. Even Descartes' critics could not escape the power and fascination of seeing behavior in this new way. Swammerdam in particular, a thorough physiatric, carefully related the behavior he observed to stimuli. He noted the contraction of the pupil of the eye when irritated by a "particle of light," the peristalsis of the intestines in proportion to their contents, and how trains of images, just like trains of muscular contractions, can follow each other "urged by one cause of motion to another."

And this emphasis is repeated by Francis Glisson (1597–1677) in England, who, I venture, could not escape knowing Swammerdam's

(Cambridge University Press, 1924), p. 184.

24. Wilhelm Reich, *The Discovery of the Orgone: The Function of the Orgasm*, trans. by T. P. Wolfe (New York: Noonday Press, 1961).

25. Jan Swammerdam, *The Book of Nature; or the History of Insects: Reduced to distinct classes, confirmed by particular instances, displayed in the anatomical analyses of many species.* With life of the author, by Herman Boerhaave. Trans. from the Dutch and Latin original editions by T. Flloyd. Revised and improved by notes from Réamur and others, by John Hill (London, 1758).

widely discussed work. Referring to the Chemiatric theories in his post-humous *De Ventriculo*, Glisson explained how "this explosion and infla-tion of spirits has now for some time past been silent, convicted by the following experiment."[26] And then he went on to perform the same sort of experiment as Swammerdam to show that muscles did not increase in bulk during contraction. His experiment with somewhat less elegance used the intact human arm submerged under water. He also stressed cer-tain aspects of Swammerdam's terminology that brought into general biology that unfortunate concept of "irritability."

In a different way, the stimulus-response paradigm is continued in the sometimes fantastic work of Thomas Willis (1621–1666), a celebrated physician at Oxford.[27] His work is an astonishing combination of worth and worthlessness, so that even contemporaries dubbed him "a lucky dis-sector" who "too soon fell in love with his first thoughts." And those first thoughts were indeed his inspiration from Descartes. Willis was little better than Descartes on the nerves, conceiving them not as tubes, but as "cords lightly strung," the animal fluids slithering down the outside of them into the muscles. His conception of the brain was even more baroque than Descartes', complete with ventricles like halls of mirrors and windows, with actual images projected on the white wall of the *corpus callosum* by the *cor-pora striata*. Images undulate about the brain, pushed hither and thither by hydraulics more fantastical than Descartes', and were stored in the folds of the cortex. The brain even produced its own light that shone out through the eyes in ancient Platonic fashion, so that he could believe an elderly gentleman who once quaveringly told him that "after an extra good bout of wine he could see to read print clearly on a very dark night."

But Willis' importance resides not in his fantasies, as Descartes' does, but in his two emphases. First, he carries through all his work the Cartesian idea of behavior as a reply or response to stimuli. He even used the metaphor of an echo, and differs from Descartes in making the periphery, as well as the brain, the seat of what Marshall Hall in 1833 called the reflex.[28] Second is his emphasis on the hierarchy in the nervous system. The cerebrum presides over voluntary motion and is higher than the cerebellum presiding over involuntary motion. Each has its own memory.

26. As cited by Fearing, p. 37.

27. Thomas Willis, *The Remaining Medical Works of that Famous and Renowned Physician, Dr. Thomas Willis*, trans. by S. Pordage. V. of Muscular Motion. VI. Of the Anatomy of the Brain. VII. Of the Description and Use of the Nerves (London, 1681).

28. Hall, "On the Reflex Function of the Medulla Oblongata and Medulla Spinalis," *Philosophical Transactions of the Royal Society of London*, 1883, *123*, 635–665.

This is the first and proper solution to a problem that perplexed many of the writers I have dealt with. Van Helmont had ascribed voluntary and involuntary motion to two occult "blasses." Descartes had hidden the problem of voluntary motion in the depths of his nonphysiological human soul, all other behavior being automatic. And Swammerdam, appalled at this mixture of science and metaphysics, had gone too far the other way in refusing to admit the distinction. Willis put the matter in the right direction, which led to considerable experimental work in the next century on the effects of destroying parts of the nervous system. The important result was to solve the problem of animate motion by classifying it according to the parts of the nervous system necessary to it.

What was happening was now becoming clear. The problem of animate motion, when separated from physics, has two solutions: correlating it with stimuli or with parts of the nervous system.

But there is another solution. And it is the morose and quarrelsome Giovanni Borelli (1608–1679), a troubled and swaggering thinker, who is the very summing up of this seventeenth-century obsession with the problem of motion.[29] In one of his early works, he had spoken of the attraction between bodies that we have come to call gravity, explaining the movements of the moons of Jupiter as a resultant between such an attraction and inertia — and this twenty years before Newton. But he lacked the calculus that Leibniz and Newton were inventing even at that very time, and the definitive statement had to wait for Newton's great *Principia* in 1687. And after a stormy life studying astronomy, fever, kidney function with Bellini, and geometry, and scrapping with the Accademia del Cimento, the scientific society to which he belonged (they met in semisecrecy and were supposed to publish anonymously, which was too much for his ego), Borelli retired to a monastery and spent his last years finishing the work for which he expected fame (and received posthumously), his *De Motu Animalium*. It was published in two parts, in the two successive years after his death, and is concerned with the problem that had persisted since the century had begun.

The first part solves much of the problem Fabricius and the Aristotelian writings had opened. Following Galileo's mechanics and Steno's ideas on the structure of muscle, with diagrams and equations meant "to ornament and enrich" his subject, Borelli showed the bones to be true levers — the length of the limb, the distance to the muscle, or differences in the center

---

29. Borelli, *De Motu Animalium* (Rome, 1680–1681).

of articulation all influence the force necessary to make the movement. When he examined the flight of birds and the swimming of fish, he first looked for the center of gravity, even as Aristotelian writings had done, but with the new Galilean emphasis. One of his sections is entitled "The Quantity of Air Acted Upon by the Wing of a Bird in Flight Is in Shape a Solid Sector Swept out by a Radius Equal to the Span of the Wing." He demonstrated that "the power of the muscles that beat the wings is ten thousand times greater than the weight of the bird." And from this he deduced that the story of Icarus is impossible since our pectoral muscles could never reach this ratio. It is to be noted that he is never concerned with the initiation of animate motion, only its mechanics.

In the second part, Borelli went on to apply mechanics to internal motions. He calculated the forces necessary for Harveian circulation, the heartbeat, and respiration, and attempted to apply mechanics to liver and kidney functions with less successful results, biochemistry being unknown. This is, of course, the exciting beginning of physiological biophysics. And thus the seventeenth-century's fascination with motion produced major discoveries in physiology as well as in physics and psychology.

My underlying purpose in this essay has been to suggest that much of modern science has structured itself out of these seventeenth-century divisions of the problem of motion. During the Renaissance many think-ers kept and nourished a mystique about motion that confused it with both life and change. Partly because this mystique was so intellectually haunting, and partly because motion by machines was becoming more and more important in the European economies, it became the central intellectual concern as the century begins. Even before Galileo disen-gaged the physical problems of mechanics from this mystical confusion, Fabricius separated out the biological problems of animal motion. He failed to find a solution, but succeeded in correlating animal motion with environment in a remarkably prescient way. Harvey also struggled with the problem, but made no advance in it whatever. What was needed was a new metaphor or paradigm for animal motion, one that would differenti-ate it from the motion of physics. And this, as I have shown, was supplied by Descartes' analogy of organisms with hydraulic sculpture. How ironic that this materialistic idea, by considering animate motion as a response to stimuli, distinguished it forever from the motion of inanimate objects! Even by 1680 it was somewhat trite to point out, as did Perrault, that, for example, the flowing of a river which "seems to seek the valley,"[30] indicating choice and desire, is in reality a wholly different kind of thing than the sense-caused movements of animals.

Three solutions followed. First, the paradigm that animate motion is a response to stimuli led directly to the notion of "irritability" and of the reflex, and thence to the stimulus-response psychology of more recent times. Secondly, the explanation of animate motion was felt to be in the nervous system, just as a machine is explained by its parts. This led immediately to the study of the localization of function. Willis' idea of the independence and separate functions of parts of the brain was pursued by Boyle, Perrault, Bohn, Chirac, Du Vernez, Preston, and others, and led to the development of neurology in the next centuries. Thirdly, another kind of explanation was found in the descriptive mechanics of the organism treated as a physical system. After Borelli, there was so little more to say of a fundamental sort that the subject, except for a brief flurry of interest in the late nineteenth century in Marey and others, did not receive further attention until modern biophysics.

The seventeenth century, then, sorted out the mystical and confused problem of motion into our several modern sciences. Perhaps the most important lesson from all this is to realize the tremendous generative power of metaphor and analogy in the beginnings of science. This is particularly evident with respect to the two kinds of motion. Physics in the seventeenth century is anthropomorphic about matter, applying animate terms like attraction, force (originally muscular strength), inertia (originally referring to an idle and unemployable person), and acceleration (to hasten one's steps) to get started. The reverse occurred with Descartes when he applied the inanimate statue analogy to animal motion.

Newton's *Principia* in 1687, coming after this history, is of course the major answer to the seventeenth-century concern with the problem of motion. Newton's laws of motion make it all the more clear that physical behavior is a quite distinct thing from animate behavior. Hardly any physicist would ever again think of the world as living because it moved, as Kepler and Campanella had done, and even as Newton was tempted to do at one time. Animate behavior is different. Its explanation resides no longer in the explanation of motion, but only in the correlation of that motion with a nervous system and the stimuli around it. This is a huge and important step.

---

30. As cited by Fearing, p. 35. Claude and P. Perrault, *Oeuvres Diverses de Physique et de Méchanique* (Paris, 1761). The quotation is from his *Essai de Physique* (1680).

# CHAPTER 8

# The Origin of Consciousness

I N THE COURSE OF TRYING TO UNDERSTAND the evolution of mind, I had for a long time been developing various notes and evidence about a new theory of consciousness. But when Robbie MacLeod invited me to bring them together into some kind of pubic coherence for an address to the APA three years ago, I had reservations. For one thing, I would have liked to have waited for more evidence. And for another, to confess such an involvement with such a taboo subject as consciousness in a world of successful behaviorism was to court its dismissal and scorn. But such was the encouragement of Robbie's request and my trust in his quiet judgment, that I ventured out with my ideas, as I do again in slightly fuller sail this morning.

First of all, let me say that in the problem itself there is a kind of reticence. For how can we think or talk about consciousness? When we try to do so, we are trying to be conscious of consciousness, and is this possible? In any such instance, when what something is, is so elusive and difficult, it is good to begin by saying what that something is not.

Most importantly, consciousness is not nearly as extensive as our language and culture have led us to think it is. Consciousness, for example, does not include simple reactivity, since there are unconscious states in which a person's behavior is still reacting to the environment in an almost normal way. All kinds of perceptual processes and constancy corrections go on without any consciousness whatever. When we speak, we are not really conscious of our speech but of our intentions. Consciousness is certainly not necessary for learning, as the literature on "learning without awareness" demonstrates. The Würzburg experiments at the turn of the century showed us that consciousness is not even the main ingredient of thinking. Even great creative thought is often autobiographically described as being non-conscious.

Adapted from a lecture presented by Julian Jaynes at the MacLeod Symposium, held June 2–3, 1972 at Cornell University. First published in David Krech (ed.), *The MacLeod Symposium*. © 1973 Cornell Department of Psychology. Reprinted with permission.

A further error we make is to think of consciousness as located in the head somewhere behind the eyes. We assume this in ourselves and in others. But we all know that this is simply an imaginary space and not a real one. Consciousness indeed has no location. Of course the brain is necessary for consciousness. But it is also necessary for riding a bicycle, and we don't ride bicycles inside our heads.

What all these criticisms do is bury piece by piece the huge and baroque nineteenth century idea of consciousness as it was professed, for example, here at Cornell. For it was in the lecture room just across the hall from where I now stand that Titchener, year after magnificent year, proclaimed that "consciousness is the sum total of mental activity happening now." It is not. It is something else.

What then is it? And here I must, for the sake of brevity, simply leap into the center of my ideas without any really sufficient preamble, hoping that they will become clearer as I go on. Subjective conscious mind is an analog of what we call the real world. It is built up with a vocabulary or lexical field whose terms are all metaphors or analogs of behavior in the physical world. Its reality is of the same order as mathematics. It allows us to short-cut behavioral processes and arrive at more adequate decisions. Like mathematics, it is an operator, rather than a thing or a repository. And it is intimately bound up with volition and decision.

Consider the language we use to describe conscious processes. The most prominent group of words used to describe mental events are visual. We "see" solutions to problems, the best of which may be "brilliant," or "clearer" than "dull," "fuzzy," or "obscure" solutions. These words are metaphors, and the mind-space to which they apply is a metaphor of actual space. In it we can "approach" a problem perhaps from some "viewpoint" and "grapple" with its difficulties. Every word we use to refer to mental events is a metaphor of something in the behavioral world. And the adjectives that we use to describe physical behavior in real space are analogically taken over to describe mental behavior in mind-space. We speak of the conscious mind as being "quick" or "slow," or of somebody being "nimble-witted" or "strong-minded" or "weak-minded," or "broad," "deep," "open," or "narrow-minded." And so like a real space, something can be at the "back" of our mind, or in the "inner recesses," or "beyond" our minds.

But how, you may ask, can consciousness be a metaphor of the world? A metaphor in its most general sense is a comparison between two things that already exist. In attempting to describe *a*, we say it is like *b* (what in

other places I have called respectively the metaphrand and the metaphier).
But metaphors are really much more than that. There are associations of
*b* that can project back and become the associations of *a*, creating a very
different *a* than we started with. Metaphor is thus generative.

Supposing after puzzling over a problem, I suddenly exclaim that I
"*see*" the solution. On analysis, this statement breaks down into a metaphor where *a* is the sudden solving of the problem, and *b* is seeing some
object. I am expressing *a* by saying it is similar to *b*. But seeing an object
has many associations, such as the space of the external world and the
multiplicity of objects of which one is being selected. These associations
project back into *a*, giving a spatial quality to the act of solving a problem.
By this trivial example I mean to indicate the way in which language and
metaphor can generate the kind of mind-space and the mental metaphor-
objects with which consciousness works.

A theory of consciousness along these lines results in several features
that are testable in everyday introspection. These include (1) *spatialization*,
the quality of things thought on of being spatially separated, even time,
where we have to spread out a before and after into a spatial succession;
(2) *excerption*, where we "see" only single aspects or parts of a thing in consciousness at any one time, just as in behavioral attention; (3) *conciliation*,
where we reconcile disparate things consciouscized into a recognizable
unity that can be recognized as past experience or future plans; (4) *the
analog 'I*,' the metaphor we have of our volitional selves which can "move
about" vicarially in our "imagination," "doing" things that we are not actually doing; (5) *the metaphor 'me*,' or ourselves as objects; (6) *narratization*,
how our analog 'I's' are always "seeing" our "metaphor 'me's" as the main
figures in the ongoing spatialized stories of our lives. All these features of
consciousness are deducible from behaviors in the physical world and are
capable of separate investigation.

Now if conscious mind is a spatial analog of the world, and mental acts
are analogs of bodily acts, and it is all generated by metaphor on the basis
of language, a rather startling deduction can be made as to the origin of
consciousness. It is one that is completely contradictory to the evolutionary solutions of this problem which I at one time — and most of you —
have believed. For if consciousness is based on language, then it follows
that only humans are conscious, and that we became so at some historical
epoch after language was evolved.

This is an extremely serious statement. Certainly it immediately directs us to the earliest writings of mankind to see if we can find any hints as to when this important invention of consciousness might have occurred. Although writing began in 3000 B.C., the first text in a language we can really understand, and which has had a continuity to modern times to be adequate to our purposes, is the *Iliad*. Following the general tone of modern scholarship, we may regard this powerful paean to anger as having been orally composed by successive generations of *aoidoi* or bards from about 1200 B.C. up to 850 B.C., when it came to be written down. The astonishing thing about it is that there is no consciousness in the *Iliad* whatever. No one thinks, plans, or decides anything — strange and disturbing as that seems. The words that in later Greek come to mean mental processes, in the *Iliad* have quite different meanings. *Psyche*, which later means soul or conscious mind, is life, or life-substances such as blood or breath. And *noos*, which later means conscious mind, is, in the *Iliad*, simply recognition. There are certain exceptions to these statements. But they are not such as to modify my main point, that the characters in the *Iliad* have no conscious minds at all. It is a behaviorist world inhabited by noble automatons who know not what they do.

What initiates behavior? The beginnings of action are not in conscious plans, reasons, and motives, but are always in the speeches of gods. In every novel situation, a man in the *Iliad* hears a voice telling him what to do. These voices, or gods, start the war in the *Iliad*. They devise its strategy and determine the outcome of every crisis. Even the poem itself is not composed by men in any modern sense, but rather by a goddess, as the first line indicates.

Who, then, were these gods that pushed men about like robots and sang epics through their lips? I suggest they were auditory hallucinations, often with visual aura, organizations of the central nervous system composed of amalgams of admonitory experiences, which could be as distinctly heard by the Iliadic heroes as voices are heard by schizophrenic patients today. And I further suggest that the physiological mechanism cueing these auditory hallucinations is appreciably similar, being the biochemical effects of stress occasioned by novel situations in which the person does not know what to do.

I am calling this different mental organization among these strange ancient Greeks *the bicameral mind*. By this, I mean that it was a mental organization in which there was a god side, which made the decisions and did the planning, and a man side which obeyed. In the trivial everyday

circumstances of his life, such a bicameral man would behave with unconscious habit, but in situations where you or I would narratize out what to
do in consciousness, such a man would hear a voice that was neurologically
impossible to disobey. And neither side was conscious in our sense.

This is a difficult conception to imagine. We cannot approach these
ancient heroes of the *Iliad* by inventing mind-spaces behind their fierce
eyes as we do with each other. Iliadic man did not have subjectivity as
do we; he had no awareness of his awareness of the world, no internal
mind-space to introspect upon. Just as the auditory hallucinations of a
schizophrenic often do more "thinking" than the patient does, so volition,
planning, and initiative were organized with no consciousness whatever
and then "told" to the individual, sometimes with a visual aura of a friend,
king, or god.

Now what this implies is that consciousness had not been developed
by the time of the *Iliad*, and that the previous millennia were also not
conscious and were ruled by the bicameral mind. So we should next turn
to history, and ask whether or not this plain reading of the *Iliad* conforms
to anything in the older civilizations of man.

Let me simply state that it does. The early civilizations up to the latter part of the second millennium B.C. are all theocracies. The evidence
that they were run by hallucinated voices called gods seems difficult to
negate. Thousands of cuneiform tablets in Mesopotamia leave no doubt
that everything — cities, buildings, and people — were owned by gods, or
what I am calling the bicameral voices. Often such owning gods are idols,
carefully dressed statues 'living' in temples or ziggurats, which I suggest
is unexplainable apart from the suggestion that they were hallucinogenic
sources of the bicameral directions that controlled the society. Similar evidence for the bicameral mind is found throughout antiquity, in Egypt,
the Hittites, later in India and then in China, and then much later in the
early civilizations of Mesoamerica and the Andean Highlands. I do not
mean that all this is worked out at present in fine detail, but rather that
all these early civilizations without exception present a consistent picture
of divinely managed societies based on auditory hallucinations from gods.

This then is what I am calling the great bicameral age, which civilized
mankind. I shall merely state without evidence here that I consider it to
have begun shortly after 9000 B.C. and that its hallucinatory aspects were
part of the early evolution of language, but that these became organized to
authoritative voices only as a method of social control, when man became

urbanized into agricultural communities. The first gods, I suggest, were dead kings whose voices were still heard commanding their people in hallucination. And the first temples were their tombs, which became places where such hallucinations could most easily be heard. The first idols were the patched-up corpses of such kings, which when withered away were replaced by statues. But all these are possibilities only if we accept the major premise of the bicameral mind.

The era of such societies, organized and obedient to hallucinated voices called gods, lasted at least into the second millennium B.C. Then comes the period in which we can see the breakdown of the bicameral mind. The reasons for this breakdown are many. As populations grew, this type of social organization became highly unstable. The development of writing, a visual means of communication, perhaps reduced the effectiveness of auditory voices. But perhaps most important were the general social upheavals that characterized the last centuries of the second millennium B.C. Half of the civilized world had been made refugees by various geological catastrophes. And in the migrations and invasions and wholesale slaughter and conquest all over the Middle East that followed, the voices of gods no longer worked as a method of social control.

It was during this period, the latter part of the second millennium B.C., that consciousness began to develop as an alternative method of social control. This development can first be seen inferentially in the artifacts of Assyria. But the development of consciousness is much more clearly seen somewhat later, in the development of Greek literature after the *Iliad*. By following the careers of certain terms, which we are calling *preconscious hypostases*, such as *thumos, phrenes, psyche*, and *noos*, we see them develop from external observations to internal sensations, which then acquire a metaphor space in which what we call mental functions can occur. Then, by the time of Solon in 600 B.C., they join together into one subjective conscious mind. And with this comes an ability to retrieve the past as a frame for present action, for volitional memory in the sense of reminiscence is only rudimentary in the *Iliad*. And with this also comes a spatialization of time, accounting for the birth of morality or what is *dike* or right for a man to do. In the bicameral age there was no right or wrong; only the hallucinated voice of a god.

The third area where the development of consciousness can be seen is perhaps the most interesting. This is the Old Testament. In its older parts, gods tell men what to do whenever a novel situation arises. But gradually the gods disappear. Moses, as Deuteronomy (34:10) tells us, is the last prophet to see Yahweh face to face. Thereafter we have *nabiim* or prophets who for the most part have only auditory hallucinations. And then these too cease. The later prophets seek wisdom. They no longer run out into the wilderness inquiring of Yahweh. And we see the same concern with right action and wisdom as occurred slightly earlier in Greek writings. By comparing Amos of about 800 B.C. with Ecclesiastes of about 200 B.C., the change in mentality is extremely clear.

Such an important alteration in mentality requires us, if we are to think responsibly, to think of what the neurology of all this might be. Certainly the simplest hypothesis about the bicameral mind would begin with the notion of one hemisphere of the brain talking to the other. There are quite a few facts that recommend such an idea. Speech has evolved such that it involves only one hemisphere, which could mean that the corresponding speech areas in the other hemisphere (which we know to be perfectly capable of speech at birth) would be free to develop the auditory hallucinations from admonitory experience called gods. Stimulation of what corresponds to the major speech area (Wernicke's area) on the nondominant hemisphere often produces hallucinations of a similar kind. The functions of the nondominant hemisphere, as determined in recent work with commissurotomized patients and others, are precisely those that characterized the functions of the gods; the spatial synthetic fitting of elements into a pattern. And if this was indeed the biology of the bicameral mind, there are important deductions to be made here as to the neurology of consciousness and introspection.

Indeed, all that is novel in what I've been saying here this morning is perhaps largely the work of my right hemisphere, since its chief recommendation as a theory of mind is that it fits together evidence from widely diverse sources and contexts. It is a theory of consciousness that is certainly presumptuous at first sight. But it does work out into testable hypotheses. Moreover, it has particularly interesting ramifications into other areas, such as child development and anthropology, as well as providing us with a new theory of schizophrenia as a partial relapse to the bicameral mind. I certainly cannot expect to be convincing in this brevity here this morning. But what I do insist is that the idea of consciousness originating in human history is a perfectly viable alternative to the much more mystical — and I think naïve — views that would hide the problem in the inaccessible reaches of primordial evolution.

# CHAPTER 9

# The Evolution of Language
# in the Late Pleistocene

I N THIS PAPER I SHALL FIRST ADDRESS the question of when language evolved, basing my answer on three assumptions. I shall then attempt the question of how language evolved, appealing to a principle of intensity differentiation of call endings and describing how this may have resulted in first modifiers, then commands, and then nouns and names. I shall then insist that this development is roughly correlated with the hastening sequence of archeological artifacts from the Acheulean to Neolithic times. Finally, since such a view demands an exceedingly swift evolution, I shall close with several possibilities of how this "leveraged" evolution, as I shall call it, could have occurred.

## WHEN LANGUAGE BEGAN

To answer the question of when language evolved, I would like to introduce below three reasonable constraints upon a possible solution.

### Survival Value

In thinking about the evolution of language, we naïvely assume that language is always beneficial. But this is questionable. If some subhuman primate could be taught vocal speech or if those who have already learned sign language could be fired up with some missionary zeal to return to the wilds to teach their conspecifics, it is not at all certain that it would have the slightest survival value whatever. In fact, if a species is fully adapted to its ecological niche, it could perhaps be shown that the sudden ability to communicate syntactically would be disastrous. At the very least,

Article by Julian Jaynes first published in the *Annals of the New York Academy of Sciences*, Vol. 280. © 1976 John Wiley & Sons. Reprinted with permission.

the sounds might attract predators; or if the communication is gestural it might position its users in more vulnerable open situations. More importantly, however, the communication itself might detract from the innate signaling systems that already have organized the successful social grouping of that species. Also, the genetically based spacing mechanisms would be altered and an outbreak of intraspecific aggression might result. Too much communication is a bad thing.

It follows from such considerations that human language developed only during an era in which some portion of the human population was being persistently forced into new ecological niches to which it was not fully adapted. For any trait that is as universal in a species and that has as precise a neurological substrate as language in man must have developed during an age when it had a great and persisting survival value. And it is certainly a requirement of any theory of language evolution that this survival value be specified with some precision.

## Behavioral Sequelae

Words are of such huge moment in the life of men that the acquisition of them and the ability to organize them into sentences that convey meaning must have resulted in very real behavioral changes; and these changes must be reflected in the artifacts left behind. This constriction will not be so readily consented to, but let me remind you of a fundamental principle of vertebrate learning: that acquiring different consistent responses to different things makes them more discriminable, and makes it easier to acquire new responses to those things.[1] This is exactly what language does. A differential lingual response to an object is a training of attention upon it. To look at an object and to name it at the same time allows a concentration upon it that otherwise would be absent. Without names for things, we cannot readily get our own or others' attentions to the right places or keep them there very long. Speechless children, such as the wild boy studied by Itard,[2] or even normal children before the advent of speech, have difficulty in maintaining attention for very long. Language is an organ of perception, not merely a means of communication.

But the effect of language on behavior goes much farther and deeper than orientation and attention. Stimuli when labeled are actually easier to

1. Julian Jaynes, "Learning A Second Response To A Cue As A Function of The Magnitude of the First," *Journal of Comparative and Physiological Psychology,* 1950, *43*, 398–408.
2. George Humphrey, *The Wild Boy of Aveyron* (New York: Century, 1932).

remember. Children who can name colors better can remember and recognize them better.[3] And what is remembered, is shaped by the terms that
express it.[4] Moreover, stimulus differences when labeled can be responded
to in a much more encompassing way: behavior can be reactions to rela-
tional concepts rather than to the actual stimuli themselves, something
impossible without words.[5] Language thus allows us to code and compare attributes of objects verbally, thereby freeing us from the momentary
perceptual impact of one attribute or another. Many workers feel this is
the very essence of cognitive development.[6] There are also many studies,
both in Russia[7] and America,[8] which show that the teaching of verbal
descriptions of various response alternatives allow children to bridge situational changes or extensive time gaps by verbal mediation, which would
be impossible without language.

And so it was with mankind when speech first developed. Just as the
psychobehavioral development of a child leaps forward with speech, so a
similar leap must, I think, have occurred when man as a species first developed language. The position can be taken therefore with some assurance
that the development of language produced a qualitatively different level
of mentality that resulted in behavioral sequelae whose artifacts we may
find archeologically.

*Brain Structure*

Any theory of the development of language must at least where possible
make some sense of what we know of brain development over these time
periods. The reason for this is that the three cortical areas involved in
language, the supplementary motor cortex and Broca's area in the frontal
lobe, and Wernicke's area around the fissure of Sylvius where the temporal

3. Meredith Kimball and Philip S. Dale, "The Relationship between Color Naming and Color Recognition Abilities in Preschoolers," *Child Development,* 1972, *43,* 972–980.

4. L. Carmichael, H.P. Hogan and A.A. Walter, "An Experimental Study of the Effect of Language on
the Representation of Visually Perceived Form," *Journal of Experimental Psychology,* 1932, *15,* 73–86.

5. Margaret Kuenne, "Experimental Investigation of the Relation of Language to Transposition Behavior in Young Children," *Journal of Experimental Psychology,* 1945, *36,* 471–490.

6. Jerome S. Bruner, R.R. Olver, P.M. Greenfield, et al., *Studies in Cognitive Growth* (New York:
Wiley, 1966).

7. Dan I. Slobin, "Soviet Psycholinguistics," In N. O'Connor (ed.), *Present Day Russian Psychology*
(Oxford: Pergamon Press, 1966).

8. Charles C. Spiker, "Verbal Factors in the Discrimination Learning of Children," *Monographs of the
Society for Research in Child Development,* 1963, *2,* 53–68.

lobe joins the parietal are in a probabilistic way[9] present in all contemporary speakers, and may thus be assumed to have been necessary for the complete development of language as we speak it today.

## Glaciation and Language

Now let us apply these constraints to the problem of when language developed. We have inferred that so dramatic a development as language had to coincide with significant ecological changes during which man's life and habits underwent significant change. This inference obviously points to the great periods of glaciation, when ice accumulated in polar zones and slid southward to cover most of the North temperate regions four separate times just as man evolved from *Homo habilis* through *Homo erectus* and *Homo sapiens neanderthalesis* to *Homo sapiens*. Each glaciation lasted roughly 70,000 years. The approximate dates of the middle or coldest part of each of these periods are without sufficient ecological challenge to provide language with the survival value that we have insisted it must have had, and may thus be ruled out as the loci of its development.

The three constraints I have mentioned taken together eliminate all but the fourth glaciation. During the first two glacial periods, man was largely an African animal and far removed from their serious effects. The third glaciation occurred in the middle Pleistocene is certainly a period when the more northern living hominids were put under intense ecological pressures. That race of *H. erectus* called Peking man is now known to have been a hunter of large game animals of considerable variety during the third glaciation. And he did this with a tool kit almost as crude as those of his ancestors in Africa.[10] But it is just because of the crudity of their tools and the primitiveness of their subsistence that makes it doubtful that language developed at this time; nor had the brain of Peking man evolved to the size and structure that we have assumed to be necessary at least for the complete development of language.

At this point, some objections could possibly be raised. How was it possible for proto-man to function, to live in caves, to hunt, to use fire, to make pebble choppers or hand axes if he could not speak? The answer is that he communicated just like all the other primates, with an abundance of visual, vocal, and tactile signals very far removed from the syntactical

9. Joseph E. Bogen, "Wernicke's Area: Where Is It?" *Annals of the New York Academy of Sciences*, 1976, *280*, 834–843.
10. Grahame Clark and Stuart Piggott, *Prehistoric Societies* (London: Hutchinson, 1965).

language that we practice today. Nor is language necessary for the transmission for such rudimentary skills as simple tool using and making from one generation to another. Indeed language might even have hindered. It is almost impossible to describe the method for chipping flints to make simple choppers and hand axes with language. This art was transmitted solely by imitation in exactly the same way in which chimpanzees transmit the trick of inserting vine stems into ant hills to get ants, or Japanese macaques the method of using leaf-sponges and other nutrient-handling tasks that have then diffused without vocal language. In our own culture, it is doubtful if language is at all necessary in the transmission of such skills as swimming, riding, or other motor skills.

*Characteristics of the Late Pleistocene*

All indications, then, point to the fourth glaciation during the late Pleistocene as the period during which speech evolved and developed. This period began about 70,000 B.C., and was one in which the climate north of the equator became gradually colder, causing dramatic changes in the flora and fauna. Its coldest part came about 35,000 B.C. The glaciation then slowly receded and temperatures became normal about 8000 B.C. The temperature changes through these periods were not steady or gradual, but were characterized by wide variations corresponding to variations in the advance and retreat of glacial conditions, all of these factors causing huge migrations of both animals and men.

While *H. erectus* had been venturing quite far outside Africa since perhaps the second glaciation, it is only during the fourth glaciation that the human population in significant numbers expanded out into the Eurasian subarctic, and then into Australia and a little later into the Americas. Population density around the Mediterranean reached a new high and this area became the leader in cultural innovation, transferring man's cultural and biological focus from the tropics to the middle latitudes. His fires and furs were a kind of transportable microclimate that allowed these migrations to take place. We are used to referring to these people as late Neanderthalers. They were not a separate species of man as was thought at the beginning of this century, but were part of the general human line, which had great variation, a variation that allowed for an increasing pace of evolution as man spread into these new ecological niches.[11] It is important

---

11. This debate continues, with recent research using nuclear and mitochondrial DNA now suggesting

here to stress both the variation and the nomadic quality of life that was spreading over such wide distances. Some tribes, certainly, were following the herds of reindeer, mammoths, horse, and bison into the forest-tundra during the winter, and returning with them onto the broad expanse of herbaceous tundra in summer. Others most likely were going in a lateral direction, from campsite to campsite whenever food might be had.

There conditions then fulfill the three constraints we have placed upon the solution. Such climatic changes as occurred during the fourth glaciation certainly provide a theater of sufficient selective pressures such that a communication system such as language would, as I shall later show, have considerable survival value. The artifacts of the cultures, beginning with an explosion of new and different tools about 40,000 B.C., fulfills the second requirement, the record of artifacts showing that changes in man's way of living were occurring at an increasing tempo. And thirdly, through evolution, the brain, particularly with the increase in the frontal lobes with Broca's area, was reaching its contemporary proportions.[12]

We have inadvertently in our discussion suggested the place in which language most likely developed. Again applying the three constraints, it would be an area in which there were sufficient selective pressures, where excavated artifacts reveal the most change, and where skulls show the increase we have referred to. This area is indeed the north temperature zone in a band from France to Spain all across Europe, North Africa, the near East and Asia, and from there spreading southward. It is interesting to consider whether or not it is possible that this Northern locus of the origination of language had any effect on just how languages were formed, or left any traces of their age in present languages.

## HOW LANGUAGE BEGAN

In the discussion I am about to attempt I would like it to be continually understood that I am painting in the broadest strokes possible. All stage theory, be it in the development of a child, an idea, or a nation, requires this qualification: stages are never really discrete and differ in different instances. They are true only in general. And this is particularly so of anything as hazardous as the present undertaking. I am describing an ideal model of which the actualities are probably variants. After all,

---

Neanderthals were in fact a separate species. — *Ed.*

12. Wilfrid Le Gros Clark, *The Fossil Evidence for Human Evolution* (Chicago: University of Chicago Press, 1964).

Neanderthal man was widely distributed over Africa, Europe, and Asia at this time. It is very likely that language developed somewhat differently and at a different pace in different ecologies and races. The problem of persistent migration and diffusion is a hugely complicating factor, demanding almost a new kind of social psychology for Neanderthal tribes. What follows therefore is not meant as any exceptionless succession. It is rather a broad working model intended to provoke a new kind of thinking about the development of language and speech.

### Stage I: Intentionalization of Vocalization

First of all, let me here glance sideways at a view very much in evidence at this conference. This is the interesting idea of the gestural origin of language,[13] an older theory recently invigorated by the teaching of sign language of various sorts to chimpanzees. I myself am skeptical of how far early hominid facial, gestural, and postural communication approached modern sign languages. But whatever the comparison, there is little doubt that at least some system of visual signals did exist as it does in most primates, that it was complex, and that it was largely composed of intentional signals rather than merely incidental signals.

This is an important distinction. An *incidental* signal is simply a concomitant of some ongoing behavior. It may or may not evoke a response in another animal, and may even be emitted when the animal is alone. An *intentional* signal, on the other hand, is only emitted in a social context, and tends to be repeated until it is turned off by the behavior of the animal to which it is addressed. Territorial bird songs are incidental signals. But the distress cries of nidifugeous hatchlings are intentional, ceasing or changing to contentment sounds at the approach of an imprinted object.[14] Threat postures and the like in primates are intentional signals, tending to continue until some change in behavior in a conspecific occurs. Intentional signals are thus a more complicated sort. I am using the term descriptively in a completely behavioristic way, and do not imply any consciousness or cognitive purposiveness in its emission.

---

13. Gordon W. Hewes, "The Current Status of the Gestural Theory of Language Origin," *Annals of the New York Academy of Sciences*, 1976, *280*, 482–504 and H. Steklis and S. Harnad, "From Hand to Mouth: Some Critical Stages in the Evolution of Language," *Annals of the New York Academy of Sciences*, 1976, *280*, 445-455.

14. Julian Jaynes, "Imprinting: The Interaction of Learned and Innate Behavior: I. Development and Generalization," *Journal of Comparative and Physiological Psychology*, 1956, *49*, 201–206.

Many monkey or ape visual signals are intentional, but almost all their vocal signals are simply incidental. They merely accompany the visual signals. Vocal signals given alone apart from the total multisensory gestalt of posture, facial expression, gesture, movement, and often touch have little significance. I suggest this was also true among early hominids such as *h. habilis* back around 400,000 B.C., who had perhaps an incidental call system of perhaps 15 or 20 cries as in a present-day anthropoid.[15] The first and important step toward speech is the generalization of the intentional signaling system from the visual channel to the auditory channel.

Neurologically, this change is tantamount to the encephalization of vocalization. It is an absolute prerequisite for speech. The incidental vocal signals of present-day subhuman primates are incidental because they are controlled by the limbic system. They are emotional expressions accompanying other behavior. The entire vocal repertoires in rhesus monkeys[16] and squirrel monkeys,[17] for example, can be elicited by electrical stimulation of points throughout the limbic circuit. Although such information is not really conclusive on this point, it nevertheless suggests that this limbic control of vocal calls was true of early hominids. The transfer to cortical control occurred, I suggest, by the evolution of additional frontal cortex in the region ventral to the cortical substrate of the already intentionally gesturing hand, thus selectively suppressing and releasing the limbic centers for vocalization beneath it.

Under what ecological pressures could this have happened? As populations of Middle Pleistocene man with their Acheulean culture migrated out of African savannas and alluvial flats into northern climates, visual signals were less effective for a variety of reasons. Such a migrant to the north during the third glaciation lived more and more in dark caves or smoky shelters, perhaps hunting diurnal animals by night in situations where visual, facial, and gestural signals could not be seen as readily. Moreover, his bipedalism and tools in themselves created new selective pressures, making it important to free the hands and body for his increasingly complicated activities. It is therefore plausible that incidental vocal signals under these persisting pressures took on the intentional function that was

15. Peter Marler, "Communication in Monkeys and Apes," in Irven DeVore (ed.), *Primate Behavior* (New York: Holt, Rinehart and Winston, 1965).

16. Bryan W. Robinson, "Vocalization Evoked from the Forebrain in *Macaca* Mulatta," *Physiology and Behavior*, 1967, *2*, 345–54.

17. Detlev Ploog, "The Behavior of Squirrel Monkeys as Revealed by Sociometry, Bioacoustics, and Brain Stimulation," in S.A. Altmann (ed.), *Social Communication Among Primates* (Chicago: University of Chicago Press, 1967).

formerly the property of visual signals only. This was a momentous step, and probably had a long evolution that was not complete until the end of the Middle Pleistocene and the approach of the fourth glaciation.

## Stage II: Age of Modifiers

The first real elements of speech were, I suggest, the endings of intentional cries first varying by intensity, and then being differentiated further. This Principle of Intensity Differentiation is central to my view of language development. An example will help us here. Let us say that man has evolved an intentional warning cry of *wah! wah! wah!* We can perhaps imagine a caveman, gesturing wildly and often impotently, rushing back to his dark cave screaming this cry at the approach of any danger. It is an innate dynamism that the intensity of such a warning signal corresponds to the intensity of the danger whether the signal be gesture or vocalization. Indeed, the same dynamism could be applied to the gestural theory as a way segmentation began. In vocalization, such intensity differentiation would be reflected little by little and perhaps more and more in the way the cry was uttered, particularly perhaps in its ending phoneme. And after a period of development, we could imagine that a dangerous approaching tiger or bear might result in *wahee!*, while a tiger or bear far off and going in another direction might result in a cry of much less intensity and develop a different ending such as a more relaxed *wahoo*. It is these endings, then, that become the first modifiers meaning near and far. And the next huge step toward syntactic language was taken when these endings could be separated from the particular cry with the same indication and attached to some other cry.

What is of crucial importance here is to appreciate that the differentiation of verbal qualifiers had to precede the invention of the nouns that they modified, rather than the reverse as is assumed by most of this audience. And what is more, this state of speech had to remain for a long period until such modifiers became stable. This slow development is also necessary so that the same basic repertoire of alarm vocalizations is kept intact to perform their intentional functions. Thus we might expect that a small lexicon of modifiers like near, far, at the river, behind the hill, etc. was developed in this way long before the specific referents themselves could be differentially indicated.

The "age of modifiers" perhaps included most of what in Europe is
known as the Mousterian period and lasted perhaps up to 46,000 B.C.
Neanderthal skulls of this time show a frontal angle of 65 degrees (ours is
nearer 90 degrees) denoting undeveloped frontal lobes. Casts of some of
the better skulls show that the lower frontal lobe where Broca's speech area
is located is not fully developed, and the Fissure of Sylvius is extremely
wide, showing an undeveloped Wernicke's speech association area.[18] It is
over the next stages late in Pleistocene times that the human brain fully
evolves its characteristic speech areas. For those who find it impossible to
think of evolution of these areas going on in so short a period, it is good
to stress again the immense migrant variety of which this natural selection
for modifier development had to work under the intense selective pressures of the coldest part of the glacial period.


## Stage III: Age of Commands

Modifiers once separated from the cries they modified become commands. Just as these endings once modified cries, now they modify men's
actions themselves. Thus as in the above example, a new cry of *ee!* shouted
to a recipient could mean nearer, while *o!* could mean further. The advantage of such commands in such an endeavor as group hunting of the huge
new mammals that abounded everywhere at that time is quite obvious.
Particularly as man relied more and more on hunting in the chilled climate, the selective pressure for such a group of hunters controlled by vocal
commands must have been immense. But the use of such modifiers in
other skills is equally important. We may imagine that the industry of
flint and bone tools was passed down by imitation, but the invention of a
modifier meaning shaper as an instructed command or self-repeated command would be of extreme importance. I would suggest that this period
corresponded to the Aurignacian period in Europe, with its much sharper
blades and other tools, which lasted perhaps to 25,000 B.C. All speech up
to this period has been holophrastic.

Two further developments possibly occurred during this long period
I have called the stage of commands. The first is interrogation; and
here, I think, we can invoke a Principle of Buccolaryngeal Response
Generalization. Just as in careful manipulatory skills we often twist the

---

18. Wilfrid Le Gros Clark, *The Fossil Evidence for Human Evolution* (Chicago: University of Chicago
Press, 1964).

tongue and mouth in a corresponding way (more often in children), so in early man, postural and gestural intentional signals, particularly when done carefully because they were less effective, generalized to the mouth and larynx, altering vocalization in a corresponding fashion. In interrogation the originating postural signal would have been the quick upward movement of the brows and look of expectant waiting common in many primate dyadic social situations. Thus, the leader of a hunting group, while raising his brows and looking expectantly, might command *nearer!* with an expectant intensity ending that raised its pitch slightly, carrying it over the distance to the hunter on the other side of the prey. And the recipient of the message might then repeat the command *nearer* over and over to himself as he accomplished this act, the intensity ending being much diminished, since it was to his own ears that he was speaking. Using our punctuation, it would be *nearer?*, with the 'reply,' *nearer*. And out of this kind of repetition it is a simple matter to derive inflectional questioning. This may also have resulted in chanting of various sorts and the beginning of primordial ritual. It should be particularly noted that placing the development of inflectional questioning as early as the age of commands, indicates a very strong genetic basis.

The second development is that of negation. It is probably of a different order. I suspect that its origin is prelingual possibly as a disgust cry. Again, a part of its development may have been a buccolaryngeal generalization from a facial, gestural, or postural signal of rejection. It then may have developed into an intentional cry as from a parent to a child to stop it in what it was doing. Toilet training, which with the progressive prematurity of birth and cave living probably now became a problem, may have been the carrier. The survival value of its use as a command in group hunting is obvious.

## Stage IV: Life Nouns

Once a tribe has a repertoire of modifiers and commands, the necessity of keeping the integrity of the old primitive cries can be relaxed for the first time so that they can indicate the referents of the modifiers or commands. Thus from the original *wah* and *wahee!* We might have *wakee!* for an approaching tiger or *wabee!* for an approaching bear, the consonant differentiation being again a buccolaryngeal generalization of imitated tiger or bear behavior. And these would be the first sentences with a noun subject and a predicative modifier. This may have corresponded in Europe to the Gravetian and Solutrean cultures, which existed between 25,000 B.C. and 15,000 B.C. The pace of language development is increasing.

Some of you may be exasperated at this point and wish to exclaim, how arbitrary! But succession from modifiers to commands, and only when these become stable, to nouns, is no arbitrary succession. Nor is the dating entirely arbitrary. Just as the stage of modifiers coincided with the making of much superior tools, so the stage of nouns for animals coincides with the beginning of drawing animals on the walls of caves or on horns and tools carved from horns. Once animals — particularly those that were hunted — had nouns that could designate them, they had a kind of extra being, one indeed that could be taken far back into the caves and drawn upon its walls. And from this time on the first animal silhouettes develop into the well known cave paintings of bison and reindeer, which I suggest, could only occur after the beginning of life nouns. The fact that such paintings rarely include men drawn with the same life-like similitude may suggest a lack of words for different men.

## Stage V: Thing Nouns

This is really a carry-over from the preceding stage. Just as life nouns began animal drawings, so nouns for things beget new things: the invention of pottery, of pendants, and ornaments, bone carvings, harpoons, and most important the invention of the barb for harpoons and spearheads. It corresponds perhaps in parts of Europe to the Magdalenian culture. By this time, the brain has the modern language areas.

## Stage VI: Names

We are now in the Mesolithic period, about 10,000 B.C. to 8000 B.C. It is the period of man's adaptation to the modern postglacial environment, keying in to specific environmental situations, to grassland hunting, to life in the forest, to shellfish collecting, or to the exploitation of marine resources combined with terrestrial hunting. Such living is characterized by a much greater stability of population, rather than the mobility of the hunting groups with their large mortality which preceded them. And thus with these more fixed populations, with more fixed relationships, and probably larger numbers in the group, we have the carry-over of nouns into names for individual persons. While noun-names may have occurred for troop leaders for special individuals earlier, it appears to me that it is the Mesolithic period in which names become universal. Once a tribe member has a proper name, he can in a sense be recreated in his absence, thought about. While rare, individual, ceremonial graves date from much earlier, this is the first age in which they become common and elaborate. But just as a noun for an animal makes that relationship a much more intense one, so too does a name. And when the person dies, the name still goes on, and hence the relationship as in life, and hence an elaboration of burial practices and mourning. The Mesolithic midden-dwellers of Morbihan, for example, buried their dead in skincloaks fastened by bonepins and sometimes crowned them with stag antlers and protected them with stone slabs. Other graves from the period show burials with little crowns, or various ornaments, or possibly flowers in carefully excavated places, all, I suggest, the result of the invention of names.

Again, I would like to emphasize that the above sequence of stages may in no particular tribe or region have been actual throughout the enormous time spans we are speaking of. Migrations and therefore behavioral and cultural diffusion were on a level far beyond anything that had happened earlier in man's protohistory. Such diffusion as applied to aspects of speech in different regions and times and evolutionary development is profoundly complex. Hence any series of stages as I have propounded should perhaps be regarded as a logical analysis to which a kind of commonality of the historical realities might approximate.

*Other Developments*

It is to be noted in the above discussion that our own sense of what is necessary for primitive communication has not demanded of us a separate stage of verbs. Words denoting actions were common among the first modifiers and commands. A modifier meaning 'running' to follow a danger call is not in a different class than other modifiers. But when turned into a command it would have an obvious greater value. Similarly, most commands have verb qualities. And after the stage of nouns, we may imagine that intensity differentiations operated upon them as well to produce the first verb declensions. It is not far from a sentence such as *mammoth nearer* to *mammoth nearers!* As the animal begins to run, letting the added *s* here stand for some primordial sound produced by increased intensity.

Prepositions perhaps came about by intensity differentiation of the beginnings of place modifiers. A modifier meaning *in cave* as in *tiger in cave!* might separate into *in cave* and *out cave* on the basis perhaps of the initial intensity of the intentional communication. It might even be possible to order an historical sequence of prepositional meanings on the basis of their ease of dichotomization.

As for syntax, there is a kind of ordering that is inherent in the development I have presented. And this ordering is dependent upon the process I have called intensity differentiation and whether it occurs at the beginning of the communication as in prepositional differentiation or at the end as in the original modifier differentiation. Most primordial syntax can be derived from this in obvious ways. I hope it is apparent here that the vowel and consonant sounds naturally produced by any primate at high intensity or low would make an extremely important study.

As for the other parts of speech, pronouns being redundant with names, would develop very late, and even in some older languages never get much beyond verb endings first differentiated on the basis of intensity. Articles and conjunctions, also because they are redundant with the paralingual or expressive behavior of language are also perhaps one of the final additions to the parts of speech.

## Leveraged Evolution

In what sense is it correct to say that language evolved through these various stages? The question points to the somewhat hazy problem as to the relationship between the innate and the learned developments necessary for language. This haziness can be clarified by a consideration of what is known as the Baldwin Effect in evolutionary theory: when some new ecological pressure or species demand forces individuals to learn a particular thing to survive, and this is repeated generation after generation, there will be a continuous selection for those biologically best able to learn that particular thing. Thus what was purely learned in one millennium can become partly innate in the next. We have already pointed out the tremendous biological advantage in learning the linguistic components in the several stages I have outlined. And thus we may assume that Baldwinian evolution was continually operating, and that successive generations were building in step-by-step the innate capacity to learn a language. Indeed this is, of course, what is evolved, not the articulated language itself — a quite obvious point that is not always remembered.

But how was it possible to have the evolution of such a thing as speech over a mere 70,000 years? We know that the evolution from the skull *H. erectus* to the Cro-Magnon type did take place during this short time. To account for this I suggest that we should speak of evolution being leveraged in this particular instance. There are several reasons for the assumption of this leveraged evolution in relation to language.

*Retarded Fetal Development*

If one plots the brain volume of fossil skulls over time, there is evident a tremendous leap from *H. erectus* with an averaged brain capacity of 1000 cc. to Neanderthal skulls as large as 1650 cc. only 60,000 year later. As the skull of the fetus enlarged, maternal mortality would select for slower fetal development or birth at an earlier and earlier functional age. The evolution of this slower gestation development was also hastened by the narrowing of the mother's pelvic outlet that was a consequence of erect posture, although this was partly compensated for by the evolution of more flexible skull bones in the fetus and of a relaxation of the pelvic ligaments to enlarge the outlet during parturition.

There are several very important results of this:

(1) It increased the death rate, since successively more and more premature infants would be less likely to survive.

(2) This increase in infant mortality increased the birth rate since the cessation of suckling and therefore lactation would allow more frequent ovulation. (The first estrus after parturition occurs in primates only after nursing has stopped — a kind of built-in birth control.) Both increased birth rate and death rate speed up the evolution of anything that the ecological pressures at the time select for. One of these may have been intentional vocalization.

(3) Another important result of this slower fetal development is the much longer period of dependency upon the mother. Newborn primates of other species can move about on the mother or on the ground around the mother by themselves. But the premature human infant must communicate its needs by its cries and obtain the mother's help in everything. In such a situation, the tremendous advantages of increased communication between mother and infant are obvious. And during this long infancy with a high infant mortality, one can see how children who responded to the mother with vocalizations would be more carefully cared for on

the one side and on the other side, that the mother who could vocally communicate and obtain vocal responses from their infants, being better mothers, would pass on their own genetic constitution through their children to the future more readily.

## Child Education

With the increased infancy caused by retarded development in the gestation period, there is also a lengthening out of human childhood with its greater need for parental guidance. The importance of language in directing children what to do or in stopping them from doing something harmful is obvious. Neanderthal children who could not understand parental commands would be much less likely to reach an age where they could reproduce. It is indeed quite plausible to think of tribes during the Fourth Glaciation simply disposing of speechless children in the exigencies of their strenuous seminomadic life. This is not natural selection but human selective breeding that could have leveraged language evolution even by itself.

## Social Organization

Language certainly changed the kind of hierarchical social organization within the tribe. The dominant male in a tribe of *H. erectus* was probably the strongest. But in the first semispeaking Neanderthal tribes, the dominant male might be the best speaker, the best able to give commands as the men surrounded prey during a hunt or in apportioning its results. It is common in social organization of primates that the dominant male does more of the mating than is his numerical share. In some instances, as in the baboons, he does most of it. If such an organization existed in Neanderthal tribes, if the best speaker did most of the mating, it would leverage the evolution of language considerably.

I have already referred to the immensely complicated problem of the diffusion of speech. But as it did diffuse, what were the consequences of this most profoundly important change in human behavior? While it must have enormously increased the human population of the world, I do not think it increased the basic size of the hunter-gatherer troop. This probably remained fairly stable at from 20 to 30 as it had for the last 100,000 years.[19]

---

19. Glynn L. Isaac, "Traces of Pleistocene Hunters: An East African Example," in Richard B. Lee and

The reason is that the group was defined by a certain hierarchical structure, and the limitation of its size was due to the requirement that the members of the community remain within sensory contact particularly with its alpha male. Language simply changed the sensory channel of this communication and made it infinitely more efficient. It did not expand those channels to include significantly more individuals.

But the spacing of the individuals and the way they live together, partly because of the technological expansion, but also because of language itself must have been considerable. There may have been changes in postural adjustments, changes in how the head was held so as to be able to hear language more keenly. The distancing between individuals in a campsite may have been much closer to hear what was said. And we do not have words to even describe the change in the intensity of relationships between the individuals that came with the kind of communication between individuals that language can encompass, let alone the intenseness of relationship already mentioned that was introduced by proper names. All the words that one might wish to use are really metaphors with consciousness, and consciousness, as I have tried to show in another work,[20] is a much later addition to the behavioral functioning of *H. sapiens sapiens*.

The advent of language also provided the paradigm known in behavioral therapy as desensitization. Speaking the noun of a feared thing, or even possibly giving it a proper name and repeating that, could little by little decrease the fear by associating that now part of it which is its word with undangerous situations. Thus the naming of animals and the consequent cave art of drawing them in places safe from them perhaps made men more courageous hunters along the banks of the Vezere and elsewhere.

Water may be another example. Almost all subhuman primates fear water, nor do any of them swim. A stream that cannot be leaped acts as a natural barrier to the movement of many anthropoid troops. Similarly the location of pre-Mesolithic campsites seems to indicate that early man shared this fear of water with other primates.[21] But in the Mesolithic era, all this changes. And I suggest this change may have been due to the desensitization of training of repeating the word for water with no danger present. And it is thus at this time that the first boats are invented

---

Irven Devore (eds.), *Man the Hunter* (Chicago: Aldine, 1968).

20. Julian Jaynes, *The Origin of Consciousness in the Breakdown of the Bicameral Mind* (Boston: Houghton Mifflin, 1976).

21. Sherwood L. Washburn and Chet S. Lancaster, "The Evolution of Hunting," in Richard B. Lee and Irven DeVore (eds.), *Man the Hunter* (Chicago: Aldine, 1968).

thereby opening up huge new ecologies all the way to the Arctic with a new kind of fishing, and permitting such settlements as the well-known lake-dwellers of Neuchatel in Switzerland.

By now it is evident that I am making language not merely one among several of the remarkable evolutionary achievements of the late Pleistocene, but the very pioneer and promoter of the rest. Chiefly this is a matter of attention, of the holding power of language upon a thing or an action, both in the direction of the attentions and actions of others and of oneself. And it will be thus no surprise to the reader when I suggest that language was also the aegis of agriculture as well. Without a word for seed, for earth, for growth, waiting, and for the ripened grain, man would not put seed in the ground and wait for the harvest. If man had had words for these matters a million years earlier, I think it would have been inevitable that agriculture would have begun then instead of only around 8000 B.C.

The chief objection to the model I have presented is its timing. The earliest languages that we know, the languages of the most primitive peoples and the most civilized, seem to have about the same complexity. And the attempts to reconstruct such languages as Indo-European of perhaps 2000 B.C., seem to be just as complex. If there has been so little change in linguistic complexity over the last 4,000 years, how could there be such a huge change in only 10 times that time span?

There are several considerations which at least dilute the strength of this objection. First, the kind of reconstructions of Indo-European on which this objection is based may rest on assumptions that exaggerate the similarity of its linguistic complexity to that of present day languages. It would be interesting to examine critically such reconstructions from this point of view. Second, given diffusion and migration, it must be agreed that linguistic change cannot be quantified, and that therefore to trace a trajectory back to prehistoric times is a questionable procedure. Thirdly, even if such a theory is forthcoming, the chances that it will be even near a linear accumulation of complexity are very small. Once the rules of language are evolved into brain structure, it is far more likely that we would have — as we do in the developing child — an explosion almost to asymptote, filling semantic space over a few millennia. And this is what I suggest took place even as man's first stable agricultural communities suddenly swelled into cities of thousands.

## Conclusion:
## A Comparison with Previous Theories

The main features of the model that I have presented are in contrast to previous proposals about the origin of language. Most have placed it historically much further back, perhaps a million years ago, and its place of origin as Africa. I instead have placed it in Southern Europe, the Near East, and Asia in the midst of a hastening sequence of technological advances during the period of the fourth glaciation. Previous models all emphasize nouns as coming first. But a central feature here is that modifiers not only preceded everything else but necessarily had to do so until they were stabilized into commands before the call system itself could be relaxed into nouns.

Most importantly for a science of archelinguistics, is its feature that each step towards language brings with it some new technology or skill. It is certainly to be hoped that closer analyses than I have been able to present here may result in a much tighter tying together of the Würm interstadial episodes, the artifacts of their cultures, and the formation of parts of speech. Indeed, it may in some plausible future be possible to read off the development of language in any area from its archeology.

One final question. While the outdated Biogenetic Law of the nineteenth century that ontogeny recapitulates phylogeny is now merely a way of entering a much more complex issue, it is nevertheless perfectly proper to ask whether or not the sequence of language development in the child in any way resembles its sequence in the species as a whole. Other models have little to say on the matter. The call-blendings of the Hockett-Ascher model[22] do not seem to be pertinent to the data on children. But looking at the present theory in its largest contour, it is at least reminiscent of Braine's distinction between pivot and open classes of words in child language.[23] The age of modifiers and then the age of modifying commands may specifically have evolved the neural basis of the pivot class during those eras, while the three successive noun stages that followed evolved the neurological structure for the open class and its relationship and differences from the pivot class. If this is so, and if verbs are not primary evolved elements as I have indicated, it could mean that the evolved neurological structure that makes language possible is not so involved with the distinction between noun phrases and verb phrases as contemporary traditions of parsing might indicate.

---

22. Charles Hockett and Robert Ascher, "The Human Revolution," in *Current Anthropology*, 1964, 5.
23. M.D.S. Braine, "The Ontogeny of English Phrase Structure: The First Phase," *Language*, 1963, *39*, 1–13 and David McNeill, *The Acquisition of Language* (New York: Harper and Row, 1970).

# CHAPTER 10

# In A Manner of Speaking

## Commentary on Cognition and Consciousness in Non-Human Species

IF WE COMPARE THE VOCABULARY between early and late Greek texts over the first millennium B.C., or between early and late Hebrew texts over the same period, a dramatic change is obvious. Early texts have no mental words. The referents of words are concrete, indicant, objective, touchable, watchable. But, in a few centuries only, the human lexicon is suddenly aglitter with a network of new subjective words that to us are equivalent to mind, belief, know, remember, imagine, aware, purpose, intention, and so forth. The referents of such words are only observable, if at all so, by a new kind of mental process currently called *introspection*, previously *reflection*, or simply and more fuzzily *thought*. And the peculiar quality of these words, in contrast to cup, run, green, river, et al. is that they create their own referents on the basis of metaphor, becoming those analog behaviors which we call consciousness.

This new way of talking about human happenings became its own theory of human behavior. Previously, it might have been said that a man seeks shelter. Now, a man seeks shelter because he wants shelter — a vacuous tautology which says almost nothing, but whose function is perhaps to help us look "inside" the man and pay attention to his consciousness rather than his motions. We like dealing with the "insides" of others, their intentions, ideas, thoughts. It is safer. It makes behavior more predictable. Most of our social interactions are now on this level. In fact, talking about other's consciousness is itself an inherent feature of consciousness. Even in this peer commentary journal, we are talking about ideas which we

Article by Julian Jaynes, first published in *Behavioral and Brain Sciences*, Vol. 1, Issue 4 as commentary on three articles on cognition and consciousness in nonhuman species by David Premack and Guy Woodruff; Donald Griffin; and E. Sue Savage-Rumbaugh, Duane M. Rumbaugh, and Sally Boysen. © 1978 Cambridge Journals. Reproduced with permission.

locate in the heads of others and ourselves. Nothing of the sort could have taken place in 1000 B.C.

This mentalizing lexicon was so useful that it spread out to describe almost all human action, even when not warranted. A person after consciousness developed may indeed want X or have an intention to Y or be aware of Z, but not all X's and Y's and Z's are preceded by wants, intentions, or awareness. The attribution of all our behavior to wants, purposes, intentions, and so forth, became so habitual that it left us with the false conviction that consciousness governs all and is responsible for everything from concepts to learning and speaking.

So excessive did this way of speaking about ourselves become that it spread to all animate behavior, until during part of the first millennium A.D., animals could be tried in court of law and proven guilty or innocent of willful misbehavior. And then it engulfed even inanimate behavior. In the Renaissance, because magnets had the ability to move and be moved, they were thought to have souls. Or even rivers seeking valleys. And after Copernicus showed that the earth really moved, no less an assembly than Campanella, Kepler, and — at one time — Newton believed that the universe was what we would call "cognitive." Even today, contemporary physicists such as John Wheeler and Eugene Wigner are making the same confusion of metaphor and actuality, proclaiming that consciousness has to be brought in as a force in the universe because of certain astonishing findings of quantum mechanics.

This wisp of history is not beside the point here. It is meant to show that we have inherited a group of mentalistic words that are as slippery as live fish and just as difficult to hold still. Moreover, there seems to exist, from their first significations to conscious processes, a hierarchy of levels of metaphoric application as we descend from human adults to rivers or magnets. I think it is obvious with this preamble that I am about to suggest that the three papers under discussion are using these mental terms on a metaphoric level, not as they pertain to actual human consciousness.

Let me immediately say, however, that my criticism is in a sense unfair, since none of the writers stresses the word consciousness. I apologize, but only halfheartedly. For I think the average reader will certainly assume that it is a consciousness like his own that is being talked about with such cognate terms as awareness, intentionality, or theory of mind.

Let me take just one part of Griffin's extremely interesting paper, his description of Gallup's experiment. That a mirror-educated chimpanzee immediately rubs off a spot on his forehead when he sees it in a mirror is not, I suggest, "clear evidence for self-awareness," at least in its usual sense. Self-awareness usually means a consciousness of our own persona over time, a sense of who we are, our hopes and fears, as we daydream about ourselves in relation to others. Our conscious selves are not our bodies, although our bodies, particularly our faces, are often emblems of ourselves. We do not see our conscious selves in mirrors. Gallup's chimpanzee has learned a point-to-point relation between a mirror image and his body, wonderful as that is. Rubbing a spot noticed in a mirror is not essentially different from rubbing a spot noticed on his body without a mirror. The animal is not shown to be imagining himself anywhere else, or thinking of his life over time, or introspecting in any sense — all signs of consciousness.

As for mental representations or images, it depends what our precise referents are. A dog seeking a particular stick thrown by his master into a high hayfield certainly has a persisting brain-representation of the stick, a visual-olfactory-tactile complex by which he will recognize the stick. But he does not introspect upon his brain-representation as we do with our conscious images.

When two chimpanzees are communicating with each other, we have a vastly more complicated situation than one chimpanzee communicating with a mirror. The experiment by Savage-Rumbaugh et al. is methodologically elegant and exciting in clearing out extraneous variables. The reader is almost impatient to suggest further studies with the same paradigm. But I do not understand the necessity of emphasizing such difficult terms as "intentionality" and "symbolic." I am reminded here of Sir John Lubbock, who, in 1888, hearing of the methods used in the training of the human handicapped, trained his dog to "read." The dog would bring him in appropriate situations any of several cards on which were printed "food," "out," "bone," "tea," and do this in a way that simulated human speech expressing human wishes. I would call this symbolic and intentional behavior, but explainable on a far simpler level than consciousness.

Even more complicated is the relationship of a chimpanzee to a videotape of actors in problematic situations. Premack's papers are always so articulate about these issues as to leave one full of doubts about one's own ideas. As he well knows, so much depends on definitions and the referents of the terms of those definitions, and also on the connotations of the terms used. "Theory of mind" certainly conjures up human intellectual processes. If the term simply means the recognition of a particular mental state in another animal and by mental we do not imply conscious, I do not disagree. But then we can apply such a phrase much more widely: to a dog that cowers to his master's scolding tone or wags his tail to praise; or to a four-year-old child who can choose appropriate gifts for a two-year-old. Both dog and four-year-old are recognizing the mental states of others, and I suggest that this is more automatic than introspective.

Although this is not explicit, all three papers seem to say that demonstrating that animal behavior can be made to simulate aspects of human behavior, simultaneously demonstrates a similarity to human conscious functioning. It is the same argument used with that other method of simulation of cognitive processes, computer intelligence.[1] But — to use a wildly dissimilar and probably inaccurate example — because Mickey Mouse looks and behaves so humanly on a screen does not mean that a celluloid film is conscious; it means Mickey is made to look conscious.

In no way do I mean to diminish the very real breakthroughs of these ingenious studies in what, with David Premack, we could call "animal cognition." They point to a new era in studying the primate mind. But we must not be misled by our labels into thinking the results identical with that metacognition we call "introspective consciousness." It would be interesting in this connection to do a reverse simulation, to run these experiments with human subjects, particularly if they had been trained in giving introspective reports by Külpe back in Würzburg.

---

1. See Zenon Pylyshyn, "Computer Models and Empirical Constraints," *Behavioral and Brain Sciences*, 1978, *1*, 1.

# CHAPTER 11

# Paleolithic Cave
# Paintings as Eidetic Images

I PROPOSE THE HYPOTHESIS that the well-known cave paintings and engravings at Lascaux, Altamira, and in about a hundred other caves in
southern France and northern Spain, dating somewhere between 20,000
and 10,000 B.C., are tracings of eidetic images rather than art in its usual
sense. The purpose of this note is to discuss whether Haber's thorough and
welcome revival of the topic sheds any light on this issue, and conversely
whether consideration of such a hypothesis suggests new ways to study
the still perplexing and inconsistent phenomena of eidetic imagery.

The arguments in favor of the hypothesis are as follows: (1) the cave
paintings cannot be art in our sense of being meant for public display or
ritual observance since they are usually located in the most difficult and
inaccessible positions inside the caves; (2) if they were drawn by artists
in our sense, we would expect to find preliminary attempts, as if learning to draw, but such are not found; (3) if drawn by artists in our sense,
we would expect a homogeneity of skill regardless of subject, but we do
not: the paintings or engravings of animals (about 90% of the total) are
of an astonishing sweep, beauty, and likeness, while those of humans are
almost entirely stick-like and not likenesses at all; and no scenery is ever
attempted; (4) the most prominent reason to think of these paintings
and engravings specifically as tracings of eidetic images is their common
superposition one over the other, as if each animal was projected on the
cave wall regardless of what was there in the first place.

Particularly because of (4) — which I find difficult to understand otherwise — I think we should take the eidetic hypothesis of the origin of
these paintings seriously. But if we do, we are assuming much stronger and
longer-lasting properties of eidetic imagery in Cro-Magnon man than we

Article by Julian Jaynes first published in *Behavioral and Brain Sciences*, Vol. 2, Issue 4 as commentary
on the article "Twenty Years of Haunting Eidetic Imagery: Where's The Ghost?" by Ralph N. Haber.
© 1979 Cambridge Journals. Reproduced with permission.

find in laboratory studies of the phenomenon today. We must posit that an individual out on a hunt with his group, perhaps stared into the dusk waiting to see the hunted animal; and then finally, either as the animal was at bay or as it was killed, registered the eidetic representation, which, after returning to the deep interior of his cave, he then by torchlight traced out with charcoal and colored ochres on the wall (or where the surface was softer, engraved with a pointed stone) — and all in disregard of what had been drawn there before. (I assume here that the deeper engraving, and scraping technique which are sometimes found, were reworkings of previous paintings — for which there is considerable evidence.) Such a picture of the Cro-Magnon painter is full of new assumptions that seem implausible from what we know of eidetic imagery in the laboratory.

It assumes that an eidetic image under late Pleistocene conditions is not "blinked away" as in Haber's studies, nor does the image "fall off" when transferred to another background. But we should recall that at least some eidetic children today can shift images to any surface at will, superimposing them over any subject, and can even change their size as they wish.[1] The last characteristic is consistent with the lack of relative size constancy in the cave paintings.

It assumes that from a brief exposure, the Paleolithic eidetic image can be maintained over longer periods than is commonly found in laboratory studies. But the duration in modern studies outside the laboratory can be longer. One investigator reported what seem to have been spontaneous eidetic images in Tanzanian children, which often lasted twenty minutes or more.[2]

A further difference is that we usually think of eidetic imagery as being a scene, whereas the cave paintings are of solitary animals without any vegetation or scenery. But one thing that all eidetic researchers agree on is that the only way for a subject to get a complete picture is to look at each part of it for enough time; parts omitted are not seen, though they may be remembered on questioning. Hence in the Cro-Magnon situation, it is only the emotionally salient target animal and sometimes only a part of the animal that is stared at and registered, not other hunters or scenic background. (The poorly drawn human figures may indeed be attempts to draw noneidetic memory images, or they may have been added a century

---

1. Jan Leask, Ralph N. Haber, and Ruth B. Haber, "Eidetic Imagery in Children: II. Longitudinal and Experimental Results," *Psychonomic Monograph Supplements*, 1969, 3.
2. Leonard W. Doob, *Resolving Conflict in Africa: The Fermeda Workshop* (New Haven, CT: Yale, 1970).

or a millennium or more later, as I suspect most of the nonpictorial slashes and graffiti were.)

Whatever these somewhat tenuous comparisons suggest, the huge difference between the Paleolithic and the contemporary situation is the emotional salience of the image. The animals on the cave walls and ceilings are life and death matters. They are those hunted for food in the desperations of the last glacial age or else dreaded predators such as lion or bear. The importance of such targets to the Cro-Magnon hunter and the waiting dangerous excitement connected with this vision of the animal is in high contrast with the bland picture-book stimuli in the usual eidetic study.

While there is no necessary reason to think that the brain of a modern eidetic child and that of a Cro-Magnon adult 15,000 years ago demonstrate the same processes in so esoteric an area, nevertheless discovery of the pertinence of these variables in the modern condition, particularly the emotional salience, would be some support for the hypothesis.

These possibilities could easily be studied by using pictures of stronger emotional and personal impact, such as food displays with hungry subjects, photographs of the subject's family in various settings after some separation as in children's hospitals, or highly desired objects such as a bicycle or other toy that we know (by pretesting) the child impatiently desires, and then comparing the results with control pictures. The waiting expectancy could be stimulated by using projections slowly brought into focus or intensity in dim light and compared with the same pictures presented for the same duration in the usual way. Moreover, dark adaptation of the subject might in itself produce a longer lasting eidetic image, since a bright surround may actually wash out the image. In the study of Tanzanian children with eidetic images of long duration, such images were usually seen one or two feet in front of the eyes *in darkness* as the child lay down for sleep.

The most interesting of Haber's results to me is that nearly all eidetic children can (and commonly do) prevent an eidetic image from forming by naming the items in the picture while seeing it. This immediately suggests that in the usual procedure, the naming of the objects in the testing for imagery (see Haber's protocols) may have hastened the fading of the image. It would thus seem that a nonverbal technique of testing for the image would be preferable, such as asking the child to trace the eidetic image on the blank easel with a felt pen or crayon[3] — even perhaps as did his Upper Paleolithic ancestors in a different way and context.

---

3. Cf. Ulric Neisser, "Images, Models, and Human Nature," *Behavioral and Brain Sciences*, 1979, *2*, 4.

One of Haber's conclusions can, I think, be questioned in part. This is that fidelity of the eidetic image to the stimulus is no better than memory, a conclusion that has a considerable history in eidetic research. My difficulty has to do with how we can compare what are almost two different modalities. It does not seem to me correct to compare the verbal replies to analytic questions about numbers of items and details, since two such different procedures are involved: the eidetic where the subject is not to verbalize, and memory where analytic verbalization is encouraged. What we really want to know here is the accuracy of depiction, not accuracy of report. Because of the verbal erasing factor, this could be better studied by again comparing tracings by eidetic children with memory drawings of the same picture by noneidetic children. I would suspect that such a study might return the accuracy criterion for eidetic imagery to its former popular favor.

To sum up, I have suggested that if the hypothesis that cave paintings are eidetic images is correct, we might find that the strength, duration, and accuracy of modern eidetic images could be increased by using stimuli of greater emotional salience after an expectancy period in dim light and asking the subject to trace out the image on a blank easel instead of verbally reporting about it. If none of these new variables proved pertinent, I think the hypothesis would be weakened.

And if one appreciates the total situation and the number of individuals involved, one might conjecture that the hypothesis would not have to be completely abandoned. We commonly call these paintings Paleolithic with the unthinking connotation that the paintings were made over ten thousand years or more of the Late Pleistocene as a cultural tradition. That this is false can be seen from the fact that there were at best fewer than 100 paintings in any one cave, which (if it were a cultural tradition over this period) would work out to be only one painting every century or two. I think this is absurd, particularly when we remember that primates and particularly human primates tend to continue and even teach a learned activity of this sort that is suddenly discovered and found pleasurable. It is thus more plausible to think of all of the paintings and engravings in these one hundred caves as being done over only a few decades by only a few Cro-Magnon persons, a unique few whose strong eidetic imagery may have been more similar to the extreme of Luria's adult mnemonist[4] than to the usual eidetic child.

---

4. A.R. Luria, *The Mind of Mnemonist* (New York: Basic Books, 1968).

# CHAPTER 12

# Remembrance of Things (Far) Past

WHEN WE REMEMBER, we are allowed into an enchanted other world where the past is magically present and time becomes like a space. We are in an enormous space whose far boundaries merge indistinguishably into imagination on every side, a space full of forgetful shadows and obscuring twilights, of meanings that gleam with feeling, and bursts of accuracy that support us, humiliate us, ennoble us, teach us. It is past and yet present. How is this possible?

This space, of course, is really a metaphorical space, a something made to be like actual space, a mind-space generated by the metaphoric associations of the language we use to describe mental acts. Sometimes this spatialized time is a line or a path, perhaps stretching from left to right. At other times it is a road yawning in front of us, or a huge darkened landscape we have just passed through. Or simply a spaceness that allows memories to be distinct. Note the necessity of the metaphors! It is an as-if space that becomes so absolutely necessary to our conscious decision-making, so real, so requisite to our efforts to find out who we are, that it often feels as real as the actual world, until the distinction blurs and we dream.

It has not always been so. The evidence of ancient writings and archeology indicates that conscious memory only began around 1000 B.C. — a mere hundred generations ago. Before that time men and women moved about in an intellectual darkness through a more confined world with a different mentality — a bicameral mind. Decisions and remembering were not conscious, but heard from another part of the brain as auditory hallucinations called gods. There was no conscious remembering then.

Ancient man did not live in a frame of past happenings and future possibilities as we do. He had no notion of a lifetime stretching between birth and death as we do. He worked his dark and brittle life through a strange and brilliant world of hierarchies and idols, commanded by divine voices from his own brain, unguessing of past or future. His was in an eternal

Article by Julian Jaynes, first published in *Quest*, Vol. 1. © 1977 *Quest*.

present untroubled by remorse or ambition, unlit by hope, untaught by regret or private thoughts.

The remembrance of things past begins in human history only as this bicameral mind breaks down. About three millennia ago, social chaos and catastrophe made this earlier mentality unworkable. And in the resulting agony of indecision, mankind learned on the basis of linguistic metaphor a new kind of mentality, consciousness.

For the first time, a man could "know himself," could remember, not simply *know that* or *know how*. For the first time, he could "see" what he had done and grope for what he should do in a mind-space generated out of metaphor. For the first time, a man could plan better than the now-silent gods what to do in a future which — because he can now remember consciously — will be forever and ever different. For the first time, a man could make a quest of his life.

For the first time! How strange that sounds to us who use memory words so loosely that we impute remembering the past to animals when they simply know their names or mealtimes, or to infants when they know their parents, or to ourselves when we simply know a telephone number or a path home through the wood. We even speak of computers as having memories! You might as well say this page has a memory since it is storing information.

These are not ever remembrances of time past. They are learnings, habits, hook-ups, imprintings, mechanics that have no pastness about them whatever. The use of the term memory for such things is only metaphoric. Habits or learnings or information storages are *like* memories because they are dependent upon the past. But it is only we human beings, living during these last three millennia, who can reminisce upon our past lives, who can wander through this hidden kingdom where the past can be reexperienced.

But with this new ability to reexperience the past in a spatialized time, to remember and plan and narratize, comes a troop of new complications, some of which are still erupting into the difficulties of modern conscious life. Our innate genetically determined emotions that we share with most mammals are changed dramatically.

Shame remembered and fantasized in this reversible mind-time expands itself into guilt, something hugely more difficult to expiate or interpret. Sexual emotion was once confined to the presence of socially adequate stimulation, but with consciousness, with memory and fantasy, it becomes a much more prominent part of life. Fear and terror, once easily dissipated, stretch out into anxiety that can last a lifetime. And all because men can now automatically and even against their wishes reconstruct and hold as if present in this new spatialized time the unalterable experience of the past and its possibility in the future.

And nostalgia too. For with time metaphored as space, so like the space of our actual lives, a part of us solemnly keeps loitering behind, trying to visit past times as if they were actual spaces. Oh, what a temptation is there! The warm, sullen longing to return to scenes long vanished, to relive some past security or love, to redress some ancient wrong or redecide a past regret, or alter some ill-considered actions toward someone lost to our present lives, or to fill out past omissions — these are artifacts of our new remembering consciousness. Side effects. And they are waste and filler unless we use them to learn about ourselves.

Memory is a privilege for us who are born into the last three millennia. It is both an advantage and a predicament, liberation and an imprisonment. Memory is not a part of our biological evolution, as is our capacity to learn habits or simple knowings. It is an off-shoot of consciousness acquired by mankind only a hundred generations ago. It is thus the new environment of modern man. It is one which we sometimes are like legal aliens waiting for naturalization. The feeling of full franchise and citizenship in that new environment is a quest that is the unique hidden adventure of us all.

# CHAPTER 13

# Art and the Right Hemisphere

RIDING HOME on the Lexington Avenue subway the other afternoon, a friend was trying to eavesdrop on two young girls in school uniforms to find out what the coming generation is thinking. The only thing he could hear was when the train lurched through a particularly noisy piece of track at which one of the little girls had to raise her voice and shouted at the other, "The trouble with you is that you're too left-brained."

When the current fashion for hemisphere localizing and the over-praise of the synthesizing right hemisphere at the expense of the poor analyzing verbal left hemisphere has gone this far, even to little girls seeking a perjorative epithet, we may be in serious intellectual trouble. We have seen so many spurious fashions in psychology come and go in this century, particularly as they influenced art theory and taste, that we certainly don't need another to drag out its unverified assumptions all over the cultural landscape.

Earlier this century it was the idea of the subconscious, of a place of stored repressed images that surge up into art and dreams. We are still hearing from artists who believe with intractable sincerity that they are painting directly from this subconscious long after such over-simple doctrine as been put aside by scientific theory.

A case in point is the current exhibition of "mindscapes" by John Randolph Carter (at the New Jersey State Museum in Trenton). Refusing to pre-visualize or draw erasable guidelines, and never erasing, Carter's vividly colored ink drawings, abstract or figurative, erotic, comic, or futuristic, are said by him to be dreamt up from the depths of his subconscious mind.

This is questionable. Free association is more chance, habit, and invention than meaningful. While these works are very interesting for what they are, such unprevisioned drawing is the resultant of too many non-psychical causations, including what by chance has been begun, then what

Article by Julian Jaynes first published in *Art/World*, Vol. 5, No. 10. © 1981 *Art/World*.

is different or can agree with that, chance proximities, the surface structure of actions and media to ever depict any "inner reality."

Is a child building a sand castle dredging it up from his subconscious
mind? Or in turning a kaleidoscope to a pleasing pattern, is that pattern an
expression of an immersed self? In one sense perhaps, but not as claimed.

Now the current fashion as in our two little girls on the subway is to
think that our abilities can be neatly assorted into the left and right hemispheres of the brain. Is this too an ephemeral idea whose time will pass?

The difference between the hemispheres is even represented in the
Carter exhibition. In one of the paintings, number 38, the left side of the
painting is drawn by the right hand, while the right side is drawn by the
left hand. Now to say that unpremeditated free association painting by
one hand or the other is the tapping into the subconscious of the respec-
tive hemisphere is to compound error. I think Mr. Carter is too intelligent
and sensible to put it quite like that. But others might, and they should
remember that drawing with either the right or the left hand is using both
hemispheres, since there is an almost instantaneous transfer of information across the interconnections between the two hemispheres in doing
anything with either hand.

It is, however, a very different matter when these interconnections
between the two hemispheres are surgically cut, as they are in some
patients as a cure for epilepsy. Such individuals with "split-brains" as they
are often miscalled (only the commissures are cut) behave with a superficial normality. But if we ask such a commissurotomized person to draw
with either the right or left hand, we immediately see in which hemisphere the artistic abilities of the person originally were.

One patient was given the drawing of a cube to copy. As in the line
drawing, his left hand guided by the right hemisphere can copy the three-
dimensional design, although somewhat crudely because the patient was
right-handed and somewhat mysteriously since it is the mirror-image.
But the right hand, guided by the left or speech hemisphere, while it can
still write perfectly well, cannot draw the object at all. It cannot because
it has been disconnected from the right hemisphere. It is interesting to
conjecture in what sense we can say that the left hemisphere, either in
this patient or in ourselves, really sees the world that is being depicted in
representational art.

Evidence such as this together with much else, as well as a consistency
with other theory such as that of the bicameral mind, certainly does lead

to the strong conclusion that it is the right hemisphere which is more active in artistic ability. It is not just a fashion, then, but something based on neurological reality and is here to stay.

That the right hemisphere is the artistic hemisphere yields an explanation of what has long been known by art historians: left and right are not always interchangeable in composition. Perhaps in the majority of paintings they are, and several laboratory studies have demonstrated this. But in others, particularly asymmetric paintings or drawings with marked lighting and perspective differences between the two sides, left and right are absolutes. The mirror image of the work is easily seen to be somehow wrong.

The illustration shows Janssens' well-known "Woman Reading." Almost all of us who are right-handed prefer the true picture. While this phenomenon used to be explained on the basis of an innate "glance curve" from left to right, I would suggest an alternative and opposite theory that I call right hemisphere preemption.

As we look at anything, everything to the left of the center of where we are looking is being seen by the right hemisphere and everything to the right of center, by the left. (This is because the left side of each eye connects to the right hemisphere and the right side of each eye to the left hemisphere.) So in looking into the center of a picture, if the focus of interest is to the left, the right or artistic hemisphere sees the intended interest of the composition before the left hemisphere, and so sees what the picture is about and likes it better than in the reverse situation. The right or artistic hemisphere preempts perception and fits the parts of the picture into a whole, something the right hemisphere does much better than the left. Moreover, since moving the eyes to the left is done by the right hemisphere (and vice versa), the immediate next glance from the center to the left focus of interest, as well as repeated glances thereafter back to the focus of interest, is done by the same hemisphere which is doing the artistic seeing and patterning, and so seems more natural than the other way.

On the other hand, note how in the mirror image of the Janssens painting, there is a sense of strain in getting over to the central figure, because moving the eyes to the right engages the left non-artistic hemisphere. Note also how the picture therefore falls apart and how the shoes intrude irrelevantly on our attention in the mirror image.

"Woman Reading" by Pieter Janssens Elinga (late 1660s), original (left) and reverse (right).

That is true, of course, mainly for right-handed people and some left-handers. But other left-handers, those with really opposite laterality, are likely to prefer the mirror image. Leonardo da Vinci would think Janssens a bad artist (unless he saw the mirror image). Artists should thus beware left-handed critics!

My line drawings on the following page of a face and its mirror image show an even stronger right hemisphere preemption. This is probably because faces have an innate schema in the right hemisphere which the Janssens, of course, does not. But the principle is the same. Most right-handers choose as happiest the right face with the smile in the left visual field — and therefore in the right hemisphere — which preempts the other side in making an overall judgment. Leonardo again would find the left face happiest. Perhaps here is some of the explanation of the enigmatic smile of the Mona Lisa. Portraitists should take serious note and sitters should beware left-handed portraitists!

This principle is of obvious importance in printmaking, and has been so in art history. Rembrandt, for example, was so careless in this respect that at least some of his etchings should be seen through a mirror to be truly appreciated. While others, like Dürer and Van Gogh, were scrupulous in etching originals in their mirror image.

But this is all the viewer's side. How about the artist? Do artists draw, paint, or sculpt primarily at the behests of the right hemisphere?

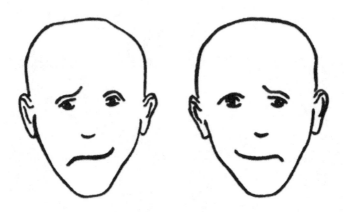

These faces are mirror images of each other. Stare at the nose of each. Which face is happier?

In music, we know that most of us appreciate music and remember it on the right hemisphere. But musicians and composers have music on both hemispheres due to their training. This is now well known. May it not be so in graphic art as well, that all artists have their art on both hemispheres due to their training and practice? If so, it helps us to understand some of the misunderstandings between artist and patron: they have a different neurology for art. And it also cautions us against over-simplification and thinking that everything artistic is the product of the right hemisphere alone.

Anyway, I hope these rambling comments might induce readers of *Art/World* to take hand mirrors along on their next visit to a gallery to test out some of these things for themselves.

And as for those little girls on the subway, I would like to tell them sometime about the glories of left hemisphere articulation and the wonders of left hemispheric analysis of life's problems — particularly amidst the thundering aesthetics of the MTA [Metropolitan Transportation Authority].

# CHAPTER 14

# Imagination and the Dance of the Self

Who am I? It's such a terribly important question to us at various times of our lives, particularly in adolescence. Who and what am I? Do I have a purpose in life? What does my life mean? Why do we have such a problem with this particular aspect of what is our real self? Why is it such an ephemeral thing that when we try to touch it, it isn't even there?

This is of course a problem that everybody has been aware of. I'd like to remind you of the greatest play that Henrik Ibsen wrote, *Peer Gynt*. In one of the great scenes in *Peer Gynt*, Peer comes out in front of the audience — he has been through all these fantastic experiences full of success of various kinds — and he comes down to the question: "What is my self?" And he takes out an onion, and he says, "Now I'm going to find what my self is in this onion." He takes off one peeling. "Ah, yes." And then there's another. And then he takes off that wrapping … "getting close to the real self"…and he takes off another wrapping and another wrapping, until… there is nothing there. It's all wrapping, and there is no single kernel or heart of self there. And of course, that is what a lot of us really want to find.

Now what I'm going to do tonight is to take you on a journey and try to pick up from where we left off this afternoon — which was a development of psychohistory, of the history of mind — and it is going to relate to what we think the self is.

Let me first say something about the self as distinguished from the bodily self. John Locke, whom I mentioned this afternoon, had a very interesting thought experiment. He says, "Imagine cutting off your finger, is your self diminished? Of course not." Therefore, whatever idea you have about your self, it is not your bodily self. And this is a very important distinction to always remember.

Transcribed and edited from a lecture presented by Julian Jaynes at the Yellow Springs Institute in Chester Springs, Pennsylvania on June 9, 1980, as part of the "Six Saturdays: Explorations in Archetypal Themes" lecture series. Jaynes presented his "Consciousness and the Voices of the Mind" lecture (similar to Chapter 19 of this volume) in the afternoon, followed by this lecture in the evening.

Now one of the very fascinating experiments that is being done — it is
continuing on — but the basic experiment is done by a man named Gordon
Gallup, and what he does is he has chimpanzees that he has brought up
with mirrors. Chimpanzees love mirrors. They look at themselves and they
learn all kinds of things and look at their back sides and look in the mirror
and so on. It's a great deal of fun for chimpanzees to play with a mirror.
So he brings up chimpanzees like this, and then he anesthetizes them,
and then puts a red smudge on their foreheads. Then he waits for them
to come out of the anesthetic, and has a mirror there, and observes what
they do.[1]

Sure enough, the chimpanzee looks at himself in the mirror and
immediately rubs the spot off. And this is taken to be definite evidence of
self-awareness by some people. I say no, this is bodily awareness.

What we see in the mirror is not the self that Peer Gynt was trying to
find by unraveling the onion — it is not the self that you would introspect
on and say "ah that's the real me." When you look in the mirror, you know
that what you see is not your real self — that is your bodily self. And that
is the first distinction I'm going to make.

Bicameral man has a bodily self. But then we come to a very big
distinction just about 1300 B.C. in the inscriptions that you can find in
Assyrian temples that is involved with the sense of time.

Now time is a terribly important thing as it comes into the human
mind. Because there are two kinds of time. One is duration. This is the
kind of time of physics, of stars, of the origin of the universe, of growth
and decay, and so on. And as I mentioned this afternoon, we cannot be
conscious of that. We have to spatialize it, we have to make a metaphor —
an analog of it — and then we can deal with time.

The other kind of time is created by mankind. I am going to call this
*mind-time*. And one of the tremendous errors of recent psychology is
their failure to distinguish between duration and mind-time. They are
very different things. You learn habits in duration time, but you introspect
in mind-time. And we can pinpoint almost precisely when this starts to
come in to human history. We first see it in these Assyrian inscriptions
I mentioned of 1300 B.C. and prior to that time. One found that a king
would say, "My god is Marduk, and I'm building this temple for Marduk."
Period. Something like that. Then in 1300 B.C. the sense of time comes in.
And a man might say, "My god is Marduk, back earlier in my life I built

1. Gordon G. Gallup, Jr., "Chimpanzees: Self Recognition," *Science*, 1970, *167*, 86–87.

another temple to Marduk, I built this temple now, 10 years from now I vow to build another temple, and so on." Like building up an onion, we get the beginnings of what I call the *autobiographical self*.

## *The Beginning of History*

This autobiographical self is very different, and it gets very complicated, because the whole sense of time, as you look for evidence of it, is connected with one's sense of historical time. We tend to think that of course everyone would think that they had a history, but this was not the case. The concept of history comes in just about this time, but in different ways in different places.

I tend to trace this particularly in the Greeks because shortly after the Trojan War, which is 1230 B.C., and the Dorian Invasions — whatever dark period that is referring to — the Greeks started to expand all over the Mediterranean. They had colonies up into Spain and perhaps even into England. And these colonies gave a sense of space that was not there before. And that sense of space builds in the metaphor of the sense of time. They seem to go together. My evidence comes from three places that show that mankind for the first time had a sense that there was a history behind it, going way back, going back we know not where.

These three places are in Egypt; among the Hebrews; and in Greece, in the Ionian philosophers. You can read in Herodotus that in Egypt there was a pharaoh named Psammetichus. In 600 B.C., he wanted to find out what was the oldest country in the world. What would you do, if you wanted to find out what was the oldest country in the world? One of the marvelous things about this story is the kind of thinking Psammetichus was doing. He said, "I will discover the original language, and that will be the oldest country in the world."

So he did this famous experiment in which he took two boys and had them brought up on cow's milk by two shepherds whose tongues had been cut out, so that the boys never heard any human speech. As it is related in Herodotus (I'm not sure if we can believe him in all the details), the two shepherds were to come to Psammetichus as soon as the boys said their first word, because that would be the word of the oldest country in the world.

According to Herodotus, it turned out that when the little boys were about two and a half years old, they went down on their knees and cried *bekos*. Psammetichus was dejected because *bekos* was not an Egyptian word. He sent his ambassadors out everywhere and they discovered that in Phrygia, which was in the northern part of Greece, *bekos* meant bread. Psammetichus then honored Phrygia as the oldest country in the world, which of course it wasn't — Egypt was much older, and it shows you can never trust experiments [laughs]. But the thinking about history and time is very interesting.

Another thing happened around this same time, 641 B.C., among the Hebrews. King Josiah put together, from we know not where, all these different parts that make up the Hebrew Testament to show something from Genesis right on to a promise — a covenant about the future. There is a very strong sense of historical time that I'm suggesting was not there before.

The third place is in the theory of Anaximander, one of the earliest Ionion philosophers. This is very interesting because it is the first scientific theory ever written down in the history of mankind. Thales, who came before him, evidently used the oral tradition but did not write anything.

Anaximander's theory described historical time. The world starts as a kind of disc spinning in space. Next it develops oceans. The oceans are all spinning around on this disk, and then at the bottom of the oceans, by spontaneous generation, small fish are born. They interbreed and change, grow into other fish, then grow into other animals that then come to the surface, and then a little bit later they climb up on land, still interbreeding, still changing, until land animals born in this manner become human beings.

I think it is fantastic that just man's thinking power at this time could come up with a theory of evolution, a theory that took until we have Darwin and Wallace in 1859 to come around again and eventually become accepted. But there it is at the beginning of intellectual thought. And while it doesn't have the mechanism — it doesn't have natural selection, of course, and I don't mean to be overplaying it — but the idea is there, and it shows this tremendous new mind-time as the analog of duration time against which man is seeing himself.

As a result of that, man for the first time has a lifetime. He can see his own death ahead of him. It makes for a very different kind of person than Achilles. Achilles never thought of his childhood, he never thought of his death — he is sort of in between these things. *We* see that around him, but he did not. He only heard and obeyed the voice of his god. Now human beings see their lives stretched out in time, as you and I do, and lots of things happen to the way we think about ourselves just because of that. Imagination is one of the things that I have titled tonight's talk. Consciousness and imagination are very much related, and I want to now consider just what imagination does to our emotional life.


## Two Types of Emotions

I think that there are basic emotions that are genetically evolved into our nature that give our basic emotions, which have nothing to do with consciousness. Animals have them and bicameral man had them. But when we get imagination or consciousness able to think about these things, to remind ourselves about these things, they begin to change.

One of the most important emotions that we have is the emotion of shame. It is really in childhood that we notice the power of this emotion. It is hard for us but think back when you were a child just how awful it was to be shamed in front of your peers. It was the worst possible thing that could happen.

By the time we are adults we have learned so carefully to fit ourselves into civilized life that we rarely experience shame. Animals have shame, dogs have shame, chimpanzees have shame. Say "no" to an animal and they have various reactions. A dog for example will put his tail between his legs and skulk away. This is a common thing that has evolved genetically into animal behavior.

Bicameral man also had shame. Shame dissipates like other emotions. Once you get the biochemistry going, the biochemistry gets used up and the emotion comes to an end. But when we have conscious man looking behind and ahead, who can imagine shame, and who can go back and reminisce about shameful incidents, then we have a new thing called guilt.

Guilt enters human history just around 600 B.C. I think you can see it most clearly in Greece and it becomes a very different kind of problem. You find that society in Greece at that time tries to deal with this guilt because, unlike shame, guilt does not go away. We do not have a way of dealing with our imagination of shame, which is what guilt is.

Around this time we see guilt referred to as an uncleanness, even as a contagion, so we see whole rituals of purification. Purification — what an absurd thing that is, unless you see it against this background that the nearest metaphor that they could find for guilt was an uncleanness.

Of course those of you who know Greek drama know exactly what I am talking about. The origin of our term *scapegoat* was an idea that was common in Greece — as well as among the Hebrews — where they literally took a goat and pinned on to him little things about the guilts that the people of the city had and sent the goat out into the desert to perish, metaphorically taking away these guilts.

We also have the idea of forgiveness coming in around this time, of course particularly with the Christian religion. And we have something called *blessing* in the Hebrew Testament. If you look back in the Old Testament it is a very powerful thing. Sons would fight each other for the blessing of their father. It's difficult for us to understand exactly what that means. But that blessing later on becomes forgiveness and forgiveness becomes a very important thing as a way of dealing with guilt.

Now if you make a statement like that, obviously you should go back and look for evidence. And I can tell you that as far as I've come is to look at the story of Oedipus. As I was saying, back in the period of the bicameral mind there is no guilt but there is shame. If you look at the story of Oedipus as it is referred to in two lines only in the *Iliad* and two lines in the *Odyssey*, it seems a very different story. Oedipus is a man who killed his father and married his mother and had two children by his mother and perhaps he felt shame by it — but he lived a life with his rather strange family until he was at an old age and died with military honors. It is not treated as though what happened was a big deal.

But when we go forward to 800 B.C., look what comes just three centuries later with Sophocles's play *Oedipus Rex*. The same story is described as a horrible thing that has happened. So horrible that Oedipus has to symbolically take the brooches from his mother's breasts and gouge out his eyes because he is unfit to look on the world. Then in the final play of the trilogy, Oedipus of Colonus has to creep away from nature because he is so horrible that the sun should not look at him lest he pollute the entire world.

This is a fantastic change over the course of just a few centuries. That is only the beginning of the kind of research I am doing into the particular matter of the changes in emotional life that occur with imagination or with consciousness.

You can also take a basic emotion like fear and show that with consciousness, fear becomes the anxiety that you and I can have. In animals, fear occurs in the presence of the fearful stimulus, but when the fearful thing is taken away, the animal is not afraid anymore except on the basis of what it has learned. In ourselves, we can go back over a fear, from our childhood perhaps, and feel anxious about it and experience a free floating anxiety that is not attached to anything.

That is something that Achilles or Hector or anyone back in bicameral times did not experience. Someone this afternoon was asking about love and hate. Well I think hate is a very conscious thing and I think it is anger with imagination added in. Once you go over your anger this becomes hatred. Achilles had wrath and anger, but he didn't have hatred. He did not hate Hector — he did not hate anybody. Hate is indeed a conscious thing that I think is the emotion of anger spread out over this mind-time. Imagination works on it and turns on it into this different kind of emotion — what I would call a feeling.

It is similar with love, although there are differences. It is a little more difficult to talk about. We have affiliation responses in animals (or imprinting, which I have studied) where animals have a very powerful impulse to stay together. But this becomes our complicated kind of love when we can imagine the loved person and go back and forth in our imagination about them.

Similarly — and interestingly — with sex. If you look at the comparative psychology of sexual behavior in animals, it is very clear that this is not an open kind of behavior that happens any time or anything like that. It is cued ethologically into certain kinds of stimuli. So you have to have just the right kind of situation in order for animals to mate.

This is a problem that happens in every zoo: as soon as they get new animals, they want to mate them and have progeny. It is a tremendous problem, because you don't know ethologically what those tiny cues are — they might be temperature or darkness or whatnot. For human beings it might be moonlight and roses [laughs], but it is this kind of thing that you find evolved into animal behavior.

I tend to think that in bicameral times mating was very similar to what it is in animals in that sense. It was cued into moonlight and roses shall I say, and not otherwise. Therefore it was not a problem in a way. Now, when human beings become conscious, have imagination, and can fantasize about sex, it becomes what we mean in quotes "sex." Which I think is a problem in the sense that it does not ever quite fit into our conscious society. We go back and forward in history from having a free sex age and then a clamping down of Ms. Grundy[2] and Queen Victoria and so on. It goes back and forth because sex to us is tremendously more important than it was to bicameral man because we can fantasize about it.

Now similarly as I mentioned with the Oedipus story and the idea of guilt, we should be able to go back into history and find evidence for this. The evidence that I found for this — and I should be studying it in different cultures — is again in Greece. If you talk to Greek art historians and you ask them to compare, for example, Greek vase painting of the conscious era with the vase painting or other kinds of painting that went on in what I call the bicameral period — either in Minoan art in Crete or the famous murals that were found in Thera — they will all tell you that there is a big distinction. The older art is chaste, there is nothing about sex in it. But then you come to the vase paintings of Greece. We often think of Greece in terms of Plato and Aristotle and so on, and we do not realize that sex was something very different. For example, they have all of these satyrs with penile erections on their vases and odd things like that. Another example are things called *herms*. Most people have not heard of them. All the boundary stones of the city were stones about four feet in height called *herms*. They are called *herms*, by us anyway, because they were just posts that very often they had a sculpture of Hermes at the top — but sometimes of other people. Then at the appropriate place — the body was just a column — there was a penile erection. I do not think we would find Athens back in these early conscious times very congenial.

These were all over the city of Athens. They were at the boundary stones everywhere. If you think of them being around nowadays you can imagine children giggling and so on. It is enough to make you realize that these people, even at this time, the time of Plato and Aristotle, were very different than we are. And if you read Plato you can find that one of the great crimes of Alcibiades — the Greek general that comes into several of the dialogues — is this terrible, frightful night when he got drunk and went and mutilated the *herms*. You can imagine what he was knocking off. This is hard for us to realize, because it again makes this point that these people are still not like us even though they are conscious. Because they are new to these emotions. I do not mean to intimate that Greek life was sexually free all over the place because I don't think that was the case. If you read Kenneth Dover's[3] classic work about Greek homosexuality, for example, you see it is very different from the gay liberation movement

---

2. A name that has been used to refer to a prudish woman since the nineteenth century. —*Ed.*
3. Kenneth Dover, *Greek Homosexuality* (Cambridge: Harvard University Press, 1978/1989).

that we can find going on in our country right now. It is a very tame kind of thing.

I don't think we really understand what is going on. There is the evidence, it is there in vase paintings, it is there in Greek times, but there is something we still do not fully understand about it. But it is different from the bicameral period. We have a different kind of human nature here, and it is against this that we look at where the self can come from.

## Types of Selves

Previously I said that there is the *bodily self* and that that is not what most of us mean by the self. Then there is the *autobiographical self* that begins around 1300 B.C. and it lasts through this Greek period that I have just discussed, in which people know that they have lifetimes, they are going to their deaths, and they see their lives patterned out. "My childhood was this, my present is this, maybe I'll be ambitious now" and so on. Things like ambition and all these kinds of things come in at this time, and this autobiographical self is a very different kind of self.

But then we come to people around Plato's time, and one finds again a different kind of self, and this is the kind of self that I call the *idealed self,* in that it is measured against ideals. I would like to make a diagram here of what I call consciousness — of an analog 'I' and the field of consciousness:

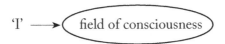

The idealed self occurs when one creates out of the field of consciousness a self and measures it against some ideal. In Plato we see many examples of this. One of the astonishing things to consider about Plato and Aristotle is that perhaps they were so great because consciousness was so new. It was so new and, as a result, everything was so vivid to them. I have often thought of how we might try to do this ourselves — to expand our consciousness, so to speak. It is one answer to say that Plato and Aristotle were simply born that way, but I don't tend to think so. I think it is because everything is fresh and new and clear that this outpouring of thought emerges, particularly in the greatness of Socrates, Plato, and Aristotle.

So we have this idealed self where people around the time of Plato, instead of just introspecting, were measuring themselves against some kind of ideal. This comes into the Christian writings when you have Jesus saying some very curious things about the self. "He who shall lose himself shall find himself, he who is first and last," and that kind of thing. It almost seems to be saying that it is a bad idea to expand your self to your entire field of consciousness. What you should have instead is a self that is more combined so that you leave places in your field of consciousness for others. If any of you are mothers you know perfectly well that when you are a mother, your field of consciousness is occupied by a child.

Just as a side note, I am rather critical of those people who talk about self-actualization. I feel that it is somewhat unfortunate because a lot of people are getting involved in human potential movements and thinking they are going to actualize themselves — to use Abraham Maslow's term — when they are not going to do anything like that at all. Because there is no particular reason to actualize yourself rather than to actualize others. Parents are of course actualizing others, and it is a wonderful thing. I just wanted to point that out before I go on.

## Origins of the Self

Where then does the self really come from? What happens as we go through history — and I feel that there is a lot more thinking to be done here — is we build up a kind of attribute network of good and bad properties. It is almost a part of our language. Some of you may know the French neo-Freudian Jacques Lacan who says "the unconscious is language." Certainly language is a terribly important part of this because in our language structure we have all these different kinds of attributes that we can attach to ourselves.

In making up a self, I am suggesting that what we do is pick out a selection of attributes and then fit them together in a kind of structure that seems correct for a particular time or a particular mood. Obviously it is changeable — changeable from day to day — but we try to hang on to it and try to make it the same and this is why for some reason it seems a little bit ephemeral.

The self is built up out of these attributes in two kinds of ways. The first is inferences from others. Your parents telling you, "Oh you're a good boy," therefore you have a good attribute going in to your self. Or a teacher saying you you are a stupid person, and "stupid" goes in as part of your self.

To take another example there was an experiment in which they told a group of children, "You can play with all the toys but not that one." And half the children did play with it and half did not. It is a rather involved experiment, but later on, they gave another task to the child in which you could not solve the task unless you cheated. And the ones that had been obedient and had not played with the toy did not cheat. They were making themselves consistent, they had already built into themselves, even in this little experiment, "I am not someone who cheats and disobeys." Whereas the children who did cheat were the ones who played with the toy. So we see this consistency even happening in children.

But this consistency is one of the dangers of the self. Particularly it happens with schoolchildren. It happens particularly with ideas of IQ, and this is one of things that is wrong with the idea of IQ. A friend of mine was walking the other day in New York City with one of America's most famous novelists, and the novelist pointed up to a floor on a high building and said "that's where it all happened."

She asked him what he meant by that, and he said that when we was 17 or 18 his mother took him there to the Psychological Corporation and had him tested for IQ. He came out to have a very high IQ and the man there told him, "You can do anything in the world that you ever want to do." And he never looked back. I don't think John Updike would like me to tell you his name [laughs], but he has had extraordinary success in many different kinds of writing and I appreciate his work.

On the other hand, I had a relative who was going to a Midwestern university and they gave him an IQ test, the horrible Otis test that has a time pressure on it. He came out to have about a 100 IQ, which is just average — not good enough for college and university. So they called him in and they said, "Look you've struggled through with your C's, and you'll have to struggle an awful lot more with your last two junior and senior years, we suggest that you drop out now and take up a trade," and so on. "Here is your IQ, you're way below the average for this university." And he didn't know what to do. His next report came and he got D's after that experience.

I realized something was very wrong here. I was a graduate student at Yale at the time, and I told him to come to Yale, which he did. I got the very best intelligence tester at the university at the time to give him a proper Wechsler-Bellevue test and he came out with an IQ of 132. He then went back to the university and got straight A's thereafter. So what we believe about ourselves then turns around and determines some of our behavior.

Some of you may know the very interesting work of Bob Rosenthal at Harvard and something called the Pygmalion effect. I don't think they did this specific experiment, but in an interesting experiment that is similar to their work, a class was given an intelligence test but the experimenters did not even look at the scores. They randomly picked half the children as sub normal and half as good intelligence, and gave these results to the teacher. And sure enough — this is random mind you — when the next grades came down, the marks all correlated.

It is a tragic thing that the teacher can get across to a student some-thing like "I don't think you're very intelligent" and so the person takes that and puts that in their selves and behaves unintelligently and does not do well in school. We don't quite understand how this is done but it is being done and it is a tragic thing.

So when we construct our selves by what we hear from others we have to be careful. If we hear someone say something casually about us, we may start worrying about it, and sometimes it takes a long time to work itself out. So the first way we build up a self is indeed by what we hear from others.

The second is what we know of ourselves from inferences about our own behavior. Much of this can be trivial as well. For example, if you are having supper and you take a second sandwich and you say, "Oh I didn't know I was that hungry." You are making an inference you see about your-self being hungry. Lots of trivial things like that happen.

I remember I had a very interesting experience at the University of New Hampshire. I was giving a talk there and someone else was giving a talk just before me. He was a Harvard professor, and I noticed how he was trembling up there. I noticed how he held his papers and they were trembling and I thought "Isn't that ridiculous — a full Harvard professor having all that stage fright?" and I was thinking rather gloatingly, "I'm glad I don't have stage fright at this point in my career."

So then I got up to give my speech. I took hold of the podium and I began to tremble and I didn't quite know what was going on. I felt scared and even as I was starting to talk I was trying to think "What is it? Why am I scared this way?" Well, the podium is above a generator in the cellar, and the whole podium shakes, but you can't see it, so just hanging on to the podium you start to shake. Then you make inferences from your trembling and go through all this narratization in your consciousness which is all completely false.

There are other more important ways of how we make inferences from our own behavior, how we label ourselves. This is where indeed our intelligence comes in — not intelligence in the sense that I was talking about earlier, but our own fastidiousness with how we can look at ourselves, how we try to understand ourselves. How we have ideals and how we measure up to those ideals. This is how indeed we can make inferences from our own behavior.

I was talking this morning with someone about writing and how you cannot predict whether you are going to write well on a particular day or not — you just have to launch yourself into it. When you do write well, that returns, and so you continue writing well, because you have convinced yourself that you are a good writer. If only we could find a way of controlling ourselves so that we could create these patterns and become more inspired or efficient.

I would also like to just briefly say something about the reality of the self. Because the self is so ephemeral, does that mean it is not real? It is real because it is what allows us to do things. There is a whole new theory being developed called self-efficacy theory. It means that what you believe of yourself is what allows you to choose certain kinds of paths or behaviors rather than others. It is what gives you confidence. It is very important to this whole concept of the self. This is why we must be very careful from these two sources that build up the self — about whether we have them just from the incidental trivia of other people, or whether we have it as true inferences from our own behavior as we try to understand ourselves.

The other selves that I just wish to briefly talk about come about somewhat later, as well as the exceptions. When we come up to the Dark Ages we find exceptions, for example, with Cicero's letters. Unless you carefully examine them, you cannot tell any difference between them and contemporary writing. If you look at Cicero's *De Senectute*, however, I don't think anyone could have written it today. There is just something slightly off about it.

Then we come to Augustine (354–430) — a remarkable man — and look at his *Confessions*. You can see how this is a progression. No one ever wrote confessions like this before. But his *Confessions* are quite different than what we might think. He is not really revealing himself. I suggest that he did not have a self quite that way. He confesses that he has committed fornication, lying, sodomy, and poetry — in that order. It is different than what we would expect. It does not quite jibe with us, even though Augustine was a marvelous, wonderful person.

But after Augustine, for 700 years there is no autobiography. Everything closes down and is very different even from what it was before. There is no development of the self until we get to the wonder of the twelfth century. The twelfth century is full of fascinating things that happen rather suddenly. But the changes in the twelfth century toward greater indivdualization happen unevenly, and there are still examples of the lack of a clear concept of an individual self.

For example, there is Herrad of Landsberg (c. 1130–1195), abbess of Hohenburg Abbey, who writes a religious tract, and then she decides to put the pictures of all of her nuns in the last part of the book, as well as a picture of herself. So there are drawings of all of her nuns with their names underneath, but every one of them looks nearly identical. And the picture of herself is also nearly identical to the sixty other people. All of the names are different but the pictures are nearly the same.

If you look at sculptures at the great cathedral of Chartres, many of the people depicted also lack individuality. It is very similar to Herrad of Landsberg. If you compare that with the cathedral at Reims, for example, the people depicted there start looking different and individual.

In the twelfth century you also have people like Saint Bernard of Clairvaux (1090–1153), for example, who writes on the seven steps to confession. And the first step to confession is "Know thyself." That Greek saying that we found way back in Solon. This is a development of consciousness as well as a development of the self.[4]

We must not think too much about the seven steps to confession. Often people think that means confession as we have it in the Catholic Church today. But it was very different. At the Fourth Lateran Council, held in Rome in 1215, they decided to make sure that every Catholic went to confession, so they put it in the law. But confession was required only once a year. That is very different than those of you who have been brought up with the Catholic training where, particularly on the East Coast because

---

4. For more on this subject see John F. Benton, "Consciousness of Self and Perceptions of Individuality," in Robert L. Benson, Giles Constable, and Carol D. Lanham (eds.), *Renaissance and Renewal in the Twelfth Century* (Cambridge: Harvard University Press, 1982), from which Jaynes draws these examples. —*Ed.*

Irish Catholicism was influenced by Jensonism, they insisted that there should be confession every single week.

But the whole idea of confession comes in here around the twelfth century. You can see the idea of individuality or the *comparative self* emerging, in which people start calling themselves "Peter the Hermit" or name themselves after particular physical characteristics. It is a very new kind of thing when you see it against the background of the Middle Ages.

Then as we come into the proper Renaissance we find this developing even more when, for example, we contrast between the Rules of Saint Francis (1223) and the Rules of Saint Benedict (c. 530). The Rules of Saint Francis are warm and somehow interior, emphasizing love and so on — all of that seems to reappear around this particular time — whereas The Rules of Saint Benedict are the more classical shaping of behavior from the outside with rules.

It is odd to think of us coming up to the fifteenth and sixteenth century and to think that people even at that time were different than we are today — that they had different selves. But I think that this also can be clearly shown. Through literature we see the idea of the self makes a track that keeps changing as it goes along.

We can find it in the seventeenth century. For example, we can make a contrast between Descartes and Locke — Descartes being part of the older side of things and Locke being part of the new side of welcoming experience and talking about the self in a very different way. Of course they were using the word soul back then, but soul, particularly as it comes to be written about by Locke and Hume and people after, comes to mean more what we might refer to as the self.

If we follow along in literature and come through Romantic literature, it all has a lot to do with the self. Percy Bysshe Shelley (1792–1822), for example, says that "the self is the mammon of literature" — by which he means that we have to get rid of the self in order to get pure inspiration. This is something which if you attach it to what I said this afternoon makes a little more sense.[5]

There is a new book out for example, *The Invention of the Self in the Eighteenth Century*[6] — I don't agree with it — but this subject is popular

---

5. Here Jaynes is referring to his overall theory and specifically the role of hallucinations in inspiration. For more on the subject see Jaynes's "The Ghost of A Flea: Visions of William Blake" in M. Kuijsten (ed.), *Reflections on the Dawn of Consciousness* (Henderson: Julian Jaynes Society, 2006) —Ed.

6. John O. Lyons, *The Invention of the Self: The Hinge of Consciousness in the Eighteenth Century* (Southern Illinois University Press, 1978).

right now, with a lot of people discussing these changes that have been going on in history both in consciousness and in the idea of selfhood.

So what we have is a complicated idea of the self. It is composed of a selection from an attribute pool that is all around us. The way we judge other people is the way we judge ourselves. The very attributes by which you construct your self is the way you construct your understanding of others. And what you do to others you do to yourself, because you cannot get away from this. What your self is and what others are are part of the same thing and you really cannot separate it. "Judge not, that you be not judged" is a very true kind of thing because how we judge others, so will we judge ourselves.

### The Neurology of the Self

Where could our ideas of the self be in the brain? There is a possibility, I've begun thinking recently, that the analog 'I' is in the left hemisphere, and this field of consciousness is a bit more in the right hemisphere — in the spatial hemisphere — and our dialog with the self is going back and forth as we constantly recreate the ideas of our selves that we turn into the self-efficacy that allows us to do one thing or another. We don't know.

But there is some evidence that is rather interesting that I will just mention for whatever it's worth. Prior to about ten years ago (when for the most part they stopped performing the procedure, at least in adults), for several decades neurosurgeons commonly removed the entire right hemisphere in certain people. The reason for this is that if a person gets a disease or tumor of some kind in the right hemisphere and just a portion of the hemisphere is removed, the person is frequently much worse off than if the entire hemisphere is removed completely.

So we have quite a few people, almost a hundred probably in the United States, who are going around with only their left hemisphere. They are an interesting and rather odd group of people. At first they seem relatively normal. But if you were to ask them, for example, "How do you feel?" they might say "With my hands." They will not be able to understand the metaphor, the whole concept of it. All of their language is what we might call "self-centered" in another kind of way. It is all "What I am going to do now," and so on. They are not interested in other people. They seem to have lost that and become very concrete. So I just put this idea of hemisphere interaction out there as a possibility for this complicated idea of the self that seems so ephemeral.[7]

[Recording ends.]

---

7. Jaynes's speculation here on the possible neurological substrates of the self is that our sense of self may be related to an interplay between the analog 'I', located in the left or language-dominant hemisphere (see also Michael Gazzaniga's discussion of the "left-hemisphere interpreter" in *Nature's Mind* [Perseus Books Group, 1992] and elsewhere), and what he refers to as the field of consciousness in the right hemisphere. Jaynes draws the example of typical deficits one might see in right hemispherectomy patients from a summary of the relevant literature in Marilee Zdenek, *The Right Brain Experience: An Intimate Program to Free the Powers of Your Imagination* (New York: McGraw-Hill, 1983). There is now a large body of literature on cognitive and behavior changes after hemispherectomy or hemisphere damage, but for one study of particular significance see Orrin Devinsky, "Right Cerebral Hemisphere Dominance for a Sense of Corporeal and Emotional Self," *Epilepsy and Behavior*, 2000, *1*, 1. The type of deficits Jaynes describes are more typical of adult patients; when a hemisphere is removed in very young children, the remaining hemisphere is better able to adapt. For an interesting case of right hemispherectomy in a three-year-old child, see Antonio M. Battro, *Half a Brain is Enough: The Story of Nico* (Cambridge: Cambridge University Press, 2000). As I mentioned in the Introduction, the ability of some people to function relatively normally with only one hemisphere provides further evidence that prior to the breakdown of the bicameral mind the two hemispheres could have operated more independently than they do today. For further discussion of the nature of the self with regard to Jaynes's theory see Brian J. McVeigh, "The Self As Interiorized Social Relations: Applying a Jaynesian Approach to Problems of Agency and Volition" in Marcel Kuijsten (ed.), *Reflections on the Dawn of Consciousness* (Henderson, NV: Julian Jaynes Society, 2006) —*Ed.*

# CHAPTER 15

# Representations as Metaphiers

W E UNDERSTAND SOMETHING by finding a metaphor for it with which we are more familiar, and the feeling of familiarity is the feeling of understanding. In such metaphors, the thing to be understood is what I have called a metaphrand, and that more familiar thing to which it is compared, the metaphier (intentionally connoting multiplicand and multiplier in mathematics). This relationship between metaphrand and metaphier is at the basis of all knowledge. New phenomena are found to be similar to previous phenomena and are brought under their rubric.[1]

To say that in learning an animal stores the results of previous trials as a "representation," and that that representation controls future behavior, is to use representation as a metaphier. It seems innocuous enough. Moreover, it does indeed seem to help us understand what is going on by making the process familiar. But where does the familiarity come from?

As conscious human beings, we have embedded in us as a result of our culture and language the idea of mind as a kind of space, containing images, ideas, and memories that are representations of previous external events. This is what it is like to be introspectively conscious. But this is not what consciousness is. Moreover, so ingrained is our habit of imagining what is going on 'in' the minds of other human beings that we tend to carry over this "ejective perception" (as W.K. Clifford called it in the nineteenth century) to anything that behaves in any way similar to ourselves. So we wrongly impute consciousness to lower animals when what we are really doing is trying to know the animal predictively on the basis of past behavior. In other words, with terms like representation we may be using our own fallacious consciousness of consciousness as a metaphier to understand animals. This is a mistake.

Article by Julian Jaynes first published in *Behavioral and Brain Sciences*, Vol. 5, Issue 3 as commentary on the article "The Meaning of Representation in Animal Memory" by H.L. Roitblat. © 1982 Cambridge Journals. Reproduced with permission.
1. See Julian Jaynes, *The Origin of Consciousness in the Breakdown of the Bicameral Mind*, Book 1, Chapter 2 (Boston: Houghton-Mifflin, 1976).

Representationalism has, of course, become central to problems of artificial intelligence and is now influencing aspects of neuroscience. But I often suspect that hidden behind a great deal of sophistication are metaphors that are not always critically distinguished as such. Metaphiers such as 'information,' 'memory,' and even 'representation' have all but thrown off their psychological meaning. We may read that, in order to build a computer that can pass Turing's test of conversing in a conscious-like manner, we must build into it a "a representational system ... an active self-updating collection of structures organized to mirror the world as it evolves" — as if this abstract simplification were really what was going on in ourselves. It perhaps seems as if this were our consciousness, but careful examination of introspective experience shows that it is not.[2] Consciousness is primarily an analog 'I' 'narratizing' in a 'mind-space,' whose features are built up on the basis of metaphors. Present computer programs do not work on the basis of metaphors. Even if computers could simulate metaphoric processes, they still would not have the complex repertoire of physical behavior activities over time to utilize as metaphiers to bring consciousness into being. Computers, therefore, are not — and cannot be — conscious.

Roitblat, in his full and interesting essay, feels it will turn the corner of an historical paradigm to take over the popularity of representationalism from AI into the field of animal learning. I certainly have sympathy for his purpose, that is, to once and for all put to rest the vacuousness of simple stimulus-response connectionism. But in this thorough interment, he is certainly stirring up old ghosts. The average reader of the term "representation" in the context of retention has as its first referent himself introspecting on an image, regardless of whether the theorist intends something nonpictorial like a matrix of propositions. Moreover, few would agree that it would be productive to use representation so widely — certainly not for the result or residue of any and all learning, as Roitblat suggests. Is something represented from the past in habituation? Or motor learning? Or in simple conditioning, as of leg flexion in the isolated ventral ganglion of a headless cockroach?[3]

If a dog, after searching a field, retrieves a stick that has been thrown, we find it easy to say that he has some kind of tactual-olfactory-visual

---

2. See Julian Jaynes, *The Origin of Consciousness in the Breakdown of the Bicameral Mind*, Book 1, Chapter 1 (Boston: Houghton-Mifflin, 1976).

3. G. Adrian Horridge, "Comparative Physiology: Integrative Action of the Nervous System," *Annual Review of Physiology*, 1963, 25.

representation of the stick because he retrieves only the stick and rejects other objects. But perhaps we find this metaphier of representation from our own private experience easy in this instance because we know so little about such searching and retrieving.

Let us consider color vision, about which we know considerably more. We used to think that color was due to the wavelength of light reaching the eye, the ensuing sensation being a representation of the colored object. But simple color-shadow experiments (known, incidentally, since von Guericke's work in the seventeenth century) show that this is not true. If a red light and a white light are projected together onto the same screen, the result is, of course, pink. If we then put a hand in front of the white projector, we get a red shadow on a pink background. But if we instead occlude the shadow from the red projector, the outcome is not what would be predicted from the actual spectral composition. We do not get a whitish hand on a pink background (as we could expect on the basis of the ingrained representationalism of our consciousness of consciousness). Instead, the hand is a sharp blue-green hue.[4] There is thus no one-to-one relationship between the wavelength of light from another object and the sensation. Color is experienced when there are certain ratios of relative activity in different color-specialized parts of the retinal field, and these ratios are weighted by comparisons with activity in the prestriate areas of the visual cortex and other neural surfaces. And when we take into account the further neuroanatomical evidence that, for each nerve fiber from a retinal ganglion cell entering the cortex via the lateral geniculate nucleus, there are a hundred or so fibers from other cortical and subcortical areas that enter at the same topographical location, we have a complexity in which the word "representation" seems lost indeed.

Feature detection work once seemed to lead to a complete representationalism. But these cellular responses have been shown to hold only under stabilized experimental conditions. Even simple perception, let alone animal memory, appears to be much more complicated and dynamic over time than the metaphiers of representation theory imply.

---

4. See Francisco Varela and Humberto Maturana, "Size Constancy and Accommodation," *Perception*, 1981, *10*, from whom I have taken this example, for a much fuller discussion; also E.H. Land, "The Retinex," *American Scientist*, 1964, *52*.

# CHAPTER 16

# A Two-Tiered Theory of Emotions: Affect and Feeling

No theory of emotions can make sense out of the psychological data unless it is absolutely clear about what is conscious in emotional experience and what is not.

Let me state briefly my own point of view.

All mammals, including ourselves, have a basic set of genetically organized affects, specific aptitudes to respond to characterizable classes of stimuli or events in certain characterizable ways. Back in evolutionary history, I believe, the core of most of these aptitudes, their "aptic paradigms," were actual overt behaviors of reptiles. But in mammals these overt behaviors have become inhibited by more recently evolved parts of the brain, leaving them more diffusely related to actual overt behavior in a more general energizing way.[1] Most emotional behaviors of mammals are thus paleoreptilian behaviors transformed on both the stimulus and the response side by limbic and cortical selective inhibition. And just as the behaviors in the repertoire of any animal cannot be set out as similar things, with the same characteristics — being different in their nature, timing, pervasiveness, situational dependence, interrelations with other behaviors, and dependence or independence of them — so mammalian emotions also cannot be set out in a linear array. A list of mammalian emotions or affects, although nonlinear and often interlocking, could start off clearly enough with the usual items like fear, anger, disgust, and the various affectional systems[2] and then end up somewhat vaguely, but no less appropriately, with those behaviors that are less commonly called

Article by Julian Jaynes first published in *Behavioral and Brain Sciences*, Vol. 5, Issue 3 as commentary on the article "Toward A General Psychobiological Theory of Emotions" by Jaak Panksepp. © 1982 Cambridge Journals. Reproduced with permission.

1. Paul MacLean, *A Triune Concept of the Brain and Behavior* (University of Toronto Press, 1973).

2. Harry F. Harlow, Margaret Harlow, and Stephen J. Suomi, "From Thought to Therapy: Lessons from A Primate Laboratory," *American Scientist*, 1971, *59*.

emotional because of their lesser intensity, such as drowsiness and curiosity. Since expectancy is common to all molar mammalian behavior, I would not include it in such a list.

Are all behaviors emotions? It is not the behaviors themselves that we denote by emotions, but their inferred organizations, which usually include four characteristics: (1) emotions have a clear variation in intensity, so that every emotion has more or less to it; (2) even if not immediately expressed, emotions are associated with a distinct class of behaviors; (3) emotions have bodily and often facial expressions, which are distinguishable from more usual states; (4) there exist distinct classes of stimuli or situations that occasion emotions.

This list is to be compared with Panksepp's list under his heading "A definition of emotions." What Panksepp has done is to suggest a theory of the brain circuitry involved that is interesting in itself, but is so restricted in an ad hoc way as to eliminate many behavioral responses that most observers would include under the term emotion.

But the real point of my commentary concerns consciousness and how consciousness, once established in history, adds something new to genetically programmed mammalian *affects* that we can call *feelings*. I believe this to be an historical change that occurred in the ancient Mediterranean and Near Eastern world sometime after 1000 B.C. which, as I have tried to show elsewhere, is the beginning of the period when human beings learned consciousness on the basis of metaphor.[3] By consciousness I mean precisely what Panksepp does in his few references to it, namely, all our introspective experience, including retrospection and imagination. Once human beings have these capacities, they can think out consciously and privately what they are to do, in contrast to a more ancient mentality called the "bicameral mind," in which what we call volition was a matter of hearing and obeying auditory hallucinations called gods.

With this metaphor-generated consciousness, there comes the metaphor of time as a space, or spatialized time, in which human beings 'see' themselves as embedded in their own histories. This human sense of a lifetime begins over the same period as the development of the idea of historical time,[4] as well as the appearance of ideas of justice, retribution, doing wrong, remission of wrongs, and forgiveness, all very curious behav-

---

3. Julian Jaynes, *The Origin of Consciousness in the Breakdown of the Bicameral Mind* (Boston: Houghton-Mifflin, 1976).

4. For evidence for this see Chester G. Starr, *The Awakening of the Greek Historical Spirit* (Alfred A. Knopf, 1968).

iors when we think of them against the background of the evolution of mammalian behavior, and all occurring in world history for the first time. The result is a new set of social and political problems. Behind these social changes are the changes in personal emotion that arise from the new human capacity to stretch out the affects over the spatialized time, or, in other words, to dwell on past behaviors or on possible future behaviors and respond to them as if they were presently occurring, with copies of the affects themselves. These are our feelings. My language here is difficult and metaphoric, because these processes are not fully understood at present. But let us consider some examples.

Shame is one of the most powerful affects.[5] It occurs in many mammals, such as canines, primates, and early man. Observation of present-day children's development or reminiscences about our own will demonstrate the tyrannous power of humiliation, of rejection from a social group, in shaping behavior to some norm or other. In fact, we have all been so shaped by shame into our customary behavior that, as adults, we rarely have this affect in its pure state. But once human beings can reminisce about shameful actions or imagine possible shameful actions, until they imagine real or possible humiliation and ostracization in a general way, we have guilt. Guilt is thus a conscious feeling that is generated from the biological affect of shame.

This is obvious, I think, in the development of consciousness in the child.[6] It is also evident in the development of consciousness in ancient history. Consider, for example, the story of Oedipus. In its earliest form (in two lines from the *Iliad* and two lines from the *Odyssey* — pretty meager evidence, I agree), it seems to be the story of a king who had killed his father and married his mother and had two daughters-sisters by her, and who (since the incest taboo is the reason the story is mentioned at all) certainly felt some shame, but then apparently lived a long remorseless life with his somewhat strange family until he was buried with military honors at Thebes. But just a few centuries later, in the fifth century B.C., consciousness has transformed the story into the tragic sense of guilt that savages its way through the great tragic trilogy of Sophocles.[7]

---

5. For the best discussion, see Silvan Tomkins, *Affects, Imagery, and Consciousness: Vols. 1 & 2* (New York: Springer, 1963).

6. See Lawrence Kohlberg, "Moral Stages and Moralization," in Thomas Likona (ed.), *Moral Development and Behavior* (London: Holt, Rinehart, and Winston, 1976).

7. On this point, see E.R. Dodds, *The Greeks and the Irrational* (Berkeley: University of California Press, 1951).

Similarly with other genetically organized affects. Fear, when consciously reminisced about and projected into the future, becomes the conscious feeling of anxiety. The affect of anger stretched out over spatialized time in consciousness becomes hatred. Excitement becomes the conscious feeling of joy; disgust, contempt; affiliation, love. And so on. All of these changes need to be carefully documented in historical data and in child development.

Perhaps most interesting are the sexual emotions, which were usually omitted from Victorian lists of the emotions (including Darwin's) because their bodily expression is primarily genital rather than facial. We do know that mating in the anthropoid apes, in contrast to ourselves, is casual and almost minimal, with observations of mating in gibbons, chimpanzees, orangutans, and gorillas in the wild being extremely rare. Paralleling these facts, tomb and wall paintings, sculpture and the writings of bicameral civilizations rarely if ever have any sexual references. All classicists will agree with this, that all Mycenean and Minoan art, in particular before 1000 b.c., is what seems to us as severely chaste. But after the advent of consciousness, say, about 700 b.c., Greek and Etruscan art is rampant with sexual references, very definitely demonstrating that sexual feelings were a new and profound concern in human development in these regions. We can perhaps appreciate this change in ourselves if we try to imagine what our sexual lives would be like if we could not fantasize about sexual behavior.

By this two-tiered theory, I mean to imply that because of our ability to fantasize, both by reminiscing about the past and imagining the future, our present affectional experience consists of far more than the basic affects of mammals. I should like to point out here in passing how well this development fits in with the James-Lange theory (with some slight shifts in terminology). We see a bear, which occasions the genetically organized affect of fear, and we run away, which we are then conscious of, turning the fear into the feeling of extreme anxiety. So the James-Cannon controversy may be resolved.

Emotional terminology is a considerable problem. We have an excessive vocabulary of emotional terms that arise from our own experience and the culture in which we live. In observing animal behavior, when we see a behavior similar to our own in emotional circumstances, we usually label it with that emotion. This is, of course, all we can do; otherwise the behavior of animals is merely topological. But if we have not made a clear distinction between the affects and conscious feelings, we are likely to make mistakes and project our own conscious feelings into the simple affects of lower animals. Panksepp is making the methodological point that we have to use our own consciousness of our own behavior to label the emotions of lower animals. True. But it certainly needs the added caution I have just outlined. The two-tiered theory also suggests that studies of hypothalamic stimulation or other presently known neural substrates of emotion in animals, although largely important for understanding basic mammalian affects, are limited in their application to human emotional experience.

# CHAPTER 17

# Four Hypotheses on the Origin of Mind

Wᴴᴬᵀ I ʜᴀᴠᴇ ᴛᴏ ᴘʀᴇѕᴇɴᴛ ᴛᴏ ʏᴏᴜ this morning is essentially a historical theory that results in a conclusion that consciousness and mind cannot be understood apart from their history. To me, all discussions of mind must be diachronic, not synchronic as most such discussions are. It is a position which I recognize is not popular or even consonant with modern philosophical thinking, but is one which I would like to urge upon you whether or not you accept the details of what I am going to present.

The problem that I start with is that of the origin of consciousness in an evolutionary sense. It is a problem that after the rise of evolutionary theory in the latter part of the nineteenth century was then regarded as massively important, indeed, imperative for the completion of the theory of the origin of species by natural selection and thereby its vindication. Evolution explained the materialistic and chance origin and proliferation of species, but how could it explain the origin of the seemingly immaterial human mind? That was and still is the problem. How could consciousness have arisen out of mere matter by natural selection?

Some, like Wallace, said it couldn't: consciousness in humans had to be imposed by a Deity. So did Darwin, surprisingly, but at the beginning of evolution as one of the several powers which were "originally breathed by the Creator into a few forms or into one," my quotation being from the last paragraph of the *Origin of Species*. And this Darwinian idea that conscious mind evolved in parallel with morphology led to a program of research into the evolutionary development of consciousness by Darwin's disciple, Romanes — a program which was quickly seen to be inadequate. Other attempted solutions followed, such as Huxley's implausible brand of adversarial proto-behaviorism or the mysticism and imprecision

Adapted from Julian Jaynes's plenary lecture presented at the 9th International Wittgenstein Symposium held in Kirchberg, Austria, August 19–26, 1984. First published in Roderick Chisholm, Johann Marek, John Blackmore, and Adolf Hubnew (eds.), *Philosophy of Mind, Philosophy of Psychology: Proceedings of the 9th International Wittgenstein Symposium.* © 1985 Kluwer Academic Publishing. Reprinted with permission.

of emergent evolution, and then in philosophy with the neo-realism of Whitehead, Alexander, Perry, and others which is unfortunately having a modern revival as a result of some of the paradoxes of "observer-partici-pancy" in quantum physics. And of course along this tortuous way, the psychologist's flippant solution to the problem of the origin of consciousness by denying that it exists at all. Coming through such an exhausting and trying history, it is not surprising that the problem has withered away its nineteenth century urgency and disappeared from both scientific and philosophical discussions. I think it should be brought back to clarify many of the problems being addressed at this symposium.

The reason for this abysmal failure to solve the problem of the origin of consciousness is because of a false and unwieldy notion of consciousness. Through history it had accumulated a huge amount of cultural baggage which would not allow the matter to be looked at properly. Some of this excess of reference was due to religious history wherein the soul became invested with all possible psychological functions which then became the properties of mind or consciousness as those words replaced the term soul. Another source of such error was due to philosophical thinking itself, that what we could arrive at as a function of mind by logical inference, that too was a part of consciousness even though such propositions had no introspective validity. So the first and proper step in this analysis is to try to loosen the concept of consciousness from the accretion of these historical mistakes.

By the infusion of logically inferred capacities into the idea of consciousness, I mean processes such as sense-perception. While we can be conscious, (though not always) of the products of sense-perception, the actual processes are in no way accessible to conscious introspection. Historically, we inferred and abstracted these processes from a realization of our sense organs, and then, because of prior assumptions about mind and matter or soul and body, we believed these processes to be a part of consciousness — which they are not. If any of you still think that sense-perception is to be equated to consciousness, then I think you could follow a path to a *reductio ad absurdum*: you would then have to say that since all animals have sense perception, all are conscious, and so on back through the evolutionary scale even to one-celled protozoa, and thence to even the amoeboid white cells of the blood since they sense bacteria and devour them. They too would be conscious. And to say that there are then a thousand conscious beings per cubic millimeter of blood in each of us here this morning is a position few would wish to defend.

Now to some of you it will seem that I am defining consciousness in a much narrower way than usual. I am. But it is part of the theory I am stating that that is what consciousness is, and not sense perceptions — as I have just stated. I do not mean that all consciousness is introspection, but it is introspectable. Consciousness is what is going on "in the minds" of any dozen people now on the street in Kirchberg, and if you should ask them to say into a tape recorder everything they are thinking about, you will not find bundles of sense-perceptions, but a stream of worries, regrets, hopes, reminiscences, interior dialogues, and monologues, plans, imaginations — all of which are the stuff of consciousness.

Why should it be that some people confound consciousness and sense perception? The reasons are several. First, as I shall be describing, consciousness is an analog of perception and so indeed can *seem* to be identical. I shall try to show that as the physical sense-organed 'I' is to a physical object, so on the basis of language an analog 'I' is to an 'object' of consciousness. And a perception can indeed be an 'object' of consciousness, though not always.

But it is surprising that sophisticated philosophers and psychologists also confound sense perception and consciousness. In psychology, psychophysics began with this error. Fechner, a panpsychist, felt he was relating the entire universe of mind with that of matter by measuring the just noticeable differences in an attribute of sensation, and so forming the famous Weber-Fechner Law. Some psychologists even today who are studying perception think they are studying consciousness. As William James pointed out long ago, sense-perceptions are abstractions we impose on experience, not intrinsic parts of that experience itself. *His* starting point was only that 'thought goes on.' And so is mine.

Some modern philosophers also perpetuate this error. I imagine it is because of the old traditions about sense data. When Russell, looking for an example of consciousness, simply says, "I see a table," that is a highly artificial and misleading choice — like saying that a b flat is an example of a symphony. Yes, he is conscious of seeing a table (which incidentally he could probably do better with his eyes closed), but the seeing of the table is not consciousness but vision and an object of consciousness, even in the midst of what he was really conscious of, his argument. Russell should have picked a more ethologically valid example that was really true of his consciousness, that had really happened, such as "When will I find time to rework the *Principia*," or "How can I afford the alimony for the second Lady Russell." He would then have come to other conclusions. Such examples are consciousness in action. "I see a table" is not. Descartes would never have said, "I see a table, therefore I am."

Just as sense-perception is not due to consciousness, so with all the variety of perceptual constancies, as size, brightness, color, shape, which our nervous systems preserve under widely varying environmental changes of light, distance, angle of regard, or even our own moving about as objects retain their same position, called location constancy — all done without any help from consciousness.

So with another large class of activities we call *preoptive*, such as how we sit, walk, move. All these are done without consciousness, unless we decide to be conscious of them — the preoptive nature of consciousness. Even in speaking, the role of consciousness is more *interpolative* than any constant companion to my words. I am not now entering my lexical store-house and selecting items to string on these syntactic structures. Instead, I have what can best be described as an intention of certain meanings, what I call *structions*, and then linguistic habit patterns take over without further input from my consciousness. Similarly, in hearing someone speak, what are listeners conscious of? If the flow of phonemes or even the next level up of morphemes or even words, you would not be understanding what I am intending.

That consciousness is in everything we do is an illusion. Like asking a flashlight to turn itself on and look around a completely dark room to see if there is light, the flashlight would conclude that the room was every-where bright with light — which would be false.

A further error about consciousness stems from the beginning of empiricism when Gassendi used the Aristotelean term *tabula rasa*, and which Locke, who was basing the first two books of his *Essay* on Gassendi's *Syntagma Philosophicum*, anglicized as the mind's "white paper, void of all characters, without any ideas."[1] Had the camera been around at the time, I suggest Locke would have used it instead as his foundational metaphor. In experience, we take successive pictures of the world, develop them in reflection, bringing into existence concepts, memories, and all our mental furnishings.

---

1. John Locke, *An Essay Concerning Human Understanding*, Book II, Chapter 1.2. (London: Routledge, 1690/1910).

But that consciousness does not copy experience can be shown very easily: (a) by examining the memories we have and noting that they are not structured the way we experienced them, e.g. thinking of the last time you were swimming; most people, instead of the complicated multi-sensory experience as it actually was, tend to see themselves swimming from another point of view — something of course they have never experienced at all; or (b) by examining the absence of memories that we should have if consciousness did copy experience, e.g. knowing what letters go with what numbers on telephones which we have stared at thousands of times, or to sketch from memory while here in Kirchberg the main entrance-way to your office building — you will find it difficult. Conscious memory does not copy experience but reconstructs it as a must-have-been.

Empiricism is also the culprit in the belief that consciousness is necessary for learning. In the old terminology, mind had free ideas, copies of what was perceived, which when things were perceived together, their copies or ideas stuck together — the association of ideas. And since this presumably went on in consciousness, it seemed clear that learning or the association of ideas was the crucial criterion of consciousness. This was explicitly stated by many early psychologists. But a huge body of experimental research in later psychology suggests that this is far from true. Learning can be found in species and preparations where no one would think it plausible that something like introspective consciousness has anything to do with it whatever. In humans, all types of learning, conditioning, motor learning, and instrumental learning or operant conditioning can be shown to occur without any awareness or assistance from consciousness. This is not to say that consciousness does not play a role in human learning, as in decisions as to what to learn, or making rules of how to learn better, or consciously verbalizing aspects of a task. But this is not the learning itself. And my point is that consciousness is not necessary for learning to occur.

One could here bring up the well-known phenomenon of the automatization of habit, for when this happens to us, it seems that the task has required consciousness at the beginning, but as the habit is perfected consciousness eases away and the task is performed effortlessly. This same smoothing out and increased rapidity of a habit with practice is universal among all animals that can learn. Generally, in this ubiquitous phenomenon, it is not the lapsing of consciousness with improved performance so much as the lapsing of forced attention to components of the task. And attention, which is the focusing of sense-perception, is not necessarily conscious. If you take two coins in either hand, and toss them across each other so that the opposite hand catches each, this is a task that will take somewhere between 15 and 20 trials to learn. And if you wish to try this this evening, and monitor your consciousness while you are doing so, you will find that consciousness has little to do with the learning that seems to go on mechanically. You might be conscious of something about your clumsiness, or the silliness of what you are doing as you keep picking the coins up from the floor, until, at the point of success, your consciousness is somewhat surprised and even proud of your superior dexterity. It is the attention which has changed. Automatization is a diminution of attention, not consciousness.

Consciousness is also not necessary for thinking or reasoning, a somewhat shocking statement. But in 1901, Karl Marbe as a graduate student at Würzburg performed the most simple and yet most profound experiment of his day.[2] Using his professors as subjects, each of whom was highly experienced in introspective experiments, he asked them to make a simple judgment between two identical looking weights as to which was the heavier. Against the background of the experimental psychology of the time, the result was astonishing. There was no conscious content for the actual judgment itself, although such a judgment was embedded in the consciousness of the problem, its materials, and technique. So began what came to be called the Würzburg School of Imageless Thought, which lead through experiments by Ach, Watt, Külpe and others to concepts such as set, *aufgabe*, and determining tendency — which I have renamed structions. Structions are structures like instructions given to the nervous system, that, when presented with the materials to work on, result in the answer automatically without any conscious thinking or reasoning. This phenomenon applies to most of our activities, all the way from such simplicities as judging weights to solving problems to scientific and philosophical activity. Consciousness studies a problem and prepares it as a struction, a process which may result in a sudden appearance of the solution as if out of nowhere. During World War II, British physicists used to say that they no longer made their discoveries in the laboratory; they had their three B's where their discoveries were made: the bath, the bed, and the bus. And this process on a smaller scale is going on in me at present as

---

2. Karl Marbe, *Experimentell-Psychologische Untersuchungen uber das Urteil, eine Einleitung in die Logik* (Leipzig: Engelmann, 1901).

my words are as if chosen for me by my nervous system after giving it the struction of my intended meaning.

Finally in this list of mistakes about consciousness, a word about its location. Most people — with possibly the present company excepted who have thought long about the problem, and so placed it 'out there' in the intellectual domain — tend to think of their consciousness, much as Descartes, Locke, and Hume did, as a space usually located inside their heads. There is of course no such actual space whatever. The space of consciousness, which I shall hereafter call mind-space, is a functional space that has no location except as we assign one to it. To think of our consciousness as inside our heads is, because of all our words like introspection, internalization, etc. a very natural but arbitrary thing to do. I certainly don't mean to say that consciousness is separate from the brain; by the assumptions of natural science, it is not. But we use our brains in riding bicycles, and yet no one considers that the location of bicycle riding is inside our heads. The phenomenal location of consciousness is arbitrary.

To sum up so far, we have shown that consciousness is not all mentality, not to be equated with sensation or perception, that it is not a copy of experience, nor necessary for learning, nor even necessary for thinking and reasoning, and has only an arbitrary and functional location. As a prelude to what I am to say later, I wish you to consider that there could have been at one time human beings who did most of the things we do — speak, understand, perceive, solve problems, etc. — but who were without consciousness. I think this is a very important possibility.

So far this is almost going back to a radical behaviorist position. But what then is consciousness, since I regard it as an irreducible fact that my introspections are as real as so-called "external" perceptions, though with a distinguishably incongruent quality? My procedure here will be to outline in a somewhat terse fashion a theory of consciousness and then to explain it in various ways.

Subjective conscious mind is an analog of what we call the real world. It is built up with a vocabulary or lexical field whose terms are all metaphors or analogs of behavior in the physical world. Its reality is of the same order as mathematics. It allows us to short-cut behavioral processes and arrive at more adequate decisions. Like mathematics, it is an operator rather than a thing or a repository. And it is intimately bound with volition and decision.

Consider the language we use to describe conscious processes. The most prominent group of words used to describe mental events are visual. We 'see' solutions to problems, the best which may be 'brilliant' or 'clear' or possibly 'dull', 'fuzzy', 'obscure.' These words are all metaphors, and the mind-space to which they apply is generated by metaphors of actual space. In the space we can 'approach' a problem, perhaps from some 'view-point' and 'grapple' with its difficulties. Every word we use to refer to mental events is a metaphor or analog of something in the behavioral world. And the adjectives that we use to describe physical behavior in real space are analogically taken over to describe mental behavior in mind-space. We speak of the conscious mind as being 'quick' or 'slow,' or of somebody 'nimble-witted' or 'strong-minded' or 'weak-minded' or 'broad-minded' or 'deep' or 'open' or 'narrow-minded.' And so like a real space, something can be at the 'back' of our mind, or in the 'inner-recesses' or 'beyond' our minds.

But, you will remind me, metaphor is a mere comparison and cannot make new entities like consciousness. A proper analysis of metaphor shows that it can. In every metaphor there are at least two terms, the thing we are trying to express in words, the *metaphrand*, and the term produced by a struction to do so, the *metaphier*. These are similar to what I. A. Richards calls the tenor and the vehicle, terms more suitable to poetry than to philosophical analysis. I have chosen metaphrand and metaphier instead to have more of the connotation of an operator by echoing the arithmetic terms of mulitplicand and mulitplier. If I say the ship plows the sea, the metaphrand is the way the bow goes through the water and the metaphier is a plow.

As a more relevant example, suppose we are a person back at the formation of our mental vocabulary, and we have been trying to solve some problem or to learn how to perform some task. To express our 'see' is the metaphier, drawn from the physical behavior from the physical world, that is applied to this otherwise inexpressible mental occurrence, the metaphrand. But metaphiers usually have associations that we are calling paraphiers that then project back into the metaphrand as what are called paraphrands, and, indeed, creating new entities. The word 'see' has associations of seeing in the physical world and therefore of space, and this space then becomes a paraphrand as it is united with this inferred mental event called the metaphrand.

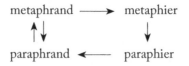

In this way the spatial quality of the world around us is being driven into the psychological fact of solving a problem (which as we remember needs no consciousness). And it is this associated spatial quality that, as a result of the language we use to describe such psychological events, becomes with constant repetitions this functional space of our consciousness, or mind space. This mind-space I regard as the primary feature of consciousness. It is the space which you preoptively are 'introspecting on' or 'seeing' at this very moment.

But who does the 'seeing'? Who does the introspecting? Here we introduce analogy, which differs from metaphor in that the similarity is between relationship rather than between things or actions. As the body with its sense organs (referred to as I) is to physical seeing, so there develops automatically an analog 'I' to relate to this mental kind of 'seeing' in mind-space. The analog 'I' is the second most important feature of consciousness. It is not to be confused with the self, which is an object of consciousness in later development. The analog 'I' is contentless, related I think to Kant's transcendental ego. As the bodily 'I' can move about in its environment looking at this or that, so the analog 'I' learns to 'move about' in mind-space concentrating on one thing or another.

A third feature of consciousness we are calling *narratization*, the analogic simulation of actual behavior, an obvious aspect of consciousness which seems to have escaped previous synchronic discussions of consciousness. Consciousness is constantly fitting things into a story, putting a before and an after around any event. This feature is an analog of our physical selves moving about through a physical world with its spatial successiveness which becomes the successiveness of time in mind-space. And this results in the conscious conception of time which is a spatialized time in which we locate events and indeed our lives. It is impossible to be conscious of time in any other way than as a space.

There are other features of consciousness which I shall simply mention: *concentration*, the 'inner' analog of perceptual attention; and its opposite, *suppression*, by which we stop being conscious of annoying thoughts, the analog of turning away from annoyances in the physical world; *excerption*, the analog of how we sense only one aspect of a thing at a time; and *consilience*, the analog of perceptual assimilation; and others. In no way is my list meant to be exhaustive. The essential rule here is that no operation goes on in consciousness that was not in behavior first.

Cognitive psychologists are sometimes justly accused of the habit of reinventing the wheel and making it square, and then calling it a first approximation. I would demur from agreement that that is true in the development that I have just outlined, but I would indeed like to call it a first approximation. Consciousness is not a simple matter and it should not be spoken of as if it were. Nor have I mentioned the different modes of conscious narratization such as verbal, perceptual, bodily, or musical — all of which seem quite distinct with properties of their own. But it is enough, I think, to allow us to go back to the evolutionary problem as I stated it in the beginning and which has caused so much trouble in biology, psychology, and philosophy. When did all this 'inner' world begin?

We have said that consciousness is based on language. This means that generations of effort to search out the origin of consciousness in animal evolution have been incorrect and in vain. If consciousness is a group of operations learned on the basis of language, then it follows that only species with language are conscious, and that means — in spite of recent questionable discussions of sign language in chimpanzees and animal communication systems — only human beings, and only at some point after the evolution of language.

When did language evolve? Elsewhere I have outlined ideas of how language could have evolved from call modification, what has been called the "Wahee, Wahoo model" which is at present in competition with several others. But such theorizing points to the late Pleistocene on several grounds: (1) Such a period coincides with an evolutionary pressure for verbal communication in the hunting of large animals, (2) it coincides with the astonishing development of the particular areas of the brain involved in language, and (3), what is unique in this theory, it corresponds to the archeological record of an explosion of tool-making, for we know that language is not communication merely, but also an organ of perception, directing attention and holding attention on a particular task. This dating means that language is no older that 50,000 years, which means that consciousness developed sometime between that date and, say, the present.

It is fortunate for this problem that by 3000 B.C., human beings have learned the remarkable ability of writing. It is therefore obvious that our first step should be to look at the early writings of mankind to see if there is evidence of an analog 'I' narratizing in a mind-space. Briefly and summarily, there is no such evidence in any writing up to approximately 1000 B.C., and this includes the older portions of texts as well known as the *Iliad*.

How then did anyone decide what to do? The evidence of many sorts in all the civilizations from 9000 B.C. up through the time of the *Iliad* clearly indicates that human beings heard voices, what we would regard as auditory hallucinations, voices called gods, emanating from somewhere in the brain, even as the hallucinated voices that occur in many normal people today, as well as in various forms of mental illness.

This is what is called the bicameral mind on the metaphier of a bicameral legislature, a word incidentally which has no good translation in German and so may be puzzling to some of you. It simply means that human mentality at this time was in two parts, a decision making part and a follower part, and neither part was conscious in the sense in which I have described consciousness. And I would like to remind you here of the rather long critique of consciousness which I began my talk, which demonstrated that human beings could speak and understand, solve problems, and do much that we do but without being conscious. So could bicameral man. In his everyday life he was a creature of habit, but when there came some kind of problem that needed a new decision or a more complicated solution than habit could provide, that decision stress was enough to instigate an auditory hallucination, which, because such individuals had no mind-space in which to question or rebel, had to be obeyed.

I think it can easily be inferred that human beings with such a mentality had to exist in a special kind of society, one rigidly ordered in strict hierarchies with strict expectancies organized into the mind so that such hallucinations preserved the social fabric. And such was definitely the case. Bicameral kingdoms were all hierarchical theocracies, with a god, often an idol, as throughout Mesopotamia, at its head from whom hallucinations seemed to come, or else, more rarely, with a human being who was divine being the head of state, as in Egypt. The evidence that these early civilizations were organized by hallucinated voices called gods, I have collected elsewhere and need not go into at this time.

So far in my talk, I have discussed two of the four hypotheses of my talk. The first, which I have spent the most of my allotted time upon as being most pertinent to this symposium, is that consciousness is grounded in the ability of language to make metaphors and analogies. The second hypothesis is that in early times, there was a different non-conscious mentality called the bicameral mind. The third hypothesis is simply that one followed the other in history.

Actually, there are two possibilities here. A weak form of the theory I am presenting would state that, yes, consciousness is based on language, but instead of it being so recent, it began back at the beginning of the bicameral mentality of hearing voices. Both systems of mind then could have gone on together, until the bicameral mind became unwieldy and was sloughed off, leaving consciousness on its own as the medium of human decisions. This is an extremely weak position because it could then explain almost anything and is almost undisprovable.

The strong form is of greater interest and is as I have stated it in introducing the concept of the bicameral mind. It sets an astonishingly recent date for the introduction into the world of this remarkable privacy of covert events which we call consciousness. The date is slightly different in different parts of the world, but in the Middle East where bicameral civilization began, the date is roughly 1000 B.C.

This dating I think can be seen in the evidence from Mesopotamia where the breakdown of the bicameral mind, beginning about 1200 B.C., is quite clear. It was due to chaotic social disorganizations, to overpopulation, and probably to the success of writing in replacing the auditory mode of command. This breakdown resulted in many practices which we would now call religious which were efforts to return to the lost voices of the gods, e.g. prayer, religious worship, and particularly the many types of divination which are new ways of making decisions by supposedly returning to the directions of gods.

In Greek literature, beginning with the Linear B Tablets, going through the *Iliad* and the *Odyssey*, through the lyric and elegiac poets of the next two centuries, to Solon, provides the clearest description of the breakdown of the bicameral mind and the development of the vocabulary of consciousness on the basis of metaphor. Such words as *thumos*, *phrenes*, *kardia*, *psyche* change from external objective referents to internal mental functions.

Another record of the same period is the Hebrew Testament of the Bible and it too is in agreement. The Prophets of Israel were those left over bicameral or semi-bicameral persons who heard and could relay the voice of Yahweh with a convincing authenticity, and who were therefore prized in their societies as reaching back to the lost bicameral kingdom. The words of such prophets should be compared with the later Books of Wisdom such as Ecclesiastes, and then, of course, with the New Testament which teaches a kind of reformed Judaism for conscious people. Recently, my associate, Dr. Michael Carr, an expert in ancient Chinese texts, has demonstrated the same development of consciousness in the language of the successive sections of the *Shijing* at approximately the same time period.[3]

But is this consciousness or the concept of consciousness? This is the well-known "use-mention" criticism which has been applied to Hobbes and others, as well as to the present theory. Are we not confusing here the concept of consciousness with consciousness itself? My reply is that we are fusing them, that they are the same. As Dan Dennett has pointed out in a recent discussion of this theory,[4] there are many instances of mention and use being identical. The concept of baseball and baseball are the same thing. Or of money, or law, or good, and evil. Or the concept of this Wittgenstein symposium, and this Wittgenstein symposium are the same thing.

That consciousness is based on language, that there existed a different kind of mentality called the bicameral mind, and that one followed the other are my first three hypotheses. The fourth I shall only mention briefly, as it is quite separable from the other three hypotheses and not germane to the symposium. It is a neurological model for the bicameral mind. It states that the neural substrate for the god side of the bicameral mind was what corresponds to Wernicke's area on the right cerebral hemisphere, and that this particular location processed and learned all admonitory information in a person's life and organized it into what are heard as auditory hallucinations in order to transfer such directions to the opposite or so-called dominant hemisphere. If we use present day schizophrenics as examples of this process (schizophrenia being a partial relapse to the bicameral mind), we do find evidence that this is so. Moreover, the increasing and I must add overpopularized findings on right hemispheric function agree with this model.

In closing, I would like to point out that if we are correct that consciousness began only 3,000 years ago, this theory opens new areas for philosophical analysis as well as offering new ways to look at many ancient

3. Michael Carr, "The *Shi* 'Corpse/Personator' Ceremony in Early China," in Marcel Kuijsten (ed.), *Reflections on the Dawn of Consciousness* (Henderson, NV: Julian Jaynes Society, 2006).

4. Daniel Dennett, "Julian Jaynes's Software Archeology," *Canadian Psychology*, 1986, *27*, 2.

philosophical problems: the historical invention and rise of ethics along with its vocabulary and of law as a replacement for the voices of gods, the development of philosophy itself as a pattern of knowledge to fill the vacuum left by the retreating gods, the historical origin of the concept of truth, and therefore of science, and of course history. I like to think that perhaps one of the reasons for the towering greatness of Greek philosophy is because the conscious world was all so new and therefore so clear, from which we could infer how our long intellectual history may work as an inhibition on our abilities and achievements.

And, of course, the greatest problem of all, the mind-body problem: the theory I have presented provides a very real solution. It restates the duality that we have been trying to understand for so long as not between mind and body, but between consciousness and everything else. This duality began only 3,000 years ago. Before then, there was no consciousness-body problem whatever. And since then human nature has been ineradicably changed.

# CHAPTER 18

# Sensory Pain and Conscious Pain

IT IS WIDELY AGREED among clinicians treating pain problems that there are at least two kinds of pain, although what pain phenomenon fit into which category is not entirely settled. The categories are usually referred to as acute and chronic or nocioceptive and psychological or, as in the present paper, sensory and operant.

Professor Rachlin has written an exciting and stimulating paper. It is particularly commendable because he has been able to spread his argument so as to bring together experimental psychology and the best of modern philosophical thinking. But the two main questions, I think, need further exploration.

*Is Chronic Pain an Operant?*

In street language this means that chronic pain is always fulfilling some purpose of the patient, either getting sympathy or a pension, avoiding work or war, reenacting a hurt-child–caring-parent relationship in surrogate, getting noticed by nurses or family, feeling important with important-sounding medicines, or, as emphasized in the paper, obtaining medication, particularly narcotics. It should be pointed out here, of course, that all such explanations in human patients are interpretations after the fact. There is no *experimental* evidence that this is the case, although I would agree with Rachlin that it often seems so.

A recent study should make us worry about oversimplified interpretations, however. In the burn unit of the Harborview Medical Center in Seattle, Dr. Alan Dimick has tried a self-administered morphine procedure. Instead of receiving from the nurse the standard dose of 2–4

Article by Julian Jaynes first published in *Behavioral and Brain Sciences*, Vol. 8, Issue 1 as commentary on the article "Pain and Behavior" by Howard Rachlin. © 1985 Cambridge Journals. Reproduced with permission.

milligrams every 2–4 hours, the patient pushes a button to receive the drug. As Dr. Dimick states the results,

> We are finding that if the patient is allowed to push the button and get his own dose of morphine, the patient usually pushes the button for a lesser amount of drugs than if the physician orders it or if the nurse gives it. And this method provides a much better pain control.[1]

I think this shows that what the patient is feeling is a combination of sensory pain and anxiety, and what is reduced by self-administration is the latter. It is well known that feelings of control over pain diminish it.[2] At any rate, it is not exactly what one would expect on the operant model.

There is also a logical fallacy here. The fact that operant training, as in the Fordyce therapy,[3] reduces pain is an important and welcome result, but it does not therefore follow that the pain was an operant in the first place. Because an alternative behavior can be learned does not mean that the original behavior was learned as well. For example, adaptation to a sensory stimulus that produces an innate response is indeed a form of learning, but that doesn't mean that the original response to the stimulus was learned. What is needed to make the point is a controlled laboratory experiment in which an introspectively real pain in a normal subject is learned in order to obtain some future reinforcement.

### Is Pain Merely Pain Behavior?

The central difficulty for most of us with Rachlin's courageous position is his insistence that pain *is* pain behavior and nothing else. As Rachlin understands it, most of us wish to say that there is a sensory pain and then our conscious reaction to it, and that psychological pain is at least an event that goes on in consciousness (where the word "in" is to be taken metaphorically). Indeed, if Rachlin wished to incorporate consciousness (or a theory of private events) in his perception of the pain problem and agree with me that consciousness was learned on the basis of language at

---

1. Alan Dimick as quoted in Driver, 1984.

2. Kenneth S. Bowers, "Pain, Anxiety, and Perceived Control," *Journal of Consulting and Clinical Psychology*, 1968, *32*.

3. For a critical review of Fordyce and other operant techniques in the treatment of pain (as well as a masterly review of the entire subject), see Ronald Melzack and Patrick Wall, *The Challenge of Pain* (New York: Basic Books, 1983), pages 333–337.

a particular point in history to obtain very specific consequences,[4] then he could call consciousness an operant (and correctly so), fitting consciousness into neobehaviorism in a consistent way. In animals pain is pain behavior, but in humans every sensory pain has its analog in consciousness as what can be called conscious pain. And then he could merge the concepts of operant pain and conscious pain.

But for this to work out to explain some of the data, the referents of that cardinal term *reinforcement*, wide enough as they already are, would have to include reinforcement by other conscious analogs, particularly ideas of the conscious self. Then we could speak of intrinsic reinforcement by emitting an operant that is consistent with some preconceived notion of who one is in various senses. So successfully functioning healthy individuals maintain their good behaviors as such behaviors are constantly being reinforced by consistencies with good and reasonable self-images — as consciousness of their own behaviors tell them, something that can only happen with consciousness. On the other hand, patients with what most of us might think of as detrimental behaviors such as pain or neurotic symptoms may learn or maintain their distressing symptoms when those symptoms are reinforced by some long-learned though perhaps erroneous self-conception.

*Phantom Pain*

Such a possibility would greatly expand the pain data that Rachlin could explain. The problem of chronic pain in amputated limbs or occasionally in breasts after mastectomy and sometimes even in teeth after multiple extractions is an example. Almost all amputees experience some phantom limb sensations. Even Lord Nelson when he lost an arm in a naval engagement at Tenerife wrote back to a friend that he could still sense his missing arm, and he took this as evidence for the existence of his eternal soul — a considerable conscious reinforcement.[5]

In recent times, approximately half of amputees have phantom limb pain of some kind and of varying durations. It is more severe in youth

4. Julian Jaynes, *The Origin of Consciousness in the Breakdown of the Bicameral Mind* (Boston: Houghton Mifflin, 1976).

5. Nelson also lost an eye but never reported on whether he sensed a phantom eye. I once knew a gaunt elderly blind man who roamed around Wiltshire with the help of a young boy. Both eyes had been enucleated. One morning he leaned over to me, stretching open one of his empty sockets with his fingers, and said, "You see — they're growing again! Just about the size of pearls! I saw them in the mirror this morning." I suggest this is an instance of phantom anatomy and its substantiation by "sensation."

(though absent in infancy) and roughly proportional to the duration and intensity of suffering before amputation. Others usually have phantom itching or cramps. To me it seems clear that this has something to do with consciousness of a body image, perhaps a denial that anything is missing in the great wish to be whole again. I recently interviewed such a case, which I think is of sufficient interest to mention here.[6]

Seven years ago, B.W., then 30 years of age, of high school education, was pushing a stalled car on the highway when a following car crashed into him. He was next conscious of his right foot and ankle being close to his right eye, and wondered what they were doing there. His pain then began. Some hours later at the hospital, surgeons first tried to save his leg but then had to amputate it just above the knee. Recovering from the anesthetic and told that his leg had had to be amputated, he denied that this was so, claiming he could still wiggle his toes and feel himself doing so in the absent leg. Two months later, because of complications, he had to have a second amputation just below the hip. He then made a complete recovery, both physically and psychologically. Presently he is well employed and is an avid amputee athlete taking part in their Olympics. He also counsels other amputees during their recovery.

But ever since his own amputation, beginning at the hospital, he has had phantom pain. This consists of a series of 10 or 15 sharp jabbing pains in the ankle or sometimes the arch of the amputated leg. At first such series occurred quite frequently, but now after seven years he may go for a month without pain, followed by a month when it happens almost every day. The pain is as severe as originally, perhaps waking him up at night, or while he's sitting down.

His wife, who is in therapy for anxiety attacks that on the surface do not seem to be related to her husband's problems, was also interviewed. She stated that during the attacks, "he almost passes out, is in a cold sweat, sometimes almost jumping off the couch with it." The wife seemed to exaggerate the pain of her husband while the husband spoke about it in a matter-of-fact way, not being particularly interested in any therapy for his phantom pain.

A possible operant scenario could be constructed, perhaps, that the husband's problems with his amputation were keeping the couple together, that his pain was being reinforced by his wife's concern, perhaps contributing to

---

6. I met with these patients in my capacity as a consultant with the Richmond Center of Charlottetown, Canada, directed by William Lawlor. I am grateful to Dr. Wayne Matheson for discussion on this problem, as well as to Dr. Frank Wheelock of Boston.

her own problems. But on further questioning, he revealed something that neither husband nor wife had realized before, that his attacks of phantom pain occurred only when his prosthesis was unattached.

While an operant explanation is possible for this particular case, it could not be complete without consciousness and the importance of a whole body image. This then would allow phantom pain to fit into operant terminology, particularly when one remembers the denial and the wiggling of toes with which his recovery began. It is as if having taken off his prosthesis, B.W. is reminded that he does not have a whole body. And then occasionally later, as if he were asking himself like an unbelieving child, "Have I really lost my leg?", the phantom pain, as an emitted response, is proof for a few minutes that the leg is still there, the momentary consciousness of which is the reinforcement. Thus, through seeing consciousness an operant, these phenomena could be included in an operant explanation.[7]

But when I consider some of the extreme debilitating forms of chronic pain, such as phantom pain in some paraplegics or after avulsion of the brachial plexus, I have to part company from reinforcement ideas. Such pain seems far too severe for an operant theory to deal with.

## An Alternative View

I would like to suggest a slightly different categorization that sorts things out in a way different from acute *versus* chronic or sensory *versus* operant. I would propose the distinction I have mentioned above between sensory pain and conscious pain. Animals and early humans had sensory pain. But with the advent of consciousness around the beginning of the first millennium B.C. began sensory pain plus its analog in consciousness, which complicates all pain with anxieties, depressions, hopelessness, anger, memory flashbacks, and feelings of attack upon the conscious self.

---

7. I should point out that there is an alternative, more sensory explanation to the case of B.W. without his prosthesis. This is that the tactile stimulation around the stump with his prosthesis on could possibly have eliminated the phantom pain. While there is no evidence that such mild tactile stimulation can function this way, there is evidence that vigorous vibration (W.R. Russell and J.M.K. Spalding, "Treatment of Painful Amputation Stumps," *British Medical Journal*, 1950, *2*), or pounding the stump many times was done a few decades ago (on the theory that "the nerves would wear out"), or electrical shock to the stump (Patrick D. Wall and William H. Sweet, "Temporary Abolition of Pain in Man," *Science*, 1967, *155*) bring relief from phantom limb pain in some cases. Perhaps such violence provides an insistent reminder to some deep level of consciousness that the limb stops there. In any case, this phenomenon of relief of phantom limb pain by a functional prosthesis has not, to my knowledge, been reported before and should be researched.

And this is complicated by the evidence that sensory pain can be delayed or even abolished by consciousness — evidence that gate-control theory would explain in a different way. This new type of pain and pain control develops in history at the same time as there are large changes in the nature of emotions.[8] Pain in the conscious human is thus very different from that in any other species. Sensory pain never exists alone except in infancy or perhaps under the influence of morphine when a patient says he has pain but does not mind it. Later, in those periods after healing in which the phenomena usually called chronic pain occur, we have perhaps a predominance of conscious pain.

*Recruitment*

But consciousness is not something floating above and apart from bodily physiology; it is part of it and constantly interacting with it, although we are not even close to understanding its neural substrate. One of the phenomena of consciousness is called recruitment, as when, for example, someone fantasizing about sexual behavior will thereby occasion physiological responses in erectile tissues, which then continue to recruit other physiological responses together with hormonal changes, the feedback from which keeps cuing the fantasy until it is difficult to turn conscious attention to other things. The process is similar in pain. Consciousness of pain, cued by a host of emotional and situational and hormonal variables, recruits sensory pain until it is difficult to turn attention away.

A common example is a patient saying that on awaking in the morning he is free of pain. But as soon as he thinks about getting out of bed, the pain begins. Then he remembers that he is ill, that he doesn't feel well the way he used to. And once out of bed he may experience low-intensity pain until the phone rings, at which time there is a sudden dramatic increase.

Or a woman who finds a lump in her breast and worries if it is cancerous. She may suddenly feel pain in the breast that may then increase in severity and even spread to the shoulder and arm over time. Later, if her physician assures her that the lump is of no consequence, there is usually a sudden total relief from the pain.[9] In this view, the difference between acute and chronic pain resides in the different ratios of sensory and conscious pain as well as their instigation. Thus the dichotomy could be

8. Julian Jaynes, "A Two-Tiered Theory of Emotions," *Behavioral and Brain Sciences*, 1982, 5. Reprinted as Chapter 16 of this volume.

9. Ronald Melzack and Patrick D. Wall, *The Challenge of Pain* (New York: Basic Book, 1983), p. 247.

sensory-instigated for acute pain and consciousness-instigated for chronic pain. So by changing consciousness through imagery or other means, one should be able to decrease the latter.

## Predictions

If this is the case, then certain dramatic predictions follow. If consciousness was learned sometime after 1000 B.C. (as I argue, Jaynes 1976), there should be no evidence of conscious pain or chronic pain in texts around or before that date. Indeed, in ancient Proto-Indo-European (before 2000 B.C.) there is no word for pain or hurt at all, although there are words for wounds and cuts. And in the oldest parts of the *Iliad*, written down about 850 B.C. but relayed by oral tradition from earlier times, there are extremely gory descriptions of bloody woundings and terrible disembowelments, but hardly any notice of discomfort so caused. Rachlin is right for ancient Troy: Pain is merely pain behavior. In contrast, one should look at Plato's *Philebus* of about 350 B.C. for a quite modern-sounding discussion of pain and suffering (as well as a remarkable description of itching beginning at 46D).

Also, neither chronic pain nor phantom limbs should appear in infants, before the age of about three, when consciousness begins to be learned. There is some evidence that this is true.[10] Also, in nonhuman animals there should be no chronic pain and no phantom limbs: Before the present proliferation of veterinarians, one used to see three-legged dogs often, but I know of no observation of such a dog turning to lick or nibble the absent leg, as would a normal dog with a hurt leg.

How does conscious pain generation work? Probably in many ways. Association and recruitment is the most obvious. Perhaps language is also a medium of such unfortunate learning. The patient asks himself, do I still hurt? And back comes the pain with such immediacy. In fact, I suggest that that is precisely what it is. Pavlovian conditioning rather than operant conditioning. In the period of sensory-instigated pain, sensory pain produces conscious pain. But sensory pain is being paired with verbalizations, such as the statement "I hurt." So that later such a verbalization, even in monitoring form, produces the conscious pain response, which then could

---

10. Marianne L. Simmel, "Phantom Experiences Following Amputation in Childhood," *Neurosurgery and Psychiatry*, 1962, *25*.

be followed by recruitment as well as perhaps being maintained by the operant reinforcements mentioned by Rachlin.

If this is so, we can see why Fordyce, at least in his original study,[11] did not ask his improving patients whether they still felt pain, since that is precisely the kind of question and solicitousness that his operant training is trying to abolish. It is a Heisenbergian situation. And yet that still remains the question to which most of us wish to know the answer.

---

11. Wilbert E. Fordyce, Roy S. Fowler, and Barbara Delateur, "An Application of Behavior Modification Technique to A Problem of Chronic Pain," *Behvaior Research and Therapy*, 1968, 6.

# CHAPTER 19

# Consciousness and the Voices of the Mind

F EW PROBLEMS HAVE HAD as interesting an intellectual trajectory
through history as that of the mind and its place in nature. Before
1859, the year that Darwin and Wallace independently proposed natural
selection as the basis of evolution, this issue was known as the mind/body
problem with its various and sometimes ponderous solutions. But after
that pivotal date, it came to be known as the problem of consciousness
and its origin in evolution.

Now the first thing I wish to stress this afternoon is this problem. It is
easy for the average layman to understand. But paradoxically, for philosophers, psychologists, and neurophysiologists, who have been so used to a
different kind of thinking, it is a difficult thing. What we have to explain
is the contrast, so obvious to a child, between all the inner covert world
of imaginings and memories and thoughts and the external public world
around us. The theory of evolution beautifully explains the anatomy of
species, but *how* out of mere matter, mere molecules, mutations, anato-
mies, can you get this rich inner experience that is always accompanying
us during the day and in our dreams at night? That is the problem we will
consider in this symposium.

*Previous Solutions*

Previous solutions have been illusory. One of the most difficult but historically interesting (associated with philosophers such as Perry[1] or
Whitehead[2]) was a vague analogy that came to be called neo-realism. It

Adapted from Julian Jaynes's Invited Bauer Lecture presented at the McMaster-Bauer Symposium on
Consciousness at McMaster University in 1983. First printed in *Canadian Psychology*, Vol. 27, Issue 2.
© 1986 Canadian Psychological Association. Permission granted for use of material.

1. Ralph B. Perry, *Present Philosophical Tendencies* (London: Longmans, Green, and Co., 1912).

2. Alfred North Whitehead, *Science and the Modern World* (Cambridge: Cambridge University Press, 1925).

seemed to be saying that because interacting matter could be reduced to mathematical relationships, in some ways like our own perceptions and interpersonal relationships, therefore consciousness originates in matter itself. Unfortunately, this much too abstract notion is having a bit of a renaissance today in a different way with some physicists because of some of the astonishing results in quantum physics.[3]

Another more popular solution was due to Darwin himself. In the last paragraph of *The Origin of Species*,[4] he implies that God created mind and body in the first primitive organisms and then both evolved in parallel together. But this sunk the problem in metaphysics, and it was soon realized that there should be some criterion of consciousness. It seemed obvious in the empiricist climate of the time that this was learning. So the question became: when did learning originate in evolution? Many people don't realize that the reason so many psychologists were studying animal learning, like maze-learning in rats, in the first two decades of this century, was to study animal consciousness on a primitive level and so trace out its evolution. As Dr. Witelson pointed out in her thoughtful introduction, this was indeed the focus of my early work for many years, but which I now see has nothing to do with consciousness. This error, I think, comes from John Locke and empiricism: The mind is a space where we have free ideas somehow floating around and that is consciousness. And when we perceive things in contiguity or contrast or some of the other so-called laws of association, their corresponding ideas stick together. Therefore, if you can show learning in an animal, you are showing the association of ideas which means consciousness. This is muddy thinking. I will be returning to this error in a moment.

Then, of course, there were other solutions — the helpless spectator theory of Huxley,[5] that consciousness just watched behavior and could do nothing. But if that is true, why is it there at all? And so there followed emergent evolution, which was meant to save us from such a pessimistic view. It was most fully developed by Lloyd Morgan,[6] although the idea goes back to the nineteenth century. A simple example is water: If you take hydrogen and oxygen you can't derive the wetness of water from either. Wetness is an emergent. Similarly, when in evolution there

3. E.g., Eugene Wigner, "The Place of Consciousness in Modern Physics," in Charles Muses & Arthur M. Young (eds.), *Consciousness and Reality* (New York: Outerbridge & Lazard, 1972).

4. Charles Darwin, *The Origin of Species* (New York: New American Library of the World, 1859/1958).

5. Thomas Henry Huxley, *Collected Essays* (New York: Appleton, 1896).

6. C. Lloyd Morgan, *Emergent Evolution* (London: Williams and Co., 1923).

is a certain amount of brain tissue, then suddenly you get consciousness. Consciousness is an emergent, underived from anything before. It is also having a renaissance in the writings of some neuroscientists today. On analysis, it generates no hypotheses and tells us nothing about any processes involved. Emergent evolution is a label that bandages our ignorance.

What I shall now present is a different kind of solution and one that has surprised me in the wealth of specific and testable hypotheses which it generates, and surprised me in the directions into which my work has been forced. But first we must face squarely the question of what is consciousness. And as a preface to that, I will first outline a few things that consciousness is not.

## *What Consciousness Is Not*

First, consciousness is not all of mentality. You know this perfectly well. There are so many things that the nervous system does automatically for us. All the variety of perceptual constancies — for example, size, brightness, color, shape, which our nervous systems preserve under widely varying environmental changes of light, distance, angle of regard, or even our own moving about in which objects retain their same position, called location constancy — all done without any help from introspective consciousness.

So with another large class of activities that can be called *preoptive*, such as how we sit, walk, move. All these are done without consciousness, unless we decide to be conscious of them — the preoptive nature of consciousness. Even in speaking, the role of consciousness is more *interpolative* than any constant companion to my words. I am not now consciously entering my lexical storehouse and consciously selecting items to string on these syntactical structures. Instead, I have what can best be described as intentions of certain meanings, what I call *structions*, and then linguistic habit patterns which take over without further input from my consciousness. Similarly, in hearing someone speak, what are you, the listeners, conscious of? If it were the flow of phonemes or even the next level up of morphemes or even words, you would not be understanding what I am intending.

Consciousness is sometimes confused even with simple sense perception. Historically, we inferred and abstracted ideas of sense perception from a realization of our sense organs, and then, because of prior assumptions about mind and matter or soul and body, we believed these processes to be due to consciousness — which they are not. If any of you still think that consciousness is a necessary part of sense perception, then I think you are forced to follow a path to a *reductio ad absurdum*: you would then have to say that since all animals have sense perception, all are conscious, and so on back through the evolutionary tree even to one-celled protozoa because they react to external stimuli, or one-celled plants like the alga chlamydomonas with its visual system analogous to ours, and thence to even amoeboid white cells of the blood since they sense bacteria and devour them. They too would be conscious. And to say that there are ten thousand conscious beings per cubic millimeter of blood whirling around in the roller-coaster of the vascular system in each of us here this afternoon is a position few would wish to defend.

That consciousness is in everything we do is an illusion. Suppose you asked a flashlight in a completely dark room to turn itself on and to look around and see if there was any light — the flashlight as it looked around would of course see light everywhere and come to the conclusion that the room was brilliantly lit when in fact it was mostly just the opposite. So with consciousness. We have an illusion that it is all mentality. If you look back into the struggles with this problem in the nineteenth century and early twentieth century, this is indeed the error that trapped people into so much of the difficulty, and still does.

Second, consciousness does not copy experience. This further error about consciousness stems from the beginning of empiricism when Locke spoke of the mind's "white paper, void of all characters, without any ideas" on which experience is copied.[7] Had the camera been around at the time, I suggest Locke would have used it instead of blank paper as his foundational metaphor. In experience, we take successive pictures of the world, immerse them in the developer of reflection, and watch concepts, memories, and all our mental furnishings come into existence.

But that consciousness does not copy experience can be shown very easily: (a) by examining the absence of memories that we should have if consciousness did copy experience, such as knowing what letters go with what numbers on telephones — although we have stared at the matter thousands of times, most of us cannot say — and countless other examples; or (b) by examining the memories we have and noting that they are not structured the way we experience them, such as thinking of the last time you were swimming — to take an example from Donald Hebb.[8]

7. John Locke, *An Essay Concerning Human Understanding*, Book II, Chapter 1.2 (London: Routledge, 1690/1910).

8. Donald Hebb, "The Mind's Eye," *Psychology Today,* 1961, *2,* 54–68.

Most people, instead of thinking of the complicated visual, thermal, pro-
prioceptive, respiratory experience as it actually was, tend to see themselves swimming from another point of view — a bird's eye view perhaps
— something of course they have never experienced at all. The conscious
memory does not copy experience but reconstructs it as a must-have-
been. This view is similar to some of the recent constructivist theories of
memory.

Third, consciousness is not necessary for learning — which I referred
to a moment ago as the mistake I labored under for so long. If we look
at the most primitive kinds of learning, such as Pavlovian conditioning,
it occurs in preparations such as the hind leg of a beheaded cockroach
for which no one would think that consciousness is plausible. And in
humans not only does consciousness not assist in acquisition of conditioned responses, it destroys conditioning once the human being is conscious of the contingences.[9]

Learning motor skills seems to happen without much consciousness
as well. This was studied extensively in the 1920s in relation to telegraphy,
stenography, and the like, occupations which were very important back
then. The learning seemed to the subjects to be "organic" — that was one
of their words. They were surprised that consciousness did not seem to
enter into this learning the way they expected it might.

A more complicated kind of learning is instrumental learning, or
operant conditioning, or we would call it learning solutions to problems.
This is the old psychological problem called learning without awareness.
Psychologists will remember the Greenspoon effect[10] and some of the
studies on the instrumental learning of little muscular movements without consciousness,[11] and many others. It is more problematical than I can
go into here, but I think that we can show that instrumental learning can
occur without consciousness.

This is not to say that consciousness does not play a role in these different types of human learning. It does, as in decisions as to what to learn, or
making rules of how to learn better, or consciously verbalizing aspects of a
task. But this is not the learning itself. And my point is that consciousness
is not necessary for learning to occur.

---

9. Gregory Razran, *Mind in Evolution* (Boston: Houghton Mifflin, 1971).

10. Joel Greenspoon, "The Reinforcing Effect of Two Spoken Sounds on the Frequency of Two Responses," *American Journal of Psychology*, 1955, *68*, 409–416.

11. Ralph F. Hefferline, Brian Keenan and Richard A. Harford, "Escape and Avoidance Conditioning in Human Subjects without Their Observations of the Response," *Science*, 1959, *130*, 1338–1339.

One could here bring up the well-known phenomenon of the automatization of habit; for when this happens to us, it seems that the task has required consciousness at the beginning; but as the habit is perfected, consciousness eases away and the task is performed effortlessly. This same smoothing out and increased rapidity of performance of a habit with practice is universal among all animals that learn. Generally, in this ubiquitous phenomenon, it is not necessarily or basically the lapsing of consciousness with improved performance so much as the lapsing of forced attention to components of the task. And attention, specifically external attention, which is the focusing of sense perception, is not necessarily conscious. Take two coins in either hand, and toss them across each other until you learn to catch each with the opposite hand. This is a task that will take somewhere between 15 and 20 trials to learn. And if you wish to try this this evening, and monitor your consciousness while you are doing so, you will find that consciousness has little to do with the learning that seems to go on mechanically. You might be conscious of something about your clumsiness, or the silliness of what you are doing as you keep picking the coins up from the floor, until, at the point of success, your consciousness is somewhat surprised and even proud of your superior dexterity. It is the attention which has changed. Automatization is a diminution of attention, not of consciousness.

The fourth thing for which consciousness is not necessary, and it may seem rather paradoxical, is thinking or reasoning. Here we are getting into perhaps the major problem in this area: the definition of our terms, particularly terms such as thinking and reasoning. If we take the simplest definition of thinking, I think we can show indeed that consciousness is not necessary for it. This concerns one of the forgotten experiments of psychology. It is indeed so simple to us today that it seems silly. And yet to me it is as important in the history of psychology as the very complicated Michelson-Morley experiment is in the history of physics.[12] As the latter showed that the aether did not exist, setting the stage for relativity theory, so the experiment I am about to describe showed that thinking is not conscious, setting the stage for the kind of theorizing I am describing here.

The experiment I refer to was first done in 1901 by Karl Marbe, a graduate student at Würzburg back in a scientific world when consciousness was being intensively studied for the first time.[13] Using his professors

12. Lloyd Swenson, *The Etherial Aether: A History of the Michelson–Morley–MillerAether-Drift Experiments, 1890–1930* (Austin: University of Texas Press, 1972).

13. Karl Marbe, *Experimental-psychogische Untersuchungen über das Urteil, eine Einleitung in die Logik*

as subjects, each of whom had had extensive experience of experiments in introspection, he asked them to make a simple judgment between two identical-looking weights as to which was the heavier. Against the background of the experimental psychology of the time, the result was astonishing. There was no conscious content for the actual judgment itself, although such a judgment was embedded in the consciousness of the problem, its materials, and technique.

So began what came to be called the Würzburg School of Imageless Thought, which led through experiments by Ach, Watt, Külpe, and others[14] to concepts such as set, *aufgabe*, and determining tendency — which I have renamed *structions*. Structions are like instructions given to the nervous system, that, when presented with the materials to work on, result in the answer automatically without any conscious thinking or reasoning. And this phenomenon applies to most of our activities, from such simplicities as judging weights to solving problems to scientific and philosophical activity. Consciousness studies a problem and prepares it as a struction, a process which may result in a sudden appearance of the solution as if out of nowhere. During World War II, British physicists used to say that they no longer made their discoveries in the laboratory; they had their three B's where their discoveries were made — the bath, the bed, and the bus. And, as I have mentioned earlier, this process on a smaller scale is going on in me at present as I am speaking: my words are as if chosen for me by my nervous system after giving it the struction of my intended meaning.

Finally, in this list of misconceptions about consciousness, a word about its location. Most people, with possibly the present company excepted, who have thought long about the problem and so placed it "out there" in the intellectual domain, tend to think of their consciousness, much as Descartes, Locke, and Hume did, as a space usually located inside their heads. Particularly when we make eye-to-eye contact, we tend to — in a subliminal way — infer such space in others. There is of course no such space whatever. The space of consciousness, which I shall hereafter call *mind-space*, is a functional space that has no location except as we assign one to it. To think of our consciousness as inside our heads, as reflected in and learned from our words like introspection or internalization, is a very natural but arbitrary thing to do. I certainly do not mean to say that

(Leipzig: Engelmann, 1901).

14. See discussions by E.G. Boring, *A History of Experimental Psychology* (New York: Appleton Century, 1929); George Humphrey, *Thinking* (London: Methuen, 1951); or David J. Murray, *A History of Western Psychology* (Engelwood Cliffs: Prentice-Hall, 1983).

consciousness is separate from the brain; by the assumptions of natural science, it is not. But we use our brains in riding bicycles, and yet no one considers that the location of bicycle riding is inside our heads. The phenomenal location of consciousness is arbitrary.

To sum up so far, we have shown that consciousness is not all mentality, not necessary for sensation or perception, that it is not a copy of experience, nor necessary for learning, nor even necessary for thinking and reasoning, and has only an arbitrary and functional location. As a prelude to what I am to say later, I wish you to consider that there could have been at one time human beings who did most of the things we do — speak, understand, perceive, solve problems — but who were without consciousness. I think this a very important possibility.

So far this is almost going back to a radical behaviorist position. But what then is consciousness, since I regard it as an irreducible fact that my introspections, retrospections, and imaginations do indeed exist? My procedure here will be to outline in a somewhat terse fashion a theory of consciousness and then to explain it in various ways.

### What Consciousness Is

Subjective conscious mind is an analog of what we call the real world. It is built up with a vocabulary or lexical field whose terms are all metaphors or analogs of behavior in the physical world. Its reality is of the same order as mathematics. It allows us to short-cut behavioral processes and arrive at more adequate decisions. Like mathematics, it is an operator rather than a thing or a repository. And it is intimately bound with volition and decision.

Consider the language we use to describe conscious processes. The most prominent group of words used to describe mental events are visual. We 'see' solutions to problems, the best of which may be 'brilliant' or 'clear' or possibly 'dull,' 'fuzzy,' 'obscure.' These words are all metaphors, and the mind-space to which they apply is generated by metaphors of actual space. In that space we can 'approach' a problem, perhaps from some 'viewpoint,' 'grapple' with its difficulties. Every word we use to refer to mental events is a metaphor or analog of something in the behavioral world. And the adjectives that we use to describe physical behavior in real space are analogically taken over to describe mental behavior in mind-space. We speak of the conscious mind as being 'quick' or 'slow,' or of somebody being 'nimble-witted' or 'strong-minded' or 'weak-minded' or 'broad-minded' or 'deep' or 'open' or 'narrow-minded.' And so like a real space, something can be at the 'back' of our mind, or in the 'inner recesses' or 'beyond' our minds. But, you will remind me, metaphor is a mere comparison and cannot make new entities like consciousness. A proper analysis of metaphor shows quite the opposite. In every metaphor there are at least two terms, the thing we are trying to express in words, the *metaphrand*, and the term produced by a struction to do so, the *metaphier*. These are similar to what Richards[15] called the tenor and the vehicle, terms more suitable to poetry than to psychological analysis. I have chosen metaphrand and metaphier instead to have more of the connotation of an operator by echoing the arithmetic terms of multiplicand and multiplier. If I say the ship plows the sea, the metaphrand is the way the bow goes through the water and the metaphier is a plow.

As a more relevant example, suppose a person, back in the time at the formation of our mental vocabulary, has been trying to solve some problem or to learn how to perform some task. To express his success, he might suddenly exclaim (in his own language), "Aha! I 'see' the solution." 'See' is the metaphier, drawn from the physical behavior from the physical world, that is applied to this otherwise inexpressible mental occurrence, the metaphrand. But metaphiers usually have associations called *paraphiers* that project back into the metaphrand as what are called *paraphrands* and, indeed, create new entities. The word 'see' has associations of seeing in the physical world and therefore of space, and this space then becomes a paraphrand as it is united with this inferred mental event called the metaphrand.

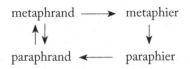

In this way the spatial quality of the world around us is being driven into the psychological fact of solving a problem (which as I indicated needs no consciousness). And it is this associated spatial quality that, as a result of the language used to describe such psychological events, becomes, with constant repetition, this spatial quality of our consciousness or mind-space. This mind-space I regard as the primary feature of

15. Ivor A. Richards, *The Philosophy of Rhetoric* (New York: Oxford University Press, 1936).

consciousness. It is the space which you preoptively are introspecting on at this very moment.

But who does the 'seeing?' Who does the introspecting? Here we introduce analogy, which differs from metaphor in that the similarity is between relationships rather than between things or actions. As the body with its sense organs (referred to as I) is to physical seeing, so there develops automatically an *analog 'I'* to relate to this mental kind of 'seeing' in mind-space. The analog 'I' is the second most important feature of consciousness. It is not to be confused with the self, which is an object of consciousness in later development. The analog 'I' is contentless, related I think to Kant's transcendental ego.[16] As the bodily 'I' can move about in its environment looking at this or that, so the analog 'I' learns to 'move about' in mind-space concentrating on one thing or another. If you 'saw' yourself swimming in our earlier example, it was your analog 'I' that was doing the 'seeing.'

A third feature of consciousness is *narratization*, the analogic simulation of actual behavior. It is an obvious aspect of consciousness, which seems to have escaped previous synchronic discussions of consciousness. Consciousness is constantly fitting things into a story, putting a before and an after around any event. This feature is an analog of our physical selves moving about through a physical world with its spatial successiveness, which becomes the successiveness of time in mind-space. And this results in the conscious conception of time, which is a *spatialized time* in which we locate events and indeed our lives. It is impossible to be conscious of time in any other way than as a space.

There are other features of consciousness which I shall simply mention: *concentration*, the 'inner' analog of external perceptual attention; *suppression*, by which we stop being conscious of annoying thoughts, the analog of turning away from annoyances in the physical world; *excerption*, the analog of how we sense only one aspect of a thing at a time; and *consilience*, the analog of perceptual assimilation; and others. In no way is my list meant to be exhaustive. The essential rule here is that no operation goes on in consciousness that was not in behavior first. All of these are learned analogs of external behavior.

Psychologists are sometimes justly accused of the habit of reinventing the wheel and making it square and then calling it a first approximation. I would demur from agreement that this is true in the development I

---

16. Immanuel Kant, *Critique of Pure Reason* (London: Macmillan 1781/1929).

have just outlined, but I would indeed like to call it a first approximation. Consciousness is not a simple matter and it should not be spoken of as if it were. Nor have I mentioned the different modes of narratization in consciousness such as verbal, perceptual, bodily, or musical, all of which seem quite distinct with properties of their own. But it is enough, I think, to allow us to go back to the evolutionary problem as I stated it in the beginning and which has caused so much trouble in biology, psychology, and philosophy.

When did all this 'inner' world begin? Here we arrive at the most important watershed in our discussion. Saying that consciousness is developed out of language means that everybody from Darwin on, including myself in earlier years, was wrong in trying to trace out the origin of consciousness biologically or neurophysiologically. It means we have to look at human history after language has evolved and ask when in history did an analog 'I' narratizing in a mind-space begin.

When did language evolve? Elsewhere[17] I have outlined ideas of how language could have evolved from call modification, which has been called the 'Wahee, Wahoo model' and is at present in competition with several others.[18] But such theorizing points to the late Pleistocene or Neanderthal era on several grounds: (1) such a period coincides with an evolutionary pressure over the last glacial period for verbal communication in the hunting of large animals; (2) it coincides with the astonishing development of the particular areas of the brain involved in language; and (3), what is unique in this theory, it corresponds to the archeological record of an explosion of tool artifacts, for we know that language is not just communication, but also acts like an organ of perception, directing attention and holding attention on a particular object or task, making advanced tool-making possible. This dating means that language is no older than 50,000 years, which means that consciousness developed sometime between that date and the present.

It is fortunate for this problem that by 3000 B.C., human beings have learned the remarkable ability of writing. It is therefore obvious that our first step should be to look at the early writings of mankind to see if there is evidence of an analog 'I' narratizing in a mind-space. The first writing is in hieroglyphics and cuneiform, both very difficult to translate, especially

---

17. Julian Jaynes, "The Evolution of Language in the Late Pleistocene," *Annals of the New York Academy of Sciences*, 1976, *28*, 312–325. Reprinted as Chapter 9 of this volume.

18. Mary Maxwell, *Human Evolution: A Philosophical Anthropology* (New York: Columbia University Press, 1984).

when they refer to anything psychological. And therefore we should go to a language with which we have some continuity, and that is of course Greek. The earliest Greek text of sufficient size to test our question is the *Iliad*. Are the characters in the *Iliad* narratizing with an analog 'I' in a mind-space and making decisions in this way?

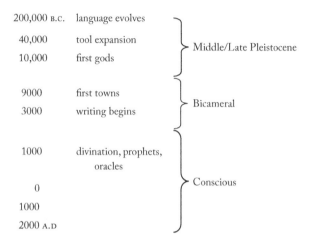

## The Bicameral Mind

First, let me make a few generalizations about the *Iliad*. To me and to roughly half of classicists, it is oral poetry, originally spoken and composed at the same time by a long succession of *aoidoi* or bards. As such, it contains many incongruities. Even after it was written down in about 800 B.C., perhaps by someone named Homer, it had many interpolations added to it even centuries later. So there are many exceptions to what I am about to say, such as the long speech of Nestor in Book XI for example, or the rhetorical reply of Achilles to Odysseus in Book IX.

But if you take the generally accepted oldest parts of the *Iliad* and ask, "Is there evidence of consciousness?" the answer, I think, is no. People are not sitting down and making decisions. No one is. No one is introspecting. No one is even reminiscing. It is a very different kind of world.

Then, who makes the decisions? Whenever a significant choice is to be made, a voice comes in telling people what to do. These voices are always and immediately obeyed. These voices are called gods. To me this is the origin of gods. I regard them as auditory hallucinations similar to, although not precisely the same as, the voices heard by Joan of Arc or

William Blake.[19] Or similar to the voices that modern schizophrenics
hear.[20] Similar perhaps to the voices that some of you may have heard.
While it is regarded as a very significant symptom in the diagnosis of
schizophrenia, auditory hallucinations also occur in some form at some
time in about half the general population.[21] I have also corresponded with
or interviewed people who are completely normal in function but who
suddenly have a period of hearing extensive verbal hallucinations, usually
of a religious sort. Verbal hallucinations are common today, but in early
civilization I suggest that they were universal.

This mentality in early times, as in the *Iliad*, is what is called the *bicameral mind* on the metaphier of a bicameral legislature. It simply means that
human mentality at this time was in two parts, a decision-making part
and a follower part, and neither part was conscious in the sense in which
I have described consciousness. And I would like to remind you here of
the rather long critique of consciousness with which I began my talk,
which demonstrated that human beings can speak and understand, learn,
solve problems, and do much that we do but without being conscious. So
could bicameral man. In his everyday life he was a creature of habit, but
when some problem arose that needed a new decision or a more complicated solution than habit could provide, that decision stress was sufficient
to instigate an auditory hallucination. Because such individuals had no
mind-space in which to question or rebel, such voices had to be obeyed.

But why is there such a mentality as a bicameral mind? Let us go back
to the beginning of civilization in several sites in the Near East around
9000 B.C. It is concomitant with the beginning of agriculture. The reason
the bicameral mind may have existed at this particular time is because of
the evolutionary pressures for a new kind of social control to move from
small hunter-gatherer groupings to large agriculture-based towns or cities. The bicameral mentality could do this since it enabled a large group
to carry around with them the directions of the chief or king as verbal
hallucinations, instead of the chieftain having to be present at all times. I
think that verbal hallucinations had evolved along with the evolution of
language during the Neanderthal era as aids to attention and perseverance
in tasks, but then became the way of ruling larger groups.

19. See Julian Jaynes, "The Ghost of A Flea: Visions of William Blake," in M. Kuijsten (ed.), *Reflections
on the Dawn of Consciousness* (Henderson, NV: Julian Jaynes Society, 2006).

20. See Julian Jaynes, "Verbal Hallucinations and Preconscious Mentality," in M. Kuijsten (ed.), *Reflections on the Dawn of Consciousness* (Henderson, NV: Julian Jaynes Society, 2006).

21. Thomas B. Posey and Mary E. Losch, "Auditory Hallucinations of Hearing Voices in 375 Normal
Subjects," *Imagination, Cognition, and Personality*, 1983, 3, 99-113.

It can easily be inferred that human beings with such a mentality had to exist in a special kind of society, one rigidly ordered in strict hierarchies with strict expectancies organized into the mind so that hallucinations preserved the social fabric. And such was definitely the case. Bicameral kingdoms were all hierarchical theocracies, with a god, often an idol, at their head from whom hallucinations seemed to come, or, more rarely, with a human being who was divine and whose actual voice was heard in hallucinations.

Such civilizations start in various sites in the Near East and then spread into Egypt, later from Egypt into the Kush in southern Sudan and then into central Africa; while in the other geographical direction, they spread into Anatolia, Crete, Greece; and then into India and southern Russia; and then into the Malay Peninsula, where the ruins of another civilization have just been discovered in northern Thailand; then later into China. A millennium later, a series of civilizations begin in Mesoamerica leading up to the Aztec, and then partly independently and partly by diffusion another series of civilizations in the Andean highlands leading up to the Inca. And wherever we look there is some kind of evidence of what I am calling the bicameral mind. Every ancient historian would agree that all of these early civilizations are thoroughly religious, heavily dependent on gods and idols.

Where writing exists after 3000 B.C., we can see these bicameral civilizations much more clearly. In Mesopotamia the head of state was a wooden statue — wooden so it could be carried about — with jewels in its eyes, perfumed, richly raimented, imbedded in ritual, seated behind a large table (perhaps the origin of our altars) in the *gigunu*, which was a large hall in the bottom of a ziggurat. What we might call the king was really the first steward of this statue god. Cuneiform texts literally describe how people came to the idol-statues, asked them questions, and received directions from them. Just why the minds (or brains) of bicameral people needed such external props as idols for their voices is a question difficult to answer, but I suspect it had to do with the necessary differentiation of one god from another.

I also want to mention that the evidence from written texts, personal idols, cylinder seals, and the construction of personal names suggests that every person had a personal god. In Mesopotamia, it was his *ili*, which in Hebrew is perhaps from the same root as Eli and Elhohim. In Egypt, the personal god which had the same function was called a *ka*, a word which has been an enigma in Egyptology until now.

In connection with the personal god, it is possible to suggest that a part of our innate bicameral heritage is the modern phenomenon of the 'imaginary' playmate. According to my own research as well as other data,[22] it occurs in at least one-third of modern children between the ages of two and five years, and is believed now to involve very real verbal hallucinations. In the rare cases where the imaginary playmate lasts beyond the juvenile period, it too grows up with the child and begins telling him or her what to do in times of stress. It is therefore possible that this is how the personal god started in bicameral times, the imaginary playmate growing up with the person in a society of expectancies that constantly encouraged the child to hear voices and to continue to do so.

This, then, is the bicameral mind. I have not had time to discuss the variations between bicameral theocracies, but all were based on strict and stable hierarchies as I have stressed. At least some of such civilizations could be compared to nests of social insects, where instead of the social control being by pheromones from a queen insect, it was by hallucinatory directions from an idol. Everything went like clockwork providing there was no real catastrophe or problem.

## *The Breakdown of the Bicameral Mind*

But such a system is obviously precarious. The huge success of such agricultural bicameral civilizations inevitably leads to overpopulation and complexity, and given a time of social and political instability, bicamerality can break down like a house of cards. Some civilizations broke down frequently, as among the Mayans on this continent. A temple complex and city would be built up, last a few centuries, and then be completely abandoned, presumably because as the society became more and more populous, the voices did not agree anymore. Then after a few centuries as tribal bands, they would somehow get together again and another temple complex would be built up. This is why we find so many of these complexes that show evidence of their people suddenly leaving them.

In Egypt we find that the bicameral mind broke down between what is called the Old Kingdom and the Middle Kingdom, and then again

---

22. Jerome L. Singer and Dorothy G. Singer, *Television, Imagination and Aggression* (Hillsdale, N.J.: Erlbaum, 1984).

between the Middle and the New Kingdom. The evidence for these dark, chaotic periods is in the hieroglyphic writings after they occurred.

But in Mesopotamia, which was the most stable civilization in the world, there does not seem to have been a breakdown until around 1400 B.C. In the graphics of the period, gods are no longer depicted. In some instances kings beg in front of empty gods' thrones — nothing like that had ever occurred before. Another line of evidence is in the cuneiform literature. There is an epic called the Epic of Tikulti-Ninurta where for the first time in history, gods are spoken of as forsaking human beings. The greatest literature of the period, which is possibly the origin of the Book of Job, is the *Ludlul Bel Nemequi*, the first readable lines of which translate as:

> My god has forsaken me and disappeared,
> My goddess has failed me and keeps at a distance,
> The good angel who walked beside me has departed.

How similar to some of our Hebrew Psalms — Psalm 42, for example.

The reasons for this breakdown are several. The success of bicameral civilizations leads to overpopulation — as I have mentioned, and as is described in texts from the period. There are various huge catastrophes such as the Thera eruption, which is well known and may be the origin of Plato's myth of Atlantis. The ensuing tsunami crushed all the bicameral kingdoms around that part of the Mediterranean. Entire nations were destroyed or dislodged, resulting in large migrations of people invading other countries, looking for 'promised lands,' a place to settle down with their gods again and start another bicameral civilization. One of the reasons that we still have problems in this area of the world, I think, goes right back to this chaotic time.

Another cause is writing itself, because once something is written you can turn away from it and it has no more power over you, in contrast to an auditory hallucination, which you cannot shut out. Writing, particularly as used extensively in Hammurabi's hegemony, weakened the power of the auditory directions. The spread of writing, the complexities of overpopulation, and the chaos of huge migrations as one population invaded others: these are the obvious causes. And in this breakdown, various things started to happen, including I think the beginning of consciousness.

The immediate results of this loss of hallucinated voices giving directions are several and new in world history. The idea of heaven as where the gods have gone; the idea of genii or angels as messengers between heaven and earth; the idea of evil gods such as demons — all are new phenomenon. By 1000 B.C., people in Babylon were walking around draped with amulets and charms, which they wore to protect themselves from a huge variety of demons. Such charms have been found archaeologically in the thousands dating from this period.

## *The Beginning of Consciousness*

And then came the development of a new way of making decisions, a kind of proto-consciousness. All significant decisions previously had been based on the bicameral mind. But after its breakdown, after the hallucinated voices no longer told people what to do, there seem to have developed various other ways of discerning messages from the gods to make decisions. We call these methods divination. Throwing of lots, the simplest kind; putting oil on water and reading its patterns; dice; the movements of smoke; a priest whispering a prayer into a sacrificial animal, sacrificing it, and then looking at its internal organs to find out what the god intends. All of these were extensively and officially practiced. And then the method of divination that is still around, astrology. It is remarkable to go back and read the cuneiform letters of kings to their astrologers and diviners of around 1000 B.C.[23] These cruel Assyrian tyrants, who are depicted in their bas-reliefs as grappling with lions and engaging in fierce lion hunts, are, in their letters, meek and frightened people. They don't know what to do. Astrologers tell them, "You cannot move out of your house for five days"; "You must not eat this"; "You should not wear clothes today" — extraordinary strictures that official diviners would interpret as what the gods meant. It is interesting to note that not only has astrology lasted, but it is being followed by more people at present than ever before.

If we now move over to Greece just following the period I have been referring to in Mesopotamia, we can trace the bicameral mind as shown in the Linear B Tablets, then going through the *Iliad*, the *Odyssey*, through the lyric and elegiac poetry of the next two centuries, as in Sappho and Archilochus, until we get to Solon in 600 B.C. Solon is the first person who seems like us, who talks about the mind in the same way we might. He is the person who said "Know thyself," although sometimes that's given to the Delphic Oracle. How can you know yourself unless you have an

23. Robert H. Pfeiffer, *State Letters of Assyria* (New Haven: American Oriental Society, 1935).

analog 'I' narratizing in a mind-space and reminiscing or having episodic memory about what you have been doing and who you are? In Greece, then, one can see in detail the invention and learning of consciousness on the basis of metaphor and analogy (as I have described above) by tracing out through these writings the change in words like *phrenes*, *kardia*, *psyche* (what I have called "preconscious hypostacies") from objective referents to mental functions.

The same kind of development has been studied in ancient China by Michael Carr of the University of Otaru. Comparing the four successive parts of the most ancient collection of texts, the *Shijing*, he found the same internalization process for such words as *Xin*, until they become the concept of mind or consciousness in China.[24]

Another area of the world during this period where we can see this rise of consciousness is more familiar to most of you. This is among peoples who may have been refugees from the Thera eruption. The word for refugees in Akkad, the ancient language of Babylon, is the word *khabiru*, and this becomes our word Hebrew. The story of the Hebrews, or really one branch of the Hebrews, is told in what we call the Hebrew Testament or the Old Testament.

Those of you who know biblical scholarship will know that the Hebrew Testament is a patchwork of things put together around 600 B.C. — the date keeps coming forward. Using it as evidence is therefore something of a problem. But there are several ways of entering this mosaic of much-edited texts to test the theory, and here I shall mention only one. If we take the purer books, those that are not patchwork but are singly authored and that can be clearly and firmly dated, and compare the oldest with the most recent, such a comparison should reflect the differences in mentality we are referring to. The oldest of them is the Book of Amos, dating from about 800 B.C., and the most recent is the Book of Ecclesiastes, which comes from about 200 B.C.

I suspect that such prophets as Amos were those left-over bicameral or semi-bicameral persons in the conscious era who heard and could relay the voice of Yahweh with convincing authenticity, and who were therefore highly prized in their societies as reaching back to the secure authoritarian ways of the lost bicameral kingdom. Amos is not a wise old man but

---

24. Michael Carr, "Sidelights on *Xin* 'Heart, Mind' in the *Shijing*," *Proceedings of the 31ˢᵗ CISHAAN*, Tokyo and Kyoto, 1983, 8, 24–25. See also Michael Carr, "The *Shi* 'Corpse/Personator' Ceremony in Early China," in Marcel Kuijsten (ed.) *Reflections on the Dawn of Consciousness* (Henderson, NV: Julian Jaynes Society, 2006).

a shepherd boy brought in from the fields of Tekoa. Probably much of his life has been spent in the fields listening to older shepherds glorying in tales of Yahweh. Asked if he is a prophet, he does not even know what the word means. But periodically he bursts forth with "Thus sayest the Lord," as the King James Bible translates it, and out pours some of the most powerful passages in Jewish history with such an authenticity that he is always surrounded by scribes taking down his words.

Ecclesiastes is just the opposite. He begins by saying that "I saw in my heart that wisdom excelleth folly..." (2:13) — a metaphoric use of 'see.' Spatialized time is something that I have not dwelt upon, but I suggest it is one of the hallmarks of consciousness. We cannot think consciously of time apart from making a space out of it. And this is very much in evidence in Ecclesiastes as, for example, in that oft-quoted but still beautiful hymn to time that begins the third chapter. "For everything there is a season, and a time for every matter under heaven, a time to be born, and a time to die" and so on, with times like spaces for everything. Historically, we could go further into the New Testament and note the even greater importance of conscious internalization and changing behavior from within in contrast to Mosaic law that shaped behavior from without.

*Four Ideas*

I can sum up what I have said so far as three major ideas about the origin of consciousness. The first concerns the nature of consciousness itself and that it arises from the power of language to make metaphors and analogies. The second idea is the hypothesis of the bicameral mind, an early type of mentality. I think the evidence for its existence is unmistakable. Apart from this idea, there is a problem of explaining the origin of gods, the origin of religious practices in the back corridors of time that is so apparent with a psychological study of history. The bicameral mind offers a possibility to tie it all together and to provide a rationale for it. The third idea is that consciousness followed the bicameral mind. I have placed the date somewhere between 1400 B.C. and 600 B.C. This is a long period and that date may have to be adjusted. But I believe this to be a good approximation.

I would add here that there is a weak form of the theory. It says that consciousness could have begun shortly after the beginning of language or perhaps at certain times and places. After all, people could create metaphors at the beginning of oral language — that is how language grew. Consciousness could have originated in exactly the same way as I have described, and existed for a time in parallel with the bicameral mind. Then the bicameral mind is sloughed off at approximately 1000 B.C. for the reasons I have suggested, leaving consciousness to come into its own. This would provide easy *ad hoc* explanations for highly developed cultures such as Sumer which otherwise are a challenge to bicameral theory. But I do not choose to hold this weak theory because it is almost unfalsifiable. I think we should have a hypothesis that can be disproved by evidence if we are going to call it a scientific hypothesis. Also, the strong theory has a vigorous explanatory power in understanding many historical phenomena of the transition period. Further, I do not see why there would be a need for consciousness alongside of the bicameral mind if the latter made the decisions.

A fourth idea that I shall end with is a neurological model for the bicameral mind. I want to stress, however, that it is not at all a necessary part of the theory I have presented. Since the bicameral mind was so important in history, responsible for civilization, what could have been going on in the brain? The proper strategy in trying to answer such a question is to take the simplest idea and set about to disprove it. If it is disproved, you then go on to something more complicated.

The simplest idea, obvious I think to anyone, would involve the two cerebral hemispheres. Perhaps in ancient peoples — to put it in a popular fashion — the right hemisphere was "talking" to the left, and this was the bicameral mind. Could it be that the reason that speech and language function are usually just in the areas of the left hemisphere in today's people was because the corresponding areas of the right hemisphere once had another function? That is a somewhat questionable way to say it, because there are other reasons for the lateralization of function. But on the other hand, it raises issues that I like. What is an auditory hallucination? Why is it ubiquitous? Why present in civilizations all over the world?

If we assume that back in bicameral times all admonitory information was being processed in some proportion of the billions of neurons of the right hemisphere, and there stored, particularly in what corresponds to Wernicke's area in the posterior temporal lobe, until it needed to be accessed, how do such complicated processed admonitions get transferred across the cerebral commissures to the left or dominant hemisphere? And what if, as I have supposed,[25] the far, far fewer fibers of the two temporal gyri are the ones involved? And in fact, recent experimental evidence with monkeys indicates that intercommunication of major parts of the temporal lobes is via the anterior commissure.[26] The transfer of such information would be more efficiently done if it were put into some kind of code. And what better code is there than human language? So, would it not be interesting if indeed what might correspond to Wernicke's area in the right temporal lobe might be the area that was involved in storing up admonitory information, processing it in such a way that it produced answers to problems and decisions (which is what the bicameral mind is), and then used the code of language to get it across to the left hemisphere, the hemisphere that speaks, obeys, and manages behavior?

At the time that I was thinking in this primitive fashion, in the early 1960s, there was little interest in the right hemisphere. Even as late as 1964, some leading neuroscientists were saying that the right hemisphere did nothing, suggesting it was like a spare tire. But since then we have seen an explosion of findings about right hemisphere function, leading, I am afraid, to a popularization that verges on some of the shrill excesses of similar discussions of asymmetrical hemisphere function in the latter part of the nineteenth century[27] and also in the twentieth century.[28]

But the main results, even conservatively treated, are generally in agreement with what we might expect to find in the right hemisphere on the basis of the bicameral hypothesis. The most significant such finding is that the right hemisphere is the hemisphere which processes information in a synthetic manner. It is now well known from many studies that the right hemisphere is far superior to the left in fitting together block designs (Kohs Block Design Test), parts of faces, or musical chords.[29] The chief function of the admonitory gods was indeed that of fitting people and functions into these societies. I am suggesting that much of the difference we can observe today between hemisphere function can be seen as echoing the differences between the two sides of the bicameral mind.

25. Julian Jaynes, *The Origin of Consciousness in the Breakdown of the Bicameral Mind* (Boston: Houghton Mifflin, 1976/2000).

26. Marc L. Jouandet, Laurence J. Garey, and Hans-Peter Lipp, "Distribution of the Cells of Origin of the Corpus Callosum and Anterior Commissure in the Marmoset Monkey," *Anatomy and Embryology*, 1984, *169*, 45–59.

27. See Anne Harrington, "Nineteenth Century Ideas on Hemisphere Differences and 'Duality of Mind,'" *Behavioral and Brain Sciences*, 1985, *8*, 517–659.

28. See Sid J. Segalowitz, *Two Sides of the Brain* (Englewood Cliffs, N.J.: Prentice-Hall, 1983).

29. See M.P. Bryden, *Laterality: Functional Asymmetry In The Intact Brain* (New York: Appleton Century, 1982) and Sid J. Segalowitz, *Two Sides of the Brain* (Englewood Cliffs, N.J.: Prentice-Hall, 1983).

In summary, I would like to again repeat these four ideas or modules of the theory I have presented. First is the nature of consciousness and its origin in language, which can be empirically studied in the learning of consciousness in children, as well as in the study of changes of consciousness in recent history. The second idea is the bicameral mind, which can be studied directly in ancient texts and indirectly in modern schizophrenia. Third is the idea that consciousness followed bicamerality, which can be studied in the artifacts and texts of history. And the fourth is that the neurological model for the bicameral mind is related to the two hemispheres. And this can be studied in laterality differences today.

What I have tried to present to you is a long and complicated story. It leaves us with a different view of human nature. It suggests that what civilized us all is a mentality that we no longer have, in which we heard voices called gods. Remnants of this are all around us in our own lives, in our present-day religions and needs for religion, in the hallucinations heard particularly in psychosis, in our search for certainty, in our problems of identity. And we are still in the arduous process of adjusting to our new mentality of consciousness. The final thought I will close with is that all of this that is most human about us, this consciousness, this artificial space we imagine in other people and in ourselves, this living within our reminiscences, plans, and imaginings, all of this is indeed only 3,000 years old.

And that, ladies and gentlemen, is less than 100 generations. And from that I think we can conclude that we are all still very young. Thank you very much.

# CHAPTER 20

# The Dream of Agamemnon

A<small>NY THEORY OF MIND</small>, any theory of consciousness, has to also be a theory of dreams. And the theory I am representing very simply says that dreams are consciousness operating primarily during REM sleep. Now what does that mean? That means that all of these things in consciousness are what are so involved in dreams. In a dream you have mind-space, in a dream you have an analog 'I' that is going around doing different kinds of things, you have narratization, and what comes into prominent importance in dreams is *consilience* — or we can call it *conciliation*. My first word for it was *compatibization* but that takes a little bit long to say. This is the very obvious thing that comes in to create a lot of the bizarreness of dreams — where things are pushed and made to fit together when they do not really — and if we had the test of our external world we would not do it because our conciliations are much more automatic in our waking life. The other features of consciousness also fit into this.

When I say that, there is sometimes some consternation as to what this means, particularly when I mention that I feel that dreams begin of course with the reticular formation getting activated in the very same way that dream experts Allan Hobson and Robert McCarley say it does, which sets the stage for this kind of cortical activity to go on.

Various other kinds of things — such as trivia of the day; concerns of the day, or of the week, or of the month; internal sensations such as all kinds of things from illnesses, stomach ache, various kinds of pubescence, perhaps leading to sexual dreams; various kinds of muscle spasms — become conciliated into an ongoing narrative.

I remember once having a very vivid dream of walking through a flat field and I didn't realize I was getting a cramp in my leg, and just before it woke me up — it was very painful — this plain that I was walking

Transcribed and edited from a lecture presented by Julian Jaynes at the 2nd Annual Conference of the Association for the Study of Dreams, held at the University of Virginia, June 17–18, 1985. In the first portion of this lecture Jaynes provided a general overview of his theory. This was omitted here as the theory is described in greater detail in the previous chapter.

on started getting mountainous, and every time another mountain would appear. This is consilience. Oddly, this is not the bottom of the matter. There are a whole lot of cognitive processes going on here that I do not understand. But turning that cramp of the pain into a mountain to climb over; it is rather strange and interesting and I think that kind of thing, but probably not so dramatic, goes on all the time.

Also external sensations such as what we used to call *incorporation*. Talking to Allan Hobson about it last month, he and William Dement feel that the experiments that you try to do in the laboratory do not seem to work out very well. Nevertheless, we have a tradition going back to the nineteenth century of experimenting on incorporation, and I certainly know that during the imagery when you are just waking up that they do have incorporation.

I had a dream when I was writing one of these chapters that I was the captain of a huge ferryboat, one that I am very familiar with at the Straits of Northumberland in Canada where I have a summer home. This is a huge boat with many decks and I was guiding it to the dry dock, and turning it at right angles, and then I woke up and I realized that this was the new chapter I was trying to work on in my book — a big unwieldy kind of chapter that very carefully I had to guide into dry dock to think about. And the reason it was a ferryboat: it was raining outside and water was rushing through the spout and so on. So I think that is an example of the kind of incorporation in dreams that come just before you start to wake up.

I was very interested in incorporation too; particularly I thought what a wonderful chance it would be to study dreams in the astronauts. After all, if you are up there whirling around the Earth, and you are free-floating weightless in space, what kind of dreams would you have? Would you have flying dreams in the usual kind of sense? It does sound so exciting and promising to think of what kind of incorporations and how you would conciliate weightlessness. Would it be a joyful kind of dream, as people have good times when they are weightless? Well after the space shuttle trip last April, one dream that I collected as one of the astronauts announced it was that as he slept weightless — as they do every night — he dreamt that he was back on Earth in his home town and people came up to him and said, "What are you doing here? You're supposed to be up in that shuttle!" So much for incorporation.

But before you dismiss what I have just said as not getting at the depth of dreams, I would like to give you another example. It is going to start off as trivial, but you will see how as you get into this dream work, it all starts to build up and conciliate together and you get the kind of thing that would indeed result in some good interpretation.

Supposing on a trivial basis, because of the reactivating system, I just happen to have something like a beach — perhaps because I am going away for the summer to my summer home which is on the beach — and a hat, and an apple. I would conciliate those and narratize those together, just as in waking consciousness, just as you perhaps have done in your consciousness right now. So in my dream I would be walking along the beach with a hat on and eating an apple.

Now let us complicate it a little bit. Let us suppose that I am coming to give a talk at a conference, and there is always a bit of anxiety about that — am I going to leave my notes behind? Because in my dream — let us add a little anxiety to the dream — I forgot to put on my bathing suit. So, suddenly I am walking along — and this is all in the dream — and then I think, "Wouldn't it be awful if people were here?" Well let us build up that anxiety dream, so suddenly the people are there. And let us say that is getting conciliated with coming to a conference, and so there are a large group of people there. And there I am — what do I do? I go and rush into the water, to preserve some kind of modesty. But at the same time it is getting conciliated with giving a talk, let us say I am afraid that I am going to get disagreed with by everybody, and that therefore I would be sort of an outcast, let us say, and then let us say that the currents that I am trying to swim against are too great, so I get swept out to sea by these currents, away from the group that I came to speak to on the beach.

Well, all of that can be fitted together by a conciliation and narratization of trivia which sets the stage and then our concerns. Our concerns can be anything: anxiety, things we have had problems with — all kinds of things then get conciliated into this structure that consciousness is building.

I think that those of you who are dream therapists can see that indeed such images that consciousness can give you can then lead you to some of the dynamics of the patient. Once you take an anxiety, which is really mostly a narratization, and turn it into a concrete image like being swept away into the ocean, it gives you something to say: "Yes, okay, I have an anxiety problem, I am afraid I am going to get a hostile reaction." It keeps you thinking about it, and in therapy I think that is something that you want people to be doing. Therefore, I don't want anyone to think that I am throwing away dreams as not being of tremendous value in therapy.

Well, this brings me to the next section of my talk. If consciousness just beings at 1200 B.C. then indeed it follows as if night from day that people have only dreamt since that time. If what I have said is true, before 1200 B.C. there should be no dreams at all, or people should have dreamt very differently before that time. So next we want to look at the historical data to see if that makes any sense.

### Bicameral Dreams

Before I begin I would like to make a distinction between what I call vicarial and translocative dreams. All of our dreams are vicarial and all of them are translocative. Vicarial means you are doing something other than lying in your bed sleeping — you have an analog 'I' that can move around and do things. It is proof of consciousness. This means vicariously that you are doing something else. If you imagine yourself swimming right now, that is vicarial — you are not really swimming. The other term is translocative. If you think in your dream that you are anywhere else except in your bed, that is translocative (in another location), and for that you need consciousness. So consciousness dreams are all vicarial, translocative events.

What we are going to see now is if dreams before 1200 B.C. are indeed of that nature. If we go back to the *Iliad* there are four dreams. They are in fact simply carryovers from the bicameral mind and the state of paradoxical sleep. In Iliadic Greek, the word for dream is *oniero* — but it does not mean dream. It is the name of a god. There is no word for dream in ancient Greek.

Now let us look at what happens in the dream that opens Book Two, the great dream of Agamemnon, which is the title of my talk. Agamemnon is asleep in his tent, and in comes a god figure from Zeus called Oneiros. It seems as though everyone assumed that Zeus and the other gods had Oneiros around them all the time because he is the messenger god that comes to them at night.

Oneiros comes in, and looks like Nestor, who was one of the generals of the army, and stands at the head of Agamemnon and tells him essentially to get up and start the Trojan War. This common phrase "at the head" is used throughout the Greek literature, used in cuneiform literature, and we cannot be sure in hieroglyphic literature, but why that phrase "at the head?" — I don't know.

Agamemnon never thinks he is anywhere except in this bed — he cannot because he is not conscious — and he is never doing anything except sleeping. The Dream says to him (dream with a capital "D," because it is the name of the god): "You are asleep Agamemnon, now hear this…" Then of course afterwards, Agamemnon wakes up and goes and tells the others, and the Trojan War begins. That is probably the most important dream in the *Iliad*. It is not translocative and it is not vicarial — it is a straight, bicameral dream.

The next dream in the *Iliad* is the "Rhesus Dream," which is a very minor reference. It just says that before King Rhesus was killed by Diomedes, while sleeping in his encampment, he gasps in his sleep, "for evil dreams stood by his head that night" — that is all it says.

The next dream, however, is a longer one. This is Achilles's dream of Patroclus, after Patroclus has been killed. Patroclus comes in, and just like Oneiros with Agamemnon, says, "You are asleep Achilles," and then he goes on and complains to Achilles that he wants his bones to be buried with those of his friends. Achilles then wakes up and tries to grasp Patroclus who then falls gibbering into the earth. This is the first time in literary history that a dead person has appeared in someone's dream. The final dream in the *Iliad* is Priam's Dream in the twenty-fourth book: "You are sleeping among your enemies" warns the god Hermes, as Hermes stands at the head of sleeping Priam and advises him to escape.

Those are all of the dreams in the *Iliad*. Having come to the idea of the bicameral dream from the *Iliad*, this is a marvelous poem to try to read for both the ancient, bicameral mentality and the modern, coming mentality — because there are little bits of consciousness in it. So in coming to that, we should now go back and look at all of the earlier works and ask, "Is this consistent?" — so that we can say that before 1200 B.C., everyone only has bicameral dreams.

Let us go over the Hebrew world. Everyone here I think knows what is usually called the "Jacob's Ladder" dream. It should not be called Jacob's ladder — it should be a ziggurat. But the Hebrew word *sullam* was probably mistranslated. It is the only time it is ever used in the Bible and it is probably a ziggurat.

Jacob has been in trouble because he cheated his brother, and he lies down to go to sleep on the hillside which is now called Beth-El. He puts his head on a pillow of stones and dreams that he sees in front of him a ziggurat with Yahweh at the top and angels streaming up and down the steps at either side.

Jacob does nothing at all. He does not say anything — he is still asleep. Yahweh does not say to him "You are asleep Jacob, listen to me," as happened with the Greeks — nothing that forthright. He simply renews the covenant and everyone who knows Biblical history knows just how important this is for the sake of Israel.

It starts with this dream, which is not a conscious dream; it is a straight bicameral dream. When Jacob wakes up, he is sure it happened right there where he was sleeping. When you wake up, you do not think the dream happened right there in your bed and look under the covers. But this happened to Jacob — and I want you to be aware of that different mentality — so that he immediately says, "This is the gate of Heaven; this is the House of God, right at this particular spot," and he anoints those stones as Beth-El, which means the house or gate of God.

That is the most marvelous dream that happened. All of us, in any kind of Sunday School or Hebrew School, all learned this dream when we were children, and yet we were never aware of what a different kind of dream that was than anything we have. And here it is indicative of this earlier kind of mentality. There are four other dreams earlier than Jacob in Genesis, and they too are all bicameral but they are not as interesting.

After Jacob we have Joseph. Those of you who know your biblical history will immediately say, "What about Joseph, he interpreted the Pharaoh's dreams, and he is supposed to be Jacob's son?" Modern scholarship — and I am talking about Professor Donald Redford of Toronto, whose books I reference in my book — has examined this very carefully and has come to the conclusion that the Joseph stories were added much later.[1] They are at least 700 years later than Jacob and come from a very different kind of source. If you read it you can see it is not by the same author; it is a very different kind of vocabulary that is being used. But they have conscious dreams.

Now if we go further away from what you are familiar with, let us go back to the first dream ever recorded in the history of the world. The earliest dream is the dream of Djoser. Djoser was the pharaoh of about 2700 B.C. in Egypt who built the great step pyramid. The dream states that when he was sleeping he suddenly found the god Khnum standing over him — which is similar to "standing at the head" that we saw in the Greek

---

1. Donald B. Redford, *A Study of the Biblical Story of Joseph (Genesis 37–50)* (Leiden, Netherlands: E.J Brill, 1970).

passage. "I am Khnum, your great creator, my arms are around you to compose your body and to heal your limbs." And this goes on in a similar vein to say how he controls the Nile and he will bring prosperity. Djoser then wakes up quickly, saying, "My heart cutting off wearies" (meaning freed of fatigue), and issues a decree that the land will then be presented to the gods to tithe for his temple, this decree to be inscribed on the stele in the temple of Khnum.

That stele is not extant, it has somehow been destroyed. We know of this dream from another stele from the second century B.C., which this dream is believed to have been copied from. Some scholars think it is a fake dream, because it is giving all these lands to the priests. It may be a combination of things. But that is the first dream ever recorded in human history.

The next dream that we have, continuing in Egypt, is the dream of pharaoh Amenhotep about 1420 B.C., and it does not say very much of interest at all. The third dream that we have is of his successor Thutmose IV, and as those of you who have traveled in Egypt may know, when you see the Sphinx, between the paws of the Sphinx is a stele. This stele was erected by Thutmosis, the crown prince, between the paws of the Sphinx. It says he was on a lion hunt, and at noon he rested between the paws of the Sphinx and had this dream. This was a thousand years after the Sphinx was carved. During his dream it is described:

> Then he found the majesty of this noble god speaking from his own mouth as a father speaks to his son ... Behold me, look at me my son Tuthmosis. I am your father, Horemakhet Kepri Re Atum who gives you my kingly office on earth as foremost of the living, and you will wear the Crown of Upper Egypt, and the Crown of Lower Egypt ... to you shall belong the earth, in its length and its breadth, all which of the Eye of the All-Lord illuminates...

Until, at the end of the stele:

> Behold, my state is like one who is suffering and all my members are out of joint, for the sand and the desert, the sun which I am, presses upon me, I have waited to have you do what is in my heart, for I know you are my son and my champion. Approach, behold I am with you, I am your guide.

As he completed this, Thutmosis realizes he was to dig away the sand under the Sphinx, which he proceeds to do. In later centuries the sand accumulated and had to be dug away again. But that stele still remains, which has all this on it. It is one of the earliest recorded dreams, and it is a straight bicameral dream. We can go on through Egyptian history and show that there are other bicameral dreams right up until the conscious period about 1200 B.C., when there are hardly any reports of dreams, but there are some.

If we go to Mesopotamia, the first Mesopotamian dream is from the Stele of Vultures, about 2400 B.C. It is again a dream that says "it stood at the head of the dreamer." It is an obviously bicameral dream, but it has certain peculiarities which I don't quite understand.

Then in twelfth century B.C. there is the so-called autobiography of the Hittite king Hattusili. In it there are more dreams than in any other document in the ancient Near East, and all the dreams are bicameral. If you read this document you might think that the king is trying to assert his authority this way, by saying that the god Ishtar spoke to him in his dreams. But they are all bicameral, whether or not you think there was some hidden purpose to it.

Then we come to the great dream of Gudea. Gudea was the ruler of the city of Lagash in Southern Mesopotamia from approximately 2144–2124 B.C. It is a complicated dream because it has several parts. In the first part Gudea is ordered to build a temple. In the second part he goes on another night to a temple of Nanshe to have this explained to him. In the third part of the dream he has a visual hallucination of what we would call a blueprint of exactly how the temple should be built.

All of this is, remember, without conscious effort. These things simply come to the person so he can relate it to others and so he can, in this case, go and build the temple. Many of these dreams have to do with repairing and building temples.

Then we come down to Ashurbanipal, who was King of Assyria from 668–627 B.C. Ashurbanipal had a garden which contained a large tree and on it hung like Christmas tree ornaments the heads of all his conquered enemies festering in the sun. He was a ferocious tyrant who collected many bicameral dreams — yet he was not bicameral himself, he never related a bicameral dream in all his writings. But always his viziers would have these bicameral dreams stating that he was the chosen one of Marduk and things of that nature. He was the person that collected these dreams and developed a tremendous library. One of the important fires in history was the burning of his palace, which paradoxically had the effect of baking the clay cuneiform tablets, preserving them for posterity. The enormous collection of cuneiform tablets excavated from Ashurbanipal's library — as many as 30,000 — has taught us a great deal, and is where the epic of Gilgamesh comes from.

## Exceptions and Anomalies

I want to mention a couple of other things in the history of dreams. First I might mention something about the anomalies here. I talked about the royal inscription texts, which are the ones you can date very carefully. But there are also literary texts. There is the great *Ludlul bel nemeqi* (translated as "let me praise the lord of wisdom"), a Mesopotamian text from approximately 1300 B.C. that has three bicameral dreams in it. It is thought to be the origin of the Book of Job. It describes the problems of Shubshi-meshre-Shakkan, a prince who Marduk is trying to destroy. Everything bad happens to him: sicknesses, boils — everything that happens to Job happens to Shubshi-meshre-Shakkan. He does not understand what he has done wrong. Then he has the first dream in which a young man comes to him, and then the tablet is broken off, so we do not know what the young man said. He has a second dream in which a man who is an exorcist comes and in the dream hears a goddess telling him which incantations to do. Then he has a third dream in which a goddess comes in and says "everything is going to be alright," and this is followed by another priest or exorcist who then brings in a tablet on which Marduk has written something to the effect of "you're going to be okay." And this is the end; Shubshi-meshre-Shakkan gets rid of all his ills.

In the Gilgamesh tablets, which as I mentioned come from Ashurbanipal's library, there are no conscious dreams, although it is from the period where there could be. But there is one stray tablet that does not belong in that series, called the Pennsylvania Tablet (also referred to as Gilgamesh P), and no one knows where it came from. It is at the University of Pennsylvania now. Scholars, buyers, and dealers want to make things as old as possible. It could be a forgery. It has a plain, conscious dream on it. It is dated as coming from about 1500 B.C. but there is nothing on it to justify that, and I am skeptical of its accuracy. It is contrary to what I am saying and I felt in honesty I should bring in this anomaly that does not fit in with the rest.[2]

---

2. The Pennsylvania tablet was purchased from a dealer in 1914, who shortly thereafter sold a tablet to Yale University. Professors Morris Jastrow and Albert Clay write, "As to the provenance of our two tablets, there are no definite data" but go on to speculate that "it is likely that they were found by

Very briefly there are two so-called "dream books" and you can some-times find in the popular literature it stated that the dream books date back 3,000 years — don't believe it. What they are referring to is that in Ashurbanipal's library, in cuneiform, there are large numbers of omen texts. These omen texts go on and on to the effect of, "if something hap-pens, then something else is going to happen," with no logical connection at all.

In a few of these tablets, the statements begin with the phrase, "If in a dream…" Now there are three words that could mean dream in cunei-form: one of them is the same word for sleep and one of them means something else, so it could be that it is not intended to mean a dream at all.

But neither in this so-called dream book or in the Egyptian one is a single dream ever mentioned. It might have the heading off to one side, "If in a dream" and then it says "if he washes his hand in his urine he will eat little; if he sprinkles with his urine his sheepfolds will expand; if he directs his urine toward the sky the son of this man whom he will begat will become important but his days will be short."

Then this follows with a whole other text in which the verb is changed and we have a series of "if he pours his urine" in various ways and places, then various other things will happen. Other tablets describe if he sits in a certain way or if enters a gate in a certain way, goes to other cities in a certain way, and so on. That is all those tablets are, and I think it is a great mistake to call that a dream book.

If we look at Egyptian hieroglyphics, there is another omen book very similar to that, although it is supposed to predate it. It is not a dream book as we would think of it. It says things to the effect of, "If you are shot in white sandals, it is bad, it means roaming the earth" — that kind of thing. It is not what we would think of as a dream book; they are just popular writings.

---

natives in the mounds at Warka, from which about the year 1913, many tablets came into the hands of dealers." Even accurately dating of the tablets from Ashurbanipal's library is problematic. Jastrow and Clay note: "According to Bezold's investigation … the bulk of the tablets in Ashurbanapal's library are copies of originals dating from about 1500 B.C. It does not follow, however, that all the copies date from originals of the same time period. Bezold reaches the conclusion on the basis of various forms for verbal suffixes, that the fragments from the Ashurbanapal library date from three distinct periods ranging from before c. 1450 to c. 700 B.C." For further discussion see Morris Jastrow and Albert T. Clay, *An Old Babylonian Version of the Gilgamesh Epic: On the Basis of Recently Discovered Texts* (Yale University Press, 1920). —*Ed.*

*Bad Dreams*

I would just briefly mention then something about bad dreams. It is very interesting that at the time we develop consciousness we have the first concept of evil in terms of demons and all kinds of ways of getting rid of evil and demons. This is just at the time when conscious dreams are coming in. There was a belief back then that if you said something you created it. For example, in hieroglyphs, in the late period there is one hieroglyph that contains a snake, and they would draw a knife through it. Because to draw that in a tomb to them meant that the snake was alive, it was creating reality. So they killed it right there by drawing a knife through it, and that took away its power.

This type of belief made them afraid to recount a bad dream, because they believed that would create it in reality. So we see rituals designed to try to get rid of the badness of a dream. And what is the badness of a dream? Well, here is the closest example I could find. You will see there is not much. The dream which I have seen repeatedly, "I saw my dead father, I saw my dead mother, I saw Shamash the King, I saw an important person, I saw a prince, I saw a dead person, I saw a living person, I saw something I did not know, I traveled to an unknown country, I ate an unknown dish, in an unknown garden."

The idea of strangeness and difference seems to be important. It is a different mentality, and it is exciting to try to understand this.

[Recording ends.]

# CHAPTER 21

# Hearing Voices and the Bicameral Mind

A UDITORY VERBAL HALLUCINATIONS exist in varying percentages in
every population in the world where they have been studied. They
are of course most notable nowadays in severely stressed individuals that
we label schizophrenic. But, contrary to what many an ardent biological
psychiatrist wishes to think, they occur in normal individuals also, and
they are not always indicative of pathology. This has been known for over
a century.[1] The most recent study shows that 71% of college students have
had at least brief verbal hallucinations at some time.[2]

*Present Cases*

I have in my files letters from about a hundred correspondents who
have had hallucinations, all the way from a transsexual who as a boy suffered considerable sexual molestation and then as an adult after a spell
of Scientology became "overwhelmed" with voices until his sex change
operation when they "abated" (her word), to milder cases, such as torpe-
doed sailors during the war who conversed with an audible God for hours
in the water.

Most of my correspondents are men, but some are women, one of
whom had a single experience:

> I remember looking to the left car window to see if someone was
> speaking to me from there. The voice told me to write my funeral (of
> all things!) and when I got out a piece of paper and pen, the words
> poured visually into my head and I was hard-pressed to keep up. I lost
> parts. It was an intense experience after which I ended up weeping.

Article by Julian Jaynes first published in *Behavioral and Brain Sciences*, Vol. 9, Issue 3 as commentary
on the article "Verbal Hallucinations and Language Production Processes in Schizophrenia" by Ralph
E. Hoffman. © 1986 Cambridge Journals. Reproduced with permission.
1. See Fred H. Johnson, *The Anatomy of Hallucinations* (Chicago: Nelson-Hall, 1978).
2. Thomas B. Posey and Mary E. Losch, "Auditory Hallucinations of Hearing Voices in 375 Normal
Subjects," *Imagination, Cognition, and Personality*, 1983, *3*, 99-113.

This mixture of auditory and Belshazzar-like visual verbal hallucination is unique in my data.

The variety of auditory hallucinations is remarkable. Another case with whom I have had much correspondence and many telephone conversations is a professor in a technical school on the West Coast. A deeply religious man, he gradually began to hallucinate divine voices a few summers ago after becoming interested in spiritualism. The voices included a god of another universe, Yahweh as a false god, Lucifer, and a variety of lesser divinities and saints, "at least 20 in all... each with a particular mood, character, history, and personality." It is the most similar case to the famous case of Schreber I have ever heard of.[3]

On the other hand, some who have had continuing long-term hallucinated voices hear only one. An example I have come to know personally is an extremely successful and happy businessman who is sometimes teased by his wife and children for spending so much time in the evening with "Richard," a superior being who "dictates" to him reams of what I consider to be boring pseudo-profundities.

Some of these cases were at some times diagnosed as schizophrenic, but others never. These letters, unsolicited, are extremely articulate, even those from individuals who are continuing to hear their voices. This is not what would be expected on the basis of Hoffman's theory.


*The Evidence in History*

Other important evidence to be taken into account by any theory of hallucinations comes from various historical personages: William Blake who insisted he could teach anyone to listen to and see angels as he did, angels from whom he heard his poetry[4]; or his teacher, the astonishing polymath Emanuel Swedenborg, whose multiple hallucinations were written down into whole shelves of books that founded a new religion; or Joseph Smith and the Book of Mormon; or Muhammad hearing the Koran; or many other examples dating back to all the prophets and oracles and *aoidoi* of history. Or in our own era, Colonel Qaddafi of Libya, born a Bedouin, who according to numerous reports hears voices from time to time and periodically goes into the desert to communicate with them.

---

3. Daniel P. Schreber, *Memoirs of My Nervous Illness* (London: W. Dawson & Sons, 1955).

4. See Julian Jaynes, "The Ghost of A Flea: Visions of William Blake," *Art/World*, 1981, *5*, 3–6. Reprinted in Marcel Kuijsten (ed.), *Reflections on the Dawn of Consciousness* (Henderson, NV: Julian Jaynes Society, 2006).

*The Evidence in Children*

The spectrum of incidence of auditory hallucinations has to include not only normal schizophrenic adults but also children. Those who have studied the phenomena of "imaginary playmates" (which should read hallucinated playmates) are convinced that such children hear the "voices" of their (by us unseen) friends in their conversations with them.[5] In my own studies, I have found that about half of the women students at a religious college had had hallucinated playmates, half of these clearly remembering the pitch and quality of the voices. One of these women still has her hallucinated playmates, now grown up like her, who appear in times of stress, their voices clearly "heard" and not imagined. She is not psychotic.

*Verbal Hallucinations in A Nonverbal Population*

A further group that must be considered in any theory of verbal hallucinations has been discovered only recently.[6] These are cerebral palsied spastic-athetoid nonverbal congenital quadriplegics who have never spoken in their lives. They must be fed, bathed, toileted, and moved by others, and they are often regarded — tragically — as "vegetables." Surprisingly, some of them are fully capable of understanding speech at a normal level. Using finger, lip, or eye movements, communication can be established with a known technique, something like the game of "twenty questions," in which the patient can indicate yes or no.[7]

When asked privately through this technique about the possibility of hearing voices, most of these patients "gave startled expressions followed by excited 'yes' signals." The voices were usually the same sex as the patient, sounding like a relative but identified as God. They spoke as from outside the patient, usually from the upper left (when hearing the voice the patient's eyes shifted to the left involuntarily), told the patient what to do and what was right, and made the patient miserable when disobeyed. Usually the voices were helpful, supporting any training program that

5. Nathan A. Harvey, *Imaginary Playmates and Other Mental Phenomenon of Children* (Ipsilanti: Michigan State Normal College, 1918); Maya Pines, "Invisible Playmates," *Psychology Today*, 1978, *12*, 38–42; Jerome L. Singer and Dorothy G. Singer, *Television, Imagination and Aggression* (Hillsdale, N.J.: Erlbaum, 1984).

6. John Hamilton, "Auditory Hallucinations in Nonverbal Quadriplegics," *Psychiatry*, 1985, *48*, 4: 382–92. Reprinted in Marcel Kuijsten (ed.), *Reflections on the Dawn of Consciousness* (Henderson, NV: Julian Jaynes Society, 2006).

7. M.V. Moore, "Binary Communication for the Severely Handicapped," *Archives of Physical Medicine and Rehabilitation*, 1972, *53*, 532–533.

was initiated. But in some patients the voice was unwanted, saying things opposite to their thoughts. The patients felt they could not communicate with the voices.

The data were checked for possible Clever Hans effects by having a second questioner who did not know the earlier results. Hamilton's pioneering and emotionally moving data are extremely rich, and I hope the research can be extended. I regard these findings as support for the hypothesis of the bicameral mind.

## *The Bicameral Mind*

It is to be noted that throughout Hoffman's substantial, thickly referenced paper on auditory hallucinations, there is not a single description of an example, except for mention of speech-intrusions in a note. Had the author been more interested in what the hallucinations said, he might have noticed the larger questions. Why are hallucinations so often admonitory, 73% commands in men and more often criticisms in women? Why are they often religious in nature? Why do criminal psychotics feel they must obey their voices — much the way Abraham did in taking his son up the mountain?

In the theory of the bicameral mind I attempt to give a much fuller explanation of these phenomena.[8] Verbal hallucinations are so prevalent in various cultures today because they were once the basis of a mentality different from the one we have now. There is evidence suggesting that this ability to hallucinate evolved along with the evolution of language during the late Pleistocene as the response part of a brain register of all admonitory information.[9] Its survival value was in directing individuals in various long-term tasks that cued their occurrence. By 9000 B.C., such voices were called what we call gods, and they produced a new kind of social control that allowed agricultural civilizations to begin. These suggestions are speculative, but they make contact with and sense of data points in archeological evidence all along the way. All early civilizations we know of seem to have been ruled by such hallucinations or gods. Space does not permit me to go into all the reasons why this would have worked then and would not work now in the conscious era. Skeptics need go no further

---

8. Julian Jaynes, *The Origin of Consciousness in the Breakdown of the Bicameral Mind* (Boston: Houghton Mifflin, 1976/2000).

9. Julian Jaynes, "The Evolution of Language in the Late Pleistocene," *Annals of the New York Academy of Sciences*, 1976, *28*, 312–325. Reprinted as Chapter 9 of this volume.

than the Bible. It is very hard to imagine what was going on in the early books if not auditory hallucinations.

Hoffman has selected one small corner of a profound and profoundly important phenomenon, neglecting all of its history, content, variety, and ubiquity. His theory is apparently based on a correlation among distressed and certainly medicated patients between hallucinations and language disorganization (I had thought that paranoid schizophrenics were the most likely to have auditory hallucinations and the least likely to have speech distortions). These patients, however, were admitted to the hospital on the basis of a set of symptoms, the two most prominent being just these. Of course they will correlate in such a selected sample. The point of my commentary is that if the true range of auditory verbal hallucinations had been considered, that correlation would have gone to zero. And that would dissolve Hoffman's hypothesis or any similar one.

# PART III

Interviews

# CHAPTER 22

# The Lost Voices of the Gods

## Interview by Sam Keen

THE HYPOTHESIS: Ancient man was virtually an automaton, who had no concept of self-fulfillment, no sense of sin or the brevity of life, no existential doubt or anxiety. He acted on orders from voices that he actually heard within his head — the voices of gods, who told him what to do and how to solve his problems. His mind was thus divided into an executive part called god, probably based in the right hemisphere of the brain, and a follower part called man.

But the gods suddenly disappeared; the voices fell silent. About the time the wily Odysseus was sailing the Aegean — as recently as 3,000 years ago — the "bicameral mind" broke down and what we call "consciousness" was born.

This radical theory of Princeton psychologist Julian Jaynes, which draws on several scientific fields for its evidence, is right now stirring up considerable dust among researchers and scholars. His book, *The Origin of Consciousness in the Breakdown of the Bicameral Mind*, has been variously characterized as bold, mind-blowing, revolutionary, monomaniacal, and ridiculous.

What is the difference between primitive and modern mind? Why did the gods grow silent and abandon man? What is consciousness, and is it a blessing or a plague? Why do schizophrenics, like ancient peoples, hear voices? Consulting editor Sam Keen asks these and other questions in a talk with Jaynes, who likens his lifetime of trying to define consciousness to the search for the source of the Nile.

SAM KEEN: Your theory about the origin of consciousness is at least audacious and perhaps preposterous. It is hard to believe that human

First published in *Psychology Today*, Vol. 11. © 1977 Sussex Publishers, LLC. Reprinted with permission.

consciousness is a mere 3,000 years old, that the ancient Greeks did not make self-conscious decisions. And it strains common sense to think that whole civilizations were directed by auditory hallucinations, by what appeared to be the voices of the gods. How did you come to such conclusions?

JULIAN JAYNES: By weaving different strands of evidence together to form a picture. There are three basic ideas that can be separated from each other, and can be independently true or false. The first is the idea of consciousness as an analogy of the world built up on the basis of metaphor, which is a means of understanding an unknown thing by comparing it to something else with which we are more familiar. The second is the idea of the bicameral mind, namely, that the minds of ancient peoples were in two parts, an executive part called a god and a follower part called man. And the third is the idea that the neurology of the two parts of the bicameral mind is rooted in differences between the right and left hemispheres of the brain.

KEEN: Let's begin with consciousness. Where did it come from? What is it? And where did your ideas come from?

JAYNES: For as long as I can remember, I have been on a quest for the origin of consciousness, as one might seek the source of the Nile, and I made a lot of false starts. I first went into philosophy with the hope that I could understand this interior space we call consciousness. But after going through Kant's *Critique of Pure Reason* and various epistemologies, I felt that we had to be out in the world gathering data to get anywhere. And that was, and is, psychology. Looking at the physiological and biological basis of mind quickly led me to ideas of its evolution. So I began the study of the evolution of consciousness by studying the evolution of learning. In my graduate training at Yale, where I went for that purpose, the faculty didn't known quite what to do with me. The mood of academic psychology at that time was behavioristic, not really biological, and I was determined to study the whole evolution of mind. I began running paramecia and protozoa through little T mazes, all in the blissfully absurd notion that I was researching consciousness.

It was only much later that I realized what a false trail that was, and that the problem of consciousness required a great deal more thinking out than simply having fun in a laboratory with the first experiment that came to mind. Studying history showed me that every age had a different metaphor for consciousness, and that the metaphors for what goes on within the mind come from the "external" world. Consciousness has been seen as a microcosm of the macrocosm, as a blank slate on which experience writes, as a camera that copies reality, as a computer. And it has been widely assumed that consciousness was necessary for learning, reasoning, forming concepts, making judgments, and that it was somehow located somewhere in the head.

I began to suspect that consciousness is a much smaller part of our mental life than we have assumed.

KEEN: What is consciousness *not?*

JAYNES: It is not the mere response to a stimulus, nor is it the "sum total of mental processes occurring now," as E. B. Titchener was wont to say. It is not necessarily involved in learning, in forming concepts, nor even in creative reasoning. Often consciousness is a hindrance to learning and performing skills. We are conscious much less of the time than we think we are. It is difficult to realize this because we cannot be conscious of times when we are not conscious. Consciousness knits itself over the gaps and gives us the illusion of continuity. Discovering how much we are unconscious is like asking a flashlight in a dark room to discover something that has no light shining on it. Nor does consciousness photograph experience and store pictures which memory later retrieves. And it does not have a location.

KEEN: For instance, learning to walk a tightrope involves kinesthetic and preconscious awareness, but the moment I start looking at myself walking the tightrope, namely, become conscious, I'm in trouble.

JAYNES: Right. Much that we do throughout the day we do unconsciously. When driving a car, I am conscious only when there's a crisis. When improvising on the piano, it goes best when I am not conscious of the process.

When Zen students practice the art of archery, they are trying to get rid of consciousness. But take a more complex example. Some of the greatest discoveries in science, such as the structure of the benzine ring, have been made without conscious processing of the data. The solutions to many problems merely come mysteriously in dreams or in flashes of intuition. Einstein often got his most brilliant ideas when he was shaving. Creative thought involves a period of preparation in which the problem is consciously worked over. But the actual process of reasoning that leads to the solution is not in consciousness. Because consciousness is not all these things, it is possible, I think, for a whole race of people to have existed who spoke, judged, reasoned, solved problems, and did most of the things we do — but who were not conscious at all.

KEEN: What remains after the striptease? Is consciousness merely reflecting on ourselves? Is it reduced to self-consciousness? *Cogito ergo sum?*

JAYNES: Consciousness is a space in the mathematical sense. As one can have operator functions in mathematics, so one can have operator functions in this space we call consciousness. When we talk about what goes on in this mind-space, we use metaphors taken from physical behavior in actual space. We speak of 'seeing clearly,' of 'deep' or 'shallow' minds, of 'pursuing' a problem or 'grasping' a solution. Just as the words we use to describe what goes on in consciousness are metaphors, so the mind-space in which these functions take place is likewise metaphorical. The subjective, conscious mind is an analog of the real world that is generated by metaphors.

When I am asked to define consciousness, I get quite academic. In defining anything, there are logically two parts: a denotative definition, in which you point at something like this chair, and a constitutive definition, in which you describe the function of the chair and how it is made. The denotative definition of consciousness is introspection. The constitutive definition is the theory I present about the features and functions of consciousness.

KEEN: One minute, please! I just felt my 'self' disappear down the cosmic drain. The thinking self suddenly has been swallowed by its functions. Consciousness is a metaphorical mind-space in which things happen in a metaphorical way that reflect the world we understand only by metaphor. It is a mirror we hold up in which we simultaneously see ourselves and the world through the medium of metaphor. Now my question: Who is Julian Jaynes? Who is the 'I' doing the thinking? What's in back of your mirror?

JAYNES: The 'I' doing my conscious thinking is a point in a relationship, like a mathematical point. It is not the self, which is a quite different construction. This is what I call an *analog* '*I*' that can move around in imagination and do things my body is not actually doing. Coming to a fork in a road, this analog 'I' can imagine itself traveling in either direction, I can vicariously observe my imagined self drinking from a stream or struggling along the high road, and can make a decision about which road to take. This analog 'I' is the agent my mind has created by metaphor who does the internal spectating.

KEEN: This sounds very much like the Buddhist idea of the void. At the heart of consciousness is nothingness. Subtract the predicates and there is no subject... So far you have described consciousness as a metaphorical space in which an analog 'I' operates. What are some of the other operations that take place 'within' consciousness?

JAYNES: I have already suggested that consciousness spatializes, it invents an 'interior' mind-space. It also represents time as having a spatial quality. You can't think of time without spatializing it, spreading it out between before and after, past and future. It also inevitably excerpts, because we can see or pay attention to only a part of what is happening at any one moment. In consciousness, we always see ourselves at the center of a story. We narratize, assign causes, and explain, in order to weave things into an ongoing story.

KEEN: You made the point earlier that every age has its favorite metaphors for understanding consciousness. When you want to understand consciousness, you go immediately to language. In the beginning is the word. We are the stuff of which poetry is made.

JAYNES: I have tried to show how consciousness is constructed out of language and metaphor. Take, for instance, the abstract concepts of science. Originally, the word 'inertia' referred to an indolent person and 'acceleration' to increasing one's steps. And now we even have concepts like charm and black holes. Even the verb 'to be' was generated from a metaphor. It comes from the Sanskrit *bhu* — 'to grow or make grow' — and the English forms, 'is' and 'am,' have evolved from the same root as the Sanskrit *asmi* — 'to breathe.' Of course, we are no longer conscious that the concept of being is generated from a metaphor about growing and breathing. We simply can't get away from metaphors.

KEEN: When did consciousness begin?

JAYNES: If we accept the proposition that consciousness is based on linguistic analogy, then the problem of when it first occurred is brought down to size. It had to be some time after the evolution of language. In my view, language evolved very late, approximately from 100,000 B.C. up to 10,000 B.C., and that means that consciousness began sometime from 10,000 B.C. up to the present. We can gather evidence about the origins of consciousness by examining the earliest writings — which began around 3000 B.C. Before 1000 B.C. they do not show any trace of an interior mind-space in which a person could imagine himself doing things or having dialogues with the self the way you and I do.

KEEN: How do you account for the presence of symbolic objects in graves? Excavations in Iraq have shown that as early as 50,000 B.C., there were shamanistic or ritual burials. This suggests some concept of afterlife, continuance of soul or spirit, or, at least, a capacity to separate the body and the person. In your terms, this would require consciousness.

JAYNES: It is a mistake, I think, to read so much into such burials, which seem to date from about 12,000 B.C. Such burials are not, I think, evidence for consciousness. You don't have to be conscious to grieve or have ritual.

KEEN: What about the cave drawings in Lascaux?

JAYNES: They are from about 12,000 B.C. If you are asking whether they could be done without consciousness, I would reply that they could, as easily as one can ride a bicycle without consciousness.

KEEN: But it seems as if the artists were projecting themselves into the hunt, into a past situation in which they killed an animal, or a future one when they hoped to. And if they were reminiscing or anticipating, they were spatializing time, narratizing, and were conscious.

JAYNES: I don't think they were projecting themselves into any past or future at all. That would be our modern conscious interpretation. Some artists of my acquaintance insist some of their best work just happens without consciously planning what they are doing. And if that can happen today, why not in Lascaux? I think the real answer to the fascinating problem presented by these remarkable drawings will be along the lines of eidetic imagery (something like lingering dream images) and not consciousness.[1]

KEEN: Let's get back to language and consciousness.

---

1. See Chapter 11 of this volume.

JAYNES: The earliest written languages we know of are in hieroglyphics or cuneiform, and these are difficult to translate unless they are very concrete. But when we come to ancient Greek and the *Iliad*, we have early writing we can translate with some accuracy.

The remarkable thing about the *Iliad* is that in general people are not conscious. They don't sit down and decide to have a Trojan war. They don't plan strategy. It is quite obvious that there are two kinds of beings that figure in the *Iliad*: there are people like Achilles, and there are a group of beings called gods. Who and what are they? The gods come into the story whenever there is a new decision to be reached. As soon as there is a novel situation to be dealt with, someone hears a voice or sees a god who tells him what to do.

For instance, when Agamemnon takes away Achilles's girlfriend, Achilles takes out his sword and starts to go at Agamemnon. Suddenly the goddess Athena twists him around and tells him no. And then, in grief, Achilles goes down to the beach and hallucinates another goddess, Thetis, who consoles him and tells him something else to do.

These auditory and visual hallucinations, occurring whenever a novel situation arose, show us the structure of the bicameral mind. Achilles, like all bicameral people, had a split mind. One part, the executive or god part, stored up all admonitory experience and fitted things into a pattern and told the follower or person part what to do through an auditory hallucination.

KEEN: Are you suggesting that all ancient people were schizophrenic?

JAYNES: In a way, yes. You could say that before the second millennium B.C., everybody was schizophrenic. Look what happens in schizophrenia. We hear voices impelling us to do something, or criticizing us. We lose our boundaries. We become automatons. Time crumbles and our mental space vanishes. These are all characteristics of the bicameral mind.

The problem of schizophrenia is complex. There is the question of diagnosis and the degree to which it is genetically determined by the lack of an enzyme which prevents the biochemical products of stress from being excreted. But let's leave these problems aside for the moment. The modern schizophrenic relapses into the bicameral mind but struggles to get back into consciousness. He is between worlds and has lost the capacity to be comfortable either in consciousness or in schizophrenia. The bicameral person fitted perfectly into a bicameral kingdom. He never learned anything different. The bicameral person was an absolutely social

individual, whereas the modern schizophrenic, having learned consciousness and being habituated to using introspection to find "himself," is cut
off from both the self and society.

KEEN: How were bicameral civilizations structured to give social support
to the hallucinated voices of the gods?

JAYNES: All of the early civilizations we know about from around 10,000
B.C. were theocracies. Society was organized hierarchically, with gods at
the head telling people what to do. How did this come about?

Civilization is the art of living in towns that are large enough so that
everybody doesn't know everybody else. When any group gets beyond the
size of 30 or so, elaborate forms of communication and social control
must be invented. I suggest that the auditory hallucinations of the bicameral mind were the means of social control. The individuals heard a command that issued from the leader or the king. These voices could "think"
and solve problems in much the way that a contemporary schizophrenic's
voices think. When the king died, his voice was still hallucinated. In this
way, dead kings became living gods. Later, idols were substituted for the
corpses of kings, and temples became the houses of the gods. It was the
authority of these hallucinations that allowed the strictly hierarchical
civilizations to begin and develop into vast kingdoms like Egypt and the
many city-states of Assyria.

The evidence that hallucinations were the support of the social hierarchy is clear. Take the Mesopotamians, for example. They had elaborate
rituals for their idols. They bathed them, took them on trips, and gave
them connubial visits to have sex with other idols. We have texts that
describe how they stood in front of them and heard the statues speak and
tell them what to do.

KEEN: Readers of the Old Testament should be familiar with this pattern.
God "spoke" to Moses and various of the prophets.

JAYNES: The Old Testament is an excellent record of the birth pangs of
our subjective consciousness. Look at the difference between Amos, one
of the earliest books written, and Ecclesiastes, one of the latest. Amos is
almost pure bicameral speech. He does not think, or ponder his words.
His thought is done for him. He opens his mouth and the voice comes
through him: "Thus saith the Lord…" By contrast, Ecclesiastes is very
subjective. He 'sees' that wisdom is better than folly. Note the metaphor

of 'seeing.' And he spatializes time ("To every thing there is a season…"). He ponders about life — metaphorically, deep in his metaphoric heart, in a way that Amos could never do.

KEEN: But others did not hear the voice of Yahweh? Amos was an exception.

JAYNES: The ecstatic prophets, the Nabiim, existed when the bicameral mind had begun to break down. Their ecstatic trances were a means of recovering the lost voices of the gods. By the time of Deuteronomy, the living voice was replaced by the law. The religion of the Pentateuch came into being because the voice of Yahweh was not being heard. In the Psalms, it is easy to hear the longing. Subjective consciousness has been born, but the mind is still haunted by its old unconscious ways and it yearns for the lost authorities.

KEEN: Nobody would deny that there were some bicameral or schizo-phrenic persons in ancient civilizations. Or even that shamans and priests encouraged hallucinated voices as a means of exercising social control. Why shouldn't we assume that the Marxist critique is correct: a mystical, or perhaps purely Machiavellian, elite controlled the theocratic structure and used the "fiction" of the voices of gods as means of maintaining power and control?

JAYNES: That is a very modern way of viewing things. Just because the voices function as a social control doesn't mean they can be reduced to that. Let's take a specific example: the Oracle at Delphi. There is no evi-dence that the priestess was used by an elite to keep everybody in line. To the contrary. In Plutarch's day, she was the daughter of a poor farmer, and even kings went to the oracles for advice. Even Plato had tremendous reverence for the Oracle, and he was a cynical man. If there was trickery, he would have smelled it out.

You have to realize that there wasn't much trickery in the bicameral world. Duplicity requires consciousness, and planning. When you hear of a trick, in ancient literature, like the Trojan horse, it is almost laughably naïve. Who would ever be deceived by a big wooden horse being given by one's enemies? But that is about the level of trickery that anybody could use before 1000 B.C. The data just don't support the Marxist critique.

You ask how I know that everybody was hallucinating? In most of these civilizations, everybody had his own personal god. In the Neolithic site uncovered at Catalhüyük, in Turkey, dating from at least 6000 B.C., almost every house had four or five rooms nestled around a god's room, which contained idols and statues of stone. To me, by definition, these little statues or idols were the gods that cued hallucinations that told people what to do.

KEEN: Why did consciousness develop? What were the events leading to the breakdown of the bicameral mind?

JAYNES: Many factors. Catastrophes, too much chaos and novelty. Sometime around 1470 B.C. the volcano on the island of Thera, or Santorini, erupted. A major part of Crete was suddenly under 1,000 feet of water. The shock waves have been estimated as 350 times more powerful than a hydrogen bomb. A tsunami 700 feet high, traveling at 350 miles per hour, smashed into the coasts of the bicameral kingdoms along the Aegean.[2] In a single day, whole populations were destroyed or became refugees. This started a series of migrations and a huge game of musical chairs, with people all around the Near East intermeshing.

This, plus the fact that writing and trading had already weakened the authority of the auditory hallucinations, led to the breakdown of the bicameral mind. People couldn't get the right directives from their voices. Ripped out of the context in the larger hierarchical group where neither habit nor the bicameral voice could support him, the refugee was forced into consciousness. Refugees and conquered people had to learn deceit to survive. They had to learn to be one thing on the inside and another on the outside, and that requires the development of imagination and the analog 'I'. These primitive operations of consciousness probably began in Assyria and were developed very speedily in a more intellectual way in Greece from 900 B.C. to 600 B.C. This was about the same time the Hebrews were also beginning to move out of a bicameral period and were lamenting the lost voice of Yahweh.

KEEN: Were the brains of bicameral people different from those of modern people with subjective consciousness? Or was consciousness merely a trick we learned, a product of a different kind of social conditioning?

JAYNES: Consciousness is learned on the basis of language and taught to others. It is a cultural invention rather than a biological necessity. However, it does have survival value, since it allows people to deal with stressful and

2. For more on the Thera explosion and resulting tsunami, see "Sinking Atlantis," *Secrets of the Dead Series* (PBS Home Video, 2008), pbs.org/video/secrets-of-the-dead-sinking-atlantis.

novel situations. So there is a modicum of natural selection at work in the emergence of consciousness.

KEEN: Let's talk about the third basic component of your theory. What was the neurology of the bicameral mind?

JAYNES: Anything as important in the history of our species as the transition from tribal to urban civilizations demands some explanation of what is going on physiologically. This raises an interesting question.. Why is the speech function in most of us represented in only the left hemisphere of the brain when most other important functions are bilaterally represented? This is even more puzzling when we consider that the neurological structures for language exist in the right hemisphere as well.

Since the proper procedure in any science is to begin with the simplest hypothesis, I reasoned that speech was in the left hemisphere to leave the right hemisphere free for the voices of the gods. This seemed a good primitive hypothesis, although I thought it was really too simple. (I should add that I was working on these ideas long before most of the split-brain research.) My hypothesis in the strongest form was that the speech of the gods was organized in the right hemisphere, in what corresponds to Wernicke's area on the left hemisphere, and was "spoken" or "heard" over the anterior commissures to, or by, the auditory areas of the left temporal lobe.

KEEN: But why should there be voices of the gods? Why would the brain organize itself in this dramatic way to deal with the world?

JAYNES: Consider the evolutionary problem. Billions of nerve cells in the right hemisphere process complex information, much of it having to do with pattern recognition and spatial fitting together of things. Some code is needed to send this information through the small anterior commissures, or corpus callosum, to the left hemisphere. And what better code is there than language? So the auditory hallucinations were the most efficient method of getting cortical processing from one side of the brain to the other. In a sense, a god is a translation of spatial *Gestalt* information into language. You might say that a god is very good at Kohs Block Test [which tests the ability to see patterns and spatial relations].

KEEN: The hypothesis is bold. What is the evidence?

JAYNES: It is complex, and I can only suggest a little of it here. Both hemispheres understand language, but normally only the left can speak. Stroke patients who have hemorrhages on the left side of the cortex cannot speak but can still understand.

There remains a vestigial god-like function in the right hemisphere. I originally predicted that the admonitory experience should be stored in the silent language centers of the right hemisphere. So I was very excited when Wilder Penfield discovered that when the right temporal lobe was stimulated, patients had auditory hallucinations.

We know from patients who have undergone surgical commissurotomy (the so-called split-brain operation) that the two hemispheres can function almost like two independent persons, which in the bicameral period were, in my theory, the individual and his god.

And, finally, we know that the brain is more plastic, more capable of being organized by the environment, than we previously supposed. The brain teems with redundant centers and can compensate for missing or injured structures. So we can assume that the neurology of consciousness is plastic enough to allow the change from the bicameral mind to consciousness to be made largely on the basis of learning and culture.

I am well aware that any model for the bicameral mind based upon the difference between the hemispheres runs the danger of oversimplification. You can also get auditory hallucinations by stimulating other areas of the brain. New research is showing that, to some degree, the brain is organized differently in every single one of us, particularly the relationship between the hemispheres. In my book I offer other models, but I still prefer the strong and simple hypothesis with which I began.

KEEN: Your theory about the breakdown of the bicameral mind reads like an intricate, intellectual version of *Paradise Lost*. In the beginning, there was innocence. Now the voices are silent, the prophets are dead, and the oracles have been replaced by computerized projections of possible future scenarios. And we are all characters in *Waiting for Godot*. What have we gained and lost in becoming conscious?

JAYNES: We have gained the ability to ask the question "What have we gained and lost in becoming conscious?" When we talk about gain or loss, we are thinking in terms of ideal values by which a human being is measured. And that has something to do with good and bad. And there was no such thing as good or bad in the bicameral world. There were only voices. All of ethics is an attempt to find a substitute for the missing voices, to find out what to do.

People in these ancient kingdoms were probably happy — if happiness is conceived of on a primitive level. Certainly a person didn't have any identity crisis. And there was no such thing as self-fulfillment.

KEEN: And no anxiety?

JAYNES: There was fear, but nothing like our modern anxiety of not know-ing what to do. Our quandary is, indeed, consciousness. Consciousness is this hesitant trying to figure out what to do that takes place during intro-spection. It's full of problems. We are still in transition, entering into the gateways of a very different kind of mentality.

KEEN: It follows from your theory that, with consciousness, we have invented the ego, imagination, and guilt.

JAYNES: Yes. And also time and history, as I will show in my next book. It is hard for us to realize, because we inevitably imagine other people as conscious, but the very idea of a lifetime, or a personal history, is a recent innovation. Certainly ancient peoples hurt with wounds, and were afraid when in danger, and knew that behavior stopped when the heart ceased beating. But they never had a sense of a lifetime stretching from child-hood to death. They never had ambition, or the opposite of ambition. They were not, as we are, persons of a thousand masks. They were obedient to their voices, sincere in the sense that they lacked the capacity for duplicity and deceit. In the modern sense in which we think about it, they did not have personalities.

KEEN: I wonder if we have really left the bicameral mind so far behind? Don't most people still hear voices? Isn't consciousness a theater filled with inner dialogue? And what is conscience but the introjected voices of the parents? And what are guilt and shame except the fear of disobeying voices we once heard? And therapy? The cure is to learn to hear the silent voices, to recover the unconscious admonitions of the superego — the gods of our childhood.

JAYNES: One of the places I would like to get more clarity in my theory is this business of interior dialogues. Most of us can have interior dia-logues with people and imagine them replying to us. But whether this has anything more than a metaphorical relationship to the bicameral mind I really don't know. I am currently working on the idea of the changes in our emotional life that accompany the transition to consciousness.

KEEN: What exactly are these changes?

JAYNES: I think that we inherit a set of basic affects or emotions that are similar in most mammals, including primates and bicameral man. Fear and shame are two examples. In bicameral man, shame was a behavior that happened and then dissipated, like a dog cringing and crawling and trying to get out of sight. The same with fear. But when we get time spatialized and have an analog 'I', and can remember and narratize, these basic affects get stretched out over time and don't dissipate. Fear that is remembered becomes anxiety, and it can pervade a whole lifetime. And shame is spatialized into guilt. That is why we have all these elaborate religious procedures of expiation and forgiveness. And now therapies — we are still inventing new ways to try to deal with this new feeling of guilt that is only 3,000 years old.

KEEN: Perhaps guilt is both a testimony to, and a replacement for, the lost authority of bicameral voices. Since we no longer have the gods, the voice of the guilty conscience gives us our only assurance that there is an authority that can punish and reward us. The internalized parent — the superego, in Freudian language — is the surrogate god. Better to be guilty in a world where there are authorities and gods, than exist beyond good or evil in the terrifying silence. So modern people have political ideology and uncritical allegiance to nationalistic leaders instead of gods. The voices of the gods are only disguised, they are not gone.

JAYNES: I don't think it is that simple. There are destructive forms of guilt, but we need to feel guilty when we have hurt somebody else, and not just shame, which is dependent on the group knowing about our misdeeds. Our internal feeling of guilt is a part of our social control. Consciousness does lead us into many quandaries. And, of course, we look around for guidance about what to do. We may consciously seek authority figures, and although it is related I would hesitate to say that this represents a direct vestige of bicamerality.

KEEN: What is the future of consciousness? You say we are in a transitional period. Between what and what?

JAYNES: I really can't say. All I can see around me is transition and movement. I find tremendous differences between bicameral and modern people, even between ourselves and the age of Chaucer. There is a difference in thinking patterns. I imagine that even if you studied dreaming, you would find that watching television has changed our dreams. But exactly what the future is going to bring I cannot say.

KEEN: Doesn't your theory suggest there is a direction implicit in the evolution of consciousness? With consciousness, we gain the ability to deliberate, to pause between stimulus and response, to decide. We are not bound by necessity. It would seem that we are becoming freer. Is history pushing us toward enlightenment, toward waking up from the illusion that we must be blindly obedient to external authorities?

JAYNES: What interests me is the metaphors you use: freedom, awakening, the passage from darkness to light. You are creating or changing consciousness by metaphors. In my value system, the effect of those metaphors is to strengthen the individual, to change consciousness for the better. But I am mostly aware of what the metaphors are doing. When you ask me what we are becoming, it is like asking me to choose one of a thousand roads. It's like asking how history is going to end up. To ask for an end or a purpose is to ask for a single path. And consciousness is always open to many possibilities. It is always an adventure.

# CHAPTER 23

# Alone in the Country of the Mind

## Interview by Richard Rhodes

THERE IS ANOTHER KIND OF LIFE, one not much lived anymore: a life of privacy and contemplation, a life sustained behind a single purpose pursued through decades. Its cost is loneliness and perhaps isolation. Its gain, whether it proceeds to obscurity or to triumph, is clarity, and resolution is its goal.

Julian Jaynes, a 54-year-old bachelor and research psychologist at Princeton University, has lived such a life, and it has served him well. Its latest result is a book, imposingly titled *The Origin of Consciousness in the Breakdown of the Bicameral Mind*. Published to no great fanfare in January 1977, the book is quietly running away to underground success — it approaches its sixth printing, with more than 20,000 copies already sold. In it, Jaynes attempts to solve an old and elusive problem, the problem of human consciousness and its origin in evolution or in time. Animals, even primates, don't introspect: men do. But when did they begin? The interior 'I' stares out on the world, looks back inward, reflects. A woman frowns and inwardly she is smiling. At our order the past returns for revision, we rehearse the future in simulations that branch like trees, daydreams sweeten our afternoons. Hardly any professionals in the twentieth century have wondered why, or how — psychology having retreated instead to illusions of mathematical rigor, to ambitions of mere control. Jaynes has wondered why since the sixth year of his life, and now he believes he knows.

His answer, embodied in *Origin*, the first of several projected books, is startling — as startling, if examination sustains it, as Darwin's dissolution of species, as Einstein's refining of light — and since the life is thus at least a life of daring provocation, it deserves examination as well.

First published in *Quest*, Vol. 2, January/February. © 1978 *Quest*.

But immediately the answer, toward which the life has led. Others have argued that consciousness is a property of matter, or a fundamental property of living things, or an aspect of learning, or a metaphysical imposition, or an evolutionary emergence, or even — the behaviorists — nothing at all. Jaynes's argument is different from any of these. Consciousness, he proposes, is a historical invention, assembled out of language no more than 3,000 years ago. Before consciousness, men were automatons guided by internal voices that they took to be the voices of the gods. The voices issued, in right-handed people, from the right side of the brain, the side that orders and patterns, from areas of the brain that now are silent except in florid schizophrenia or electrode probes. These are three mated theories, each one of which may stand or fall on its own; Jaynes unifies them in the bold, ornate title of his book.

He is not forbidding, but rather a friendly, man, with a manner and with inflections similar to Tony Randall's. His office in the Princeton psychology building is cluttered; he smokes small cigars and loses their ashes absentmindedly on the floor. He works on Saturdays and Sundays as well as on weekdays far into the night. He takes walking tours, as Englishmen did a hundred years ago, or visits his mother in his house on Prince Edward Island. A woman he once loved burned to death in her unelectrified rural house; another woman in his life was institutionalized. His voice is unexpectedly deep for so tenor a face, and the face is weathered rather than lined. He has been a teacher for 23 years, first at Yale and then at Princeton. He found consciousness in a forsythia bush when he was six years old.

RHODES: Were you an introspective child? Did you read a lot?

JAYNES: Yes, I was a very introspective child, and no, I didn't read a lot. I liked to be out doing things. I played baseball, I went hiking, I very much liked carpentry. But I remember that I had a whole other world that I never shared with anybody else. Not a fantasy world, but thinking about the mind, questioning. When I was six — I was supposed to be raking leaves — I stopped in front of a forsythia bush. The color yellow. It came to me with tremendous suddenness that I could never know, even though we had the same word, if another person saw the same yellowness of those flowers inside his mind in exactly the same way I did.

Mind has been a problem of philosophy since philosophy began. The traditional solution was metaphysical: there is mind and there is matter. William James jettisoned this dualism at the beginning of the twentieth century: "There is no aboriginal stuff or quality of being," he wrote, "contrasted with that of which material objects are made, out of which our thoughts of them are made." But he failed to specify where mind is lodged. Psychology since James has looked for mind in molecules and even attempted to deny its existence. Jaynes, in *Origin*, proposes a simpler explanation: that consciousness is an analog map generated point by point by the world, and the elements of its generation are words. Metaphors, as all words originally are. Outside, the world; in here, within me, my mind. But inside the skull is no mind-space, except metaphorically; inside the skull is brain, neural tissue, though it may be 'broad-minded', 'narrow-minded', 'deep', 'open' — you see the metaphors at work. So, as children, learning language, we learn to construct an 'interior' world modeled on the exterior, and live 'inside' our heads.

Jaynes's argument in *Origin* is Socratic; each step proposes agreement, and if you agree with one, then you are more than casually committed to the next. Thus, if consciousness is dependent on language, if consciousness is language applied to the construction of a mind-space and an analog 'I', then consciousness could not have preceded the development of language in man, but must have followed it. And language development in *Homo* is generally accepted to have begun only 100,000 years ago. Consciousness must therefore be a more recent invention.

Man without language is easy: a superior primate. Man without consciousness is hard to compass. Jaynes proposes homely experiments to demonstrate that even today we are not conscious nearly as much as we imagine: of the number of teeth in our mouths, of whether the door in a familiar room hinges left or right, of ourselves when watching television, of our actions when driving a car. He cites the psychological truism that some kinds of learning proceed more rapidly when we are not conscious than when we are: playing the piano, hitting a ball. And that other kinds of learning — Pavlovian conditioning, for example — require consciousness not at all.[1] "At this point," he writes, "we can at least conclude that it

---

1. "If a light signal immediately followed by a puff of air through a rubber tube is directed at a person's eye about 10 times, the eyelid, which previously blinked only to the puff of air, will begin to blink to the light signal alone, and this becomes more and more frequent as trials proceed. Subjects who have undergone this well-known procedure of signal learning report that it has no conscious component whatever." (*Origin*, page 32)

is possible — possible, I say — to conceive of human beings who are not conscious and yet can learn and solve problems."

This much of Jaynes's theory may eventually find acceptance among his colleagues, although those who look for mind in neural substrates, in molecules, in the firings of nerves will be dismayed. Have already been.

RHODES: How has your profession received your ideas?

JAYNES: An absolute range, from people who feel they're very important all the way to very strong hostility. I gave an invited address to the American Psychological Association in 1969, in a ballroom large enough for chandeliers, and all of ten people came. It made no stir whatever, because people weren't interested in thinking along these lines. If I'd spoken back in 1895, people might have stood up and paid attention, because I'm attacking a problem that they had been dealing with since Darwin and Wallace in 1859: How can you get mind out of molecules of matter evolving? Evolution explained how, out of matter, you could get everything up to human beings, but how out of matter could you get this internal introspection that isn't molecules? One reviewer, a clinical child neurologist, called me up the other day and said, "Well, I don't believe a word of it, and I don't think you meant me to." I didn't know what to make of that. On the other hand, my theories are taught in the introductory psychology course at Princeton, and are going into textbooks under the heading "Controversial Issues." When I get a hostile reaction from psychologists, I think it's because each specialist believes his own specialty is going to offer the answer. When someone comes along and says consciousness is in *history*, it can't be accepted. If they did accept it, they wouldn't have the motivation to go back into the laboratory the next day and go through all the petty, petty, humdrum things that are daily done in psychology. American psychology is sadly in the grip of a stereotyped perception of itself. It wants to ape theoretical physics.

If consciousness as a learned function seems shocking, the bicamerality of the mind must seem radical and even bizarre. Primate systems of control — signing, unconscious learning, dominance ranking — were adequate, Jaynes thinks, through the millennia of man's life as a hunter-gatherer roving in small cohesive bands. But the development of agriculture, the collecting of men into villages and then towns and then cities, required something more. The stress of novelty activated the chemistry that evoked

auditory hallucinations, and the voices told unconscious men what to do.
The mechanism is still there, latent in our brains. LSD sometimes reactivates it, as does the stress that leads in some susceptible individuals to
schizophrenia; and schizophrenia is usually also accompanied by a terrifying diminution of consciousness. From *Origin*:

> Now we must not make the error here of supposing that these auditory
> hallucinations were like the tape recordings of what the king had com
> manded. Perhaps they began as such. But after a time there is no reason
> not to suppose that such voices could 'think' and solve problems, albeit,
> of course, unconsciously. The 'voices' heard by contemporary schizo
> phrenics 'think' as much as, and often more than, they do. And thus the
> 'voices' which I am supposing were heard by [ancient peoples] could
> with time improvise and 'say' things that the king himself had never
> said. ... Thus each worker, gathering shellfish or trapping small game
> or in a quarrel with a rival or planting seed where the wild grain had
> previously been harvested, had within him the voice of his king to assist
> the continuity and utility to the group of his labors.

Jaynes found the bicameral mind first of all in the *Iliad*. He took up
the study of Greek to trace Greek words for mind back to their origins. By
the time he got to the *Iliad*, the words had become concrete, but there is
no word for mind in the *Iliad* at all. He was familiar with the theory that
the *Iliad* as not the work of one man, Homer, but rather a transcribed version of an oral epic passed down by illiterate poet-singers. Boldly — some
classicists have said simplistically — he decided to take the poem literally.

*Menin aedie Thea*, it begins: "Of wrath sing, O Goddess!" To say, writes
Jaynes, "that the gods in the *Iliad* are merely the inventions of the authors
of the epic, is to completely misread what is going on. The characters of
the *Iliad* do not sit down and think out what to do. ... It is one god who
makes Achilles promise not to go into battle, another who urges him to
go, and another who then clothes him in a golden fire reaching up to
heaven and screams through his throat across the bloodied trench at the
Trojans, rousing in them ungovernable panic. In fact, the gods take the
place of consciousness."

And then Jaynes went looking for traces of the bicameral mind in the
ancient world, in the kingdoms of pyramids and ziggurats. He found idols
with enlarged, hypnotic, preternatural eyes before which men did not
kneel but stood straight, as if receiving instruction. He found cities without walls and doors without locks: because consciousness is necessary for

deceit. He found other books he believes to be bicameral: "Thus saith the Lord," says Amos again and again in one of the earliest and least-revised books of the Old Testament. And in *Origin* he concluded:

> Each person had a part of his nervous system which was divine, by which he was ordered about like any slave, a voice or voices which indeed were what we call volition and empowered what they commanded and were related to the hallucinated voices of others in a carefully established hierarchy.
>
> The total pattern, I suggest, is in agreement with such a view. It is, of course, not conclusive. However, the astonishing consistency from Egypt to Peru, from Ur to Yucatán, wherever civilization arose, of death practices and idolatry, of divine government and hallucinated voices — all this is witness to the idea of a different mentality from our own.

But bicameral civilization was rigid. It could not countenance too much change. When change came — cataclysm in the eastern Mediterranean or the Spanish invasion of Peru — it broke down. Written language weakened it as well, and the mingling through trade of different peoples whose voices were in conflict. And so, in the eastern Mediterranean, around the second millennium B.C., the voices stuttered and faltered and finally failed. But civilization was by then too highly organized for men to revert to primate bands again. They turned instead to divination — if the gods won't speak, ask guidance of the *I Ching*, of the bones, of the entrails, of the floating oil. The thrones of ancient art came to be depicted as empty, the gods flown, and men took to their knees in supplication: *Unto thee will I cry, O Lord my rock; be not silent to me: lest, if thou be silent to me, I become like them that go down into the pit.*

And then — I am greatly compressing Jaynes's discussion, and his evidence — consciousness dawned, in Greece first of all, and wily, conscious Odysseus was worshiped at altars throughout the land. Jaynes: "In a word, Odysseus of the many devices is the hero of the new mentality of how to get along in a ruined and god-weakened world." The Golden Age of Greece was the first exuberant flowering of the modern, conscious mind.

Here is, at the very least, an extraordinary, sustained invention, mythical in scope. It absorbs the story of Genesis, of Adam and Eve guided by God until they ate of the Tree of Knowledge and looked upon themselves with new eyes and were driven from Eden. It absorbs the *Iliad* and the *Odyssey*, and volumes of ancient history and literature. It examines archaeology and psychology, linguistic theory, and the latest research in the neurology of the brain. And who is this man of such sweeping invention? By what route did he come to this range?

Julian Jaynes was born on February 27, 1920 in West Newton, Massachusetts. His grandfather had been born in the eighteenth century; his elderly father, a respected Unitarian minister in suburban Boston, remembered the Civil War. His mother was much younger than his father: she is 92 today. He was the second of three children, and his father died soon after the last child was born, too early for Jaynes to remember him.

RHODES: Was your childhood happy?

JAYNES: I've never been able to decide. As you know, my feeling about memory is that we're constantly narratizing, as I call it in *Origin*. Fitting things into patterns. In the ultra-reality of life, which is exceedingly complex, the pattern probably isn't simple enough to call happy or unhappy. My immediate response is, yes, happy. Then I think back, oh no, miserable. Then I remember thinking, as a child, "Gee, I'm fortunate." It must have been a combination of both. What some would think a disadvantage, growing up in a fatherless home, didn't seem so at the time. There was a single parent and a father who was spiritually present, so to speak, and he didn't have any faults because he wasn't there to show them. So I can't put a label on it.

Jaynes's mother was heir to a legacy from her father, a gregarious and ebullient Boston steel merchant, but the legacy had been badly invested. "He gave the business away," Jaynes says, "and the investments he left my mother were wool and elevated railways, just the very things that started to fail badly." In the 1930s, Jaynes's mother converted the house in West Newton into a boardinghouse for students at a nearby preparatory school, and the summer house on Prince Edward Island into a hotel. "So we were financially secure, though I wore hand-me-downs until I was 22. But there was still a security about it. Poverty was a game, really, that you just played until it ended."

As an adolescent, Jaynes discovered a talent for mathematics, but it came too easily to engage him: consciousness was already the problem he hoped to solve. "It was just as I began college that I decided to go into philosophy and literature, very much with the idea of examining the problem of consciousness." He started at Harvard, later transferred to McGill, and there, during a course on Kant's *Critique of Pure Reason*, incensed that the instructor refused to discuss whether Kant's categories of mind were scientifically valid, he decided to switch to psychology. "For two years," he adds, self-mocking, "to try to solve these problems, and then I was going to go back into philosophy. As you see, I'm still here."

Graduate school at Yale introduced Jaynes to the psychology laboratory, where he looked for consciousness in learning. From *Origin*:

> My first experimental work was a youthful attempt to produce signal learning … in an especially long-suffering mimosa plant. … That expected failure behind me, I moved on to protozoa. … A first suggestion of positive results was not borne out in later replications. After other failures to find learning in the lower phyla, I moved on to species with synaptic nervous systems, flatworms, earthworms, fish, and reptiles, which could indeed learn, all on the naïve assumption that I was chronicling the grand evolution of consciousness. Ridiculous!

He completed his Ph.D. work at Yale in 1950, but then idealistically refused his degree on the ground that it was nothing more than a mandarin's union card. He was not the first to have done so — Arthur Schlesinger Jr. and the renowned George Lyman Kittridge are two others who come to mind — but his refusal has plagued him ever since, barring him from academic advancement and tenure despite respected research and publication. He was the first man to study maternal imprinting of hatchling birds in the laboratory — Konrad Lorenz had studied it in the field — and he has published 46 scientific papers and several books. His salary at Princeton is $4,000 a year, less than the salaries of graduate students he supervises. Characteristically, he balances out the good and ill. "I did have an awfully hard time getting jobs, and some of my friends never forgave me, but I also seem to have picked up a reputation as a maverick, and perhaps earned some respect for my stand." Of the Ph.D. he recently told a *Time* interviewer: "It's a ridiculous badge. My brains are my credentials."

He spent the next three years — 1950–53 — in England, living on savings, thinking and studying at Salisbury, near Stonehenge, and then returned to the United States as an instructor and lecturer at Yale. He came down to Princeton in 1964 as a research associate. "I don't know how I lived, but my criterion has always been my sense of productivity, whether I'm doing what I think I should be doing. No matter what the salary, that's what makes me or anyone else feel well about himself."

Doing what he should be doing took precedence over marriage:

RHODES: Did you choose not to marry?

JAYNES: When I was younger I did, because there was work I wanted to do and I wanted to be free to do it, to follow wherever my ideas might lead, and I didn't want to think in terms of responsibilities.

Rhodes: So one of the things you accepted was a certain amount of loneliness in your life.

JAYNES: That's very true. I think I mind it more now that I'm older, partly because middle age is a different world. People my own age are very much embedded in families. But certainly I don't think I'd have written the book I've written, or come to the ideas I did, had I not had this freedom to move around, to drop everything and just go somewhere where nobody knows me and think and work. That kind of living doesn't fit very well with being married. But I expected to be married last year. She decided our age difference was too great, I'm sorry to say.

The life is private, even closed: it foliates in the work. One crucial quality of creativity is an ability to hold fast to confusion until confusion comes clear; in the middle of middle age Jaynes begins to find clarity where confusion reigned before. He expects his theories to be tested. He believes they will stand.

He is working now on a second book about consciousness, tracing the consequences of consciousness in the Greek and modern world. One consequence, he thinks, is that biologically based emotions became feelings: animal shame became guilt, animal connection became human love, animal fear became human anxiety, and what philosophers have called, often with sadness, the "human condition" was born into the world. Another consequence was a sense of inner time, the time of the mind that expands and contracts with the intensity of experience, to the ticking of no physical clock. Still another consequence was a change in the quality of our dreams: we appear now as actors in our dreams, move to the stage of other places from where we lie conscious and asleep. The bicameral dream keeps us on the stage where we sleep: Jacob's ladder, Jaynes thinks, was a bicameral dream, Jacob sleeping on the ground as the angels ascended and descended above him, and so are the nightmares of children where monsters visit their beds.

He and his students have interviewed scores of children for another idea Jaynes is researching about the development of consciousness in children. The evidence so far is that children are not fully conscious until they are about six years old. Before that, they have little sense of time, and dream bicameral dreams, although they learn tricks of language to disguise the difference: "I think," or "in my mind." At about three or four years of age, Jaynes has discovered, possibly 50 percent of children have imaginary companions, voices they "hear" that are different from their own. Parents indulge such voices or scold them away, and, living in a conscious community, the child learns consciousness and the voices fade. "In bicameral times," Jaynes theorizes, "these voices would have been encouraged, and they would grow to be personal gods who would relate the child to other gods. But even today, imaginary playmates are quite often valid auditory hallucinations. I met a young woman recently whose imaginary playmates had come back to her, particularly in the stress of exams, to tell her what to do. They had grown up along with her. It turned out that she had been taken care of while a young child by a schizophrenic grandmother who hallucinated all over the house."

RHODES: Is she then a schizophrenic?

JAYNES: She would be diagnosed so if she went to a hospital.

RHODES: A schizophrenic is someone who is distressed by his bicamerality?

JAYNES: That's a good way to put it. We really should drop the word and stick to describing symptoms. William Blake had auditory and visual hallucinations. So did Joan of Arc. But seeing their work, who would dare to label them mentally ill?

Whether Jaynes's theories stand will depend on evidence and further research, not on one's opinion of them. They are radical, though well within the traditions of science — he is no Velikovsky or von Däniken bending the facts to sweeten preconception. And scientific truth has often, at first, seemed bizarre: bizarre that the earth revolves around the sun, bizarre that the species are not fixed but shift to the opportunisms of time and place, bizarre that light is a limit that alters physical time, bizarre that the solid continents drift like floating islands, opening and closing the seas. It is hardly more bizarre that man might once have been bicameral, or that the supposedly unique human trait of consciousness might be something humans have only recently learned.

Learned and are learning, because in Jaynes's larger view, to which he turns his attention in the last chapter of *The Origin of Consciousness in the Breakdown of the Bicameral Mind*, we live still in transitional times. Vestiges of bicamerality, he attempts to show, still mark the modern ground: religious possession, hypnosis, schizophrenia, possibly poetry and music as well. And in larger scope too: in the dogmas of churches, in dialectical materialism, even in science itself:

> But over and behind these ... other causes of science has been something more universal, something in this age of specialization often unspoken. It is something about understanding the totality of existence, the essential defining reality of things, the entire universe and man's place in it. It is a groping among stars for final answers, a wandering the infinitesimal for the infinitely general, a deeper and deeper pilgrimage into the unknown. It is a direction whose far beginning in the mists of history can be distantly seen in the search for lost directives in the breakdown of the bicameral mind.

Jaynes's search also. One of the paradoxes of that search is that Julian Jaynes, a man with deep respect for religion applying the methods of science to discover the origin of religion, may, in locating divinity in neurological tissue, be contributing to religion's discrediting. He prefers to believe that he is not. "One of the things I'm trying to protect," he told me near the close of our interview, "by identifying its sources, is the function of religion in the world today. The voices are silent. True. But the brain is organized in a religious fashion. Our mentalities have come out of a divine kind of mind." Where they might be going, Jaynes chooses not to speculate, except that he believes consciousness continues to change and develop through historical time. Our sensibilities are different from the sensibilities of our forefathers: different metaphors make different minds.

Search. This dedicated and boldly speculative life has been organized for search, and search has been its meaning. And perhaps search is all, all and everything and the nearest men can come to certitude: the healthy, confident motion of an open mind. It unites us. Yellow we see, forsythia bushes everywhere: the child who feared his isolation has proposed a common bond.

# CHAPTER 24

# Princeton University Interview

Q: How did you first come to your theory on the origin of consciousness?

JAYNES: I guess about six years ago a whole bunch of tributaries and rivulets were all starting to come together and to go along one particular track and out of that came this very different theory of the origin of consciousness.

One has to see this against the background of the whole history of this part of psychology that goes back to when the theory of evolution came in the middle of the nineteenth century. Because everybody — including Darwin — everybody thought, "OK, so, human species have evolved by natural selection and so on, and the mind just goes along with that and has evolved too." Therefore you found a whole group of people following Darwin who were trying to study the evolution of learning in animal species and saying that this is the evolution of mind and consciousness. No one was really being very accurate about what they meant by consciousness.

What happened to me was, I spent the first part of my scientific career following along in that same error, until I began to see that this isn't going to solve the problem of where consciousness came from. I realized that I had to start off from different criteria about what consciousness was. Well, I came to a new theory of consciousness — that consciousness is very much based on language, on the nature of linguistic metaphor, on the ability to tell stories, on the ability to have analogs of yourself, and to create a kind of metaphoric space — which is this space we assume somewhere behind our eyes and ourselves, and behind the eyes of someone we're looking at — and in that space we do various operations that help us decide what we're going to do.

If that is so, then it means that this problem of the origin of consciousness — that Darwin thought went all the way back to protozoa, and that

Transcribed and edited from an interview with Julian Jaynes by two Princeton University students for a university radio program. From the Julian Jaynes Archives held at the Department of Psychology, University of Prince Edward Island.

other people think goes back to the origin of mammals, when the cortex evolves, or some other kind of neurological mechanism — that this is all wrong. Consciousness developed in human culture after the evolution of language. And then I started off like in a detective story to try to find out where that would be, because that means it would really be sometime between 10,000 B.C. and the present.

Q: How do you define consciousness?

JAYNES: Here let me be a little bit academic and say there are two kinds of definition, as logicians like to speak about it: the denotative, which means you point to something, and then there's the connotative, or constitutional, or "what is it made of?" kind of definition. I'm prefacing what I'm about to say that way because what I'm going to say I think will be a little bit unsatisfactory to you when you hear it at first.

Denotatively I simply define consciousness as what you do when you introspect. I simply ask you to think of something in your past or something in your future or anything like that and everybody knows what those words mean — that's a good denotative definition. You point to it by asking somebody to introspect and nobody has any difficulty with it. That's the denotative definition.

The constitutive definition is that we have these metaphors that we — in culture and in our childhood — build up into a kind of metaphorical space that we assume — and I like to compare it more to mathematics than to a box in which you stick memories and so on.

When we introspect on a memory, or something in the future we are going to do, or anything at all, we get this funny feeling of space. It's not like the space out there and yet it is spatial. And we have a little analog of ourselves in that space. You can imagine yourself being miles away now, you can imagine yourself in the future or in the past, and so on. And you have analogs of everything else — these things called ideas, whatever they are.

Now this whole thing — which we call consciousness — can be looked at and can be examined and we can get certain things out of it such as an analog self or the quality of spatialization, and we can try to do experiments and study those things. This is just the beginning of trying to look at these things because this is a very new way of looking at consciousness.

One of the most important things is that consciousness isn't nearly as important as the nineteenth century thought it was — or that most people walking in the street think. If you ask the man in the street "What is consciousness?" he'd say "Oh consciousness is my mind — wow, it's everything." But it isn't, it's a very small part of mentality. And it comes in to help guide you around in what you're doing, but it's astonishing the number of things that everybody does in which consciousness does not come in at all. We're learning things constantly — right here and now, as we're talking here in my office, we are learning things about each other, we are training each other in this conversation — and we're not aware of this at all. I hope we're being aware of what I'm talking about — at least I'm trying to be aware of that as we go on, but I'm not conscious of gestures that I'm using and so on.

Q: So this consciousness is guiding the automated reflexes?

JAYNES: I think that's too simple a way to look at it. What's left over isn't just automatic reflexes. There's a lot of learning — one's ordinary behavior is not just reflexive behavior. You're adapting yourself all the time to all the different cues, to everything that's going on around you constantly. It feels automatic because we're not conscious of it, we're not aware of it.

What consciousness does is to come in on top of all this when you need it. If you are trying to decide, for example, where you want to go to lunch today; there are various alternatives and possibilities and you become conscious of that. At the time you are conscious of that you're not conscious of other things, and you don't have to be.

Q: What do you call everything that isn't consciousness?

JAYNES: I refer to that simply as mentality. I'm trying not to make an important thing about what kind of names we give to it. It is the organization of behavior. Of course the theory that I've been involved in is indeed going back and discovering that mankind in all its early centuries of civilization was going on without consciousness at all — building the great civilizations that are behind us all and everything we're doing.

Q: That was you said about 10,000 B.C.?

JAYNES: Okay — to go back to the detective story about trying to find out when consciousness evolved. Ten thousand B.C. is when man left tribal life. Before that he was living in tribes of let's say roughly about 30 — very similar to modern primates, only much more developed and using tools.

Language had evolved probably between 100,000 B.C. and 10,000 B.C., and at 10,000 B.C. suddenly man becomes agricultural. There are various theories and debates going on at the present time among scientists about the actual causation. Some people think it is because the glacial ice had retreated northward bringing very different kinds of climates to the Near East — that's part of it certainly, though there are probably other reasons.

But for whatever reason, what happened was mankind suddenly was no longer tribal, he was now living in cities of 200 at first, but then they immediately explode into thousands. This is the beginning of what we can call civilization. I'm using civilization not in turn of phrase of being good or anything, but simply in terms of man being able to live in cities. It is an accomplishment, and this began just about 10,000 or 9000 B.C.

I felt that the origin of consciousness — if you try to establish the extreme dates — it would have to be from about that time up to somewhere closer to the present. When I examined this I thought, "Wouldn't it be nice if we went back to the first writings of mankind and found that they had a different kind of mind." Well, I didn't think this would turn out.

The first writings of mankind begin around 3000 B.C. and they are in cuneiform, hieroglyphic, and hieratic, and each of these is a very difficult language to translate — even now. It is dying for computers to be put upon this task, because each of these are a group of symbols — 500 perhaps — in which each one of them, for instance — I'm thinking of one in cuneiform that is seven different syllables and about six different words — appears exactly the same. The only way you can decide what that symbol means is by its context. When it comes to anything abstract it is extremely difficult to translate.

So we really have to go back to a language that we have continuity with and this is Greek. If you go back and look at the *Iliad*, it is a very interesting task from the point of view of examining the mentality. People are not conscious the way you and I are. They don't sit down and think and plan out what to do. Instead, they hear voices — voices called gods. They see visions and hear voices that tell them what to do. These voices called gods are indeed the agents that plan the Trojan War, that decide everything that is to go on. It is very hard for we who are conscious to go back and try to imagine that Achilles doesn't have any of this inner space that we do. He does not have a mind-space behind his eyes; he doesn't imagine a mind-space behind other people's eyes. We absolutely cannot identify with him, and try to feel what it is like to be him as we do with everybody else. It's a very different kind of thing. Achilles is not conscious, he has a different mentality in which it's like he has two sides of his mentality: one which is himself speaking and the other these auditory voices — hallucinations — that he hears. This is what I'm calling the bicameral mind. The word bicameral is simply a metaphor from two houses of a legislature — an upper and a lower house.

There was this kind of mentality, not conscious, in which in every novel situation, the very novelty of the situation built up a little bit of biochemical stress that then triggered in the brain an auditory hallucination.

Q: So essentially it was happening inside the mind?

JAYNES: Yes — inside the brain. We have to be very careful of the language here.

Q: And there was a biochemical basis for it?

JAYNES: Yes. Just as there is nowadays. Any of us, if we were backed into the corner, losing everything we have in our lives that is valuable to us, and people crossing us one way or another, we would build up biochemical stress and begin hearing auditory hallucinations.

This is of course what happens in schizophrenia, except the schizophrenic patient is one who, genetically, has a lower threshold for such things. Perhaps we can talk about schizophrenia a little bit later because there are lots of qualifications, so perhaps I better save that. But I'm saying that the quality of the auditory hallucination was just as it is in a modern schizophrenic patient, as it is in many of us, who may at one time have heard auditory hallucinations. Just as clear as it was to Joan of Arc, or to many other people through history — perfectly normal people — who hear hallucinations directing them, telling them what to do.

I think the bicameral mind is the kind of mentality men had going way back to the beginning of agriculture — 9000 or 10,000 B.C. I think language evolved with hallucinations being very much a part of it. Then when mankind moved to a civilization it was because he could hear hallucinations from his king or tribal chief, this growing into hallucinations from gods — when the chief died you still could hear hallucinations from him.

From 9000 B.C. up to 1500 B.C. this was man's mind. All the early civilizations, wherever you go — civilization starts in Mesopotamia, spreads to Egypt, spreads to the Hittites, then we can go over to the Indus Valley, go over to the Yangtze, and the Chinese, go over to the early Mexican civilizations 1000 years later, or the civilizations of the Peruvian Andes that end in the Incas — all of them have this similarity of gods. Have you ever thought, "That's an odd idea — where can this come from?"

We are so used to thinking in terms of atheism and from our particular religious heritages, which doesn't really apply to the question as I'm trying to phrase it. When you go back in history, it isn't God, it is always the plurality — thousands of gods everywhere. What can all that mean? I'm saying, very simply, that these were auditory hallucinations that everybody had — to one extent or another — and these auditory hallucinations were organized in the brain, that the brain was coding things back into language, that the person only can hear. This guided him and told him what to do whenever a novel situation came up.

The evidence for this, if we look at these early civilizations, wherever we go, there are always things like idols, figurines, statues of various kinds, that I think were hallucinogenic — or allowed a person to hear an auditory hallucination more easily.

If one takes the theory that I'm working on, and applies it to schizophrenia — a part of schizophrenia is a partial relapse to the bicameral mind. One can say that everybody before 1500 B.C. was schizophrenic. There was no such thing as madness before 1000 B.C. If you go back and look for it, you can't find it. You can find such things as idiocy, but there is nobody set off from the community — the way we do with mental patients today — until you get into the period I regard as conscious.

Another very interesting thing to look at here is Plato. Plato, when he was a young man in the *Phaedo*, has one of the most beautiful passages in all his works about the various kinds of madness. He has four kinds — all based on visitations of the gods more or less. We don't know whether Plato believes it in the literal sense or in the mythical sense. But regardless, "madness is a blessing." It is regarded as good. He says that between the word *manike* and *mantike* — two Greek words at the time, with just the addition of the 't' to one — one means madness, the other means prophecy. He says they are exactly the same thing.

When Plato comes to write *The Laws* — his last work — he has a conception of madness that is just like ours. It is very different from his earlier writings and it is indeed now that the family should take care of mentally ill people — people who are *manike* — that these people can't take care of themselves and that they have completely wrong ideas: that they can fly, or that they are gods, or something else.

In Plato's own lifetime, the whole concept of mental disease is starting to develop. It is something that scholars should really go into in more
depth. My reading is from Plato, and that is most of the evidence that I
am familiar with. That is 400 B.C. — then right after that, in the first century B.C. and the first century A.D., you find the development of schizophrenia the way we come to think of it.

One of the interesting things is that they had another word for schizophrenia called *paranoia* — not our paranoia at all. Paranoia coming from
two words: *noia* meaning mind and *para* meaning beside. It really meant
having another mind beside your own directing you. The word paranoia
meaning madness goes on up until about the second century A.D. in Rome
and then it disappears. It was only in the nineteenth century that the
German psychiatrist Karl Kahlbaum invented it for a persecutory kind
of illness.

In the bicameral period, the voices you heard were usually helpful. You
had been trained, from the age of four, when children start to hallucinate
quite a bit — even in our culture they hallucinate but we immediately get
them out of that — but back in the bicameral times the child of four was
taught that he or she would be hearing the voices of gods and so on. These
were organizations of all admonitory experience that told him helpful
things: encouraged him to do the right thing and told him not to do the
wrong thing.

But in conscious times, children are not brought up this way. In fact,
children are brought up not to hear the voices. Another place you can
find this is in the Old Testament. The Old Testament of course is the
story of the breakdown of the bicameral mind among the Hebrews and its
replacement with consciousness. If you read for instance from the oldest
parts of the Old Testament, such as the Book of Amos — Amos is almost
a bicameral man — and compare it with something like Ecclesiastes.
Ecclesiastes is a very conscious man.

They ask Amos who he is and he says, "I am not a prophet, I'm just a
poor Shepard boy," as the King James version has it, "I'm just a gatherer of
sycamore fruit." Then he says wait, wait — here it comes, and in the King
James version he says, "Thus sayeth the Lord, thus sayeth Yahweh." And
out comes this long speech that I don't think Amos understands himself.
And this is like the bicameral man. It's not exactly that, because the voice
is not telling him personally what to do, it's telling all of his people, all of
his country what to do. This is very much prized in the life of his time,

which is 800 B.C. Of course these scribes are following Amos — Amos is illiterate — and they are writing down everything he says very carefully. Then if you go to Ecclesiastes, he's the person who says, "In my heart I see the understanding…"

Q: So what he's done then is internalized the gods?

JAYNES: I think consciousness is a lot more than the internalization of gods. I think it is really this creation of a metaphorical space in which you have an analog of yourself and the world and so on.

Q: An inner space…

JAYNES: An "inner space" in quotes — it's not a real space. Although we feel as though it's a real space. It's astonishing when you think that right here and now — the three of us are sitting in my office here — I can't help but think that behind your eyes there's a little space in there, and behind my eyes there's a little space — every time we introspect, there's a little space in there. We know that that's not true — it's something we assume. Just as in mathematics, we put down various postulates and make deductions from it. Those postulates don't necessarily have to be real, and yet they are what makes mathematics work, and it's the same thing with consciousness.

Q: What was the thing that brought that about? Was that space there and the conscious man, as opposed to bicameral man, stumbled on to it, or did he create that space? What happened, how did he manage to do that?

JAYNES: That is an historical question. It happened in the second millennium B.C. — toward the end of it. There is a whole confluence of causes that caused the breakdown of the bicameral mind, of these bicameral kingdoms, in Mesopotamia, for example. They didn't work anymore, because there was an era of such social chaos that we really can't imagine it. We have to imagine most of the civilized world suddenly in utter chaos. One of the things that happened then was the volcanic eruption and subsequent sinking of the land space around the island of Thera that we realize now is the origin of the myth of Atlantis. But what this did was to cause a tsunami that was so vast that you can hardly imagine it, roaring all over that part of the Mediterranean. The eruption had a force that some scholars regard as like that of a hydrogen bomb. This is being estimated now by geologists — it's very interesting work.[1]

But this started a whole series of migrations that in Greece results in the Dorian invasions that nobody knows anything about, it results in the invasions of Egypt by the Peoples of the Sea — all these migrations start happening as everybody is moving in on everybody else.

Now this is one of the causes — there are other causes. But towards the end of the second millennium B.C. mankind is really in bad shape. The kingdoms have toppled, you can't trust your gods anymore, your kings aren't there, and everybody is in migration. Everybody except in one place: Assyria. And Assyria starts mopping up and makes the first really cruel, brutal kingdom.

There are historical facts that all this happened. Now I am saying that it is out of this chaos mankind first learned consciousness — created it. You can plot these changes. In Mesopotamia in 1300 B.C. we find the first literature anywhere in the world which contains all this crying after lost gods, just as we have in the Psalms, for example. "When am I going to see god face to face again? As the hart thirsts after the water brook, so longs my mind after you, oh gods," as Psalm 49 says. It is exactly 1300 B.C. in Mesopotamian literature that this first comes in. Then this becomes almost a totality of what is called the "Wisdom Literature" of Mesopotamia. This has a complete continuity into the Psalms of the Old Testament.

Q: OK so you have all of these cataclysms and people trying to recover what worked before — it's not working anymore. How was it then that something new came out of that, and this big change happened? Is it because the gods stopped talking to people?

JAYNES: The gods probably did not stop talking right away, but they probably told people very maladaptive things to do. Not quite as badly as in modern schizophrenic patients, but probably it was very maladaptive to do what these voices told you to do. Remember what the voices were: They were syntheses, amalgamations, in a very careful way, of all the admonitory experience that you had from parents, kings, viziers, and that kind of thing — all stored in the brain, reorganized, and put into linguistic code.

---

1. For more on the Thera explosion and resulting tsunami, see "Sinking Atlantis," *Secrets of the Dead Series* (PBS Home Video, 2008), pbs.org/video/secrets-of-the-dead-sinking-atlantis. The devastating tsunamis in Indonesia in 2004 and Japan in 2011 provide a modern context for the destructive force of the even larger Mediterranean tsunami. — *Ed.*

It's being done in the temporal lobe of the right hemisphere. This is the god part of the bicameral mind.

Then suddenly you have terrible chaos — nothing like this has happened before — so all this admonitory experience doesn't work — it can't tell you what to do. And so you have to think of different ways of doing things. We are trying to solve some of these problems, and we are only partially there.

Let me give you an example. Suppose you are a member of a small community, or a city-state that is suddenly toppled, and some group is invading and comes in and starts taking over, speaking another language. Let us say that they are raping your wife. Based on your admonitory experience, you'd hear voices directing you to kill these people — in which case you'd be killed yourself.

Now if you had another self inside, and you could say to yourself, "I will just wait until I can get you outside in the dark, when you are not looking at me" — that kind of thing would be of great advantage in such chaotic times. The capacity of long term deceit is very important, and I think it is one of things that starts off consciousness.

Of course in our ordinary life, deceit is a strong word, but we are not being totally honest with everybody — nor should we be. It isn't necessarily deceit, we have all kinds of things that we do — in courtesies and so on — in which we have a little self inside ourselves. These are all metaphoric terms of course. That is our "real" self. We can delay various kinds of gratifications or we can think about things we are going to do in our imagination. This is something that bicameral man could not do. It became very important in this social breakdown to develop this.

It is very primitive when it happens in Mesopotamia. But when it happens in Greece a few centuries later, then it really starts to expand — Greece teaches the world. China comes later. We tend to think of Chinese and Indian civilizations as the most ancient in the world — they are very old, they are older than Europe — but in the development of civilization, China comes about 1,000 years after Mesopotamia and India about 500 years after.

Q: So there would be a huge selective advantage to having a conscious mind...

JAYNES: Yes.

Q: The conscious mind can deal with these cataclysms that the bicameral mind can't … was the creation of that inner space a biochemical reaction to something?

JAYNES: Obviously there have to be brain changes going on as we go from the bicameral mind to consciousness. The biochemistry of consciousness or even the neurology of consciousness is something we really don't know anything about. We really are just making bad guesses at it right now. I think we understand a little more about the bicameral mind because there are areas in the brain that, if stimulated, even now, trigger auditory hallucinations. These predominantly are the areas of the non-dominant hemisphere — which in most of us is the right hemisphere — corresponding to the speech areas of the dominant hemisphere. If you stimulate what would correspond to Wernicke's area on the right hemisphere, people hear voices somewhat similar to what we might expect auditory hallucinations would be.

Q: Did perhaps bicameral man begin to realize that the voices of gods he was hearing were really hallucinations and that he himself was the god?

JAYNES: No — I know what you're saying. This is a question that comes up very often. I think auditory hallucinations have a very unique quality, a very special mechanism in the brain that is completely different from consciousness and antithetical to consciousness. Consciousness is a difference. It is not that man had been hearing voices and suddenly he realizes that the voices come from his own brain, so then he internalizes it and then experiences them as his inner thoughts instead. I really don't think that is the case.

I don't know what kind of internal neurological inhibition of areas of the right hemisphere went on — but I think it did happen. I think consciousness is something that is built up out of language. It is a matter of ascribing something inside oneself, but first there is the internalization of feelings, of becoming aware of internal sensations when one is about to do things.

Q: So rather than bringing what was outside in, it is simply becoming aware of what was…

JAYNES: Becoming aware first of internal sensations but then building on to them little tags: "Oh, that's a memory" — which it isn't at all, it's all made up. You start thinking of a memory, and think "the memory is inside me." That is a brand new idea, and actually a memory isn't inside you — it's nowhere. Actually this space you and I introspect on isn't inside you — it's nowhere. Nobody wants to say that 2 + 2 = 4 is located in any particular place — it just isn't. It is the same way with consciousness and the same way with memories, and so on. Of course for all these things there are neurological events that are going on that are correlated with them.

But back in these very important times, so full of human agony, when mankind was going from the bicameral mind to consciousness, it was not simply a matter of internalizing the voices that you heard. It was a matter of getting rid of the voices, and in their stead, slowly going through the process of inventing things inside oneself.

First they are organic sensations. In Greece it was the *phrenes* — the lungs. There was the heart, and other internal kinds of feelings that people then ascribe volition to. Instead of the god making them do something, it was my *thumos* — my heart or my lungs — that's what made me do it.

Then you have linguistic things being built up of putting memories, for example, in the lungs. I'm talking now about Greek literature back in the *Iliad* and following the *Iliad*. The word *phrenes* — from which phrenology comes — this was one of the early words for mind and it originally meant lungs. You can follow it along in the Greek literature from the *Iliad*, through the *Odyssey*, through the Elegiac and lyric poets — Sappho, for example. Sappho is a fascinating person to look at because she is the first person to talk about love being a tempest inside oneself. She talks about her heart being torn apart by the tempests of love that she has within her. Nobody ever talked that way before. That is part of the internalization that is going on. But it is not the internalization of the gods; it is the creating of this internal world.

This progresses until Solon in 600 B.C. — this man that we should know more about. Solon talks about mind and consciousness exactly as you and I do. We only have about 50 or 60 lines of his writings left — they are all in fragments. But we know about him from other writings. He was a poet-ruler of a part of Greece in 600 B.C. He was someone who traveled extensively. He had probably been to Mesopotamia — which already had some type of proto-consciousness — and when he went back to Greece, all his writings are consistently talking about mind and consciousness the way we do.

It is astonishing, because if you take the very preceding writers, they are not nearly as far advanced in consciousness as Solon is. Of course, one has to immediately say here that there are probably a lot of Greek writers we know nothing about; everything of theirs has disappeared.

All during this time we must also remember that there were many oracles throughout Greece, Mesopotamia, and so on, that told people what to do. These were people, who, like the prophets in the Old Testament, could still hear the voices of the gods and direct mankind.

If one takes the whole history of oracles — it is a fascinating thing how this develops. This is mankind trying to keep in touch with the gods that have disappeared from ordinary mentality as man has become conscious. The ways and means and rituals by which mankind have been trying to get back to the voices of the gods and the old feelings of certainty, ever since the breakdown of the bicameral mind, are of course as legion as all of our religions and all of our methods of induction ceremonies to get into various kinds of trance states or various kinds of inspiration.

Q: Is music in any way related to this?

JAYNES: Music — a fascinating subject. Why is music so moving and wonderful to us and why do we have music connected with most of our religions? Music as an induction ceremony is something that can lead us into meaning.

The experience of music happens to have a neurological location directly next to and into those areas that, in the theory of the bicameral mind, the gods spoke from. Music, in most of us, is processed in the right hemisphere, in the right temporal lobe, right next to what corresponds to what we call Wernicke's area.

I think the reason music is so often used in all of our most important moments and our religious ceremonies — and not just in ourselves but throughout all tribes, always music as a kind of induction into something that is going to happen — this is a building up of excitation right next to what used to be the place where the voices of the gods were organized and came out as auditory hallucinations.

Q: What about dreams?

JAYNES: There is another fascinating subject. It is something we do every night, and we find it impossible to think of somebody who really never dreamed at all. Dreaming to me is one of the most conscious experiences possible. Dreaming is simply consciousness in REM sleep.

If the theory that I've been talking about is correct, this would then mean that mankind before he was conscious — that is before approximately 1000 b.c. — didn't dream the way we do. And I've gone back and tried to look into the literature to find out if this is the case, and it turns out that it was. Why scholars have never remarked about this I don't know.

It isn't that they didn't dream completely. It is that their dreams were utterly different than ours. They are indeed what I would call "bicameral dreams." They are visitations by gods, angels, and what not that come and tell people what to do. And the dreamer never imagines that he's anywhere else except in his bed

Throughout the *Iliad* there are four dreams. One of the great ones is with Agamemnon at the beginning of Book Two. Oneiros comes to Agamemnon and tells him what to do. Agamemnon is never anywhere except in his bed. Another example is the famous Jacob's Ladder dream in Genesis. Jacob lies down on a pillow of stones and dreams right there that he sees a ladder — it is probably the stairway of a ziggurat — going up to Heaven with Yahweh at the top and angels going up and down the side. And Yahweh says to him, "I am the God of Abraham and of your fathers and I shall be your God and I shall protect you too." When Jacob wakes up he thinks it happened right there, he never moved. He then anoints those stones Beth-El, which means "House of God" — because that's where it happened.

Now you and I almost never have a dream like that — except very rarely. When we dream, we are often far away in some other land, some other country, in some other situation, and we are doing things. It's very different.

Q: We even see ourselves doing it.

Jaynes: We do sometimes, which is part of consciousness. So the whole change in mankind of how he dreams parallels how man thinks and indeed the whole development of consciousness.

If one were to try to look over these last 3,000 years, which are the years since the bicameral mind broke down — since the invention of consciousness and its development — one can see that all around us are the remnants of our bicameral past, in terms of all of our religious heritage, as well as reactions to what we have lost in not hearing these voices of certainty anymore.

For example, one can take the whole history of politics over this time. There is no question about politics in the bicameral world — that is what it was. After the bicameral world, we have to invent new ways of governing. So, if we take the broad view of history, we find we go into a dictatorship this time, an aristocracy this time, and a democracy this time. I think of course mankind is learning just what kind of government is best. But these are slow and agonizing things and the whole history of wars and battles is indeed this history of mankind trying to solve this problem of governing. You can almost look at nationalism as one kind of replacement for gods at one time. That is slowly disappearing and we are becoming more of a world culture now.

There are a lot of other things that can be interpreted this way. One can take the whole history of logic that really begins in the concept of *logos*, or reason, back just at about 400 or 500 B.C. in Greece, and follow this up to modern times, coming out in mathematics and other things.

Let's take the large view. Mankind up to 10,000 B.C., had what I call a "tribal mind" — not conscious, not bicameral, but developing language. From 9000 B.C. to 1500 B.C., this was the period of the bicameral mind that organized mankind into civilizations and had great inventions and everything else. Now from 1500 B.C. — or 1000 B.C. — to 2000 A.D. is what we can call the subjective conscious period of mankind. It is not very long. It is only 3,000 years. Let us try to think of 100,000 A.D. We've only been 3,000 years into subjective consciousness. We really don't know if we are changing now but I of course regard us as in a transitional period. From the bicameral mind and you can say "to what?" — it is not necessarily in the cards as far as to what.

Q: That is what evolution is all about; you don't know what the next step is going to be. There are a hundred directions you could go.

JAYNES: It is very difficult to know how biological evolution is going now. In a certain sense, biological evolution is perhaps even going backwards, in the sense that we are developing better ways to deal with genetic illnesses. This allows people who in an earlier age would have died off and not gone on to procreate — now they do live in our society, and the number of people who will have inherited illnesses such as diabetes is increasing, and will continue to increase. Medical people are very worried about this. So in a certain sense we don't really know what is happening with biological evolution.

But our cultural evolution — our cultural development; the development of what is going on in consciousness is largely a cultural thing, taught to us in childhood, in which we do various things, have various operations that go on in this mind-space that we have learned, and need language for. The possibility is that indeed this can change and be very different in 100,000 A.D. — that is a very likely possibility.

Well, if one looks back at all these ancient kingdoms and how they were organized and the bicameral mind that was responsible for this, and we look at all its ruins around the world today — how the ziggurats have crumbled into the dust, and how the fires where Hector's body was being burned have flickered and are out — all this, that was the business of the gods ... the gods have now migrated out of what I have called the posterior part of the temporal lobe of the right hemisphere, outside the skin, into temples, and churches, and heavens, where we still seek them. Leaving us uncertain, seeking archaic authorization, looking around for what is right and wrong, looking around for tests of logic and reasoning — leaving us conscious.

And when we think that this consciousness, this invention of spaces behind everybody's eyes and in ourselves — and all this thing that we do when we are conscious of another person — this is the most human thing about us. And that humanity is really only 3,000 years old. And that is less than 100 generations. From which I think we can conclude that we are all still very young.

# CHAPTER 25

# Psychologist Concentrates
# on How We Think

Interview by Beth Macklin

THE GREAT PYRAMID, long hailed as one of the engineering wonders of the world, was constructed by builders without consciousness, says author Julian Jaynes.

Jaynes, a Princeton research psychologist, contends that "ancient people" — including Abraham and other patriarchs of the Old Testament — could not "think" as we do.

Instead, he believes after years of research, they obeyed auditory hallucinations — voices of gods originating in the right hemisphere.

"Only in about the last 3,000 years has mankind operated on a basis of what I refer to as 'consciousness' (introspective experience)."

A fellow psychologist has put Jaynes in the category of Freud and Jung for the "far-reaching" theories he expounded in his 1977 best seller, *The Origin of Consciousness in the Breakdown of the Bicameral Mind*.

Jaynes started a series of eight lectures here Monday, based on the research he did for his book and since. The series will continue through Thursday at noon and 7:30 p.m. at Hope Unitarian Church, 8432 S. Sheridan Road. The public will be welcome at a charge of $25 for the set of either noon or evening lectures.

He began pondering the problem of consciousness, Jaynes said, "at age 7, when I thought about what was going around in my head and wondering whether the same thing or another set of experiences was going on in the heads of other people I knew."

As he did his undergraduate work at Harvard, then went on to McGill and the University of Toronto, and finally to Yale University, Jaynes dug first into literature for the answers he hoped to find.

First published in *Tulsa World*, Oct. 7, 1980. © 1980 World Publishing Co. Reprinted with permission.

He subsequently tried and discarded mathematics and philosophy ("because philosophers are not good at looking at evidence") and turned to psychology.

"Consciousness," he says, comes to the average individual "somewhere between the ages of 3 and 6. Learning to walk or talk is not a reflective process. A child walks because someone he loves, usually the parent, calls to him. If he falls down on the way, he scrambles up and tries it again."

Seeking out the origins of consciousness, Jaynes said, he first worked on the theory that it spread down even to the simplest one-cell bodies and evolved from there.

"It was only when I scrapped that idea and started at the other end that I began to find the answer. Consciousness is in the human culture only.

"Motherhood conversation is so terribly important."

As the child is learning to talk, Jaynes believes, "the verbal community with which he is surrounded is where the magic happens.

"So, with all due respect to the liberated woman, my prejudice in [illegible] influence of the mother on the child I think she ought to be there all day long until the child goes to school, and then she — both parents, in fact — ought to continue the process in the hours after the child comes home from school."

Jaynes is intrigued with an experiment undertaken in a northeastern state, where children separated from their parents for any reason other than death are being taught by means of tape cassettes made by the parents.

"A parent reads the lessons into the recorder and the cassettes are played for the child in school. The experiment has shown they learn so much faster when the teaching voice is one that is familiar to them: one of their parents'."

Jaynes does not equate intelligence with consciousness. "I don't like the concept of intelligence because it is too mushy — too difficult to define limits clearly."

In Jaynes's opinion, chimpanzees are the most intelligent of the animal species. He has watched with great interest the experiments with Washoe, the chimp that has been taught human sign language.

"The great hope was that she would be able to pass along sign language to a younger chimpanzee, but when one was placed in her care, she taught only a couple of signs, and that was it."

When films of Washoe 'speaking' in sign language were shown to a group of deaf people, Jaynes said, "they just laughed and laughed. They said she 'talked' like a drunk human, slurring the words she attempted to convey by signs.

"What chimps have learned is amazing, but it's not nearly what a four-year-old child knows."

Jaynes believes his research will prove helpful in dealing with schizophrenics, "because that's what schizophrenia is: people hearing voices that tell them what to do, and it's the wrong thing. It would even prove helpful in dealing with 'normal' human beings, because we all have this pull within us between wanting to be our own person and wanting a voice — not of authority, but of authorization; someone to make the rules for us, whether it's an army officer or the church. That's how people fall prey to a Jim Jones (leader of the Guyana suicide group) or an Ayatollah Khomeini."

# CHAPTER 26

# Portland Radio Interview

Q: So Dr. Jaynes, when did your book come out, *The Origin of Consciousness in the Breakdown of the Bicameral Mind*?

JAYNES: Back in January of 1977, although the copyright is 1976. My publishers thought my book would immediately plummet to the bottom of any sales list, so they only had a run of about 5,000 copies. Both the publishers and I were quite surprised how many people did buy the book.

Q: I have here a copy of an article in *Time* magazine that appeared March 14, 1977 in the behavior section on the theory that you put forth in your book. It's entitled "The Lost Voices of the Gods."[1] What is this theory?

JAYNES: Well, in fact the publishers wanted me to title the book something like that, or "The Death of the Gods" and I insisted on the title that I have. The theory can perhaps be put in two or three sentences by saying that for a long time we have thought in psychology that consciousness was something biological, that was inherited, that probably developed by emergent evolution or something like that, with the growth of the cortex back in early mammals. And I had been spending all my life trying to pursue what this origin could be in animal behavior, until I realized just how confused I was about what consciousness was. Well, when we turn around and define consciousness properly, and then go and look for it in the earliest literatures that we can obtain, we find that it disappears, it simply is not present in the central older parts of the *Iliad*. And then you ask, "How did they make any choices, any decisions, if they couldn't introspect?" — which is what I'm saying consciousness is: introspection. And you find they didn't introspect, instead they heard voices telling them what to do, voices called gods, that we nowadays would call auditory hallucinations.

---

Transcribed and edited from a radio interview with Julian Jaynes dated April 19, 1982. From the Julian Jaynes Archives held at the Department of Psychology, University of Prince Edward Island.
1. John Leo, "The Lost Voices of the Gods," *Time*, March 14, 1977, 51–53.

This is what I call the bicameral mind, and consciousness arose when this bicameral mind broke down because it was no longer efficient to deal with chaotic situations around 1000 B.C.

Q: Now I picked up from the article that your theory has something to do with right brain/left brain cooperation or interaction, and that's of course a relatively popular subject now.

JAYNES: Unfortunately — it is almost too much of a fashion. I was at the beginning of this fashion because I had laboriously come to the idea that the neurological model for the bicameral mind is the right hemisphere or the right speech centers, particularly on the temporal lobe, speaking literally to the left hemisphere. When I say literally I mean it is organized into language and this is what an auditory hallucination is.

I first came to this theory back in early 1960s, thinking that this particular neurological model — the right brain/left brain — was much too simple for anything as complicated as this, and one finds that William James in his great two volume *Principles of Psychology* is even mocking such ideas way back then. But as the data started coming in, on the differences between the right and left hemisphere — all of the functions that are ascribed to the right hemisphere are precisely those functions that would be needed by these things called gods in the right hemisphere to civilize mankind. So I was given tremendous encouragement by lots of data — everything from the so-called split-brain data to clinical literature and so on. Before that time, the right hemisphere was simply looked on as a spare tire in case something happened to the left hemisphere. But now we know it's a very different thing — it has very special cognitive, spatial, synthetic, facial recognition, music — all of these functions are primarily right hemispheric functions.

Q: It seems to be from what I've picked-up and heard, in addition to what you've mentioned, that right hemisphere function is looking at things in the "whole" form. Would that be one of the attributes that would give the voices the feeling of being omniscient and all-knowing?

JAYNES: Well I'm not sure I would say it's the right brain that sees things in whole because the left brain does too; it's simple Gestalt psychology and perception. This kind of real perception of wholes probably goes on on a deeper level of the brain than the cortex. But what we mean by thinking of the right hemisphere as more holistic is that it fits things into patterns

— into a holistic pattern — we should just leave out the word "percep-tion." It is indeed something that fits things into patterns versus the left hemisphere which does not do so nearly as well.

Q: The left hemisphere sees the detail?

JAYNES: The left hemisphere sees the detail, can work with the detail, and breaks up a pattern and looks at its different parts, and the right hemi-sphere is fitting things together. Even as I say that, I hope that it can be concluded that we need both, and when I called right brain/left brain thinking or analysis a fashion, I meant that I think the fashion has gone a little bit too far. The other day in the New York train a friend of mine heard one little girl say to the other, and they were about 11 years old, "Oh the trouble with you is you're too left brained." Well, when this fashion gets down to the 11-year-old level, I think we may have cause to worry, because the left brain, that can analyze and pick apart problems to see what they are, is so important to us. The right brain is more emotional, more involved with fitting things together. For example, if a child comes home and the parents are arguing — and it has nothing to do with the child — if the child is responding in a holistic, right hemisphere manner, it's going to be very bad for the child. Whereas if the child can use his left hemisphere and analyze the problem and see that this has nothing to do with him, he is going to be in much better shape.

What I'm really trying to say is that in some parts of education they are thinking now, "How can we educate the right brain because all of our education is for the left brain?" Well, I'm really not in favor of going that far with this new fashion. I think we should go very slowly. We are using the right brain every day. Everyone listening to this program is using his right hemisphere for lots of functions. So we don't want to think that it is this great, unused territory, because that isn't the case.

Q: Assuming that the theory of the breakdown of the bicameral mind is correct, what consequence or significance does it have for people who are living today?

JAYNES: Well, we all have vestiges of this ancient mentality called the bicameral mind, in which people heard hallucinations called gods — all of us have vestiges of that still with us. One of the vestiges is of course schizophrenia, which is a partial relapse to this older mentality. I'm very glad that my theory is being taught to schizophrenic patients in some clinics now, because it makes the patient feel so much better about what is happening to them. Before, if you hear voices and experience the crumbling away of consciousness, you could never try to explain to anybody what was going on — this would build up the panic even more. But once the patient realizes, "No, you've been under a lot of stress, and it means that your consciousness is just sort of conking out here, and you are relapsing to an earlier mentality, and this is what these voices are" — it makes them feel much more comfortable with themselves.

So that's one kind of result, but an even more important result is the realization that consciousness is learned on the basis of metaphor. When we realize that consciousness is learned and that we are teaching it to every new generation of children, it means that the sky is open to try to develop and understand new kinds of techniques of really teaching consciousness. I think this is extremely important, but if you ask me specifically what we should do, I would have to pause because I honestly don't know. I've only gone so far with this theory and I certainly would like help from others to do further theoretical analysis.

Q: I'm sure you've had a degree of criticism. Does it fall into general themes of criticism? If so, I'm wondering what they are and what's your response?

JAYNES: Well, usually it's somebody that wants to find something wrong and thinks that they have. For example, a major review of my book in a psychological journal was all about chimpanzees and mirrors and was just terribly wrong. Some other criticisms are about particular texts from particular periods, and these are well taken criticisms. I have a great skepticism about the translation and dating of ancient texts. I'm very careful about their dating. Most people — even classical scholars — are not, as if mankind has always been the same, so you don't have to worry about what the precise date of the text is. But that is indeed my territory, to make sure of the date, and then see the chronological flowering of this internal life that we have.

So the criticisms are extremely varied. I've had some very positive responses and of course some very negative responses. One very brief review simply said, "If Freud opened a can of worms, Jaynes has opened a barrel of snakes" — that was it, just that sentence.

I've covered a great deal of territory, and I have to have made some mistakes somewhere. But I think once you realize the problem of the origin of consciousness and then when you see the entire picture — fitting the Bible into this, ancient literature, all of the gods in ancient times, and poetic inspiration, even today, it all fits together into this grand pattern that needs a great deal more development in many of its areas.

Q: What would it take to convince you that the theory is wrong?

JAYNES: That's a good question. I think it would take several things. If somebody could show that no one has auditory hallucinations, or did have them in these ancient civilizations, that would certainly wipe out the basis for the bicameral mind. There are thousands and thousands of cuneiform tablets that have never been read, never translated. If a proper translation of them could be achieved, where they said something like Ecclesiastes says, "In my heart I see that wisdom excelleth folly" which comes from about 200 B.C. — if that were dated at 2000 B.C., I would at least know that my dating was indeed wrong.

There are ways of testing the theory. The idea that the right hemisphere is involved in auditory hallucinations can be tested, and it has been, by Dr. Buchsbaum at the National Institute of Mental Health in Bethesda, Maryland.[2] And indeed it corroborates the idea that in schizophrenics — perhaps not in all but in most — it is the right temporal lobe that is being activated during auditory hallucinations.

Q: On this program we've featured programs on music, and I'm personally interested in what goes on inside a person when they hear music. We've heard from a man who spoke a bit about the anatomy of the hearing system, but I think that what goes on inside the brain is uncharted territory — they are beginning to develop ways of getting pictures of which area is activated and so on. What are your thoughts on what happens with music, and were the voices of the gods all in words or did they have other forms, such as musical form?

JAYNES: I think they all had meter and this is the origin of poetry. And music was often an accompaniment of various kinds of religious rituals when they are trying to get the gods back, and we do know that the

---

2. M.S. Buchsbaum, D.H. Ingvar, R. Kessler, R.N. Waters, et al., "Cerebral Glucography with Positron Tomography: Use In Normal Subjects and In Patients with Schizophrenia," *Archives of General Psychiatry*, 1982, *39*, 3, 251–9. For a review of more recent studies confirming Jaynes's neurological model, see Marcel Kuijsten, "Consciousness, Hallucinations, and the Bicameral Mind: Three Decades of New Research," in M. Kuijsten (ed.), *Reflections on the Dawn of Consciousness* (Henderson, NV: Julian Jaynes Society, 2006). — *Ed.*

musical area is indeed in the right hemisphere, right in that same area in which the gods spoke from, according to this hypothesis of the bicameral mind. So that's another place where it fits very exactly.

Now, most of us who are not musicians are indeed hearing and enjoying music using our right hemispheres. But if you are a trained musician, what you're training consists of is training music to the left hemisphere, so that you have music in both your hemispheres. I often think of what is wrong with modern classical compositions — such as Webern and Schoenberg and the 12 tone scale and things of this kind — is they are very intellectual, very left hemispheric, only trained musicians can like it, because the right hemisphere cannot respond to it. So I wish we could get away from highly trained composers coming out of universities, who have trained music into both hemispheres and are writing left hemispheric music, whereas most of us want to hear music with our right hemispheres, so we do not "understand it."

Q: Well, Dr. Jaynes it's been fascinating talking about your theory, and the book is entitled *The Origin of Consciousness in the Breakdown of the Bicameral Mind.* Thank you.

JAYNES: Thank you very much, Steve.

# CHAPTER 27

# Baltimore Radio Interview

ROBERT LOPEZ: Let's start with your theory, which is an interesting one — a provocative one — and I take it that it's not universally accepted, because I also have in the studio this morning another book that's just come out this year called *The Universe Within* by a popular science writer Morton Hunt. *The Universe Within* is a fairly good summary of cognitive science — where psychology is today, and it has been changing in the last few years — and Julian Jaynes isn't in it anywhere. Why? Are you being ignored or what happens?

JULIAN JAYNES: My work, my approach, simply does not fit with what he was trying to do, which was simply to give a rather superficial, I'm afraid — at least the parts that I've read of this book — it doesn't go into cognitive science's problems very deeply. It goes along the surface of certain things that have been found — some of them have been known since the nineteenth century as a matter of fact. But there is a fashion now, called cognitive science, and it used to be called the study of the higher mental processes. Well, none of this faces the problem that I've been spending my entire life with, and this is the problem of the origin of consciousness. This is a problem that came to the fore, well really in 1859, when Darwin and Wallace had just published their epoch-making ideas on natural selection and evolution. And then the problem was, "How can you get all this interior mind and all this space that we introspect on — how can we get that out of mere natural selection, as was described in *The Origin of Species*?"

LOPEZ: So you figure if little green blobs in salt water somewhere aren't conscious, and we are conscious, and there's been an evolution between us and them over many millions of years, then how did consciousness evolve?

Transcribed and edited from a WIYY Baltimore radio interview by Robert E. Lopez (1953–2005) with Julian Jaynes, November 6, 1982.

JAYNES: That's right, and that's the problem. And what I was going to say was, then that problem, nobody could work with it — it was just shelved around 1910 and in came behaviorism. And cognitive science is sort of on the last end of behaviorism, and it doesn't want to even look at this problem of the origin of consciousness. If you look up the index of Mr. Hunt's book you won't find evolution there either.

LOPEZ: Why don't you tell us what consciousness is? I always thought I knew what it was but after your book I found out I didn't.

JAYNES: Well I thought I knew what it was too all the time that I was trying to study the evolution of animal behavior, and thinking that consciousness was learning, or solving problems — all of these things you can show consciousness is not. It is not necessary for these things. And my first chapter, which I think is probably one of the most difficult chapters in the book, tries to sort out what consciousness is not. And then when you really have teased away from this global, rather sloppy idea of consciousness that most of us have, just exactly what it is not, then I think it becomes clear that consciousness is indeed this metaphoric analog thing we do when we introspect. I would define it technically as an analog 'I' — that is an analog of oneself — narratizing (which simply means telling stories through time), in a mind-space. And all of these things — this is the most difficult part of the book — all of these things are based on metaphors of our actual behavior. It can be hard to describe in just a few sentences, but I like to compare it to mathematics, in the sense that it is artificial — we make up mathematics and then it turns around and works for us. Well I think that human beings at one time learned consciousness on the basis of metaphor, on the basis of language. And then we have this analog space, which we do these analog behaviors — whatever it is we're doing when we introspect. It is not something that is genetically, biologically there, it is learned. And this is the very important basis on which I was working.

LOPEZ: I want to back up a little here, because this is as you say the most difficult concept of the book. You've just said in a few sentences what you took an entire chapter to explain. Let's talk about *analog* first — the terms you're using: *analog* and what you mean when you say that consciousness is a metaphor of the real world. I think you're talking about imagination aren't you?

JAYNES: Imagination is part of consciousness, indeed. But I wouldn't separate imagination even from reminiscent memory — it's actually all the same quality of thing. Supposing I was trying to solve a problem and then I wanted to have words to describe getting the solution. I'd say, "Oh my goodness, I see the answer now — I see the answer now." Well, you're not seeing anything in the sense of opening your eyes and looking around the world right now. It's an analog of that kind of "see." It's like another little self inside of you that is suddenly doing this "seeing" into the problem. Use of that word "see" is an analog of this exterior seeing that we and all animals do. So it's an analog in that sense, and it's built up because we do have language that can make these constructions that become consciousness in that way.

LOPEZ: So then these pictures that we see in our head are representations of the real world. You mentioned in a place when you think about how to get from here to the store, you run through a map in your mind. And that something is not real — that's a representation of the world that you build up over your experience.

JAYNES: That's right. And it's like a metaphor. It's a metaphor in poetry — you say, "something is *like* something else." So that little map that you have of going to the store is like you're actually going to the store. And what we do in consciousness is, let's say that you're deciding "Should I turn right or left at this particular block to find the shortest way?" Well in your imagination you would go through that to figure out which is the shortest way. And this is what consciousness is doing all the time when we make decisions. It helps us make decisions of this sort.

LOPEZ: Now you also point out that a lot of things we do in everyday life we do without being conscious of them, and indeed there are some things we couldn't do if we were conscious of them.

JAYNES: Yes I think so.

LOPEZ: Now driving is something you do and you're not really conscious of it most of the time.

JAYNES: You're not. Very often — if somebody is driving to work today, they may be talking to someone or they may be listening to this program. We hope that they are being conscious of what this program is about, but at the same time they are automatically making all of the adjustments that are necessary to drive a car down the road. But then supposing they suddenly had a flat tire, their consciousness would switch off from this program and then they'd have to be conscious and think about what to do next. We're constantly doing this.

LOPEZ: Now we want to hold on to this point because this figures later in the theory — this idea that we do a lot of things in everyday life on autopilot, unconsciously, until something unexpected happens. And then suddenly our consciousness snaps on to deal with the problem. So we want to hang on to this process that happens and we'll talk about it later. Now on the other hand, you say that playing the piano is something that you really can't do consciously — if you were conscious of all the fingers going here and there you'd mess it up.

JAYNES: That's quite true. Anybody who plays the piano realizes that. Of course consciousness comes in at the beginning of learning to play the piano, but then these things become automatic. But even if you don't play the piano, just try to be conscious of what you're saying the next time you are in conversation. What is it that you are conscious of? If right now I were conscious of each word as I started to say it I'd simply have to stop talking. Instead it's a different kind of thing — I'm conscious of an intention, a meaning I'm trying to get across, and automatically the words slip out. And I think so much of what we do is like this and it shows you that consciousness is not nearly as extensive as most people think it is. It isn't all cognition, it isn't all of mind. It is this process that comes in when something novel happens and we have to figure out what to do about it.

LOPEZ: I would like to throw in a couple of other points. One thing I don't think you mention in your book but that occurred to me — when you get into a situation where you're making a cup of coffee and you're not thinking about it, you're not conscious of what you're doing, and suddenly you pick up a bottle of ketchup and pour it into the coffee. That shows you that you're definitely not conscious all the time. Something called "selection error" — where you're doing something automatically but at the wrong time.

JAYNES: I think we've all had experiences like that.

LOPEZ: Also we should make a distinction here that when we're saying we're not conscious of much of what we do; we don't mean unconscious as in "knocked out."

JAYNES: No.

LOPEZ: You call that something else.

JAYNES: That's right. I try not to use the word "unconscious" at all. I don't want to slip over into Freudian terminology either because I'm in disagreement with Freud. I talk about things simply being not conscious. Nobody is conscious right now of their breathing, until they suddenly can make themselves so. It's a hard thing at first to appreciate, simply because we have in our culture and language these words conscious vs. unconscious, meaning "knocked out," and therefore we think all mental activity is conscious. This isn't true. I tend to talk about just simple reactivity, or one could come up with any number of words, such as the automatic pilot — to go back to your metaphor — that most of us are on, for most of what we do during the day.

LOPEZ: Now you say that at one time, something like 3,000 years ago and then further back, that human beings were not conscious, that their minds did not have the imagination, the consciousness that we do.

JAYNES: This was an astonishing discovery to me. That when I came upon this new definition of consciousness, which I felt was correct — although there's lots of loose ends and lots more to work out about it — that consciousness is based on language. Then to get the idea to go back into history and now you have a handle on it, you can see what it is you're looking for. And we go back to the earliest writing of human beings, to look at them from this point of view: do they have this analog 'I', do they decide things by making pictures in their minds in this kind of way? And when you look at the earliest writings of mankind, such as the *Iliad* in Greek, it's really quite astonishing that there is no consciousness there in the older parts of these poems. There are exceptions — and listeners who know the *Iliad* and have read it in the original know that there are exceptions — but in the older parts of it, as agreed upon by most classical scholars, there is no consciousness in this kind of way.

LOPEZ: Now what do you mean? How does this show up in writing?

JAYNES: You read it, and then you look at all the terms that later come to mean "mind," and you see that they mean something else. And then you find that in these writings there's a different kind of mentality — a mentality that very, very few of us have nowadays, a mentality that we're calling the bicameral mind, which means simply that instead of figuring out what to do as you and I do, whenever there was a novel situation, a person heard a voice — an auditory hallucination — like Joan of Arc heard her voices, like William Blake and Immanuel Swedenborg, or, in a negative way, like modern schizophrenic patients hear voices. These voices were called gods. This was indeed what gods were. They were I think auditory hallucinations coming from a certain part of the brain. This is what we call the bicameral mind, and it is a kind of mentality that characterizes not just Greek civilization, but all of the civilizations before approximately 1000 B.C.

LOPEZ: In your book you describe the two hemispheres of the brain, and how certain brain functions are separated — that one side of the brain does some things better than the other side does. When you talk about the bicameral mind in ancient times, you're referring to a time when the two hemispheres of people's brains did not operate in as integrated a manner as they do today. It was almost as though people had two minds in one head. Is that accurate?

JAYNES: I don't like to say it quite that way. I like to say that the bicameral mind is a phenomenon that you find there in the texts, and the neurological model of it, at present, is that it is indeed the difference between the two hemispheres. That the part of the brain that these voices that I've just described come from …

LOPEZ: The gods?

JAYNES: Yes … come from what in the right hemisphere corresponds with the speech areas of the left hemisphere. This is the neurological model for the bicameral mind. When I first was trying to figure out what the neurology of the bicameral mind could be, I think anyone — any child even — would immediately think, "Could it be the right hemisphere talking to the left hemisphere?" Well that sounds so simple. Well, what you do in science, when you're first thinking out these things is to take the simplest hypothesis and then try to shoot it down. Well, I took that hypothesis — this is back in the 1960s — and the more I looked at it, the more the evidence seemed to show that indeed the right hemisphere did have those functions that a god would have to have, in order to create civilizations back in those early times. A lot of things started to fit together, so this is still the neurological model that I'm proposing for the bicameral mind. I'm making a bit of a fine distinction then between the bicameral mind and the neurological model of the bicameral mind.

Lopez: I'd like to run something by our listeners here from the book about how the brain works today. You go into great detail about what happens when a lesion is present on one side of the brain which disturbs a function. The right hemisphere for example is involved in things like creative thinking, pattern recognition, and dealing with novel situations. This side of the brain is probably where the voices of the gods came from. And you note a spatial pattern test — Kohs Block Test — where a person is shown a simple geometric pattern and is asked to take blocks and duplicate the simple pattern. So it's like putting together a simple jig saw puzzle, and normal people can do it without any difficulty. But you say patients with brain lesions in the right hemisphere, the pattern recognition side, find this extremely difficult — so much so that the test is used to diagnose right hemisphere damage. And in commissurotomy patients — this is where the two hemispheres of the brain have been separated surgically so that they don't communicate back and forth — you say in these patients, the right hand, which is controlled by the left hemisphere, cannot succeed at all in putting the design together with the blocks. But the left hand, which is controlled by the right hemisphere, can do it easily — in the same person, a minute later. And you say that frequently the left hand will try to help the right hand do this.

Jaynes: There is some excellent film of these patients, and it's just astonishing. It's very difficult to believe as you watch these patients, when the left hand can do it better than you and I can do, and the right hand just stumbles along and can't do it at all. I like to make the comparison of putting these blocks together into a pattern with what the gods — by which we mean the right hemisphere — did in organizing these early civilizations. It seems like quite a jump to make the metaphor of something as simple as Kohs Block Test and something as grand as organizing these civilizations, but ultimately I think they are both right hemispheric functions.

LOPEZ: In ancient times, before 1000 B.C., people would go about their daily lives, their habitual tasks, as we do driving, but when they ran into a problem or a novel situation, then the gods so to speak, in the right hemisphere of the brain, would speak to them or tell them what to do? Could you explain this?

JAYNES: Let's look at what happens nowadays. Let's say we have a person that we call schizophrenic. These people are put under enough stress so that they suddenly start to hear voices, usually negative, that tell them what to do. I think that any of us — if we were pushed into the corner far enough, and stripped of our securities — any of us could occasion this ancient thing that is still there in the brain of hearing a voice telling you what to do. What I think happened is that back in bicameral times, just the stress of making a decision set off, biochemically, certain kinds of hormones and so on in the bloodstream that triggered the hallucination. I think that is the mechanism of it. And one can study this mechanism nowadays in schizophrenic patients, and some of the biochemistry of hallucinations. Looking at it from that point of view, I don't think it's difficult to understand simply because we have a great deal of it today. And one way to look at what I'm saying is that before 1000 B.C., everybody had hallucinations that are often given the label of schizophrenia. But that's sort of the wrong way to put it because you had a society where culturally that was what was expected.

Hearing voices doesn't work nowadays because the individual has been brought up in a conscious society and has learned consciousness. If you took a schizophrenic patient and you brought them up in a society in which you would expect to hear gods, then it would work. To understand this is not difficult because it is present today and has been present throughout history. But what is difficult to understand is how all of this could have worked together to build a civilization. The question is constantly being asked of me, "How is it then, if everybody is hearing hallucinations, that everybody isn't hearing something different? How is it that everybody agreed?" That is a much more difficult thing to understand, but I think it can be made plausible. All of us today, as we go through our daily activities, we all have expectancies with which we are all in agreement, there are tacit assumptions, so that we are all in the same kind of culture. Back then I think the gods, built up in the right hemisphere, also were part of these social expectancies. That's the side of this theory that takes longer to understand.

Lopez: Well if you think about the rigid hierarchy of ancient civilizations, and even some modern civilizations, you can see how the king or leader would be having his hallucinations, and he would probably be in that position at least in part because his hallucinations are very effective for him, and brought him to the top. His hallucinations can then be passed down through the hierarchy to everyone else.

Jaynes: That's right.

Lopez: You say that in a hierarchical civilization like ancient Egypt, the king or god-king would be considered a god by the people because they would hear his voice in their head. They wouldn't hear a god's voice but their king's voice, as though the king were giving them commands.

Jaynes: This was certainly true in ancient Egypt, where the pharaoh himself was divine. This is exactly what that means when we say the pharaoh was divine. His voice was heard by viziers and so on down the line. But in all of these civilizations actually, just as there was a strict hierarchy of people, there was a strict hierarchy of the gods. Each person had his own individual god, that then was in a hierarchy with other gods, and so on. It's a complicated hierarchical system that seemed to have worked — it worked up to a point. Then of course occasionally it would break down and the whole civilization disappeared.

Lopez: I want to focus on perhaps a minor point that you make in your book, but a startling one. You say that in some parts of the ancient world, archaeologists have found large numbers of small hand-held clay tablets, a little larger than a pocket calculator, that look like an effigy of a god. They look a little like E.T. [from the movie *E.T. the Extraterrestrial*], come to think it. They have very large eyes.

Jaynes: E.T. is a very good example of an eye-idol of Tell Brak, for example.

Lopez: Let's get into the subject of eye idols with big eyes and what they were for. You say that archaeologists have not been able to come up with decent explanation for why there would be so many of these all over the world.

Jaynes: That's right. If one goes back and looks at idols all across the world, one finds that in many — not in all, but in most of these instances — their eyes are often as much as twice the size of normal eyes. They are very predominant in the face. Now when an infant is looking at its mother, the infant looks at the mother's eyes, not at the mother's lips, when the mother is talking. Similarly, when we are in conversation, we look at the person's eyes, not at their lips. So I think that large eyes of this sort probably helped with hearing the bicameral voices. This is what idols were. They were not statues of gods; we can find in their literature very definite statements that these were gods. This is a difficult thing for us to understand: how could human beings make statues and then think that those statues themselves were divine. Well, one answer to that is that people were not conscious back then — they did not think logically the way you and I do. They could believe this because they were not conscious. In fact, they didn't even believe the way we do; I shouldn't have even used that word.

LOPEZ: I think you would say that the gods in their head simply told them to do this and they did it?

JAYNES: That's right.

LOPEZ: And they did everything the gods told them?

JAYNES: Absolutely. Everything that was done was done under the guidance of the voices.

LOPEZ: So they would think they were obeying their voices in creating the statues. You show historical records of rituals in which this was practiced.

JAYNES: Yes.

LOPEZ: Then the statues would speak to them or would evoke hallucinations as though they were the gods. They would think the statue was the god speaking to them.

JAYNES: You have read my book very well.

LOPEZ: But we're not doing half as good a job at bringing this out on radio as you do logically step-by-step in your book. Because this explains the whole notion of temples, why you go to a temple to worship, why people would have idols in their homes — as in ancient times everybody had an idol in their home, their household god, and archaeologists find this everywhere.

JAYNES: Yes.

LOPEZ: And this is the origin of the whole idea of a church, a house of worship, and the whole idea of gods — period.

JAYNES: That's right, yes.

LOPEZ: So this is not only about the origin of our consciousness but also about the origin of religion?

JAYNES: It is. It's a very important new way to look at human nature and to look at the problems of human nature — when you realize that consciousness brings with it many, many new kinds of problems. This is of course something that I'm going to be dealing with in my next book, which I hope will be out in a couple of years.

LOPEZ: Has that been six years in the writing so far?

JAYNES: Yes, I wouldn't say in the writing but in the research.

LOPEZ: I want to back track a little bit to the idea of a god-king. You take this back to very early times, before any kind of civilization was around, when you had tribes or clans. The leader of the clan, just like the head gorilla or the head baboon in a troop of baboons, would be a dominant male. And you say that because we were bicameral, when humans developed language, then the leader's voice could be heard in a person's head, out of sight of the leader — that they would hallucinate their chief's voice telling them what to do. Then after the chief died, they still heard his voice for a long time, and they thought that somehow he was still alive and talking to them and telling them what to do from beyond death. So this is the origin of eschatology — of life after death.

JAYNES: That's true. And the origin of God.

LOPEZ: Could you elaborate on this a little bit, because I don't think I explained it very well?

JAYNES: I think you explained it quite well. Of course this part is just speculation because we have so little to go on. One has to go back and try to think of how language evolved and what happens when language first comes to let's say Neanderthal man — it's all right to use that term rather loosely here. Once language had evolved and human beings were going around in bands of twenty to thirty people, having a voice that was being repeated in their head would have been very useful to keep somebody working at a task. I try to paint a picture in the book of how this gets developed up to the time we get to the large civilizations.

LOPEZ: Well I guess the point is when you get into a civilization where many thousands of people are all out working the farms and doing tasks to make the civilization work and progress, they are all hearing the voice of their leader or their god-king telling them what to do. The orders that have been passed down, like in a military hierarchy, reverberate in a person's head literally as a hallucination and keep them doing the right thing instead of wandering off or doing whatever they would do.

JAYNES: This might sound impossible to people who don't know the modern clinical literature, but there are people today, many of them in mental hospitals, who are hearing voices constantly, all day long — sometimes good voices and sometimes bad voices. I'm thinking of one particular patient who sews aprons and cooks, and so on, and every single step of the way is dictated by a voice that she is hearing all the time. She has practically what was then a bicameral mind. So to show the plausibility that this could have happened, we look at various psychological cases today and we can see these same mechanisms operating.

LOPEZ: Let's talk about the breakdown of civilizations that were based on this hallucinatory hierarchical system. One of the big mysteries of the study of the ancient world is how large civilizations like the Mayans could just collapse — seemingly overnight — and it's hard to say what happened to them. There have been theories that they overextended their irrigation or there was a sudden disease. You think that perhaps the civilization became too large for the bicameral system to function?

JAYNES: That's a good way to put it. The bicameral mind, as we said earlier, is a strict hierarchical kind of organization. It is indeed like a house of cards, and if there's too much chaos, too many problems, then the whole thing breaks down. Once it starts breaking down then that's the end of the civilization at that particular time. By the end of civilization we mean that people can no longer live in the big cities, they have to go back and live in tribes. And as we look around the ancient world, we can see that this is indeed what happened. Among the Mayans that we just talked about, it seemed to have a certain period. It might be even just a few centuries, where they built a huge temple complex, and then things would get too complicated. The bicameral mind doesn't work under huge complications, so then they would go back to living as tribes in the jungle — until they formed a critical mass again, and the hallucinations would start agreeing again, and they would build another temple complex, and so on. And this accounts for the rise and fall of civilizations not only in Mesoamerica but also in the Andean Highlands. It seemed to have happened rather quickly in these areas.

LOPEZ: An interesting side note on this is how a few hundred Spanish conquistadors managed to take over the entire Inca civilization.

JAYNES: I'm suggesting of course that one of the reasons why Pizarro might have been able to conquer the Incas is because Pizarro was a clever, conscious person, as were his few soldiers, whereas the Incas were perhaps partly bicameral, listening to their gods, and couldn't understand deception, and therefore could be manipulated in this way.

LOPEZ: When we talk about the bicameral mind, to use a metaphor, we're discussing the innocence of humankind that is handed down to us in the legend of the Garden of Eden. That people really didn't know the difference between good and bad under the bicameral mind. They simply did what their gods told them to do and they didn't know any better. Now let's talk about the bicameral mind — how did this come to breakdown? How did we become conscious people?

JAYNES: We have to leave this continent and go back to the Mediterranean area. The bicameral mind broke down in Egypt. This is what was going on between the Old and Middle Kingdom and between the Middle and the New Kingdom — for those of you that know Egyptian history. In Mesopotamia, it doesn't seem to have broken down, except here and there occasionally. But then around 1500 B.C., a lot of things start to happen that all coalesce and start this huge breakdown of the bicameral mind in this area. These particular things are the invention of writing that weakened the auditory basis of these hallucinations; overpopulation, because these bicameral civilizations were so successful, they spread and grew everywhere; and also the chaos that was caused by a huge eruption of the island of Thera, that destroyed a number of civilizations in the ensuing tsunami.

This is, incidentally, the origin of the idea of Atlantis. There was a huge volcanic eruption on the island of Thera that caused the land to sink beneath the sea level. The eruption caused a tremendous tsunami that smashed into all the bicameral civilizations around this part of the Mediterranean — that resulted in a lot of migrations, refugees fleeing and going into other lands, and so on. This chaos that started around 1500 B.C. and lasted for the next four centuries, as people were invading other people's lands, and everybody was looking for a promised land of some kind to start a new bicameral civilization.

In this chaos I think there are three places, three ancient civilizations, where we can see very clearly the breakdown of the bicameral mind and the coming of consciousness. The first of these I think is in Mesopotamia, where the breakdown can be very clearly dated, particularly if you look at Assyrian culture. The rise of consciousness is not so spectacular there, but certainly the breakdown of the bicameral mind is, and you find literature that talks about "Where have the gods gone?" and "Why aren't the gods speaking to me anymore?" and various kinds of real statements that the gods no longer are speaking to us. This is another reason why this chaos is occurring.

The second place is in Greece, and if we follow along from the *Iliad* through the *Odyssey*, then through Hesiod and the lyric and elegiac poets, and the next century and a half up to about 600 B.C. with Solon, we can very easily trace out this building up of these interior spaces, this mechanism like mathematics that is consciousness. We can see this being built up in the poetry particularly of these periods until we get to 600 B.C., when it seems people are like you and I are now. They are talking about their minds inside of themselves and thinking of something inside while doing something different outside. That type of thing occurs at 600 B.C.

Then the third place is probably the most accessible to everyone, and this is among a group of refugees that were looking for a new land — where they came from we're not quite sure. But the word used for these travelers in Akkad, which is the old language of Babylon, is the word *khabiru*, and this becomes our word Hebrew. And the story of one branch of the Hebrews is indeed what is told in our Old or Hebrew Testament. Now when you look at the Hebrew Testament, you can look at what are supposed to be the oldest parts and indeed there you find that god and man are both very human, both talking to each other, and God is a physical presence in the world. And then as you follow along consecutively we have Moses and, as Deuteronomy says, Moses is the last person that God spoke to man-to-man. Then we have the age of the prophets. The prophets are the people who can still remain partly bicameral and hear the voice of Yahweh, and therefore are dictating it to scribes that write down this very precious material of getting back to the gods and the bicameral mind. Then the age of prophecy dies out and we have the Books of Wisdom leading into a different kind of religion, which is the New Testament, which could be looked at indeed as a kind of reform Judaism for conscious human beings. As everybody remembers, Jesus in one place says, "You have heard, 'an eye an eye, a tooth for a tooth', but I say unto you," — even in your consciousness, if you are thinking these things — "that too is not the right thing to do." It makes a very interesting distinction to think of the Old Testament as really describing this agonizing period right during the breakdown of the bicameral mind up to consciousness in the Books of Wisdom, like Ecclesiastes, and then coming into the effort at reforming Judaism, which Jesus was trying to do.

LOPEZ: There are a few things that go on in the Bible that are interesting when interpreted in terms of your theory. One of them is the notion of false prophets. You point out a place in the Book of Jeremiah, where Jeremiah is having almost a duel or a contest with another prophet, both of them claiming that Yahweh is speaking to them, each of them saying opposite things — and this happens throughout the Old Testament.

JAYNES: That's right, yes. And there are probably many, many prophets at this time. Some of them were probably simply like modern-day schizophrenics and were perhaps just saying gibberish. But some of them indeed were making sense. Some of it is beautiful poetry. But all through the Old Testament there are references to the "sons of *nabiim*," which is the Hebrew for prophet, and many scholars have had great trouble with what this means — "why does this word for prophet have this ambiguity back then?" Well, the word for prophet isn't our word for prophet, it really did mean somebody who had this speech coming from within them, that seemed to be a light from within with another kind of speech — some of it not making sense at all and some if it indeed making sense. It's a new way to look at the Bible, and when one does, one has to use an aid such as the Anchor [Yale] Bible or the Encyclopedia Britannica to date these things and to understand where they came from, because they don't come from the same place at all. They were put together sometime around 640 B.C. But when one does, it becomes a very dramatic, exciting, and

profound story of the beginnings of our consciousness, and more specifically our moral consciousness.

LOPEZ: I want to bring in one loose end here. You say that over time, generally speaking — it didn't happen at a uniform rate of course everywhere
— but generally speaking, the voices of the gods went from something
that a person would obey automatically, then they became fuzzy or perhaps several voices would be speaking at once, and it became harder and
harder to understand what the gods were saying to you. Later, most people
couldn't hear the gods at all and only the prophets could. And still later,
even the prophets couldn't hear the gods anymore, and we get into divination, or looking at omens and trying to guess what the gods are saying to
you through signs instead of hearing their voices.

JAYNES: Exactly. Most of our divination today is in the form of astrology
— it's in all our newspapers. We see this start back in Assyria. When the
gods are no longer heard you have to figure out what the gods are telling
you by these absurd kinds of methods.

LOPEZ: So you have civilizations ripping calves open and looking at their
livers for signs of what the gods say.

JAYNES: Yes. It all starts back then as an attempt to get back to the bicameral mind.

LOPEZ: There are a couple of additional points I want to cover and then
we are going to be accepting calls from listeners. Dr. Jaynes, you brought
up a term in your book that impressed me because it's a nice concept to
describe something that is a problem that many people today have: *the
quest for authorization*. I also want to solicit comments from you about a
term you brought up: *cognitive imperative*. What does that mean exactly?

JAYNES: I think we all are walking around with belief systems inside ourselves as to what we are, what is possible for us, what the world is, and
so on. It's a belief system inside ourselves by which we know things. It
isn't like a belief that you can always articulate. Some of these of course
are good but some of them also are very big limitations in ourselves. If
we "know" ourselves as not being very intelligent, for example, this will
determine what we will be. We have a cognitive imperative that has this
negative quality and it puts up a barrier in front of us. But if we have the

opposite cognitive imperative, that will be helpful to us. Of course one has to be careful here that one isn't going too far and one is constantly testing out reality here. It's just like when Roger Bannister ran the first four minute mile, then it was known that one could run a four minute mile, and then sure enough many runners were able to run a four minute mile.

LOPEZ: I'd like to share what I got out of it that I think makes use of this concept. Let's say that you and some friends hear that a house is haunted, and you have an opportunity to spend a night there. So the group of you go to this place that you've been told is haunted, and you spend the night there, and a few creepy noises occur. Each time anything happens in the house — a creak, a knock, a noise — you interpret it as ghostly activity because that's the cognitive imperative that brought you there.

JAYNES: Very good.

LOPEZ: You're set up to believe a particular thing, so there's a strong tendency to interpret things according to what you already believe — your preconceived ideas or expectations. As you know this plays a role in hypnosis as well. It used to be that people had different expectations for what it was like to be hypnotized and they would behave differently under hypnosis than they do today. Hypnosis has undergone an evolution.

JAYNES: That's correct. There have been changes through history from when hypnosis first began with Mesmer. The phenomenon of hypnosis has changed dramatically because people have been led to expect something different. And this is indeed the collective cognitive imperative that I've been talking about. It is of course operating everywhere. In the context of the bicameral mind, if you were raised in a culture that had the belief system that you would hear a voice telling you what to do, the chances of hearing a voice would be more likely. Hypnosis is an excellent place to see the operation of the collective cognitive imperative, as well as to see hypnosis as a vestige of the bicameral mind, where the authority figure, instead of the god, is the hypnotist himself. This relationship between a person under hypnosis and the hypnotist that gives the hypnotized individual the amazing extra ability to control some of their bodily functions in a way that they couldn't do while conscious is indeed going back to this relationship with the bicameral mind.

LOPEZ: This quest for authorization …

JAYNES: Very important. It is to me one of the lessons that I feel this theory presents. When you realize that our entire civilization was based on a relationship with authorities — whom we could not disobey — called gods … and that obedience to these gods was indeed what we should do. Then over the space of a millennium — which is not a very long time when you are considering the long evolution of human beings — and in this space of time we lost these authorities. Suddenly we are thrust out on our own, with this consciousness where we can imagine every kind of thing going on, and in this we are seeking for lost authorities, for an authorization for what we do. This is what ethics is about and of course what our religions are about. Most of us I think in the darker places of our lives do indeed need religion, and to have the support of a kind of mythology perhaps, underneath some of the more tragic patterns of life as it goes on.

But we need authorizations in other things as well. I would think one of my authorizations, for example in writing my book, was the idea of scientific truth. Where does that come from? I didn't make that up. The idea of truth comes from the society in which I live, my training, and so on. This is something I've always wanted to do and I get the feeling that "Yes, this is the right and good thing to do." It's almost a search for the lost gods. There was a strong religious basis for science just a century ago. It isn't so apparent now, but I still think it's going on in the guise of having this big truth that we are trying to seek in the universe.

LOPEZ: So then to break it down, because we no longer have the gods whispering in our ear telling us exactly what to do, as we did only 3,000 years ago, we still hunger for that certainty — to be absolutely sure. And this explains why large groups of people, in places like in Germany in the 1940s, can do terrible things, absolutely certain that they are right. It also explains why people now join cults. The cults suck them in with a cognitive imperative: "chant this so many times and you'll get what you want," or "follow this leader and you will find bliss." They set you up with the cognitive imperative to believe that you will get what they promised they'll deliver to you. And then you find yourself absolutely certain, completely convinced that this leader knows the absolute truth, and all you have to do is obey and everything will be okay.

JAYNES: Yes, that's right.

Lopez: And all of us have a deep hunger, in one way or another, for something like that.

Jaynes: I think so.

Lopez: That's very dangerous in people, and that's an important concept that comes out of your book.

Jaynes: Yes.

Lopez: Okay you're on the air and what is your question or comment please?

Caller 1: Let's go back to something in the Bible: Moses came down with the edict that the Jews should abandon all false idols and accept this faceless God — the God of Judaism and Christianity.

Lopez: Who was up in the sky ...

Caller 1: Right. Was this representative of a change from the bicameral mind, or were they just trying to supplant a new religion?

Lopez: Dr. Jaynes we're talking about when Moses tells his followers to throw down their false idols and follow this one God up in the sky, and what that means in terms of your theory.

Jaynes: When we go from the true bicameral period, in which everybody was hearing voices in this hierarchical fashion, then we go through a stage of monotheism, in which we have everything being combined down to one God. This first happened in Egypt with Akhenaten, and then just 100 years later with Moses, and Yahweh says "You will have no other gods before me." Going from many gods to one god is a pattern that happens in many parts of the world. If I could mention a person that has recently written me — a very brilliant man who just went through what we could call a psychotic episode, in which he had ten different divine beings arguing about him. This just happened last month. As he got better, all of these voices shrank down to one single voice, and now he just hears one voice, which is that of a Rabbi asking questions. But this pattern that occurred in this particular person in the last few months bears similarities to what happened in history, first in Egypt with Akhenaten and then among the Hebrews with Moses, as well as elsewhere.

LOPEZ: You also point out in your book that the Hebrews at one time killed the bicameral people that were around them.

JAYNES: There are instances in the Old Testament, with Elijah at one point, and there are a couple of other instances of slaughtering these "sons of the *nabiim.*" We don't know exactly what this means, but these were probably people we would regard as raving schizophrenics in sort of a group or pack outside of the city. These are very hard to explain.

LOPEZ: So there was a form of competition between the newly emerging conscious people and the remaining bicameral people, and the conscious people won.

JAYNES: The conscious people won, but also the people who could get to the voices — the prophets also won. If you read the two books of Samuel — the difficulties between Saul, who was conscious, and Samuel, who still hears the voice of Yahweh. You see it's Samuel who wins out. Because again, as we were talking about previously, about longing for authorization — somebody who has the fierceness of a fanatic and says "I know what is right to do," and really has this bold type of character, he can sometimes lead people better than someone who is more conscious and has doubts and reservations and sees all of the possibilities. This is I think what Saul was in the tragedy of those books.

LOPEZ: Thank you caller.

CALLER 1: One more point... Does Dr. Jaynes offer some explanation for the ability of the adherents of some religions to walk on hot coals unscathed as a verification as the power of their religion?

JAYNES: I have to say I don't know the scientific data of this phenomenon. I'm very surprised when I run into it, I just don't know enough about it.

LOPEZ: It would seem to me to be a very powerful form of the placebo effect, which has been demonstrated — when people are being told they are being given a pain killer, their perception of pain does decrease.

JAYNES: It also stimulates the endorphin system. Of course under hypnosis one can indeed change blisters from burns, and this gets back to the general bicameral paradigm: this extra control over the body that the gods had over bicameral man, and we have lost with consciousness. But I just don't know enough about the phenomenon specifically of walking on coals to give an explanation.

LOPEZ: Thank you caller.

CALLER 1: Thank you.

LOPEZ: Dr. Jaynes mentioned to me that he is working on a second volume — the first volume being *The Origin of Consciousness in the Breakdown of the Bicameral Mind,* if you're just tuning in. Dr. Jaynes, what have you been working on lately that you haven't published?

JAYNES: Well when consciousness comes into the world around 1000 B.C., everything starts to change. There is a huge change in human nature. One of the first things that happens is that we have spatialized time — time made into a space, metaphorically. If anybody thinks of time right now, they immediately are taken into a space. And time is not this space. We cannot think of time except as a metaphoric space. When we start doing this, back around 900 or 800 B.C., then we start having lifetimes. We know of our own death for the first time. We can plan, have ambitions, and even have an individual self — as we didn't during the bicameral era. At the same time, our emotions — because we now can fantasize about them — change dramatically. One can show that we go from shame culture — shame is a biological affect that one can find in most mammals as well as bicameral man — and this becomes guilt. One can fantasize about shame — about this rejection or humiliation for doing something wrong.

LOPEZ: Without actually being punished.

JAYNES: Yes indeed. And it happens with other emotions. Fear becomes anxiety. At the same time we have a huge change in sexual behavior. If you try to sit down and imagine what your sexual life would be like if you couldn't fantasize about it, it's a hard thing to do, and you probably would think it would be much less, and I suspect it would be. If we go back to bicameral times, and look at all the artwork, wherever we look, there is nothing sexual about it. There is no pornography or anything even reminiscent of that at all. It's what classicists call chaste. But when we come into the first conscious period, for example in Greece from 700 B.C. up to 200 or 100 B.C. — the sexual life in Greece is difficult to describe because we are taught of great, noble Perician Athens and we don't think of the sexual symbols ... phalli of all kinds were just simply everywhere. This has been well documented now but it's not something that's presented to schoolchildren.

LOPEZ: You mean then that the erotic pottery that we see in ancient Greece was a result of new found consciousness and the resulting new found fascination with sex?

JAYNES: The ability to fantasize about sex immediately brought it in as a major concern. There is something I don't understand about it... these phalli or erections were on statues everywhere. They were on the boundary stones called *herms* around the city of Athens. And yet they weren't unusual to these people, as it certainly would be in Baltimore today if you had these things all around the streets. It seems that sex had a religious quality, which is curious. There were a lot of very odd and different kinds of things that were happening.

To get back to the overall interview we're having today — one of the things I'm trying to get across is that people no longer think that mankind is everywhere the same or has been the same through history. We have changed dramatically. Human beings even during the time of Plato and a little bit before were very different than we are. They responded differently. Their emotions were much more raw and on the surface. For example, there are stories of the tragedies that were performed — some of the tragedies were too terrible, at the end people would be shaking and they couldn't go home — they couldn't move. They had to outlaw some of the tragedies because they were having these tremendously powerful effects on people.

LOPEZ: Let's get to this patient caller on the phone. You're on the air — your question or comment for Dr. Jaynes.

CALLER 2: So are you saying that God is created in people's minds?

JAYNES: It worries some people that God is simply an invention of human beings. It seems to destroy our religious faith. What my theory does is explain all the huge numbers of gods that you find further back in history. You could have a belief that goes beyond history and imagine that there is a creative God, a creative intelligence that creates human beings through evolution and so on, and then starts revealing himself to human beings step-by-step, first as a personal God, then with monotheism and Moses, then through Jesus, depending on what your faith might be. So it doesn't really destroy the profound basis for whether or not there is a God behind the universe. It is explaining the historical phenomenon of the multiplicity of gods in ancient history.

LOPEZ: Is that it caller?

CALLER 2: Regarding your discussion of hypnosis, I've heard that sometimes they hypnotize people to take them back to past lives. Are they really going back to past lives or is that just something that is planted in their minds?

JAYNES: No, I don't think that they are going back to past lives. There is no evidence for reincarnation; there is no evidence for going back to past lives. There is even no evidence that somebody under hypnosis can go back to the age of two, for example, and remember what it was like. They can act as if this was so, and one of the important experimenters in this field is Dr. Martin Orne at the University of Pennsylvania. He has shown that, for example, if you take a hypnotized person, who let us say learned English only at the age of six and knew German before — this is a particular case — he hypnotized this person and took him back to age 6, then 5, then 4, and at the age of 4 this person said "No I can't understand English"— in perfect English. This shows that the character of what happens in hypnosis can often be much more like play acting and what the person thinks it should be like.

LOPEZ: It seems our minds are very good at creating metaphors and analogs, and little worlds within it. Thanks for your call. Dr. Jaynes, we were getting into things that you're doing now that are not in your first volume, that you haven't published. You were talking about the awakening of sexuality coinciding with the newly learned consciousness.

JAYNES: That's right. I was mentioning the tragedies. They had to be placed in distant lands or among myths to divorce it from daily life, particularly in Athens. And each tragedy wasn't a Greek tragedy as we've come to know them — they were all trilogies. They went on for the day and they resolved themselves, and then what followed was called a phallic farce. And this was something that we couldn't stand on the stage today — it was as sexual as possible. If you can imagine the great tragedies of Sophocles for example — going from Oedipus Rex into Oedipus at

Colonus all in the same day, followed with these farces in which people would be cavorting on the stages with great, artificial phallic erections to make people laugh after all this profound tragedy. That is how tragedies were presented in Greece. It was very different than what we see in our contemporary society.

You can also look at homosexuality as perhaps a part of this, in the sense that if you try to trace back the origin of homosexuality, it does not seem to occur in the bicameral world, and, apart from rare exceptions, it does not occur frequently in animal behavior. And here it is in Greece that we get almost like a ritual form of homosexuality that seems to occur for the first time in history. This is something I've only begun to research recently.

LOPEZ: There is a source you cite a number of times in your book, *The Origin of Consciousness*, I believe the title is *The Greeks and the Irrational?*

JAYNES: A superb book by E.R. Dodds. I would advise everybody to read it.

LOPEZ: That book describes some crazy things that the ancient Greeks — what you would say are the bicameral Greeks — would do. For example, when a member of the family dies, they would continue to feed the corpse for quite some time. They would put a tube in the corpse's mouth and feed it soup, because the corpse, in their bicameral mind, was crying out for soup from beyond the grave. That's strange.

JAYNES: A lot of strange things were going on back then. The more I read about these things in the context of the theory that I've started out with, the clearer it becomes to me. I should immediately say, however, that while there was this increase in sexuality in Greece — it certainly happened also in the Etruscans of the same period, and I have looked at that — it does not seem to happen as much among the Hebrews. Of course the documentation we have in the Old Testament is not as clearly dated as we have in Greece. Much of even the Pentateuch comes from 550 B.C. and not before. But the difference may be that we have this raw, monotheistic God among the Hebrews, who was a moral God — this is why I call that chapter "The Moral Consciousness of the Khabiru" — whereas in Greece it was a more intellectual kind of consciousness, that allowed all this fantasy and imagination that resulted in great philosophy and great science, as well as this increase in sexuality. These are some of the things I'm working on right now and trying to understand and come to a larger picture of before I commit them to paper.

LOPEZ: I want to go back to the evolution of hypnosis. We mentioned that at one time people would automatically forget what had happened while they were hypnotized and now they don't unless they are told to. You did a brief history of hypnosis as it related to your theory, and you noted that hypnosis has gone through an evolution in the 200 years or so that it has formally been around — that the things people do under hypnosis have changed, simply because the expectations about what hypnosis would produce have changed. Can you elaborate on some of the things that have changed?

JAYNES: Well, in one period for example, when something called phrenology was around, they thought a certain bump on the head was associated with reverence, and they found that just by touching that bump on the head, people would fall to their knees and start to pray. Well, you don't find anything like that now. This is because at the time, this is what the person expected — the person had this cognitive imperative saying that this was part of what hypnosis was at the time. Previously I mentioned Martin Orne, and he came up with the term *demand characteristic*, which means that what the subject thinks the hypnotist wants him to do is very often what he does. In some of his experiments he would say things that were quite untrue, such as that under hypnosis a person's right hand is going to be paralyzed while under hypnosis, and if he just happens to hear that before being hypnotized, then sure enough that often happens. One of the things that is happening now in hypnosis research is — because it is being taught in psychology courses and being talked about, such as on this program — everybody is learning more about it, and so it is becoming very standardized, because we are all learning what happens in hypnosis. Even though we could make up other things and those things would happen.

LOPEZ: You point out that the expectations about what hypnosis would do or what it would feel like grew out of the metaphors that the hypnotist used to describe what it was. When it first began it was called *animal magnetism*?

JAYNES: This is because Mesmer was very infatuated with Isaac Newton and the idea of gravity, and celestial bodies all attracting each other. Well, he jumped to the metaphor that there is this same kind of attraction between people, and then he went to the metaphor of the magnet, and at first called it *magnetism*, and then he called it *animal magnetism*, which was this attraction that he thought he was able to demonstrate. He actually used iron filings and things like this. Just as you can create static electricity by rubbing a glass rod, so he started rubbing patients, and indeed they became hypnotized. All of this kind of thing that we now know is quite unnecessary in hypnosis.

LOPEZ: But it worked exactly the way that he told the patients it would work?

JAYNES: If you don't believe in hypnosis, hypnosis probably isn't going to work for you. If you do believe in it, then it will. And if you believe it is such-and-such a thing, then that is what will be happening to you in hypnosis.

LOPEZ: And this is a vestige of the bicameral mind?

JAYNES: Yes.

LOPEZ: Let's go to the calls. You're on the air...

CALLER 3: There's a concept in biology, "ontogeny recapitulates phylogeny," which says that a child's development from an embryo through adulthood goes through the same stages that human evolution did. I was wondering what Dr. Jaynes thinks of this with regard to his theory?

JAYNES: Yes, another way of phrasing this would be, "Does a child go through a bicameral stage before consciousness?" Would that be the kind of thing that you're thinking?

CALLER 3: Yes it is.

JAYNES: Well, let's go back to the idea of the biogenetic law Haeckel proposed in the 1850's that ontogeny recapitulates phylogeny. This has been shown not really to be true. It does point at something that should be stated more along the lines that animals later in evolution go through certain embryonic states that previous animals have gone through, rather than an exact kind of recapitulation. Now in terms of my theory, we have to look at data when we look at children, you have to study this. Actually children do go through something like a bicameral stage — this is what the data shows. I think that back in the bicameral world, every child had an imaginary playmate and the imaginary playmate grew up, as the person did, to be the person's personal god, which then fit himself with the cognitive imperative into the larger hierarchy. Now in modern times, anywhere from a third to half of children have imaginary playmates. And researchers, such as Dr. [Dorothy] Singer, who has studied this very carefully at the University of Bridgeport, feel definitely that children are hallucinating these voices, just as schizophrenics do, just as Joan of Arc did, and just as bicameral people did. This is the beginning of the bicameral mind. If such a child was brought up in a society in which this was expected and normal, then this person would become a bicameral person.

I have one instance of a young woman in Virginia who told me how she was brought up by a schizophrenic grandmother who was hallucinating, and she started having different imaginary playmates — a different one in each room — that all spoke to her, until her mother quit her job to come home and train her out of this, and she sent the grandmother to a mental hospital. And the mother was successful. But she said that whenever she gets into times of stress, all of her imaginary playmates come back, "and they are all grown up like me, and they all stand around trying to tell me what to do." I think that is how things happened back in the bicameral period. So we do find that some children are going through things like this. There's nothing wrong with imaginary playmates — this was an extreme instance. If there are mothers listening and their children have imaginary playmates, it's very often a good thing for a child.

Lopez: So the woman, when she was young, was responding to the cognitive imperative that her schizophrenic grandmother was giving her that the playmates were real and that she should listen to them for advice. Had this continued, it's possible that as she grew into adult, whenever she met with a situation where she had to make a decision, she would rely on these imaginary playmates to give her advice.

Jaynes: Right, these imaginary playmates are grown up and they are interfering with her life. She told me that she was driving along in the car and was stopped for speeding and had all of her imaginary playmates in the back seat. She probably would be diagnosed as schizophrenic even though she isn't. It's just this curious thing. She's going to college and so on, and the reason she came to talk to me was she wanted to know whether it was learned or if it was innate. I didn't answer properly because I didn't realize what somebody else told me later — that she was going to get married and perhaps she didn't want to have children that were going to go through the same thing that she went through.

LOPEZ: I've never heard of anything like that.

JAYNES: If doesn't fit in to the usual categories of mental illness or not, yet there are all these different kinds of cases that one can find if one goes and looks for them.

LOPEZ: And yet you're saying that there's nothing supernatural or para-psychological about this?

JAYNES: No. Imaginary playmates are a perfectly healthy thing for many children to have. Some very great people have had imaginary playmates.

LOPEZ: Okay thank you caller — very interesting point. You're on the air.

CALLER 4: I was just wondering if the interest in UFOs and the second coming was a search for some kind of external authority?

JAYNES: Yes, I think it is.

LOPEZ: Everybody hopes that the UFOs will come down from outer space and tell us what to do and solve all of our problems?

JAYNES: Yes. I think what we've had in the last century, particularly since the theory of evolution, is an erosion of ecclesiastical authority, and our beliefs in a kind of divine superstructure of the world, and life after death — that's the general trend, although we find the opposite in fundamentalist groups. We do find this kind of groping after other kinds of authorities and other kinds of religions. The caller who called previously and was asking about previous lives under hypnosis and going back and proving reincarnation — I feel that is another one. But UFOs — wanting people to come down from outer space and to be gods again, yes, I think it's part of this search for authorization.

LOPEZ: Thanks for your call.

CALLER 4: Thank you.

LOPEZ: You're on the air.

CALLER 5: Hello, first of all I'd like to congratulate Dr. Jaynes on his fascinating theory.

JAYNES: Thank you.

CALLER 5: My question is, religions first started as polytheistic and then changed to monotheistic religion, and this history has included many stories of miracles. How do you explain these miracles?

JAYNES: How do I explain the miracles that have been reported, such as in the New Testament?

CALLER 5: Yes.

JAYNES: Well if you look at many of the healings that Jesus performs in the New Testament, they are things that we are beginning to understand as possible now not on a religious basis. Many of the illnesses we have are what used to be called functional illnesses — they are due to us imagining things. You can heal many things through just imagery. This is one of the things I'm very interested in now — how training ourselves in certain kinds of imagery about ourselves, our problems, or our relationships can help us to find better ways of dealing with the world. What Jesus could do, with his tremendous, powerful authority, was take someone who let's say was going through this interesting phenomenon of possession — of being possessed by a demon — and simply by his authority say "Out!" This still can happen today. We don't get possessed by so-called demons in North America as much today, but one does find it in places like Brazil and some of the polyglot religions down there, and the same kind of thing happens. When we talk about miracles in the Bible, such as healings, I think these are things we are rediscovering now that have perfectly natural explanations. Some of the others I don't think have enough of a historical basis to regard them as phenomenon to explain.

LOPEZ: Thanks for calling in.

CALLER 5: Thank you.

LOPEZ: Dr. Jaynes, we just have a couple of minutes left, and I'd like to thank you for talking with us about *The Origin of Consciousness in the Breakdown of the Bicameral Mind*. Is it just now out in paperback?

JAYNES: Yes, it's just now out in paperback.

LOPEZ: And it's been out in hardback for about six years, if you want to delve more into this. Thank you very much for being on the show today.

JAYNES: Thank you.

LOPEZ: I wanted Dr. Jaynes to be off the line to say this. The reason I spent two hours on the phone today, and talked with him at such length about this theory is that if he is mostly right, about what the theory is, this man will be as important to psychology — understanding the evolution of the human mind — as Darwin was for understanding the evolution of species. The theory could be wrong, but if you read the book I think you will come away largely convinced as to its veracity.

# CHAPTER 28

# Prying Open the Barrel of Snakes

## Interview by Timothy J. Stafford

JULIAN JAYNES'S BOLD THEORY challenges a great number of old assumptions about ancient history, religion, archaeology, linguistics, anthropology, psychology, and philosophy. It is nothing short of an attempt to rewrite most of human history. It is then no surprise that a great number of questions have arisen concerning all facets of this multi-dimensional theory. However, the sad truth of the matter is that most of these questions have not been addressed to Jaynes himself. The few interviews available with Jaynes are less than satisfying, so this interview can be viewed as an attempt to answer questions that have appeared most often in reviews and discussions.

The interview was conducted via cassette tape on February 14, 1984. Jaynes's responses here are essentially verbatim answers to selected printed questions. It is hoped this interview will provide a further dimension to his theory that cannot come even from a first reading of *The Origin of Consciousness in the Breakdown of the Bicameral Mind*. If nothing else, his complete candor here supplies an important further illumination.

STAFFORD: Did you expect a certain amount of ridicule when you released the work? Why do you think the work is so controversial?

JAYNES: No. I did not expect ridicule, nor have I run into ridicule. I've run into rejection, as well as acceptance. I think the usual intellectual reaction to my book is interest, but a fear of accepting it all. The theory is fairly "total," by which you turn around and interpret something else. This is

Interview with Julian Jaynes by Timothy J. Stafford. In Timothy J. Stafford, "Prying Open the Barrel of Snakes: Historical Conceptions of Human Consciousness and Julian Jaynes's *The Origin of Consciousness in the Breakdown of the Bicameral Mind*," thesis presented to the Faculty of the Department of History, East Tennessee State University, 1984. Reprinted with permission.

quite a break for psychologists, for instance, to accomplish. Cognitive psychology and information theory are really the last remnants of behaviorism. There psychologists are so involved in their own experimental paradigms — which are partial — that they don't want to have to consider something like consciousness. If they did, then they would have to go back and repeat most of their experiments to determine when mental processes are involved with consciousness and when they are cognitive functioning that has nothing to do with consciousness. There is little experimentation going on at the present time which pays attention to introspections. And I think this is one of the huge deficiencies in contemporary psychology. But I think that this will change. There is a kind of feeling — not just with me or people who are following my theory — that consciousness is going to come back as the very centerpiece of psychology and what cognitive psychology should be studying.

Religious people also find the book controversial. Orthodox Christians sometimes feel as if the theory were explaining away all religion as nothing but the fancies of the right hemisphere and that therefore there are no gods and that this has to be a strict atheist position. Zionists, also, find much of the book hard to accept, even though my chapter on the Old Testament is simply the well-known higher biblical criticism of the late nineteenth century. But it *isn't* really anti-religious. A theologian from a Southern Baptist Theological School wrote me a very interesting letter recently. He described a seminar there which had been organized to look into my book and in which they were wondering at first if I was the Antichrist. This particular theologian had been appointed the devil's advocate. He later wrote me that the more he thought about it, my theory was perfectly consistent with positing a real god that does his creation through evolution and then reveals himself through stages of monotheism, The Books of Wisdom, and then the return as a human who dies and leaves human beings to relate to God in a new way, namely faith. I found this letter very welcome because I don't like to injure anyone's religious belief.

Classicists, of course, go from one fashion to another like psychologists do. Some time back, when Millman Parry was alive, the emphasis was on oral poetry which was composed and spoken at the same time; who or what Homer was is simply not important. It's now the fashion to employ the compromise position and say there was a poet named Homer, who although he was using all the older materials, somehow put all this together with great artistry. These "unitarians" feel that I have stepped on their toes in going back to the Parry position. Also, around the turn of the century, it was the fashion to divide up the *Iliad* into various layers of antiquity as Walter Leaf, whom I refer to in the book, did. The same thing was done, of course, with the Old Testament and the Priestly, Elohist, and Yahwehist strands interwoven with each other. I feel this is good scholarship, but the fashions have changed, and you don't find modern scholars doing that. When I came along with my fairly brief overview of some of these problems, it caused quite a controversy among people in one school or another.

Other sources of controversy would include Freudians. I do understand why all this controversy occurs. I think anything as large as this theory, with so many implications, most of which are not mentioned in my first book, would always beget such controversy.

STAFFORD: How much of the misunderstanding and/or controversy surrounding your theory involves semantics concerning the term "consciousness?"

JAYNES: This is quite true. If you go to conferences among neuroscientists on consciousness, you find them defining it in the sloppiest kinds of ways — as all awareness, perception, and everything else. And I think I've explained in my first chapter why that is completely inadequate and can get one nowhere. Also there are people who like to build computer models of feedback systems and label it "consciousness"; this is upsetting to me, because it isn't making the fine distinctions we have to make if we are ever going to have a science of consciousness.

STAFFORD: Are you familiar with any of the support you've received in the academic community, such as from Jerome Singer, Endel Tulving, Daniel Dennett, and others?

JAYNES: I know them personally, but I don't know their work completely. Dennett was a discussant at a recent talk I gave at McMaster University, where he dealt with what is known as the "use-mention" problem. This is one of the criticisms some of the people at MIT have taken, that I'm confusing the concept of consciousness with consciousness. And of course that's not so; I am fusing the two. I'm no more confusing the two than Newton confused the fall of the apple with the attraction of the tides to the moon. Consciousness is a fusion; it's an invention that is constantly expanding through metaphor. Dennett used the example of baseball: the concept of baseball and playing baseball are precisely the same thing. Philosophers have a little armory of criticisms they like to trot out when they see an opening, and this is indeed what some of the early criticisms of the book were. I think people who have made this specific criticism have done so on a very superficial basis. This is what Gliedman is referring to at the end of his article.[1]

STAFFORD: Why do you feel that no reviews of the book so far have been adequate? Which are the best in your opinion?

JAYNES: I suppose I feel none of the reviews have been adequate because there are none that place this theory against other possible theories of the evolution of consciousness. There is not a single one that offers any kind of alternative whatsoever. Most of the reviews — especially the longer ones — try to go into the evidence I cite and make some judgment about its adequacy, but they're not seeing the forest for the trees and I feel rather sorry about that. Other reviews have often tried to single out one thing and say, "this is the important part of the book," and then try to show its weakness. This kind of thing is a game, I'm afraid.

Which are the best? That's too difficult to answer because some of the short ones have been so very helpful and some of the long ones have not been; it would be very self-biased if I picked out any. One of the shortest was one of the most interesting; this was in the *Hartford Courant*. I'm not sure I'm being entirely correct here when I say that the review was in only a couple of sentences: "When you've finished laughing at the title and have looked into the book, you will find that if it is said that Freud opened a can of worms, one can say that Jaynes has pried open a barrel of snakes." Whether to take that positively or negatively, I'm not quite sure.

STAFFORD: Were you troubled that the *Time* article[2] left out your theory of the nature of consciousness?

JAYNES: It's interesting that you picked that up. John Leo, who wrote the *Time* article, later wrote me a letter of apology saying that his editors cut out all the three and four-syllable words he used in trying to explain the theory, so that it could be more easily grasped.

---

1. John Gliedman, "Julian Jaynes and the Ancient Mindgods," *Science Digest*, 1982, *90*, 84–87.
2. John Leo, "The Lost Voices of the Gods," *Time*, March 14, 1977, 51–53.

STAFFORD: John Gliedman mentions the Egyptian manuscript "Satire on the Trades" (2000 B.C.) and that you acknowledge that this is "one of a number of literary discrepancies" that may force you to move the origin of consciousness back.[3] If this is true, what does this do to your original theory, especially your examination of the *Iliad*? Can you identify any of the other discrepancies?

JAYNES: Gliedman didn't mention that I told him about a dinner I shared with William Simpson, a professor of ancient Egyptian literature and translator of this particular manuscript and others. We were discussing my theory, and I was asking him specific questions about consciousness in Egypt with which he was very quietly but firmly disagreeing. Gliedman showed me a new edition of Simpson's book, and here this new translation is added in at the end as if to contradict the bicameral theory. I doubt the translation. I am trying to learn more hieroglyphics now and am working on a grant whereby I can hire a hieroglyphics expert. Once you know how these translations are made, it is really a great deal of guesswork and often reading into the texts our modern mentality.

STAFFORD: Gliedman also says you are "… the first to acknowledge [the] blockbuster theory falls short of proof — right now." Explain.

JAYNES: I don't remember saying "short of proof." I wouldn't talk about proof, but rather about evidence and patterns of evidence, and the theory does not fall short of evidence. Perhaps I was speaking of degrees of certainty; my theory certainly isn't comparable with mathematical logic. One has to look at these things carefully, and there may indeed be ramifications of the theory that are unexpected. For example, it's entirely possible that American Indians may have developed differently from other ancient peoples. All this requires a lot of work and needs to be looked into with a fine tooth comb.

STAFFORD: How would you answer critics who claim your theory is framed in a very mechanistic, behavioristic way?

JAYNES: "Mechanistic" is a metaphor of course, a much over-used metaphier of something that is a machine. I don't like to use it because the paraphiers and paraphrands have a non-lifelike feeling to them, and in physiology, it's simply the wrong metaphier. This refers to the Renaissance

---

3. John Gliedman, "Julian Jaynes and the Ancient Mindgods," *Science Digest*, 1982, *90*, 84–87.

practice of trying to deal with quantifiable entities; of course, any science would like to achieve a relation between quantifiable variables. I think it has been possible to do this with the qualitative variables of consciousness, and in this respect, the theory is not mechanistic.

As for my views being behavioristic, that's a rather difficult thing to say about a book about consciousness. "Behaviorism" can indeed mean quite a few things. I think people who have prejudices against behaviorism use the term more like a broad brush with which to tint things a certain way. Behaviorism was a kind of "cleansing" of some of the great errors that were being committed about the nature of consciousness that followed Fechner, Wundt, and Titchener; it was an interesting kind of disciplining. I remember this when I was a graduate student so well. As such, it has been helpful to my thinking in realizing how many things we can do without consciousness.

STAFFORD: Let me divide your book into two sections for the time being, the first dealing with your theory of the nature of consciousness and the second with the bicameral mind and the historical origin of consciousness. How would you answer critics who praise your believable and commonsense approach in section one and criticize in section two what to them seems a flagrant and unnecessary application of this theory of mind to history?

JAYNES: I don't know of any such critics. I would be interested to read them because I think the most important part of my book is indeed the theory of consciousness. This is the section that has to have more development, is the most fascinating, and also the most helpful part in terms of the future of human nature. But, certainly I would think Book II is necessary to show what I mean. I should mention here that there are really two forms of the theory. One is the "strong" form, that consciousness followed the breakdown of the bicameral mind in the Near East. The "weak" form could say that consciousness developed on linguistic metaphor earlier, and that as a way of making decisions it followed along like a twin with the bicameral mind until the latter was sloughed off about 1000 B.C., leaving consciousness on its own. That would be a weak, almost unfalsifiable form of the theory. If I had written it that way, perhaps the edge of the criticism would have been dulled, but I think it is part of a scientific responsibility to go out on a limb and present things in their strongest fashion so that if they can be disproved, they will be disproved.

STAFFORD: What is your reaction to the criticisms of Jacques Barzun?[4]

JAYNES: I remember this long review as having many of the mistakes of other reviews, such as confusion of the bicameral mind with the neurological model. To me, these two things should *always* be kept distinct. The evidence for the bicameral mind is in all ancient texts. Anyone who doubts it should go read the book of Amos and all the other materials from these particular periods and ask themselves what is going on. The neurological model of the left and right hemispheres is something different, and it has to be tested on its own grounds of neurological evidence.

There are really four separate ideas in my theory: one is the theory of consciousness, the most important; two is the idea of the bicameral mind, for which there is the most evidence; three is that one follows the other (and the dating of this transition), and four is the neurological model for the bicameral mind. This is the order of importance of these ideas, and if one keeps them separate, one begins to see the picture a bit more clearly. I feel that one of the mistakes I made in writing the first book was not to make this very clear. When people start thinking that the bicameral mind *is* the two hemispheres, I feel I was wrong in using the word "bicameral."

I also remember the review as being very respectful, but particularly selective in what it chose to discuss, with a heavy and sometimes superficial emphasis on the *Iliad*. I remember, as I do with so many reviews, feeling that he had sort of skimmed through the book without reading the footnotes and had not in particular realized that the *Iliad* is a contaminated document in the sense of being an historical record of the Trojan War. So many older people who know their classics find it very difficult to think in such terms. In my chapter, I mention many exceptions and remember realizing that Barzun simply had not read the footnotes, and was trying to protect an older view of the *Iliad*. If I remember, he made some rather embarrassing mistakes about things in the *Iliad*; he also didn't understand my analysis of how thought can go on without consciousness and attacked some things he only thought I said, but was simply mistaken about. Incidentally, this review came out six months before the book was published in Britain and certainly diminished interest in the book there when it did come out.

---

4. Jacques Barzun, "Doing Without Knowing," *Times Literary Supplement*, May 18, 1978, 558–560.

STAFFORD: What are the weak points of your theory? In the words of Sam Keen,[5] if you were a critic of your own theory, what would you criticize?

JAYNES: I think if I were to criticize the theory *as it is written in the book*, I would go into the theory of consciousness itself; it's so incomplete. And were I rewriting the book today, I would indeed say so much more. I would go into modes of consciousness, such as the verbal and the perceptual modes, and even a musical mode. There are three quite different things. We can also have a bodily mode — this is also a different kind of consciousness.

STAFFORD: Have you changed or modified any of the ideas in the book?

JAYNES: I think there would be some changes of emphasis, as I said about the types of consciousness, but no big changes. I would say more about the features of consciousness, such as *concentration*, which is the analog of attention, and *repression*, or the disposal of things in consciousness. I don't like the Freudian overtones of the latter feature, but I think we have developed, through history, ways of doing this.

STAFFORD: Are there any areas in which your theory tries to explain too much?

JAYNES: It is certainly possible, but it has to be tested in each individual case. It is certainly not a complete theory of poetry, nor of hypnosis, nor of all the ills that beset our many societies today, but it does, I think, cast a new light on these problems that should be considered in any complete theory.

STAFFORD: What do you feel is the place of your theory in the history of Western thought?

JAYNES: I would really rather not answer that. It's simply something that others will have to decide. ... If I were forced to answer that, I'd say its significance lies in solving the mind/body problem, since I can't see that there is a mind/body problem if the theory as I've stated it is correct. The problem is the difference I talk about in the beginning of the book between what we introspect on and what we see outside of us that is

---

5. Sam Keen, "The Lost Voices of the Gods," *Psychology Today*, 1977, *11*, 58–60. Reprinted as Chapter 22 of this volume.

public — this goes back to Descartes and Locke. To me, that is the mind/body problem, and it is explained by the theory.

STAFFORD: Why does the theory have to apply to every group of people in the world if the bicameral mind and consciousness are cultural inventions?

JAYNES: Whenever there was a civilization, it was always under the aegis of the bicameral mind. However, some of the American Indian groups were breaking down far more frequently than in, say, the Near East; this is the case with the Mayans. The Aztecs, for example, had all the evidence of being bicameral at one time, following the voices of their gods; but then the gods stopped speaking to them — this is recounted in the Spanish records. After that time they turned to complicated methods of divination in order to find their gods, which is why they greeted Cortés with such enthusiasm. So, in different parts of the world, there can be different stages of the bicameral mind or the breakdown, and this doesn't necessarily lead to consciousness. Some either reverted to a chaotic civilization or went back to a tribal existence in the forest of existing — as the Aztecs were doing — on the basis of divination and very curious practices.

STAFFORD: Have you ignored modern pre-technological societies in your search for evidence of the bicameral mind?

JAYNES: This is the anthropological question, and there is a whole chapter in my next book on the subject. It's a little complicated, but I certainly haven't neglected or ignored them. Essentially, what I'm saying is that many of the so-called "pre-technological" societies or hunter-gatherer tribes are breakdown products of previous bicameral kingdoms throughout Africa, the Americas, and elsewhere.

STAFFORD: Some have said you show pro-Western bias in your writing and that you fail to address integration. How do you answer this?

JAYNES: The reason I couldn't go into China was because the dating there is very difficult and I don't know Chinese. I also don't read Sanskrit; the dating of the Veda and Upanishads that I do refer to is very difficult.

STAFFORD: Can a being be unconscious and still have a concept of 'self'?

JAYNES: He wouldn't have a concept of self. Non-conscious or bicameral people would have bodily identities — they would use the personal pronoun 'I' — but they wouldn't have the kind of autobiographical self that you and I do. We go back in our memories and reconstruct our past and present to construct our future; *that* is consciousness. I will probably have a chapter on the self in the next book.

STAFFORD: Can you think of any historical examples (other than your own) of the idea that human consciousness is a recent historical development, or that it was a social (as opposed to evolutionary) phenomenon spurred by the development of language?

JAYNES: Since my book appeared, people have shown me paragraphs from other books that possibly suggested this. The late Walter Kaufmann, a good friend of mine, read my book and then showed me a page of Nietzsche. Indeed, it sounded very similar, not in details, but concerning the notion that consciousness is somehow learned, although I think Nietzsche had it very wrong. Other people have sent me works from Rudolph Steiner and Jung, claiming they said something similar. I've even received letters from the Rosicrucians that I don't quite know what to do with. So yes, there have been suggestions of this, but only in passing reference without any emphasis on it or attempting to work out the details.

STAFFORD: Is it possible that a great number of the world population is nearly "unconscious" according to your definition?

JAYNES: No, I wouldn't think so. As I have said, I hope to be writing on the anthropological question also in the next book. About the problem of degrees of consciousness or whether we can mention it, I don't know how to solve this very difficult problem at the present time.

STAFFORD: Have you considered in this connection the possibility that future or present personalities might use your theory to justify a wide range of actions, remembering the examples of Jesus, Darwin, Nietzsche, and the like?

JAYNES: No, I don't think so. I can't see that at all, unless it were to justify developing more understanding of each other and more consciousness in children, something which I'm interested in doing by perhaps teaching analogies and the use of guided imagery. But as far as the things that happened with Darwin and Nietzsche? No, I don't think that anything like Social Darwinism or Nazism could come out of my book … I'm pausing here, because although the Nazis used Nietzsche, you certainly can't say that Nazism came out of Nietzsche.

STAFFORD: It appears to me that the history of ideas can be identified, using your terms, as nothing more than a succession of metaphiers, paraphiers, and paraphrands that have been used to describe (and often castrate) what historian Franklin Baumer calls the "perennial ideas" and their offspring.[6] What do you think?

JAYNES: Yes, indeed, in one sense, I do think the history of ideas could be identified as a succession of metaphiers, paraphiers, and paraphrands, but I wouldn't say "nothing more than that." But that these metaphiers recur through history and could be called "perennial ideas" I think is quite possible and could be a program for the history of ideas. However, we should remember that we are not dealing with single ideas traceable through history but a complicated matrix of ideas.

STAFFORD: You say that in the process of the breakdown we "became our own gods." Isn't this another version of the existential line that modern man is alone in the world and must learn to take responsibility for his own actions?

JAYNES: I think one could say there is a partial accord with existentialism in my theory.

STAFFORD: You refused your doctorate at Yale in the 50s, describing it as a "ridiculous badge," then accepted it some 30 years later. What made you change your mind? Have you changed any of your ideas about academia?

JAYNES: As far as I know, there's no such thing as a graduate school anywhere in the United States today. Instead, we have the apprentice system (although if someone can write a thesis on my book, perhaps I'm wrong). I felt we should get rid of the Ph.D. degree in the 50s because 95 percent of the people who received their doctorate never did any original research; even their thesis hadn't been original research. This is why it's so ridiculous, because according to every graduate catalog in the country, this is what the Ph.D. is supposed to mean. I still think the hypocrisy should stop. Someone should come to a university to get a graduate education, go

6. See Franklin L. Baumer, "Intellectual History and Its Problems," *The Journal of Modern History*, 1949, *22*, 3.

out and do ten years of research, send in their papers to the university, say-ing "I think now I'm ready to be awarded a further degree" (if somebody wanted that) and then on the basis of those publications, get one.

That's precisely what happened to me at Yale, except it was the people at Yale who very kindly copied and bound my articles and then put me through their committees. I would have been embarrassed to refuse it after all they had done. Because I am working with patients now in some clinics, it is a good thing to have a doctorate degree for your relationship with them and with the hierarchies of various clinics and hospitals.

STAFFORD: What do you think of the monist school and the myriad inter-pretations which attempt to reconcile quantum physics, consubstantia-tion, and consciousness?

JAYNES: You're referring to those who use quantum physics to say there is a force called "consciousness" in the universe. I feel this is very confused. They should not be talking about "observer participancy," which is the way John Wheeler refers to it, but about the participancy of the *recording instrument* in what you find. Their use of consciousness simply isn't valid. These very competent theoretical physicists are *not* competent when they come to psychology.

STAFFORD: What themes will the second volume address? Do you envi-sion a series of Julian Jaynes consciousness books?

JAYNES: My next volume will open up with ideas of time, and then discuss emotion, feeling, the importance of moving from shame to guilt, and from fear to anxiety, and also changes in sexual behavior. There will probably be two chapters on dreams and a theory of dreams, showing that dreams are consciousness operating mostly during REM sleep on hosts of different reactivations. This is where conciliation, one of the features of conscious-ness, shows its controlling power. I'm not sure if the chapter on childhood will come into this book or whether it will be a separate one.

STAFFORD: Has there been any recent physiological research that you're aware of which has a bearing on the theory?

JAYNES: The neurological model for the bicameral mind, as you know, implies the right hemisphere talking to the left. Dr. Monte Buchsbaum of the National Institute of Mental Health has been doing studies of positron emission tomography (PET) on schizophrenic patients as they're hallucinating, and this research shows that the right temporal lobe experiences *much* higher activity during the hallucinatory minutes. I regard this as confirming evidence for the neurological model of the bicameral mind.[7]

STAFFORD: Why is it appropriate to use modern schizophrenics and split-brain patients as virtual models for ancient bicameral man?

JAYNES: I don't use them as virtual models. I use them to support a neurological model for bicameral man, to show that right hemispheric functions are similar to those the gods must have had, and to show that modern schizophrenic voices do have a commanding, religious quality. One uses schizophrenics because auditory hallucinations are at the heart of the idea of the bicameral mind. These are our examples of auditory hallucinations, and they're all over the world. Why? Why should schizophrenia be genetically transmitted worldwide? How did this evolve? Under what kind of selective pressures did it come into being? The answer is the bicameral mind.

STAFFORD: You have said that psychiatrists like your theory. Can you mention any specific cases?

JAYNES: I certainly didn't mean that all psychiatrists like my theory, since Freudians certainly do not. But in various clinics, some psychiatrists are teaching the theory to their schizophrenic patients. When schizophrenics understand that the voices they've heard go back to a mentality that was perfectly normal at one time, it makes them feel a lot better and relieves some of the stress which then helps in the cure of the patient. This is being done in two clinics in California, one in Canada, and one in Denmark. I have many letters from schizophrenic patients who have written how much they have been relieved to understand that hearing voices should no longer be called "craziness," but a partial relapse to an earlier mentality.

STAFFORD: Have you recognized any affinities between your theory and those of the "gods" of psychology — i.e., Freud, Jung, James, etc.?

---

7. M.S. Buchsbaum, D.H. Ingvar, R. Kessler, R.N. Waters, et al., "Cerebral Glucography with Positron Tomography: Use In Normal Subjects and In Patients with Schizophrenia," *Archives of General Psychiatry*, 1982, *39*, 3, 251–9. For a review of more recent studies confirming Jaynes's neurological model, see Marcel Kuijsten, "Consciousness, Hallucinations, and the Bicameral Mind: Three Decades of New Research," in M. Kuijsten (ed.), *Reflections on the Dawn of Consciousness* (Henderson, NV: Julian Jaynes Society, 2006).

JAYNES: It's difficult to critique them all. Of the three, I like William James the most. The other two are what I would call German romantic psychiatry, based on a Sturm und Drang philosophy of the unconscious full of repressed sexual wishes in Freud or full of the archetypes in Jung that press up and out into dreams and neuroses of waking life. This is all a little too nineteenth century for me. I don't think we have an unconscious in that sense; we have what I would call a "non-conscious." Most of our thought processes, such as deciding my words right now, are non-conscious; they just come out. Barzun misunderstood this. Even though he described the phenomenon, he didn't understand that you're conscious of your intention of what you want to say, but you're not conscious of going into your lexicon, picking out particular words, and sticking them into a syntactical structure.

STAFFORD: What have been your greatest influences?

JAYNES: I started to say "behaviorism," but that's misleading. I went to graduate school to be a comparative psychologist studying the evolution of consciousness in animals, but I had to keep quiet about consciousness because I was at Yale, the best behaviorist school in the country. It gave me good training, however, because I was trying to imagine what some of my professors could mean by saying consciousness didn't exist. What possibly could they mean by that about themselves? I came to the conclusion that they simply weren't telling the truth; it was a pose that had become such a hardened fashion that the word "consciousness" simply was not talked about.

# CHAPTER 29

# Library of Science Interview

In 1977, Julian Jaynes, then a lecturer in psychology at Princeton University, shocked the scientific world with a revolutionary theory about the origin of consciousness. The minds of ancient people, he asserted, differed radically from our own. According to Jaynes, the actions of ancient men were orchestrated by the hallucinated voices of gods, and consciousness arose only after language and societies achieved a certain level of complexity (around 1000 B.C. in the Middle East). Bringing to bear a wealth of evidence from ancient literary texts and archaeological artifacts, Jaynes constructed a compelling theory through which all of paleoanthropology and ancient history could be reinterpreted.

With the re-release of *The Origin of Consciousness in the Breakdown of the Bicameral Mind* (including a new Afterword by the author), we talked with Julian Jaynes about his theories and current interests.

Q: Has there been a growing acceptance of your views?

JAYNES: There have been very extreme reactions ranging from "It's all wrong" to "Oh, we've known that all along." In general, there is a growing acceptance of the book in terms of the number of universities using it for courses, but it has not been truly assimilated into experimental research.

Q: Does this reluctance stem from the notion of saying other cultures differ from ours is somehow wrong?

JAYNES: Yes, in anthropology there's a particular prejudice against showing a difference between ourselves and other cultures; and of course I'm showing an enormous difference between ancient people and ourselves. It's only when you realize how different these people were from ourselves that ancient writings make any sense... I'm shocked at what translators do. Their idea of a good translation is what sounds like us! And that's exactly the wrong thing. What is needed is a *science* of translation instead of simply making it sound like modern writing. Such modernized translations have hindered generations of archaeologists and anthropologists from understanding what ancient individuals were like and the true nature of their societies.

Q: Recalling how people reacted when Darwin reduced man to a product of evolution, do you think some people refuse to consider your theory because they are unwilling to accept that consciousness also has a traceable origin?

JAYNES: To think of the mind as not having always been there or not imposed by God is very difficult to countenance. Even scientists want to think that consciousness was there in the beginning, even though the evidence shows exactly the opposite.

Q: Is the difference between modern consciousness and the ancient bicameral mind a difference in the "software" or the "hardware" of the brain?

JAYNES: The software. In gross appearance, you couldn't tell the difference between the brain of a modern person and the brain of a bicameral person. But there would be a difference in the fine structure, just as there's a difference in the fine structures of the brains of those who know English and those who know French.

Q: What is included in the new Afterword?

JAYNES: A clarification of some of the confusions aroused by the book and a brief look at some of my current research. This has to do with changes in human nature that accompany the emergence of consciousness — for example, the discovery of time, the invention of reminiscent memory and therefore the self, as well as the dramatic change from a biologically organized affect system common to all mammals, to our difficult and unique emotions. These changes include the development of our anxiety out of fear, guilt out of shame, and our panorama of eroticism out of simple and unemotional mating.

# PART IV

# Discussion

# CHAPTER 30

# Consciousness and the Voices of the Mind: Yellow Springs Institute Discussion

Q: Have you said anything that could be of help in treating schizophrenia?

JAYNES: I think so. There is a clinic in Copenhagen that is trying to develop a whole method of treatment on the basis of the idea that schizophrenia is indeed a partial relapse to the bicameral mind. But of course in the schizophrenia patient it is very different than what it was like to have a bicameral mind because the person has learned consciousness and is trying to hang on to consciousness while he is going through this panicky situation. And the voices haven't been trained into the right hemisphere in the proper way. But one of the ways in which I think it's been helpful — there is a clinic out in California, that when the schizophrenic patient is in contact with a psychotherapist, they are teaching them this theory, and I've received lots of letters that have been exceedingly gratifying from schizophrenic patients, or former schizophrenic patients, who said how grateful they were, because this takes away the craziness. Before, psychiatrists didn't want to deal with auditory hallucinations — it was all just crazy. But now, it all makes sense. It makes sense to think that the stress of the modern world on our learned consciousness can in some people bring out this earlier kind of mentality, which made a lot of sense back then.

Q: What about for instance a patient who was paranoid but was not schizophrenic? Could his ideation be on the same basis?

JAYNES: I really can't answer the question. I really don't know. There are lots of difficulties here and I certainly don't mean that all mental illness is a relapse. I'm really saying that when you have a patient that is hearing

Transcribed and edited from a question and answer session following Julian Jaynes's "Consciousness and the Voices of the Mind" lecture (similar to Chapter 19 of this volume), presented at the Yellow Springs Institute in Chester Springs, Pennsylvania on June 9, 1980, as part of the "Six Saturdays: Explorations in Archetypal Themes" lecture series.

auditory hallucinations and has what is called "the dissolution of the ego" or what Jung called "thought deprivation" — all of those things fit together. Consciousness is breaking up and into that vacuum comes auditory hallucinations.

Q: If I understand the argument, it goes something like this: It's possible that people could not have been conscious; we are conscious; it's true, apparently, that people had a bicameral mind and heard hallucinations and we don't routinely hear such hallucinations; so therefore, the people who heard hallucinations were unconscious. Now would it be possible or simpler to say that people in the *Iliad* had a bicameral mind but perhaps also consciousness? I don't see the connection between the consciousness/unconsciousness and bicameral/non-bicameral.

JAYNES: I could rephrase it in this way. There could be a weak form of my theory that would say that mankind was both conscious and bicameral at the beginning of civilization, and then as civilization became more and more complicated the bicameral mind couldn't work anymore and it broke down just leaving consciousness. And you could never prove or disprove that. The point of a scientific hypothesis is to get it out on a limb so you can disprove it. And then when you can disprove it, then you go back to that. I am out to get at the origin of consciousness. I think there is a lot more work to do. I've just talked about metaphor and analogs — I've just scratched the surface or opened a little keyhole into a huge area that I think is going to be developed, but all the things we base metaphors on, and analogs, and so on — and it's just a beginning — I want to know the source of that. And if I say, in the weak form, that consciousness began somewhere further back, well we're right back at the beginning again — we still have the problem: how can you get this inner experience out of mere matter in evolution?

Q: What about the experience of hearing voices when one is just waking or going to sleep? Does that mean we still have residues of the bicameral mind?

JAYNES: I was discussing this with a reporter this morning and he has had that experience. Does that come from the right hemisphere? Is this a mapping of the bicameral mind? I honestly don't know. All of us have internal conversations by which we figure out what we're doing, and it can have that quality. But an imagined voice is different than an auditory hallucination. An auditory hallucination has an external quality to it. Whereas in that hypnogogic state of going to sleep, we generally know that's part of us. I don't know whether that's related or not, we've got to do a lot more research on this.

# CHAPTER 31

# Consciousness and the Voices of the Mind: Tufts University Discussion

Q: Do you see vestiges of bicameral hierarchical structure in our political system? In other words, wherever we see a hierarchy, is that a vestige of bicamerality?

JAYNES: I think it has something to do with the fact that all social animals are involved in building hierarchies — not just ourselves, but chickens in a barnyard as well as gorillas. So this hierarchical business of social individuals being in a hierarchy — this is common to all social mammals. Now, I'm hesitant about saying this about some of the things that go on in politics, but yes, it is related. I'd just like to say it is related rather than being an actual kind of identity.

Q: If we're so young in consciousness, what does our adolescence hold in store for us?

JAYNES: I could be a pessimist, but I'm not — I am an optimist. I am very interested in the human potential movement — this is one thing I am speaking about tomorrow night in Bedford, Massachusetts. I should pause a little bit to say that some of this human potential movement is not exact and is full of a lot of flaky things. Some of it though is quite good and I think there is an enormous future in people realizing how much they can control themselves, and how much perhaps they can change themselves and change their ways of thinking. We all know the concept of psychosomatic disease; well let's reverse that to psychosomatic health if we can.

Q: You seem to be focused on Western civilization, but how about Eastern civilizations, particularly India and China?

Transcribed and edited from a question and answer session following Julian Jaynes's "Consciousness and Voices of the Mind" lecture (similar to Chapter 19 of this volume), presented at Tufts University on October 14, 1982.

JAYNES: India and China, these supposedly ancient civilizations — they're not. They come long after Mesopotamia. We somehow grew up with the idea that India and China are these very old civilizations, but civilization happens in China really about 1200 B.C. — quite some time after these huge cities in Mesopotamia. India is a little older than that, but not much. But another problem comes in getting sufficient materials, because in India and China there hasn't been this sense of time and history that we have had. In India, many of the *Veda* and *Upanishads*, some of the greatest of them were not written down until 1850, when British colonels went into India to rule and didn't have anything to do. They became scholars of this material and wrote it down — it was still being repeated in the temples orally. So it isn't as authentic to its time.

Somewhat the same thing in China but as you perhaps know, Chinese archeology is booming right now. The new regime — this is part of their whole effort to give a historical basis to China. They are making some mistakes, saying that there was never any diffusion from Mesopotamia, but most scholars don't agree with that. But that doesn't matter — they have discovered just loads of stuff that has been buried there. So, we'll be able to deal with that much better than we can right now.

But I think the same things went on. If you compare the *Veda* and *Upanishads*, you find the same contrast between a non-conscious literature, with people hearing voices, and a very conscious literature. If you look at China, there isn't really any bicameral literature in Chinese because we're suddenly there with Confucius and the *I Ching* and things like this, but there are other things like idols that make us think that indeed they were bicameral about 1200 B.C. with the Shang Dynasty and then things began to change.[1]

Q: Do you have any hypotheses on why and when consciousness occurs in infants?

JAYNES: The question really should take a whole different lecture on the development of consciousness in children. Let me say that I'm trying to investigate this empirically with some of my students and it is not an easy thing to do. But remember what we mean by consciousness — it is the ability to introspect, to have this narratizing ability, to think before and after. If anybody here has children, you certainly know how at times you

---

1. See Michael Carr, "The *Shi* 'Corpse/Personator' Ceremony in Early China," in Marcel Kuijsten (ed.) *Reflections on the Dawn of Consciousness* (Henderson: NV, Julian Jaynes Society, 2006).

say to a young child, "Now think about what you are going to do, stop and think a little bit," or you might remind the child, "Do you remember what we did last summer? Remember this place, remember that?" — training memory and so on. These are empirical questions that I think we have to do a lot more studies on. I can give you one example that came from my being in a restaurant in Princeton, where I saw a little boy — I guess he must have been six — tagging along behind his mother, who seemed to be cross with him as she went up to pay the bill. He simply tugged on her coat and said, "Can I say it in my mind?" And the mother turned around crossly and said "Yes." And the little boy just stood there and a glaze came over his face. So we turned that into an experiment. We started doing various things and finding out when children can say things to themselves and sing things to themselves in their mind, and it turns out to be about four-and-a-half — it is pretty clear. Now what does that mean? Does that mean consciousness? I'm not sure, we still have to work at it.

Q: Why do you suppose that consciousness developed from the bicameral mind? Would it make you more fit for survival?

JAYNES: Yes, it has tremendous survival value. But I don't think it has a biological, genetic basis. However, if you are a follower of E. O. Wilson, he has recently come out with some statements that in only a period of 1,000 years you can change the gene pool a little bit. But I don't think this is an evolved kind of thing. But I'm very sure that those individuals since that time who were conscious and could get along in a conscious society are those who would reproduce more, and those who were not conscious would not be as successful. But there are a lot of problems there. I don't like to base my case on evolution because that puts it in the darkness again. Once you say "consciousness is evolved and it's innate in a child" then you don't have to do any investigation anymore, it just sort of grows. Instead I am taking the more radical position that indeed it is learned, and we want to find out how it is learned.[2]

---

2. More recently, research has confirmed that the human brain is still evolving, that genetic changes can move through a population more rapidly than previously believed, and that the rate of human evolution has been greater over the past several thousand years than it was over the past several million years. These findings suggest there could have been a slight genetic component to the primarily cultural transition from bicamerality to consciousness. See Patrick Evans, et al. "Microcephalin, A Gene Regulating Brain Size, Continues to Evolve Adaptively in Humans," Science, 2005, *309*, 5741, 1717–20 and David Biello, "Culture Speeds Up Human Evolution," *Scientific American*, Dec. 10, 2007. — *Ed.*

Q: If consciousness is learned from generation to generation, does this imply that there are bicameral groups today — hunter-gatherer societies, for example?

JAYNES: The answer is no. The last two possibilities have recently been destroyed. They were two bands in the Amazon. The Brazilian government is moving in there and they are doing farming and everything else there. But that doesn't mean that there aren't a lot of things to look for. I tend to think that there were many bicameral civilizations going on in Africa, for example. There were the Nok, back around 500 A.D. We are just digging up the idols that they used. To me this means almost by definition that they were bicameral. What you find is that they had breakdowns. So what each hunter-gatherer tribe has now is a whole history — as long as ourselves — and many of the practices they have perhaps came from a time when they were a part of a bicameral kingdom. I feel that is an interesting hypothesis, to see if we can have an archeo-history where we could go to a hunter gatherer group and try to get back what it was like 1,500 years ago. We are dealing with very long periods of time here. That's a very good question.[3]

Q: You said something very briefly in passing in reference to chimpanzees. I recently read a book that mentions attempts to intercommunicate with chimps. If we ever manage to, if they could learn our language, they would be the first species to learn another species' language. Well, without having to buy into that, since you did mention chimps, I wonder if you had

---

3. Over the past decade, new information on uncontacted tribes has emerged. In 2004, the Sumatra-Andaman earthquake and resulting tsunami brought renewed attention to two pre-modern tribes, the Sentinelese and the Jarawa, living on the Andaman and Nicobar islands in the Indian Ocean. While the Jarawa have seen increased contact over the past decade, the Sentinelese have continued to resist all contact with the outside world. Uncontacted tribes have also been discovered in the Amazon rainforest in Brazil and in the mountains of Papua, New Guinea. In cases of tribes where contact has been established and is welcomed, it is unfortunate that they have not been studied by anthropologists familiar with Jaynes's theory. However, the research that has been done nonetheless supports Jaynes's theory in a variety of ways. For example, the Jarawa and a neighboring group, the Onge, are described as having beliefs that the dead live around them as spirits. This suggests auditory hallucinations and indicates vestiges of bicamerality. As mentioned in the Introduction, other studies suggest that some tribes lack the modern concept of time, which Jaynes argues is one of the features of consciousness. See Adam Goodheart, "The Last Island of the Savages," *The American Scholar*, 2000, *69*, 4, 13–44; Madhusree Mukerjee, *The Land of Naked People: Encounters with Stone Age Islanders* (Houghton Mifflin Harcourt, 2003); and Chris Sinha, et al., "When Time is Not Space: The Social and Linguistic Construction of Time Intervals in An Amazonian Culture," *Language and Cognition*, 2011, *3*, 1. Similar evidence for vestiges of bicamerality in tribes studied worldwide in the late nineteenth and early twentieth centuries is described by the French anthropologist Lucien Lévy-Bruhl in *Primitive Mentality* (AMS Press, 1923/1975), which was part of Jaynes's source material. — *Ed.*

anything to say about inter-species language or what the consequences are for the mind of other species learning language?

JAYNES: One of my former students from Princeton here... good question, and how am I going to answer it? In the use of the word language, some people use it very loosely — they talk about bees' language, things like that. I don't like to use it that loosely. I prefer communication systems. Chimpanzees have huge communication systems full of gestures, cries, and everything else. So I wouldn't like to talk about us learning their language — although I have friends of mine at the Philadelphia Zoo that do just that, they learn all the different ethological signs and go into the chimpanzee cage and communicate with them. But it's not the communication of information; it's the communication of emotions and feelings and things of this sort. Now if we get back to the groups of people that have been trying to teach chimpanzees language — the Gardners and there are a whole group of them — and there is still a great deal of controversy. It would be very interesting particularly if we could get a female chimpanzee to teach it to her young, which has not happened, although they have looked into that. Or if it would go back into the wild and try to teach it to others and nobody has tried that. It seems to fade out in the chimpanzees unless it's constantly reinforced. But I'm sure the consequences of it would not be overwhelming. I think for the individual animal, the consequences are things like increasing perceptions. I think our words for things increase our perceptions. If I have a word for lectern, one can see it more clearly. So I think in particular Washoe would go through a magazine and make signs for what the things were, and I'm sure it made it much more attention-getting to him than a normal chimpanzee looking through a magazine who probably wouldn't have paid much attention to it.

Q: Your theory seems to discredit the reality of religious experience before consciousness. Could you give me your opinion of the reality of religious experience after consciousness?

JAYNES: Does the theory destroy the reality of religious experience? Let me just describe to you a letter that I received from a theologian at a Southern Baptist college, where they were reading my book and indeed my book was being damned as the Antichrist and most of them wanted to burn it. But he was very nice, and he said I don't want you to think that even of yourself, because here's how it all fits together for me. Assume there is some kind of God that we don't know very clearly, a God that can create in time — although time doesn't exist for him — create in evolution and so on. Then slowly he reveals himself to human beings in a series of successive steps, to get the human beings to where he wants the human beings to be — remembering that there is no time in God. So first of all, he has human beings evolve language here, then he reveals himself to each individual as their own personal god, then he turns to monotheism, with Moses and others — even Akhenaton for example can be brought in here. Monotheism wasn't something that was going on at this period — the idea of there being one god, not many. And then we have the prophets that are relating God to human beings. Then the end of the prophets comes — which I think this theory explains and I don't think any other one really does, why the prophets just suddenly die off. And then because he is a Christian theologian, God comes to Earth in the person of Jesus, who goes through a human life, and is trying to teach more about God's purpose to human beings, then is crucified and dies, and then is forcing human beings to relate to God in terms of faith. "The evidence of things unseen," as Paul says. All of that you see can then fit into a Christian interpretation, if you want to think of indeed a God outside of all this. So I don't want people to think that I'm trying to be anti-religious in what I've been saying.

[Recording ends.]

# CHAPTER 32

# Consciousness and the Voices of the Mind: University of New Hampshire Discussion

Q: Was the shift away from the bicameral mind caused by a genetic mutation or was it culturally induced?

JAYNES: It is the latter. I do not think there is time for genetic change here. Although if you read E. O. Wilson and Charles Lumsden's *Genes, Mind and Culture*, they talk about changes to the gene pool over a 1,000 year period. However, from my knowledge of evolution, the transition occurs too fast. I am placing it as a cultural thing — that consciousness is learned. Now, you may say, "How can we block off these voices that are coming from the right hemisphere?" Well, we can understand that neurologically. You can have whole areas shutting down for awhile and then relearning and getting recircuited. So I do say it's cultural. One of the causes of the breakdown of the bicameral mind is writing. Once things were in writing, there isn't that power to the auditory voice. If it's in writing, you can turn away from it, and it no longer controls you. Another was the catastrophes and then all the invasions that were going on at the time. The gods simply no longer worked as the societies became too unstable.[1]

Q: What is the next stage beyond consciousness?

JAYNES: I wish I knew. Standing back and looking at it from the whole point of view of evolution — what a short period this is, back to 1000 B.C. It does make one interested in what will happen to consciousness 3,000 years from now. I think consciousness is changing. I think at least the content of consciousness is changing. I think you can see changes in the nature of the self, and selfhood. Back at time of Chaucer the self was very

Transcribed and edited from a question and answer session following Julian Jaynes's "Consciousness and Voices of the Mind" lecture (similar to Chapter 19 of this volume), presented at the University of New Hampshire on April 28, 1983.
1. See note 2 on page 290.

different from what it is now. Back in the twelfth century it was also different, and back earlier in the Middle Ages it was very different. These are the kinds of things you can see in more recent history and if you carry that trajectory on to our own time and ask, "What is it that's happening in our own time that is of interest?" Well, unknown signs are television — what is it doing? We're not quite sure. And video games. There is going to be a big spread in the use of video games. What will that do when so many children are going to be using video games? And computers. At the same time, look at some of the other things we have. We have something called the human potential movement. So much of it is slush, I'm afraid, and yet it is so popular. Some of it is good. Some of it is more seriously studied and does change people and does help people. But the amount of interest is quite astonishing — I occasionally speak at some of these conferences. And what does that do to consciousness, when we are so conscious of consciousness and learning different ways of changing it? I think that is very helpful, in terms of the history of psychiatry, I think it is a very helpful thing. These are the things to look at. And to remember that, although we are in bad times now because of our [weapons] technology, it isn't because of our psychology. We are generally less aggressive now, I think, as people, then we were before, during the Middle Ages. I think there is less cruelty and there's more kindness and more consideration of other people. Out of all that, I hesitate to make a prediction, but it's interesting to think about.

Q: How is consciousness related to activity in the brain?

JAYNES: It's a good question. I have not touched on that problem whatsoever. I have given you no neurological model for consciousness. I simply don't know.[2]

Q: I was surprised to discover that the Buddha and Confucius were supposedly contemporaries. And they were both not very far from the beginning of the Greek civilization. I wonder if that conjunction fits into your development in the transition from bicamerality to consciousness?

JAYNES: The fact that Confucius and Buddha and Solon — and many important people — that they were all contemporaries, that all this was

---

2. Recent advances in brain imaging technologies have now made the neural correlates of consciousness a viable topic for research. In one recent study, French neuroscientist Renaud Jardri and his colleagues investigated brain areas involved in inner speech and self-awareness. See Renaud Jardri, Delphine Pins, Maxime Bubrovszky, Pascal Despretz, Jean-Pierre Pruvo, Marc Steinling, and Pierre Thomas, "Self-awareness and Speech Processing: An fMRI Study," *Neuroimage*, 2007, *35*, 4. — *Ed.*

happening during this particular period, is flabbergasting. Now what happened in China with Confucius? China becomes bicameral — and we can find this with their practices and so on — in 1500 B.C. but only lasts about six centuries. This is the Shang dynasty and then the Zhou come in and conquer them. We find lots of evidence for divination. A colleague of mine, Professor Carr, who is working in this particular area, shows that there is a change in language in China towards the mind just as there is in Greece at just about the same time.[3] Until we come to Confucius who is very conscious indeed. That is about 500 B.C. which is precisely the same time as Solon.

Now is this something magical, that you can get these two things happening at the same time? There are problems here, but we've got to remember that there were trade routes through the high waters of the Yellow River — although some patriotic Chinese historians don't want to say that because they want it to be completely independent. But there was trade from Mesopotamia coming this way. One can only say this is through diffusion somehow — I don't know. But it's a good point.

Q: What is going to be in the second volume?

JAYNES: Well, the second volume is going to take up about where I've left things off tonight. It will start with an analysis about our human sense of time, and then go into what a new sense of spatialized time does to the human being. The human being for the first time has a lifetime. Bicameral man, not being conscious, couldn't go backwards and forwards in consciousness because of he didn't have consciousness. He never worried about his death, just like an animal doesn't. But now we have lifetimes — people know their births and know that they have deaths to come.

Another subject I will discuss is affect systems. By affect I mean biologically, genetically organized emotions, such that we share with all mammals, and which have a genetically based way of arousing them and then getting rid of their byproducts. But then these become something — and we really don't have the terminology for it, so I'm going to call them feelings right now, and by that I mean conscious feelings. We have shame, for example. It is very important and powerful — if you remember your childhood, and the importance of fitting yourself into the group without being humiliated. This becomes guilt when you have consciousness

---

3. See Michael Carr, "The *Shi* 'Corpse/Personator' Ceremony in Early China," in Marcel Kuijsten (ed.) *Reflections on the Dawn of Consciousness* (Henderson, NV: Julian Jaynes Society, 2006).

operating on it over time. Guilt is the fear of shame. We also see the emergence of anxiety, which is built on the affect of fear.

Then you have the same thing happening with sex. I think mating was pretty perfunctory back in the bicameral period, just as it is with most of the primates. It isn't an obvious thing in any of the anthropoid apes — like the orangutans, the gorillas, the gibbons, and the chimpanzees. It is not all that obvious. And I think it was the same thing in the bicameral time — there is nothing really "sexy," if I may use that adjective — in the bicameral paintings and sculptures. But just after this period, beginning in 700 B.C., the Greek world is a pornographic world if ever there was one. It's astonishing what happens. [At museums] most of these vases are not upstairs where children can see them, they are usually kept downstairs. At the same time this isn't just a matter of artifacts; it is a part of their behavior. There is evidence of brothels beginning here, homosexuality perhaps begins at this same time, and we have various kinds of laws to regulate these things. It is something we don't understand though, because it isn't quite like our sexuality — it has a religious basis. It is very strange and odd, this almost religious basis. You have the tragedies, like the Oedipus plays, put on as a trilogy, and it was always followed by a phallic farce, for example. This seems extraordinary to us, because it destroys the whole beauty of these plays.

All that was going on in Greece, and was going in with the Etruscans — who didn't leave much writing, but they left us enough so that we have a pattern and know that there was group sex going on and things like that. We don't find it so much among the Hebrews I think because the Hebrews — who in some places were monotheistic and in other places were not — had a very powerful God saying "thou shalt not" and so on — follow the law. At least we don't have evidence for those behaviors.

So we have for the first time increases in sexual behavior and the emergence of guilt and anxiety. Think of that: anxiety, sex, and guilt — if anybody wants to be a Freudian, this is where it begins [laughs]. Because then you had to have psychological mechanisms of controlling this. I mentioned something about repression — that's one of the things that comes into play here — but all these methods of forgiveness and the whole concept of sin beings at this time.

I will also have a section on dreams. The interesting thing about dreams is that we see a dramatic change between the bicameral and conscious periods. Before the development of consciousness people had bicameral dreams, and after the development of consciousness people have conscious dreams. I define modern dreams as consciousness operating during REM sleep. During the bicameral period, everyone hears voices whenever they have a dream, but this is infrequent after the development of consciousness. So those are some of the topics I'll be discussing in the next book.

Q: Did you consider this shift to be attributable to an integration of the bicameral mind at any point, as opposed to the breakdown?

JAYNES: Did I regard this as an integration of the bicameral mind, such as an integration of the god-like function...?

Q: More facilitation between the hemispheres, yes.

JAYNES: I think we do have more facilitation between the hemispheres — this gets back to the person who asked me if I had a model for consciousness. I really think the breakdown of the bicameral mind was a silence of the gods — a shutdown of those parts of the right hemisphere. We know with schizophrenia, for example, that the voices come and go. It's astonishing how you can get rid of the voices in schizophrenia. The schizophrenic himself cannot get rid of the voices. But in some cases — and this has been done — if you make a suggestion to a schizophrenia patient: "Here is brand new medicine, take it and it will get rid of the voices right away" — and he takes it and it gets rid of the voices, at least temporarily. It is curious how this can be under the control of social suggestion but not under the volition of the individual patient.

It could be called an integration of the hemispheres. Right now, I could ask you to be conscious of language or I could ask you to be conscious of music. We know one is based in the left hemisphere and one is based in the right hemisphere, and you can go back and forth with no difficulty. This has to be going through the corpus callosum and anterior commissure.

Q: Is creativity a harking back to the bicameral mind?

JAYNES: Creativity in the bicameral time was the bicameral mind. Nothing could be more creative than the right hemisphere that ordered these civilizations and planned its buildings. People would have visual dreams that were just like blueprints, which of course I'm thinking are indeed the function of the right hemisphere. That was creativity. Nowadays, yes the right hemisphere is more involved in artistic and creative things, certainly with music. But I think both hemispheres are involved. Let's take composing, for example, which is a very creative process. Those of you who are not musicians will tend to process music mostly in the right hemisphere. But if you are a musician, and you become a composer, you will process music on both temporal lobes. So you can think of a great composer like Beethoven — the struggle is between the left hemisphere which is more concerned with the structure and the right hemisphere which is the source of inspiration. So in that sense there is more integration.

Q: In the shamanistic tradition — which seems to go back as far as 10,000 B.C. — they seem to have ideas of death and intermediaries. Do you think that comes later?

JAYNES: The question was in regards to the shamanistic tradition, which the questioner believes goes back to 10,000 B.C., and their ideas of death, and so on. Now, when you say the shamanistic tradition, I think I know what you are referring to, and if they say that [regarding their concept of death], I don't think they have the data to show that — because we don't know the tradition. What we find are shamans in various primitive groups. And what are shaman? They usually go into trances and hear voices — although not all of them do — and come back. They may be healing someone by going into this trance or perhaps deciding what the tribe is going to do. But when we talk about a shamanistic tradition going back to 10,000 B.C., I think we have to say that is not known. There is no writing that shows that. There is the bicameral mind that is going back to that time, but not in a shamanistic kind of way. The earliest writing starts in 3000 B.C., and everything before that is inference.

# CHAPTER 33

# Consciousness and the Voices of the Mind: McMaster-Bauer Symposium Discussion

Q: I would just like to raise a terminological question. Do you make any essential difference between the word "consciousness" and the word "self-consciousness"?

JAYNES: Absolutely. Consciousness should not be equated with self-consciousness. There are at least three senses of the term. Self-consciousness has a trivial sense of embarrassment, or fear of what others may think of you, which I am sure is not what you mean. A second and most important sense is the consciousness of self as in answering the question "Who am I?" The self is the answer. It is an entity or structure of attributes given by our culture and imbedded in our language that is learned into our personal history which we infer from two sources: what other people tell us we are and what we infer from our own behavior. Many recent experiments in social psychology provide evidence for this statement. The self is not in any sense the analog 'I' which is contentless. The self is an object of consciousness, not consciousness itself. As such, the self is not a stable construction, but changes dramatically through history and among nations, as well as in child development, and even over the course of a day, depending on one's excerpts and how one narratizes them.

But here, as in many topics relating to mind, we must carefully locate those fuzzy areas of polyreferential confusion where what seems to be the same word is used to denote two or more quite different referents. Thus self properly is the psychological self I have just described. But the word is also used in trivial reflexive senses as when we say "the word itself" or say that "a fly washes itself." And an extension of that usage occurs when

Question and answer session following Julian Jaynes's "Consciousness and Voices of the Mind" lecture (Chapter 19 of this volume), presented at the McMaster-Bauer Symposium on Consciousness at McMaster University in 1983. First published in *Canadian Psychology*, Vol. 27, Issue 2. © 1986 Canadian Psychological Association. Permission granted for use of material.

we say we see ourselves in a mirror. We don't. We see and recognize our bodies or our faces, not our selves. When pigeons[1] or chimpanzees[2] are taught to recognize their bodies (note how much easier it would be to say "themselves," and how erroneous!) in mirrors, it has nothing to do with consciousness or self-awareness in its human sense. When such a chimp, because of its mirror training, rubs off a spot on its head it has seen in the mirror, it may be no different essentially from rubbing off a spot on its arm without a mirror.[3]

There is a third sense of self-consciousness that occurs mostly in philosophical discussions and is a rather musty way of indicating self-observation of our own thinking or introspection. Such introspection is one type of narratization in which consciousness — and you remember I called it an operator as in mathematics — is operating twice. We are conscious of our own consciousness. Consider a schoolboy taking an exam fantasizing a romantic daydream about a girl across the aisle. Then when someone makes a noise, perhaps, or he notices a physiological reaction incongruous with the situation, he suddenly realizes he is daydreaming and must stop and return to the exam if he is to pass. Here is consciousness operating twice. From the schoolboy's point of view, it can be diagrammed as:

$$\text{'I'} \to (\text{me and girl together})$$

which changes to:

$$\text{'I'} \to [\text{'I'} \to (\text{me and girl together})]$$

and so ceases, where 'I' in single quotes always stands for the analog 'I' and the arrows for those analog abilities designated as narratization.

It is an extremely functional process, making us able to prevent ourselves from being commandeered by fantasy — as happens in dreams. Conscious processes and content are introspectable (which is being conscious of our own consciousness), and even sometimes introspection itself (which is being conscious of being conscious of being conscious). As such, introspection can be used as a denotative definition of consciousness, that

1. Robert Epstein, Robert P. Lanza, and B.F. Skinner, "'Self-awareness' in the Pigeon," *Science*, 1981, *212*, 695–696.

2. Gordon G. Gallup, Jr. "Chimpanzees: Self-Recognition," *Science*, 1970, *167*, 86–87.

3. See Julian Jaynes, "In A Manner of Speaking: Commentary On Cognition and Consciousness in Non-Human Species," *Behavioral and Brain Sciences*, 1978, *1*, 578–579. Reprinted as Chapter 10 of this volume.

is, a definition by pointing at it. But we must not make the mistake of thinking that all consciousness is introspective because it is introspectable.

Q: Is there a more objective way of pointing out consciousness?

JAYNES: Right now let us take any ten people out there on the street and ask them when they next hear a clock strike to tell us all what they had been thinking of in the previous minute. The resulting reports are the basic material of consciousness and what we are trying to understand. That is bedrock and an objective denotative definition of consciousness. It is an experiment I do with my class each year.

Q: I think this is a related question. Some people would say that consciousness is all awareness while you are just talking about self-awareness. Could you comment?

JAYNES: *Awareness*, like the word *experience*, is an extremely slippery word that immediately confounds attention, perception, and consciousness, and by doing so buries the problem all over again in a morass of undefinitions. It stealthily crept into our descriptions of behavior more and more during the behavioristic era as a rather sly surrogate for the deposed and banished consciousness, and has been causing multireferential havoc ever since. It is interesting that in the midst of that era, Webster's *Collegiate Dictionary* (5th ed., p. 215) tried to distinguish between consciousness and awareness by saying that consciousness "applies primarily to that which is felt within oneself," while awareness "applies to that which is perceived as without." I would be happy to agree with that if others would as well and stick to that distinction. But too often awareness slides around everywhere and takes on associations of internality, which confuses it again with consciousness. I therefore try to avoid the term. There is nothing that the word awareness can refer to that cannot be expressed in more precise terms. And we should do so.

Now, back to the question. Am I just talking about self-awareness? The more precise term here is self-consciousness, which I think is what you mean. The question then becomes similar to the last part of the first question where I noted that all consciousness, while being phenomenally located internally, is not self-consciousness. I can be worried about what my young daughter is doing staying out after midnight again. That is certainly consciousness, certainly narratizing in mind-space, and I think of it as going on in me — even though such phenomenal location is arbitrary — but I can't see how that could be called self-consciousness or self-awareness.

Now, as to those who wish to call consciousness all awareness. What could that mean? Probably consciousness as I have described it plus all sense perception. This is very deceptive, and it gets back to the question I mentioned in my talk: Is sense perception consciousness?

First of all, consciousness is not necessary for sense perception. We must be crystal clear about that. You can notice this in your everyday life, all the countless things you do when you are thinking of something else, very obviously being guided by hosts of perceptions. And if you do still hold that consciousness is necessary for perception, you will have to carry it over into animal behavior and down the evolutionary tree — as I meant to emphasize in my lecture — until you will have to impute consciousness to protozoa, since they react to objects and so have sense perceptions, and so to the white blood cells circulating right now in your body. To me that is a *reductio ad absurdum.*

Second, while sense perception is not due to consciousness, we are of course conscious of what we perceive. Consciousness, this narratizing in a mind-space, would be useless otherwise. I perceive the blackboard. So can an animal. But I can be conscious of the blackboard as I perceive it, a kind of extra dimension that a non-human animal does not have. But that is a poor example. It is difficult to hold one's consciousness steadily on a perception — like a Zen meditation discipline. If I try to keep conscious of the blackboard, I lose it quickly: I start narratizing around it, noting its location, thinking of what is written on it, remembering other black-boards, wondering how it's made nowadays, and so forth. What is more, I think I can be conscious of the blackboard more easily by closing my eyes. Perception often can be slightly inhibiting to consciousness.

Q: I think I agree that consciousness and perception should be separated and that they have been squeezed together by many psychologists. But why do you think this is so?

JAYNES: There are several reasons. The simplest is that consciousness as I said is an analog of external perception and so is easily mistaken for perception. After all, it is mapped onto sense perception almost as its template. We can "perceive" an idea or a subtlety using the same word as perceiving a tree. Sharing the same terminology, it is no wonder the two kinds of perception are confused.

Another reason is that even the casual use of mental words inappropriately can produce convictions in us that are quite mistaken, and this goes on non-consciously. If a boxer is knocked out, we might say, lacking a better word, that he is knocked unconscious. This automatically and irrationally gets us to assume that everything before the punch was conscious — which we know is untrue. It's as if having a blackout in a city means that everything in the city is white. We should say the boxer is knocked unreactive or senseless.

Language also plays this trick on us when we try to describe animal behavior. If a moth keeps flying into that light up there, and someone asks us, "Is the moth aware of the light?", we might say "Yes," lacking a better word. The moth is aware of the light, which translates for some people into consciousness, spiraling us back into the same confusion. The proper description is that the moth flies into the light and nothing more. No projected internality, please. It is reflex machinery.

And a further reason is strictly academic history. So-called experimental psychology was begun in Germany by physicists and physiologists who were strict metaphysical dualists (even if some of them called themselves panpsychists) and who knew and cared nothing about the evolutionary problem or animal behavior or human behavior for that matter. Their perspective is therefore very distorted. Fechner, a physicist, is an excellent example. By studying just-noticeable differences in stimulus intensity, pitch, or brightness, he thought he was studying the elements of consciousness and so relating the universe of mind and the universe of matter, as in the famous Weber-Fechner Law. And this led into what William James — whose emphasis you remember was so opposite, on the *stream* of consciousness — called the dreary wasteland of psychophysics. Even today some students of perception suppose they are studying consciousness when they are simply studying perception — which we share with all animals.

Q: Some modern philosophers make that mistake as well.

JAYNES: I imagine it is because of the artificial analytic traditions begun in 1920 by two Cambridge friends, G.E. Moore[4] and Bertrand Russell, about what used to be called sense data: consciousness sits in its space in the head waiting to be fed sense data through the apertures of the sense

---

4. G.E. Moore, *Philosophical Studies* (London: Routledge & Keagan Paul, 1922).

organs. When Russell,[5] looking for an example of consciousness, simply says, "I see a table," that is a highly artificial choice, and really incorrect reporting. It is not "I see a table" but his knowing he sees a table that is what he is really meaning. It is his consciousness of seeing a table that he is talking about, not the bare perception. This can be diagrammed thus:

$$\text{'I'} \longrightarrow \text{I see a table}$$

Russell thought his consciousness was the second term alone, where really it was both. He was being conscious of the perception as part of an argument. Russell should have selected a more ethologically valid example that was really true of his consciousness, that had really happened, such as "I think I will rewrite the *Principia* now that Whitehead's dead," or "How can I afford the alimony for another Lady Russell?" He would then have come to other conclusions. Such examples are consciousness in action. "I see a table" is not.

Let me give another hypothetical example from our ten subjects out there in the street. Suppose one of our subjects was hurrying to an intersection just as the light turned red against her. Her consciousness indeed would have recognized she had to stop at the red light. If she crossed she would be jay-walking, which is wrong. And she remembers she is a good person. Except she shouldn't have stopped for that fudge sundae — and with walnuts on top too! And now she might be late getting home, because there goes the clock, and now invalided Cousin Sally will be worrying I've been in an accident. Punishment for breaking my diet, I'm sure the police have made this particular red light longer than it used to be, probably just to be mean to me — and to poor Cousin Sally. Oh! There it turns green. Nothing less than all that and more.

And so if a psychologist or a philosopher comes along and says consciousness is awareness or sensation, and "seeing the red light" is a good example of consciousness, it is as absurd as saying a B-flat is a good example of a symphony. Seeing a red light cues consciousness: the sensation is a node between one conscious string and another.

I hope some of you will try that experiment tomorrow of monitoring your consciousness when you hear a clock strike. See if you have just been thinking of a perception.

---

5. Bertrand Russell, *Analysis of Mind* (London: Allen & Unwin, 1921); *Philosophy* (New York: Norton, 1927).

I could add that even Watson and the early behaviorists would agree with my point here. In saying that consciousness does not exist, they certainly did not mean sense perception.

Q: Are you a behaviorist in animal behavior?

JAYNES: I am a strict behaviorist up to 1000 B.C. when consciousness develops in the one species that has a syntactic language, namely, ourselves.

Q: Was there humor in the bicameral period?

JAYNES: There was jeering at individuals who do something different from expectation in the bicameral world, shaming them. It is a method of social control that has its parallel in other social mammals' ostracism of an aberrant member of the group or as children on a playground may mock a child who is different. It is not humor in our sense. It is usually cruel and it is usually excluding somebody from the group. The theory I am working on is that this is what humor grew out of as human beings became conscious. We today have clowns and comics who almost always are portraying people we don't respect for various reasons. We are really excluding such portrayals from ourselves as we laugh at them, and we like to do this in a group, suggesting its ancient innate origins of social ostracism. But I haven't traced it out with any thoroughness. It is an excellent problem for research.

Q: Did everyone hear the gods?

JAYNES: Yes, I think so. Except possibly the deaf. But deaf bicameral people may have had visual hallucinations of gods directing them by gesture, even as modern deaf schizophrenics often do.[6]

But perhaps you meant to ask if it wasn't just the leaders that heard the gods. The literary data that we have historically is indeed mostly about leaders or important people. But there are other kinds of evidence that show that everyone heard gods. Idols used to facilitate hallucinations were everywhere and of all sizes, not just in palaces and temples. Ordinary people had idols, and idols were buried with them. In some excavations of cities, every family dwelling had a shrine. Thousands of cylinder seals from many sites in Mesopotamia show a person being led by his personal god

---

6. J.D. Rainer, S. Abdullah, and J.C. Altshuler, "Phenomenology of Hallucinations in the Deaf," in W. Keup (ed.), *Origin and Mechanisms of Hallucinations* (New York: Plenum, 1970).

into the presence of a higher god. Then we have the names of ordinary people that have the name of their god imbedded into their name. *Kainesut,* which translates as "The King is my *ka,*" is an Egyptian common name that in bicameral theory means "I hear the King telling me what to do." I think everybody fitted into these hierarchical, tightly knit organizations because everybody did indeed hear voices that controlled them.

Q: Did the role of conscience change between the bicameral period and consciousness?

JAYNES: In one sense, the bicameral mind was conscience, hearing what to do from gods, but the idea of conscience today is like a faint and wayward echo of it. I have been surprised recently to find that conscience in this sense is a relatively modern notion, having been begun, I think, by Thomas Aquinas in the thirteenth century as practical moral reasoning, and then heavily emphasized by Calvin in the sixteenth century as an innate subjective mode of moral revelation. In the seventeenth century, the King James translators of the New Testament, no doubt influenced by Calvin, translate *suneidesis* as "conscience" when it should probably be "consciousness." But it is not until the beginning of Romanticism with Rousseau that "conscience" becomes "divine instinct" and "the voice of the soul." It is interesting that this occurs just as poetry is beginning to turn back to some bicameral-like admirations.[7]

I remember as a young boy asking my mother how I could tell the difference between right and wrong. She told me softly to listen to my conscience. I tried but nothing ever happened. I concluded that either I was too wicked to have a conscience or too good to need one. I have been wavering between these two positions ever since.

Q: Was there any difference in moral developments in the bicameral mind?

JAYNES: I think you are saying it too weakly. There is no such thing as morality in the bicameral world. Ethics and morality are things that we have to learn in our societies to replace the dictates of the gods. The first replacement for the gods in holding a society together, however, was sheer legality without real morality. A work by the early sophist Antiphon even says that laws and customs are to be obeyed only when disobedience is

---

7. See Judith Weissman, "Vision, Madness, and Morality: Poetry and the Theory of the Bicameral Mind," *Georgia Review,* 1979, *33,* 118–148; "Somewhere in Earshot: Yeats' Admonitory Gods," *Pequod,* 1982, *14,* 16–31.

liable to be detected. It would be contrary to nature *(physis* as distinguished from *nomos* or convention) not to injure someone if you would benefit thereby and would not be caught.[8] The idea of a morality apart from legality only begins to appear in Greece in the fifth century B.C., as in Sophocles' *Antigone,* and then of course in the Socratic *Dialogues* with sudden and tremendous sophistication. But because there is no universal natural basis for morality in large conscious civilizations, because we cannot derive any *ought* from a scientific study of what is, we commonly return to our bicameral heritage for our authorization, basing our ethics on the writings of the last people to hear bicameral voices, such as the Bible in Judeo-Christian societies or the Koran in Islam.

Q: Do you consider any possibilities of nutritional effects resulting in changes of consciousness that came about around the agricultural period?

JAYNES: Is there a nutritional determination of some of these changes in mentality? I know that there are several theories about specific geographic areas, but I suspect they are promoted by a tendency we all have to wish simple materialistic determinations rather than complex cultural ones. Materialistic determinations only seem simpler, but they really are not. And the evidence for them is usually weak and local. They could not explain the geographically extensive changes I have been referring to.

However, you did phrase your question as if to entertain the possibility that in the change from a hunting and gathering economy to agriculture back around 9000 B.C., there may have been nutritional changes — more carbohydrates perhaps — or ergot on cereals — that could produce more hallucinatory activity. I am skeptical, but it should be investigated. If schizophrenic patients have more carbohydrates in their diet, do they tend to hallucinate more? And conversely, would such patients be helped by being on an all-meat diet? I don't know.

Q: How about the pyramids of Egypt? Surely the pharaohs who built them as their tombs were thinking ahead to their afterlife, and that would be consciousness.

JAYNES: This is what is called the presentist fallacy. You are phrasing the situation as if ancient Egyptians were like ourselves. They were not. The pharaohs of 2500 B.C. did not build the pyramids for themselves. You must remember that the volition of a bicameral person was his auditory

---

8. See G.C. Field, *Plato and His Contemporaries* (New York: Dutton, 1930).

hallucination or god, and so the volition of each pharaoh was Osiris, the chief god, who was his *ka* or bicameral voice. Osiris commands the building of the pyramids to his glory in the same way that a millennium later Yahweh with great architectural detail commands Moses to build an ark and a tabernacle to his glory (Exodus 25–27), or as the Greek earth goddess Demeter commands that a temple be built at Eleusis to her glory,[9] or in many other examples. In Egypt, however, when the pharaoh dies — as we would call the process — he is absorbed into his *ka* and then both are absorbed into Osiris as is depicted many times on funeral walls — even perhaps as Jesus after his resurrection is absorbed into the unified Trinity.[10]

Q: What about pain? Pain is certainly conscious and ancient people and animals surely feel pain.

JAYNES: Most pain theorists today agree that there are two fundamental types of pain in ourselves, variously called acute and chronic, nociceptive and operant, or sensory and functional. In our work this same distinction is between sensory pain with its associated pain behaviors and conscious pain, and they follow each other in history.[11] Animals and bicameral people just have the former; we always have a combination of both. We have sensory pain and also are conscious of it, fear it, recruit it, extend it out, amplify it with our conscious concern, interact with it, re-enact it. Using this distinction, one can enter into a greater understanding of many human pain phenomena such as the effectiveness of placebos, some phantom limb pain, and chronic pain for which no neural basis can be found. Pain in ourselves is always a complex interaction between the physical stimulus that causes pain behavior and the conscious reactive component to it which we might call the conscious suffering.

Q: Are there any matriarchal societies in early civilization?

JAYNES: There is no clear evidence of matriarchies in early civilizations of the Near East at least. In our research the more common thing is a world ruled mostly by female gods and masculine hearers of those gods. I suspect this is because children were brought up almost exclusively by women.

9. Homeric Hymn to Demeter, lines 271 ff.

10. Julian Jaynes, "The Meaning of King Tut," *Princeton Alumni Weekly*, 1979, June, 16–17. Reprinted in Marcel Kuijsten (ed.) *Reflections on the Dawn of Consciousness* (Henderson, NV: Julian Jaynes Society, 2006).

11. Julian Jaynes, "Sensory Pain and Conscious Pain," *Behavioral and Brain Sciences*, 1985, *8*, 61–63. Reprinted as Chapter 18 of this volume.

That is what the *Iliad* is. Evidence for this bicameral gender arrangement goes back to the Hacilar and Catalhüyük cultures in Anatolia of about 6000 B.C., with their pudgy and strange idols of what are often called mother goddesses. But there is no evidence that these were matriarchies on the human level. There were, of course, several ruling Queens of Egypt, such as Hatshepsut, but I don't think that makes a matriarchy any more than it does today in the British Commonwealth because a woman is head of state.

Q: Before a child can use language, does this mean that the child is not conscious?

JAYNES: Yes. The idea of consciousness that I have just presented should be tested out in child development. My students and I are trying to do that at Princeton. One needs language for consciousness. We think consciousness is learned by children between two-and-a-half and five or six years in what we can call the verbal surround, or the verbal community as B. F. Skinner calls it. It is an aspect of learning to speak. Mental words are out there as part of the culture and part of the family. A child fits himself into these words and uses them even before he knows the meaning of them. A mother is constantly instilling the seeds of consciousness in a two- and three-year-old, telling the child to stop and think, asking him "What shall we do today?" or "Do you remember when we did such and such or were somewhere?" And all this while metaphor and analogy are hard at work. There are many different ways that different children come to this, but indeed I would say that children without some kind of language are not conscious.

Q: If you ask a person what he was thinking about yesterday, would this be something that did not ever happen in the bicameral world?

JAYNES: It would not happen in the bicameral world. Supposing I asked you what you were thinking of five minutes ago. I think you would find it difficult to reply. You have to tag these things in the time domain to remember them. There was not any such thing in the bicameral world, no spatialized time in which we locate lives and actions. This idea of reminiscent memory, what Tulving[12] calls episodic memory, is built on consciousness. You don't find a bicameral Achilles saying things like "When I was a

---

12. Endel Tulving, *Elements of Episodic Memory* (Oxford: Clarendon Press, 1983).

child" or "Back in Greece what did I do at this time?" or anything of that sort. The bicameral world goes on in a relatively continual present.

I should add that of course bicameral people knew, *non-consciously knew*, where they were, had come from, and were going, and what they were doing over a short time frame. So does a dog or a pigeon over a short time. Otherwise no behavior could be completed. This particular time frame is what William James and others have called the specious present.[13] That is a much more primitive type of immediate and non-conscious retention which all vertebrates and many invertebrates have as well, and appears to be very carefully evolved to vary for particular behaviors.

Now add to that for bicameral man the use of language as a retention device. Having verbal formulae or rote epithets, such as "the war-loving Danaans" or "the horse-taming Trojans" or "much enduring god-like Odysseus" (all examples from the *Iliad*) for peoples, persons, places, or gods, gave him a much greater capacity for these immediate knowledges by cueing off these verbal associations.

The bicameral epics themselves, composed by formulae and by rote from generation to generation, can be viewed as retention devices and a huge step toward episodic or reminiscent memory. But it is only with consciousness, of course, with its spatialized time in which events can be located, that we achieve remembering in its full sense.

Q: In the model here, does one side of the brain have the attributes of consciousness, since it is making the decisions in terms of the voices of the gods sending it over to the left side?

JAYNES: Narratization, but not with an analog 'I,' seems to have taken place in the right hemisphere, since I have assumed the early epic narratives are right hemispheric.[14] Therefore some of the attributes of consciousness begin, if this model is correct, in the right hemisphere. That is a very perceptive question and one which needs to be explored, particularly in relation to the previous question.

Q: Do you think there might not be some sculptors, painters, and particularly composers who would dispute the idea that language is required for consciousness?

13. William James, *Principles of Psychology* (New York: Holt, 1890), pp. 609ff.
14. Julian Jaynes, *The Origin of Consciousness in the Breakdown of the Bicameral Mind* (Hougton Mifflin, 1976/2000).

JAYNES: The assumption of your question, I think, is that consciousness is necessary for art and music. I don't think it is. There was a great deal of art and music in the non-conscious bicameral world, all originated by those neural organizations and resulting cognitions called gods. Texts specifically refer to gods dictating how idols are to be carved or buildings built. Look at the meticulous detail that Yahweh goes into in building the ark or the tabernacle in Exodus that I just mentioned. If you talk to composers and painters today, and I have on these matters, many of them don't have the feeling that consciousness is doing the composing or painting any more than consciousness is giving me the words I am presently speaking. As I mentioned in my talk, I am narratizing an intention in consciousness, what I have called a struction, and then the words just come. So in artistic expression of any kind. I have just received a letter from a contemporary composer who asked me if he is schizophrenic because he simply hears his music and transcribes it.

Q: That isn't quite what I meant. I meant that consciousness doesn't seem to be all language.

JAYNES: I understand you now. Yes, the content of consciousness is far from being all language. You or I can right now imagine a triangle in mind-space, color it red, and even slowly turn it around in our consciousness. There is nothing linguistic in that. But it takes language to get us there, to set it up in our imagination. I did not mean that everything in consciousness is made up of language. Language creates a mind-space on the basis of metaphor and analogy in which you are 'seeing' the triangle, as well as the analog 'I' which is doing the 'seeing.' The particular things you are conscious of, music, sculpture, triangles, are often not linguistic at all.

Q: Why in some cases does the right hemisphere say good things and sometimes bad things?

JAYNES: In schizophrenia, which I suggest is a partial relapse to the bicameral mind but mixed with a great deal of stress, some patients hear good voices, but the majority today hear condemnatory harsh voices. One hospitalized 40-year-old patient whom I interviewed and who will probably remain hospitalized the rest of his life, hears all day the Queen of Heaven in a rose garden, constantly telling him what a good boy he is; he is extremely gentle and constantly smiling. While another, a former parochial high school principal, heard a deep voice associated as God telling

him how unworthy and sinful he is and to fall down and break his teeth
and sometimes not break his teeth (he came to the hospital with broken
teeth). We suspect of course the difference perhaps is due to a doting
mother in the first case and a punishing, inconsistent father in the second.
But we do not know, and the problem should be possible to research.

Q: How do you define thought and feeling?

JAYNES: Both of these terms are polyreferential, as are most words for
mental acts. I would like to use "thought" just for consciousness, for what
we are doing in consciousness at any time. But usually this involves a
non-conscious substrate that is solving structions on an almost continuous basis. Most people would call that thinking. I use thought loosely and
not as a technical term.

   "Feeling," however, I do try to use technically — by which I mean with
a precise referent. And perhaps I shouldn't because it has several other
referents, the prominent of which have to do with touching and believing, which I feel are entirely separate. In a theory of emotions that I have
proposed elsewhere,[15] I suggest that we, like other mammals, start with a
complex of evolved basic affects that, with the advent of consciousness,
become the basis of our feelings. That is, a feeling is the consciousness
of an affect, thus stretching it out in time and making it difficult to get
rid of. So around 700 B.C. in Greece, shame becomes guilt; fear, anxiety;
anger, hatred; and so on. And, as I mentioned before, pain becomes suffering. The evidence for these changes is in the dramatic transformations
of behavior and customs in the first millennium B.C. This is what I have
called the two-tiered theory of emotions.

Q: You said — this was in connection with imaginary playmates — that
the bicameral mind was innate. Why then aren't we all bicameral?

JAYNES: Innate does not mean inevitable. It means an inborn potentiality
that can be made actual in a particular environment. It is the distinction
between genotype and phenotype. The social, verbal, and behavioral environment of a child today, and the peer pressure to be and think like other
children, does not encourage or reward a child in a bicameral direction.
Back before 1000 B.C., that social, verbal, behavioral environment plus

---

15. Julian Jaynes, "A Two-Tiered Theory of Emotions," *Behavioral and Brain Sciences*, 1982, 5, 434–435.
Reprinted as Chapter 16 of this volume.

peer pressure would encourage the child's imaginary playmate towards the status of a personal god and a full-fledged bicameral mind.

To say this another way: A child from bicameral times brought up in our culture would be normally conscious, while a modern child if brought up in the Ur of 3000 B.C. under the sovereignty of Marduk in his *giginu* in the great ziggurat would be bicameral.

Q: I still can't believe all this, saying that ancient people are not conscious like we are. How can you prove it?

JAYNES: There are really two questions there. First is the difficulty of believing ancient people were not conscious. I certainly understand the problem, which is why in my book I call it "preposterous,"[16] for so it seems at first. The reason it seems preposterous is because of all the everyday functioning we have packed into our concept of consciousness, thinking of it as all perception, all mentality. That is why I spent so long at the beginning in trying to straighten out the term to its true and original meaning.

To say this another way, we tend to infer that anything that acts like us is conscious because the inference of consciousness in others is so habitual, going on not only in all our social life but in consciousness itself as we narratize about our relationships. It is very difficult to suspend that habit of projecting consciousness in thinking about ancient civilizations or even in animals close to us or even in newborn infants.

The second question was how can it be proved. To stretch a comparison, I can imagine someone back in 1859 complaining to Darwin that it is preposterous to say that species were created by chance and natural selection without any purpose whatever. Look at all the evidence for the purposiveness of God's creation — everywhere! It can't be chance and selection. How can you prove it?

The answer in both cases, evolutionary theory and bicameral theory, is to try to state the hypothesis as clearly and factually as you can, and then evaluate how the data, all the data you can find, may fit in. For evolutionary theory, we look at the fossil record and current situations of speciation where we can observe them; for bicameral theory, we look at ancient texts and artifacts and current mental phenomena as they may be illuminated

---

16. Julian Jaynes, *The Origin of Consciousness in the Breakdown of the Bicameral Mind* (Boston: Houghton Mifflin, 1976/2000), p. 84.

by the theory. In both cases the theory must explain the data more completely and parsimoniously than any alternative.

Q: Do you think you have done that?

JAYNES: I know of no alternative of equal explanatory power that maps on to all the evidence. But it is only a beginning. I know there will have to be adjustments and revisions. There is so much left to do. So much more sheer theoretical analysis of consciousness itself, particularly of narratization that covers so much so thinly, so much more accurate translations of ancient texts, so much in studying the development of consciousness in children, a taboo subject for so long, or the variety of mentalities in hunter-gatherer groups, all of whom have partly learned consciousness by now in their contacts with civilizations. But I think it is an opening in the right direction into which psychology should go.

Q: How did you come to this theory?

JAYNES: How do I narratize my arrival at these views? As one who had gone down many blind alleys in search of the origin of consciousness in lower species with simpler nervous systems, until I realized more and more that I — and most others who had preceded me on such a quest — were confused in a way we did not understand. So I decided to change directions and attempt to trace back in human history the mind-body problem as a way of alleviating that confusion. I traced it back until it disappeared in some of the works ascribed to Aristotle, then in some of the pre-Socratics, and then vanished in the *Iliad*. What did that mean? I then felt for a long time like someone in a dark room, stumbling about, bumping into strange unrecognized objects while feeling for a light switch or chain, not even knowing if there was a light. And then it happened and the light went on. Consciousness is learned on the basis of language, and right at that time — at least in the strong form of the theory. And so many things were suddenly clear. It was not biologically evolved. Other ideas about the metaphoric nature of consciousness, which I had been harboring for a long time, joined up with that and the theory began.

Q: What are dreams in this theory?

JAYNES: Dreams are consciousness operating primarily on neural reactivations primarily during REM (rapid eye movement) sleep. (And let us remember that the presence of REM does not necessarily indicate dreaming.) The same features of consciousness that function in waking life function in dreams as well: narratization, the analog 'I', mind-space, excerption, and particularly that feature of consciousness not so noticeable when awake because it's so automatic, consilience (what I call in my book conciliation — consilience is Whewell's,[17] better term for my intended meaning of mental processes that make things compatible with each other). Consilience is the conscious analog of perceptual assimilations where ambiguity is made to conform to some previously learned schema. Consilience is in mind-space what narratization is in mind-time, making things compatible with each other.

The neural reactivations which are narratized and consiliated into dreams are instigated by excitation from the pontine region of the brain stem — as is now well known.[18] They are usually related to recent events or recent conscious thoughts or feelings, some by chance neural causation, others by association, some utterly inconsequential as a shiny color or an abstract spatial relationship, perhaps others through our conscious concerns of what has happened or might happen, sometimes in a jumble, sometimes not depending on one's physiological state. These occur together with internal (posture, blood flow, visceral, etc.) and external stimuli (temperature, light, sounds, etc.) impinging on the sleeper — what in the older dream literature was called incorporation. Consciousness tries to narratize and consiliate it all together into a story.

An example: Suppose among these reactivations you have independently an apple, a seashore, a straw hat: you will consiliate and narratize them together (even as you probably did as you were conscious of them as I said them) so that you dream you are walking along a beach in a straw hat eating an apple. Now add in the external stimulus of cold because your blankets have fallen off, and you may then notice in your dream that you are naked. Rationalization (in its old-fashioned sense of simply making things reasonable) is a kind of narratization and occurs in dreams as well. So you rationalize your sudden nakedness by realizing in your dream that you are going swimming. Or if you have some sudden stomach indigestion, as you swim in your dream, the ocean may suddenly roughen

---

17. William Whewell, *Theory of Scientific Method* (R.E. Butts, ed., Pittsburgh: University of Pittsburgh Press, 1858/1968).

18. J. Allan Hobson and Robert W. McCarley, "The Brain As A Dream State Generator: An Activation-Synthesis Hypothesis of the Dream Process," *American Journal of Psychiatry*, 1977, *134*, 1335–1348.

with turbulence. But then add in a spontaneous reactivation of something really disparate such as a calculus of metaphor you were trying to invent on a blackboard last night, and if this can't be consiliated or narratized into what has gone before, the scene of the dream abruptly changes perhaps to a classroom and you are having a new dream. So dreams are fashioned by consciousness and change when consilience becomes impossible. Sometimes we may have very bizarre consiliations, as with a feeling and a quite inappropriate scene or activity making a dream that makes no sense and often can't be reported.

Q: Then you don't believe in dream interpretation?

JAYNES: Occasionally some ongoing concern or anxiety can be teased out from the tangle of dream ingredients, sometimes with striking imagery, but it is usually something you have been conscious of the day before. Such imagery thus symbolizes a problem and can help keep one's concentration upon it. Apart from that, dreams have no necessary interpretation, but they can be and are being used projectively as Rorschach cards in therapy. And it can be an interesting game for anyone to try to sort out the particular elements which were consiliated and narratized into their various origins in recent conscious experience.

Q: What about animal dreams?

JAYNES: They are not dreams in our sense. What you see in the fluttering paws and mouth of a sleeping dog are pure reactivations instigated as before by the giant pontine cells but without consciousness, without any consilience or narratization with an analog 'I' — or perhaps I should say analog Fido. Even the well-known experiment of lesioning parts of a cat's pontine brain stem, so that the usual REM sleep muscle inhibition does not occur,[19] does not result in these animals' "acting out their dreams" as is commonly said, but in acting out their stereotyped reactivations — if that is how to express it.

Q: Can introspection occur in dreams?

JAYNES: Sometimes, yes. Such occasions are what are called "lucid dreams."

---

19. J.C. Hendricks, R.M. Bowker, and A.P. Morrison, "Functional Characteristics of Cats with Pontine Lesions During Sleep and Wakefulness and Their Usefulness for Sleep Research," in W.P. Koella and P. Levin (eds.), *Sleep* (Basel: S. Karger, 1977).

Q: But if dreams are consciousness and consciousness only began about 1000 B.C., then no one should have dreamt before that time.

JAYNES: No one did dream before that time in the way you and I do. Let's look at the data. In the *Iliad* are four dreams, although they are not called that: there is no word for them in the *Iliad*. The most important one is at the beginning of Book II, important because it renews the Trojan War. Agamemnon is asleep in his tent. Presumably, he is in REM sleep. In comes Oneiros, a god messenger from Zeus, whose name comes to mean "dream" in later Greek. Oneiros appears as the much admired Nestor, "stands at his head," tells Agamemnon he is asleep in his bed, and then proceeds to deliver his message, and departs, after which Agamemnon awakes, arises, and tells the others. Agamemnon never thinks he's anywhere else except on his bed or doing anything except sleeping. He can't because he is not conscious, which is what he would have to be to dream himself somewhere else (translocative) and doing something else (vicarial) as we do in our dreams. It is what we call a bicameral dream, similar to what goes on in the waking mentality of ancient times. Such dreams are very rare today but they occasionally occur with profound effects. Descartes had one and it changed his life.

All four dreams in the *Iliad* are of this type. If we go over to the Hebrew world, the famous Jacob's Ladder Dream is a bicameral dream (Genesis 28:10–22). Jacob's dream takes place exactly where he is sleeping and he does nothing except hear Yahweh at the top of probably a ziggurat rather than a ladder, with angels streaming up and down its steps, as Yahweh renews the covenant with him. So sure is he that the dream happened where he was sleeping that he anoints the place as Beth-El, place or house of God. Three other dreams are mentioned prior to this in the early chapters of Genesis and they are all bicameral. The Joseph stories that follow, according to modern scholars,[20] come from around 700 years later and they are not bicameral.

In the cuneiform literature, we have dreams going back to 2500 B.C. and in hieroglyphics back to the dream of Djoser in 2650 B.C. All are bicameral with one possible exception where the translation is in question.

Going the other direction in time, dreams after the *Iliad* rapidly become first vicarial, the person's analog 'I' in his dream doing something other than sleeping, and then translocative, that is, they take place somewhere other than where the person is sleeping. All of us today have

---

20. Donald B. Redford, *A Study of the Biblical Story of Joseph (Genesis 37)* (Leiden: Brill, 1970).

vicarial translocative dreams, which are consciousness operating primarily during REM sleep.

I regard this development, this definite historical change in the nature of dreams, as one of the great confirmations of the strong form of the central hypothesis of the origin of consciousness in the breakdown of the bicameral mind.

Q: Does this theory relate to therapy in any way?

JAYNES: I think there are some obvious inferences to be made. As for schizophrenia, the theory of the bicameral mind in simplified form is at present being taught to hallucinating patients in several clinics both here and abroad. It relieves a great deal of the associated distress of "being crazy" by getting the patient to realize that many of his or her symptoms are a relapse to an older mentality that was perfectly normal at one time but no longer works.

In the treatment of neuroses, the theory provides a strong theoretical framework for such consciousness-changing procedures as the cognitive therapies of Beck[21] or Meichenbaum,[22] reframing or restructuring, the use of guided imagery, paradoxical therapy, and various visualizing practices. Most of what are diagnosed as neurotic behaviors are, of course, disorders of consciousness, or more specifically of narratization and excerption. Therefore, narratization and excerption must be retrained for the patient to obtain relief. Such renarratization is actually what is going on in most therapy, even in analysis of either the Freudian or Jungian variety. And it doesn't matter whether or not the renarratization is existentially veridical so long as it is believed and redirects behavior into more adaptive modes.

---

21. Aaron Beck, *Cognitive Therapy and Emotional Disorders* (New York: International University Press, 1976).

22. Donald Meichenbaum, *Cognitive-Behavior Modification* (New York: Plenum, 1977).

# CHAPTER 34

# McMaster-Bauer Symposium on Consciousness: Response to Discussants

## Julian Jaynes

FIRST OF ALL I WOULD LIKE to say how honored I am to be the Bauer Memorial Lecturer this year. This has been somewhat historic for me, and particularly made so by the caliber of the discussants. George Ojemann, from Seattle; Jonathan Miller, from Britain; and Dan Dennett, from Boston. It is a flattery that has to be appreciated in terms of the many differences that I am sure we do have. I would like to thank them very much for coming.

In my talk, I presented four central ideas, and I was describing them to you in their order of importance. They turn out to be the order in which I came to them. The most important part of the entire theory is the first, the idea of consciousness, what it is, what it is not, and how it developed on the basis of metaphor and language. Now, had I been a discussant of this work, I would have pointed to a certain incompleteness here and stress, as I did in the question period, how much more analysis of the features, modes, and functions of consciousness needs to be done. The discussants were kind to me in not zeroing in on that.

One theme that seemed to be present in all three discussions was the issue of the brain. The model of the brain in respect to the right and left hemispheres is, of course, not the bicameral mind; that is a common misperception. It is simply a model that can be dispensed with; every mention of the brain could be taken out of the book and everything else could still stand. It is, however, something I couldn't help speculating about.

Julian Jaynes's response to comments by Daniel Dennett, Jonathan Miller, and George Ojemann on his "Consciousness and the Voices of the Mind" lecture (see Chapter 19 of this volume), presented at the McMaster-Bauer Symposium on Consciousness at McMaster University in 1983. First published in *Canadian Psychology*, Vol. 27, Issue 2. © 1986 Canadian Psychological Association. Permission granted for use of material.

Let me say a few things about George Ojemann's very interesting presentation of fascinating data. He began by saying that I had said that we shouldn't look for the neurological model of consciousness — I never in the world said that. He must have misunderstood me when I may have said to him last night that there is no neurological model of consciousness in my book. I simply do not know what it might be, and I think one would be premature. So I thought it was both very courageous of him and enthralling that he tried to present one.

Now there were things along the way that I felt troubled about. He talked about consciousness in a way contrary to some of the things I said. As I was stressing during the lecture and question period, I think we should define consciousness very carefully. I think he was referring to the ideas of Sir John Eccles and Sir Karl Popper when he talked about collective consciousness being out there in the public domain. To me this is a metaphor of a metaphier applied to something like this, but I think to call it consciousness is to confuse the issue. His later distinction, however, between consciousness and conscious experience is more interesting, although I think he is confusing consciousness and awareness or reactivity in his first level. His "conscious experience" with its episodic memory is precisely what I call consciousness. Perhaps if I changed the title of my book to "the origin of conscious experience in the breakdown of the bicameral mind," he could find it more to his interest. I prefer to remain with consciousness as Locke and Descartes and most other people — including behaviorists — would define it, as what is introspectable.

George also mentioned consciousness in animals. I felt I was showing that indeed this isn't possible since it is based on language. Then he went on to present the thalamocortical activating system as a neurological model for consciousness, and pointed to its ancient evolution, thereby inferring that there is a very ancient source of consciousness, and that it is present in animals generally. While the neurological model is not completely contradictory to anything I said, his inferences most definitely are.

Now, behind his inferences is the assumption that the functions that are at certain anatomical sites of the brain today have always been there. Yet I think we do know that this is not necessarily so. For example, consider the speech areas of the brain: language is established in them. Therefore I do not see why other parts of the brain cannot have other functions established in them, so that what we find there today may not be at all the record of what happened previously, even though that particular structure or tract may have had a very ancient kind of evolution. That is why this extremely interesting thalamocortical activating system model is not inconsistent with what I have said. Indeed, I would certainly agree that it has to be involved with the neural substrate for consciousness today in some way. I did not mean, incidentally, to give the impression that consciousness only involves the language areas of the brain — we know that is not true. But I did suggest that is where the development of consciousness got started long ago.

Dan Dennett was of course mentioning that he felt the brain was what I didn't want to give up. I don't feel I am going to, but that is not the really essential thing. I liked it that he singled out things in my book that other people haven't, like the idea of concepts as classes of behavioral equivalence which are not usually conscious. He is the first person to ever mention it, and when one has taken a long, long time plowing through the minefield of one's confusions to finally reach a clarity that results in only a simple couple of sentences, it is gratifying when a prominent modern philosopher like Dan notices it. I was also appreciative of his brilliant discussion of the use-mention criticism of the theory.

He went on to speak of optional features in the theory, such as the optionality of hallucinations. Yes, I would find it difficult to dispense with hallucinations. They practically define the bicameral mind. Hallucinations seem to be simply a close reading of the data, the historical data, in the sense of trying to understand religion and the history of religion. If it isn't auditory hallucinations in all these ancient texts, then there has to be some other explanation for it. What is it that is happening in Amos? Is it just concocted by somebody for the sake of controlling the people at that time so that they fit into the Judaic system? Jonathan Miller was perhaps suggesting such a Marxist explanation. I disagree on two grounds: the text internally has a strong authenticity of reporting as to who Amos is, contrary to any Marxist interpretation, and secondly there exist many other instances of such messages from gods all over the world in every early civilization and even today.

The metaphor of hardware/software is a good approximation that in the change from bicamerality to consciousness the hardware remained the same, but the software changed. But it is only an approximation. When we change the software of a computer, we are not changing anything in the chip, but changing what goes into it. But in the brain, any experience changes the ultrastructure to some even minute extent. This is particularly true in development where we know that the brain undergoes permanent changes as a result of experience. For example, the infant starts off with an ability to recognize a huge variety of phonemes. Then after the child is embedded in its language and culture, say by about age 4 or 5 years, it loses even the possibility of recognizing about a third of possible phonemes. Now, I do not mean that the neonatal preprogrammed structure of the brain changed in going from the bicameral mind to consciousness. But the later structure of the infant brain does change due to experience. In my book, I entertained the possibility, and only the possibility, that there could have been some kind of genetic change, since perhaps half the people of the world were killed off in this particular period and it seems likely that these might have been the most bicameral. But natural selection is not what I wish to emphasize, but rather learning. If you had a child in the bicameral world and brought it up in our culture, I think he would be like you or me. I think if you took any child today, and could give me an island and 200 actors and let me construct a culture with an expectation of hearing voices the way I have described it, that I could bring up a modern child to be bicameral. Thus, I am emphasizing the importance I give to child development and early education in children in this whole matter of consciousness and perhaps in the matter of how some different parts of the brain can work.

In Jonathan Miller's fluent discussion, I think I detected a tendency to let certain word-usages, personifications, and error-by-associations do the labor of intellectual argument. For example, to call verbal hallucinations imaginary is to me a serious confounding of two very distinct phenomena. Auditory hallucinations are not the same as imagining someone speaking to you. They come at a person; they are usually definite and discrete. And it is simply not true in my experience or in the literature that schizophrenics in general label their auditory hallucinations as such, although some perhaps call them hallucinations. This is not the common thing. If you go into mental hospitals and talk to hallucinating patients, you will not find that many of them do so unless their disease is lessening. But there are other qualities that are indeed like the bicameral mind in terms of their religious quality, the power that they do seem to have, and it is different from just having an imaginary voice. It is a phenomenon that has to be paid attention to, brought into psychology and studied further. We went through a whole period of Freudian psychiatry, mostly where this was not paid attention to at all, and you cannot find very many really good studies about hallucinations in schizophrenia.

One deduction that follows from what I have put forward as the neural substrate for the bicameral mind is that present-day verbal hallucinations may originate in the right temporal lobe in many cases. This can be empirically tested. While no definitive results have yet been obtained, several lines of research implicate brain functional laterality effects in schizophrenics. For example, in some positron emission tomography studies patients showed higher glucose uptake (and therefore increased functioning) in the right temporal lobe while hallucinating.[1] I must add, however, that later studies have indicated that the neurological basis of hallucinations may be more complicated than such a simple picture. But several other studies agree with the conclusion that in schizophrenia we have what can be considered as either a right-hemisphere overactivation of function or a left-hemisphere deficit.[2]

Another place where Jonathan seemed to be begging the question was where he said the *Iliad* is, after all, a work of art; as if that meant it was consciously composed. Here as elsewhere Jonathan has missed the point by a rather wide margin. Art today in any medium is partially and sometimes almost entirely of non-conscious origin — even as in my lecture I tried to emphasize about ordinary speaking. Of course we use consciousness today in art to criticize and judge and reshape the products of non-conscious creation. But for bicameral times, a case can be made that art originated completely in the god-side of the bicameral mind. Many texts — cuneiform, hieroglyphic, Greek, Hebrew, Sanskrit — bear this statement out. How to build pyramids, temples, tabernacles, and how to carve idols were literally dictated by gods down to the last detail. And poetry also. The first line of the *Iliad* demonstrates the origin of the poem: "Sing goddess of the anger of Achilles" — although as I mentioned earlier, conscious elements were added later in the first millennium B.C. It is extremely important to understand that this is oral poetry recomposed on the basis of story formulae and descriptive formulae and repetitions by the

1. M.S. Buchsbaum, D.H. Ingvar, R. Kessler, R.N. Waters, et al., "Cerebral Glucography with Positron Tomography: Use In Normal Subjects and In Patients with Schizophrenia," *Archives of General Psychiatry*, 1982, *39*, 3, 251–9.

2. Pierre Flor-Henry, "Lateralized Temporal-Limbic Dysfunction and Psychopathology," *Annals of the New York Academy of Sciences*, 1976, *28*, 777–795; Raquel E. Gur, et al., "Brain Function in Psychiatric Disorders," *Archives of General Psychiatry*, 1983, *40*, 1250–1254. For a review of more recent studies confirming Jaynes's neurological model, see Marcel Kuijsten, "Consciousness, Hallucinations, and the Bicameral Mind: Three Decades of New Research," in M. Kuijsten (ed.), *Reflections on the Dawn of Consciousness* (Henderson, NV: Julian Jaynes Society, 2006).

*aoidos* and altered and reshaped by audience reinforcement over almost half a millennium in many locations.

Of course, we do not have to use the *Iliad* at all to illustrate these issues. If we go back earlier to the so-called Linear B, the earliest kind of Greek that we can translate and that predates the Trojan War by several centuries, it is clear that there was a strict hierarchical structure just as in Mesopotamia. At the top is the *wanax*, which in later Greek means a god; the land of his state is the *temenos*, which later means land sacred to the gods; and the chief steward of the wanax is the *basileus*, which later means king. The texts do not, however, give you evidence for hallucinations directly, but rather for a firm hierarchical structure so similar to bicameral theocracies in Mesopotamia at the same time.

Also, Jonathan disagreed with me about "imaginary playmates" or hallucinated playmates as they should be called. Following Freud, he feels they are adversary fictions, which to me is an adversary fiction itself. I do not think that such a phrase is true to the phenomenon at all, and could only be used by those who had never studied such children. Dorothy Singer has extensively studied the phenomenon of imaginary playmates. On the basis of her findings, she is convinced that indeed such children are hearing voices and carrying on conversations with them.[3] Other investigators also agree that the phenomenon involves true verbal hallucinations.[4]

My own research into hallucinated playmates has unfortunately been restricted to adult memories of childhood by questionnaire and to parents' observations. I would like to interview the playmate directly via the child, which is probably rather difficult to do if one is a stranger, and unfortunately I have not been able to do this. I think I can summarize the kind of things I have found by describing a seminar on imaginary playmates that I gave at a southern women's college. We went around the room to determine who had had such playmates, and it turned out that over half the young women had had imaginary or hallucinated playmates — an incidence slightly higher than normal, perhaps because the college had a religious basis and the seminar participants may have been somewhat self-selected. Such playmates were of enormous variety: old and young, dour and joyous, elaborate and simple: "Pookie" who had to be met off a certain daily train by her human friend and then brought across a field to the child's house to play and have lunch, her place set at the table, and

---

3. Jerome L. Singer and Dorothy G. Singer, *Television, Imagination and Aggression* (Hillsdale, N.J.: Erlbaum, 1984).

4. Nathan A. Harvey, *Imaginary Playmates and Other Mental Phenomenon of Children* (Ipsilanti: Michigan State Normal College, 1918).

later returned across the field to a returning train, to be helped aboard by a kindly conductor as the child waved goodbye to nothing that anyone else could see; or at the other extreme, a man in a black cloak who sometimes brought his brother — about which I felt I shouldn't inquire further. Then I asked each of them if they had heard the imaginary playmate "like an outside voice," and half of those who had had such playmates said yes, the others said they could not remember or that "I was just told I had an imaginary playmate, but I really can't remember." Most of those who remembered hearing the playmate could then imitate it. After the seminar, one woman who looked worried came up to me and wished to talk alone. She explained that she hadn't raised her hand because this was much too serious for her. When she was a child, her mother and father were very poor and they both had to go to work, and she was left at home in the care of a schizophrenic grandmother. The grandmother was hallucinating voices in different rooms of the house, and she learned to hallucinate playmates, a different playmate for each room, and carried on conversations with them just like her grandmother had with her voices. I think that is interesting because it is the verbal-behavioral surround that you give to a child, full of its expectancies, that possibly related to the ontogeny of the bicameral mind in antiquity.

She then went on and said that when her mother realized what was going on, she quit her job, sent the grandmother to a mental hospital, and came home to train the child out of these "playmates" — which was successful up to a point. But she added that now that she is grown up, she has this problem. When she gets into periods of stress (and she seemed to be undergoing stress at that very time) all her imaginary playmates come back, and they are all grown up like her, and they all stand around and try to tell her what to do. Then she followed this with a question that I, a rather unthinking bachelor, didn't understand. She asked me if this was innate or learned? The question took me by surprise, and I'm not sure how I answered. It was only later that a friend suggested to me that this young woman was probably considering marriage and did not want to have children if this was innate and if they would have to go through the same thing she had experienced. I hope I answered correctly by explaining to her that it was as most behavior is, both innate and learned, and that innate in this instance means a potentiality and not a necessity.

I do not think this is the time or place to argue whether or not my views should be relegated to the compost-heap of unfashionable anthropologies as Jonathan covertly suggested, but I would like to finish this response to the discussants with a few remarks about Lévy-Bruhl. He is having something of a small renaissance now in anthropology because he has been so despised by the now ageing Boas School, of which Margaret Mead was the best known. I once inadvisedly brought up the name of Lévy-Bruhl to Mead at dinner, and I thought she was going to be ill. We quickly changed to another subject. The reason that Lévy-Bruhl still begets this visceral reaction is because, working with Durkheim's[5] concepts, he set out to show that primitive peoples were very different mentally from ourselves, were governed by "representations" (something like what I call collective cognitive imperatives), and were "pre-logical." To the Boas School, all peoples everywhere were the same mentally. Student anthropologists were forbidden to study mental differences, and such ideas as in Lévy-Bruhl seemed to lead to racial prejudice of the worst kind. And they may have, back in the first quarter of this century.

This is no longer true. Once we realize that human mentality is partly learned, and particularly that our mentality, consciousness, is mostly learned in the verbal community and expectancy surround and peer-pressure imagery of ontogeny, the matter is entirely in a new perspective. I do not particularly agree with his Durkheimian concepts, and there is a problem in selection of material, but Lévy-Bruhl's books are excellent reading for the data they present.[6] These are collections of descriptions of the first meetings of many different primitive peoples with Western observers.

Once we realize that a child from any of these mentally different bands and tribes brought up in our own society would be mentally just like ourselves, we are in a position to begin a true anthropology of mind — if it is not too late.

To state in a few sentences my own point of view, I think that the majority of hunter-gatherer groups today are the result of several different routes of history. Many, the majority perhaps, have been a part of a bicameral theocracy one or more times; hence the ubiquity of references to "the ancestors" and a host of shamanistic practices and rituals. (We should remember that there were many bicameral theocracies around the world at various times, rising up and periodically breaking down, not just those I have mentioned.) Other bands perhaps may have been like other primates, being neither bicameral nor conscious, and may have or have

5. Émile Durkheim, *The Elementary Forms of the Religious Life* (New York: Free Press, 1915/1965).
6. Lucien Lévy-Bruhl, *Primitive Mentality* (AMS Press, 1923/1975) and *How Natives Think* (New York: A.A. Knopf, 1926).

not learned such practices from others. But in the last millennium, and much more intensively in the last three or four centuries, almost all such tribal peoples have been taught a conscious mentality by trade, conquest (particularly in the nineteenth century and during World War II), and association with other conscious peoples, including other conscious tribes, missionaries teaching a soul-body dualism, and anthropologists themselves mapping our language onto theirs. The last possibly truly isolated tribe was in the Amazon and has been in contact with Brazilian anthropologists only in the last few years.[7]

Anthropologists once had the assumption that if you find a hunter-gatherer tribe nowadays, it is in a stone age similar to a pre-civilized era. This is not true. Each has had a history just as long as we have, and perhaps a complicated history of going through a bicameral phase somewhere, then breaking down, migrating somewhere else, and perhaps going through another bicameral phase, perhaps for a time mingling with conscious people. As well, so much comes in by diffusion — that difficult concept in anthropology that still does not have a good theoretical base, but appears important in many of the features of civilization found in hunter-gatherer groups.

A final note. Jonathan Miller, I think, stated that writing was an attribute solely of the leaders. I don't think this is true to the evidence at all. Read the letters to underlings and the stelae set up to give commands to the public in Mesopotamia. Recently, in a remote newly opened mine in Mount Sinai, there has been discovered the writings of the names of goddesses scratched on the mine walls that have been clearly dated by scholars to about 1500 B.C. I doubt if Mesopotamian leaders worked in the mines, although there is much left to understand on this topic.

Well, these are the points that I felt I should cover. I am going to close here and leave further discussion to other people. Again, I would like to thank our discussants for being so generous with their time and effort in coming here this afternoon.

---

7. See note 3, page 291.

CHAPTER 35

# McMaster-Bauer Symposium on Consciousness: Panel Discussion

Julian Jaynes, Daniel Dennett,
Jonathan Miller and George Ojemann

DENNETT: Since I have two microphones, one for each part of my mind, even if not parts of my brain, maybe I'll make a point or two first. The hardware/software distinction has to be handled very carefully because of course (if anybody doesn't realize this already) we do know enough about the architecture of the brain to know that there isn't a CPU (central processing unit) and a bunch of registers in it, and so we don't store a program in the brain's registers. All I mean by software in this context is really, I think, what Julian wants. Of course, even in a computer, to put some software in you must make a physical change in the computer. The change can be thought of as more or less isolated — packed off into some memory somewhere, maybe even off on a disc or on tape, but that is irrelevant. A software change — a change in "concepts" — *is* a physical change; it is a transient, temporary, change in the microstructure of the system. You can "undo" the change with more software — you don't need to use a screwdriver or a file. And, similarly of course, if we are going to be good materialists, we must suppose that when a child, say, grows up in one part of the world and learns French, this is embodied in very subtle changes in the physical structure of that child's brain, which nobody of course would be able to determine by a microscopic examination of that brain, even though those changes are in there. Now just as if you raise a child in France, the child learns French, and if you raise a child in the United

Panel discussion following Julian Jaynes's "Consciousness and the Voices of the Mind" lecture (see Chapter 19 of this volume) and subsequent lectures by Daniel Dennett, Jonathan Miller, and George Ojemann at the McMaster-Bauer Symposium on Consciousness at McMaster University in 1983. First published in *Canadian Psychology*, Vol. 27, Issue 2. © 1986 Canadian Psychological Association. Permission granted for use of material.

States, the child learns English, so if you raise a child in the post-bicameral world, the child "learns consciousness," and if you raise the child in the bicameral world, the child "learns bicamerality." Those are different software configurations of the hardware, and, of course, at some micro level those are all hardware changes because you can't put the software in without making tiny changes in structure. So, I think we can use a sort of biologized version of the term software here, if we like, to mean the sort of thing that Julian wants.

JAYNES: Thank you, I really like that.

DENNETT: Another comment I am a little reluctant to enter into because if I really got going on it, I would take half an hour. I think I know how to do most of what you want to do without the hallucinations.[1] But it is nowhere near as exciting, although it still seems to me to be very interesting. I will just say a few things to sketch it out, and then tonight perhaps we will thrash it out for hours.

JAYNES: I would like to.

DENNETT: Here is my very boring alternative. Why couldn't the voices you make so much of just be a phenomenon that we all know anyway, the familiar sort of obsessive memory, like having a damn jingle running through your head? That is not a hallucination. Advertisers are very good at writing jingles that once they get in your head, stay there. You keep hearing them, but you don't have to suppose it is a hallucination. It is just a memory which gets triggered under various circumstances and it might be memory of admonitions that were particularly impressive when you first heard them, for instance. Now that is just the first step. I take it that when you recall a jingle, you don't call it a hallucination.

JAYNES: I wouldn't say so, no.

DENNETT: Well, I would take that slender phenomenon and build on it in various ways. There is a whole side to Julian's book which none of us

---

1. At the time of this discussion, the occurrence of auditory hallucinations among the general population had not been widely studied. Since then — and initially inspired by Jaynes's theory — many studies have documented a higher than expected occurrence of auditory hallucinations in a wide range of normal (non-psychotic) populations including children, students, the elderly, individuals under stress or in isolation, and others. See Marcel Kuijsten, "Consciousness, Hallucinations, and the Bicameral Mind: Three Decades of New Research," in M. Kuijsten (ed.), *Reflections on the Dawn of Consciousness* (Henderson, NV: Julian Jaynes Society, 2006). — *Ed.*

has discussed which is perhaps my favorite part of all, and that is the relationship between consciousness and control, and the idea that the crisis for which consciousness is the ultimate stabilization is a crisis of control where individuals who had been controlled by leaders, more or less the way bees are controlled by the queen bee (or among mammals, the way mole rats are controlled by the queen mole rat), could no longer be so controlled. At some point in history, Julian says, social organizations got too large, groups of people got too large, and their projects became too complex for that sort of monolithic control to be practical, and so ordinary people had to become self-controllers for the first time, and this was a real crisis for them. I think that idea can be extrapolated in very interesting ways. It is a project I have been working on myself, but I will not say more about it right now, or I will go on for an hour.

OJEMANN: Perhaps then I will say something about the neurologic model, since that stirred up a bit of discussion. It seems to me that there were really two major points in Dr. Jaynes's book that this bears on. One is his suggestion that consciousness, in the main at least, involves an analog of the world in words, which I believe was his terminology slightly paraphrased. I think for that there is fairly good neurologic evidence. You can show a lot of behavioral changes that we would interpret as alterations in consciousness that occur in parallel with alterations in at least the phenomenon that is so hard to study, that one calls inner speech.

I think that when you turn, however, to what I see as the second point — that is, was that phenomenon something that was learned three and a half millennia ago? — I think the evidence is very poor from a neurologic standpoint. I think if you identify the likely substrates of consciousness and inner speech as the thalamocortical reticular circuits playing on language cortex that produce events essential to the inner speech and that alter or modulate your attention to verbally codable information, those seem to be structures which have been there for a long time — more than three or four millennia. While one cannot say for sure that there wasn't some change in their function at that point, it appears that these are systems that are present much earlier in the animal kingdom, at least in their anatomic features. At best you can say that in man they have been adapted to special needs related to language. That is where I think the quarrel comes. You look at the anatomic substrate and say, all right, the thalamocortical part of it is present for such things as motor learning in cats, is adapted in man with a little more lateralization, but at least the basic mechanism of this is present much earlier in the course of evolution. You look at language cortex. Well it is not there in monkeys, but you can begin to see changes in chimps and orangutans. You can certainly see it as a much more rapidly evolving system, but not evolving in the course of three millennia, but over a much longer time course. So, it is not that this is a system that is not changing, but it is changing over a time course that is so much longer than the one proposed by Dr. Jaynes that it seems unlikely that there was some learned event so recently ago that changed it. So while I tend to agree with the first point, that is, that language is the essential thing for most of conscious experience, I have trouble with the second.

If I can close with the Joan of Arc comment. The data on Joan of Arc ran like this. Remember, Joan of Arc's heart did not burn. One of the few conditions that would make a heart not burn is calcific tuberculous pericarditis. Of course, tuberculosis was very common at that time. A common sequel of someone with tuberculous pericarditis is to have tuberculomas in the brain. A common sequel of a cerebral tuberculoma is temporal lobe epilepsy, and there we have the hallucinations that changed history.

MILLER: If I may just make the point here about what William James calls medical materialism.[2] In a sense, I am taking issue here with both you and Julian for trying to see all this in terms of brains rather than societies. I think that most of the things that you are describing about the transformations and changes that have taken place in human self-consciousness could be perfectly satisfactorily described in terms of the development of cultural artifacts, through the medium of which we succeeded in building up elaborate representations, not only of the natural world in which we live, but also of ourselves in the social world. Writing, far from being a sort of fire extinguisher which puts out the hallucinated voice, provides a more manageable way of moving counters around in the menial game of describing your own personality. Without writing them down, your thoughts are nothing more than a fugue of forgettable sentences. Here we are, all scribbling away, not able to marshal our own arguments unless we remember what the others have said; we can't even remember what *we* thought unless we jot it down.

One of the points that Jack Goody makes in his book *The Domestication of the Savage Man* (1977) is that the most insignificant thing that emerges with writing is that you write down lists and tables. Once you start doing

---

2. William James, *The Varieties of Religious Experience* (New York: Modern Library, 1929).

this, you can have very elaborate degrees of reflectiveness. I would attribute most of the changes that took place to writing, as you do indeed, but for very different reasons. The reason why writing did it — and I think that McLuhan's[3] version of what writing did is nonsensical — is that it enabled us to visualize our thoughts and therefore to play much more sophisticated board games with psychological reality.

JAYNES: I like what you are just saying. But when you use the metaphor of writing "putting out" the voices, I would suggest that it is only one of the things. I am not trying to waffle here. Every large event in history has multiple causes and so likely did the breakdown of the bicameral mind, as I am sure you understand. This event here this afternoon has multiple causes.

MILLER: In connection with that, I'd like to modify what I said about the cunning conspiracy of priestly kings who manipulate, as it were, the public relations office of the gods. That is not what I meant at all. I am not suggesting that the priests deliberately invented the gods in order to control society. I am not saying that there was a design conference in some ziggurat where they said, "Well, let's run this up the flagpole and see how it comes out!" What happens is that theological imagery gradually evolves; and people find themselves under its hegemony. The same thing happens in complex literate societies. We know, for example, that the structure of the Anglican Church in England in the sixteenth century resulted in an authoritarian structure which exerted political control over society at large.

All we know is that when there are social crises, due to catastrophic crop failures, for example, there is often a change in political authority, and with the upset *political* authority there is often a collapse of the theological system, which is, after all, a constitutive part of the social structure. It's nothing to do with hallucinated voices!

JAYNES: There are some data which I think are relevant here. When you look at the writings in the period from 1400 B.C. to 600 B.C., those that are not simply factual but are more meaningful to us do talk about wanting to get back to the gods. Where have the gods gone? They don't call them voices. This is very distinct in the Hebrew hymns, for example, and it is very hard to know what Psalm 42 would mean otherwise:

3. Marshall McLuhan, *Understanding Media: The Extensions of Man* (New York: McGraw-Hill, 1964).

> As the hart pants after the water brooks,
> so pants my mind after you, o gods ...
> when am I going to see gods face-to-face again?

This is the proper translation of this Psalm, and it is not an isolated example.

MILLER: I think to use your own apparatus of metaphors and metaphrands and so forth, what is going on here is an elaborate way of representing in the idioms and currencies of the time, a sense of loss, nostalgia, or something of a previous stability which in fact is best often personified. It is easier to do it, we still do it today without being bicameral. It's a way of representing things. It is still in political cartoons personified. I think that this is the "in" poetry and is often the best way of carrying the message across, but not because such poems with their personifications are the residue of actual direct experiences of personal address inside the head.

JAYNES: I do understand your point of view. You are saying it is all metaphorical and poetry, related in fact to the loss of some kind of reality which could be this authoritative structure. I, of course, am preferring to take the historical data absolutely literally. They meant what they said.

DENNETT: There is a time and a place for metaphor!

# CHAPTER 36

# McMaster-Bauer Symposium on Consciousness: Open Discussion

Julian Jaynes, Daniel Dennett,
Jonathan Miller and George Ojemann

QUESTION FROM THE AUDIENCE: I would like to address this to all the participants. Harry Jerison in his book *Evolution of the Brain and Intelligence* (1973) a number of years ago suggested that consciousness was the highest level of abstraction of the sensory input and that's the level we work at. I was wondering if this fits into your model, Dr. Jaynes, and what the various participants think about this?

JAYNES: The statement was that consciousness is the highest level of abstraction. I don't think that means very much. It's like saying that a concert performance of a Beethoven sonata is the highest level of physical exercise: it may be, but such a statement doesn't tell us much about music or its forms. Let me add that I have a great respect for other aspects of Jerison's book.

My view of consciousness cannot be easily translated entirely into terms of abstraction. The analog 'I', narratization, and mind-space are certainly powerful abstractions of the highest order, and therefore Jerison is partly correct. But as Dan Dennett pointed out, about a bee having a concept of a flower, there has to be some kind of abstraction in the nervous system of the bee for it to be able to recognize flowers. And the bee is not conscious. So, to try to define consciousness in terms of pure abstractions may be confusing the issue, rather than clarifying it.

Open discussion with all of the panelists following Julian Jaynes's "Consciousness and the Voices of the Mind" lecture (see Chapter 19 of this volume) and subsequent lectures by Daniel Dennett, Jonathan Miller, and George Ojemann at the McMaster-Bauer Symposium on Consciousness at McMaster University in 1983. First published in *Canadian Psychology*, Vol. 27, Issue 2. © 1986 Canadian Psychological Association. Permission granted for use of material.

DENNETT: I would want to add two things to that. First of all, I think we should always be suspicious of any evolutionary argument which starts using the word "higher" and seeing a gradual upward progression. Here we have "higher" doing two jobs for us: one is where we are going up the phylogenetic scale, and the other is where we are going up, up, up in the familiar, if somewhat threadbare, idea of higher abstraction. I don't like either progression in this case. On any account of abstraction that I would be happy with, I think a lot of our unconscious mentation involves abstractions that are greater, or more abstract, than those contents that are consciously accessible to us. So if I took Jerison's definition seriously, I would be in the awkward position of having to say that I have absolutely no access to my most conscious thoughts!

MILLER: Why use the word abstraction? I prefer to use Craik's notion of the brain as an internal model-maker, as something capable of maintaining a high degree of constancy in the face of the variation in the sensory input.[1] What we mean by a successful internal model of the world is one that remains stable in the face of an otherwise bewildering flux of sensation.

OJEMANN: I think one can show a dissociation of abstract skills and consciousness. In the reports of the people who have had major hemispheric strokes in the language area, in the course of their recovery what they tell you is that as their internal speech comes back their consciousness comes back, but their consciousness is now constricted: it is now concrete, they have lost a lot of the abstract ability that they had before. I think in that sense you can dissociate them, and if you consider abstract ability a higher function, then in that sense consciousness is not the highest function of the human brain, because it can be there in a setting where the other is gone. Perhaps the conclusion from all of this is that for once the panel agrees!

Q: I would like to ask a question about the use of some Biblical stories to support the idea of God or the right hemisphere speaking to people. The question is addressed to Julian Jaynes and Jonathan Miller. I am not familiar with stories from other cultures, but in the Old Testament, especially in the story of Amos, since that was the figure you chose, God did not choose to speak to someone very high up in the hierarchy. In fact, what's typical of Biblical stories is that God rarely speaks to kings. He doesn't

---

1. Kenneth J.W. Craik, *The Nature of Explanation* (Cambridge: Cambridge University Press, 1943).

like to speak to kings. God speaks to people who undermine the social order, rather than people who should preserve it.

Second, it's clear from a lot of the descriptions from the Bible, that God hardly ever speaks to everybody — except in unusual cases such as the Revelation on Mount Sinai. There are people who are chosen as prophets; they're select. He doesn't speak to the ordinary man. In fact, when individuals challenge the prophets' authority and unique qualifications, as in the tale of Korah in Numbers, they are destroyed by God: but God doesn't speak to them to tell them that he is going to destroy them. The premise has always been that prophecy is a very select calling in the Bible. Also, the Biblical Hebrews' notion that the "idol-worshippers' actually believed that their statues in fact spoke to them seems to have been based on a misconception of what it was these statues did — what purpose they served — in the surrounding cultures. Kaufmann[2] in commenting on the ancient religion of Israel claims, in fact, that ancient Jews were so far removed from idolatry that they no longer understood what it was that the idol-makers believed in. Kaufmann says of the Jews that their view of idolatry was laughably simplistic. The ancient Jews thought erroneously that idolators, in fact, believed that their icons would speak to them, something which I think you, Dr. Jaynes, believe as well. Kaufmann, however, asserts that in idolatrous societies, the icons behaved more in the way that Jonathan Miller claimed a picture of the Pope or an icon of Jesus behaves to a believing Catholic. These icons were simply icons that represented a deity, not real gods themselves that anyone in those idolatrous societies actually spoke to. I suspect in those societies maybe people believed gods did speak to kings, but I don't know very much about those societies. I only know a little about Biblical literature.

JAYNES: If I could first reply to that. Indeed, such statues are definitely called gods in the Hebrew Bible.

Q (CONT.): That's right, but erroneously…

JAYNES: I am not making judgments. I am just looking at the whole series. Nor am I just looking at the Jews. The evidence for idols, a truer term than icons, during the time period of the Hebrew Testament is considerable. Else why would so many of the prophets inveigh against them? Idols are particularly evident in the early books, from the *elohim* or gods that

2. Yehezkel Kaufmann, *The Religion of Ancient Israel*, M. Greenberg translation (Chicago: University of Chicago Press, 1960).

Laban accuses Jacob of stealing[3] to centuries later when the Philistines
after defeating Saul run and tell their *atsabim,* their idols, before they tell
their people.[4] To call such god-idols merely icons like pictures of the Pope
is a serious misreading of the texts and contradicted in many passages.[5] It
is a further instance of the presentist fallacy referred to earlier in connection with the Egyptian pyramids.

Q (cont.): I'm sorry, maybe I misunderstood. Didn't you say that, in fact,
the bicameral period is the period in which people hear gods and that
Amos was indeed representative of the bicameral mind?

JAYNES: I did not use the word representative. Amos is a shepherd brought
in from the fields of Tekoa who is unusual for his time because he hears a
voice that has this authenticity.

Q (cont.): Amos is not unusual among the prophets.

JAYNES: He is unusual among the Hebrews of the time, which is why the
scribes are following him around.

Q (cont.): Every prophet is unusual among the people of his time. He is
not unusual among prophets in hearing voices and he is prototypical of
the prophets that supposedly came either before or later.

JAYNES: You are talking as if there are a huge number of prophets.

Q (cont.): Not at all. You are talking as if there were a huge number of
people who heard voices and there is no such evidence.

JAYNES: I think you misunderstood me. Because I didn't mean to say that
this is the bicameral period. Prophets, just as the oracles in Greece, are
these special people who have this remaining ability which was highly
prized by the societies as they were groping towards consciousness after
the end of the bicameral period.

Q (cont.): I just see this as being very slippery. Let me try to understand
what it is that you are saying again. Then I will stop. The evidence that
you have for a bicameral period, where people hear voices, you claimed, is

---

3. Genesis 31:30.
4. I Samuel 31:9; I Chronicles 10:9.
5. See, for example, I Chronicles 16:26.

based among other sources on evidence of these Biblical writings. Among these writings that you mentioned was Amos. Now if Amos is unusual, then what is it that you are basing your evidence on and why bring Amos into it altogether?

JAYNES: You can leave him out… Amos is in 800 B.C. This is late. The evidence for the bicameral mind is in all Greek, Hebrew, cuneiform, hieroglyphic and other ancient texts of the second and third millennia B.C., as well as the archeological remains from that period and earlier all the way back to the ninth millennium B.C.

DENNETT: I am not sure, but as I understand Julian, the prophets, all of them, were not themselves living in a bicameral age — they were bicameral throwbacks of the earlier bicameral age — living in an age which was essentially like our age, the conscious age — and so that is what makes them special. They are the dinosaur-links, as it were, to our bicameral past.

Q (CONT.): I just think that you can't play this kind of game — the attitude that is presented here. In our age if someone told us that they heard the voice of God, we would not follow them, there would not be scribes going around preserving their words for centuries. You can't say Amos was a throwback to the bicameral age and then say that everybody else in the society is like us. If everybody else was like us, Amos' writings would not be kept — any more than the rantings of any other lunatic who tells us they hear the word of God.

OJEMANN: I would like to make two comments on that. First, the following of prophets who hear the voice of God and having these words recorded by scribes quite clearly does happen in our age: one need only take the example of Joseph Smith and the rise of the Mormon Church as one of many. The second comment I would like to make, and I think this might be the right place for it, is to raise an issue with Dr. Jaynes. He indicated that this right-hemisphere effect on hallucinations was the origin of religion. At least that is what my notes say, although they may not be correct. There is only one study that I know of that has looked at the effect of brain lesions on religious performance. That is the study of Bear and Fedio on people with temporal lobe epilepsy.[6] That study suggested that left temporal lobe epilepsy is associated with increased religiosity. I

---

6. David M. Bear and Paul Fedio, "Quantitative Analysis of Interictal Behavior and Temporal Lobe Epilepsy," *Archives of Neurology*, 1977, *34*, 454–467.

just wondered if Dr. Jaynes wanted to comment on that or relate that in any way to his idea.

JAYNES: Could I simply ask you a question on that point, because I wish to defer to you in the matter. Left-lobe epilepsy would mean some foci of epilepsy in the left hemisphere?

OJEMANN: That is correct.

JAYNES: Could this then mean that the right hemisphere was taken out of a certain amount of inhibition and therefore could have been, what will we say, overactive, resulting in activity manifesting as increased religiosity?

OJEMANN: Bear and Fedio don't interpret it that way. They interpret it as hyperactivity in the left temporal lobe responsible for this picture of hyperwriting, hyperreligiosity, and hyperintrospection. On the other hand, your interpretation might be a correct one, but it is not the way they have interpreted it.[7]

MILLER: To amplify on that. Again, I would like to dispose of this medical materialism. If you are going to talk about prophets, seers, shamans, and so forth, I think we can do so without having to get into conjectural neurology — we don't need to think about bicamerality or about tuberculomas or temporal lobe epilepsy. As far as I can see, it's much more helpful to take social factors into consideration. In other words, even if one accepts the fact that certain people "hear" or claim to hear voices, what one wants to know is why it is that at certain times and in certain societies, such people are credited with oracular authority — and that in other societies they are just as likely to be locked up. I find I. M. Lewis's analysis

---

7. Other studies have found hyperreligiosity associated with both right and left temporal lobe epilepsy. See for example "Sudden Religious Conversions in Temporal Lobe Epilepsy" by Dewhurst and Beard (1970) and "Hyperreligiousity in Temporal Lobe Epilepsy" by Tucker and Novelly (1987). Important here is the fact that handedness is often not reported, as the left hemisphere can often be the non-dominant hemisphere for language in left handed patients (see S. Knecht, et al., "Handedness and Hemispheric Language Dominance in Humans," *Brain*, 2000, *123*). Other studies have reported a greater instance of hyperreligiosity in cases of epilepsy in the non-dominant (usually the right) temporal lobe, such as Roberts, Robertson, and Trimble, "The Lateralizing Significance of Hypergraphia in Temporal Lobe Epilepsy," *Journal of Neurology, Neurosurgery, and Psychiatry*, 1982. As Jaynes suggests, an interaction between the left and right temporal lobes seems likely. A right-left temporal lobe interaction has also been found during auditory verbal hallucinations (see *Reflections on the Dawn of Consciousness*, pgs. 116–126). Also relevant here are cases of psychosis resulting from temporal lobe epilepsy (S. Nadkarni, et al., "Psychosis in Epilepsy Patients," *Epilepsia*, 2007). Only Jaynes's bicameral mind theory accounts for why the right temporal lobe would be implicated in both hyperreligiosity and auditory verbal hallucinations. — *Ed.*

much more fruitful.[8] He identified the social types who displayed oracular powers and showed that in certain contexts, unfortunate and often alienated individuals could graduate from the status of hysterical victims to the role of prophets and shamans. In other words, in societies which looked upon seizures with awe and dread, an afflicted individual could sometimes manipulate his or her defect to advantage; so that affliction becomes the royal road to social importance. What we are dealing with here is the social and cultural significance of charisma — beautifully described by Max Weber in his *The Sociology of Religion* (1964).

Q: May I ask a question?

MILLER: I hear a voice!

Q (CONT.): I want to preface my question with the comment that this has been such an intellectual feast that I feel somewhat of an ingrate asking for more, but Jonathan Miller's last comment really gives me an opportunity to ask if the panel could say something about the role of the spontaneous transcendental experience in the context of the evolution of human consciousness. The reason I raise this is one, because I am greatly interested, and two, perhaps our guests may not know that Hamilton was the place in which Dr. Richard Maurice Bucke, a psychiatrist, first started work on his book *Cosmic Consciousness* (1901), which does attempt to explain, in somewhat Darwinian terms, that human consciousness is evolving and there are forerunners who have these somewhat mystical experiences. I wonder whether the panel might want to comment.

JAYNES: That is a difficult question to answer succinctly, but let me try. I have been speaking of consciousness as a human product, an ability that is learned in history in order to cope behaviorally in a civilized world. If I am correct, Dr. Bucke is assuming the existence of a cosmic consciousness, a higher form of consciousness out in the universe that some special individuals can approach and be a part of. So-called transcendental meditation has a similar belief. Such notions to me are unnecessary metaphysical suppositions that are not in agreement with general scientific principles of parsimony and evidence.

---

8. Ioan M. Lewis, *Ecstatic Religion: An Anthropological Study of Spirit Possession and Shamanism* (Harmondsworth: Penguin, 1971).

Q: We've been talking about the disappearance of the voices of the gods away back in time, and yet it seems to me that Carl Jung took very seriously the archetypes and other products of our unconscious. Could you help me understand the relationship between this and the Jungian concepts?

JAYNES: I would reply that Jung had many insights indeed, but the idea of the collective unconscious and of the archetypes has always seemed to me to be based on the inheritance of acquired characteristics, a notion not accepted by biologists or psychologists today.

DENNETT: I just have one more remark to that. One might try to salvage the Jungian idea in the face of the simple unacceptability of its Lamarckian underpinnings, by a hypothesis about very persistent regularities in the social environment which would create the sort of effect that Jonathan has just been talking about. That way you could make an honest, non-mystical hypothesis out of a notion like the collective unconscious. You would have laundered quite a lot out of it, but then you might find it serviceable.

Q: Presumably at any moment an individual would either be bicameral or not. I would just like to pin it down to the individual animal at the moment: it is agreed, isn't it, that a person either is or isn't conscious?

JAYNES: It really does depend here on the historical period you are talking about. Consciousness and a kind of bicamerality can exist together. For instance William Blake indeed had hallucinations of his poetry and many of his paintings are direct hallucinations as well, and at the same time he was indeed conscious in the way he related to and talked to people.[9] And there are many other examples such as Emanuel Swedenborg and several individuals that I have interviewed recently. So you can't say in general that people who hear voices in the modem era are not conscious.

Q (CONT.): Let me explain why I am asking this. As you know, people now believe that most systems in the developing individual brain go through a critical period in their development, and during that period, for example in the system dealing with vision, they have to receive an appropriate input from the environment; if not, then the behavior the system is destined to deal with develops abnormally. Now, supposing there were a number of

---

9. Julian Jaynes, "The Ghost of A Flea: Visions of William Blake," *Art/World*, 1981, 5, 3–6. Reprinted in Marcel Kuijsten (ed.), *Reflections on the Dawn of Consciousness* (Henderson, NV: Julian Jaynes Society, 2006).

systems, perhaps working in parallel, that together were the substrate of consciousness, and that they had a critical period; would you now be able to say — and perhaps you could look into your own material and answer this — whether you could suppose that the environment could be pinpointed into a number of items which, if they were absent, would not result in this total system developing appropriately, and that this would result in the absence of consciousness, as you defined it? If the inputs from the environment were present during the critical period of development, then you would have consciousness.

JAYNES: I think that is a very interesting statement, particularly the idea of parallel development of different neurological systems. I am sure the truth is not as simple as I have presented it this afternoon. Uneven parallel developments could indeed build in considerable complications. That there therefore could be a people brought up in a certain environment that during critical periods for certain lines of development did not get the necessary input, thus resulting in some kind of deficient consciousness, is a provocative and important hypothesis. It is the kind of idea that empirical studies of different cultures would illuminate. But I suggest that the idea of consciousness will have to be developed a little more finely in order to study such questions. The science of the development of consciousness in children over the last three millennia, whether or not based on some partial innate substrate, is an important project for the future.

OJEMANN: The issue of critical periods and their impact on brain development obviously is a very essential one to this, but I put a couple of cautions in here. It seems to me that what we know of critical periods is that where they have been clearly shown is in sensory systems. Whether that can be generalized beyond sensory systems I don't think we know. Secondly, they have been shown only under very, very adverse environments and whether the environment when the world was in all that trouble got bad enough, three and a half millennia ago, I don't know. I will crawl out on a limb and say that I would guess that if one is willing to accept at least some of the neurological model that I proposed as a basis of conscious experience, that there probably isn't much of a role for critical periods. The brain mechanism for conscious experience in that model is available as hardware for a variety of learning situations.

I will also respond to something that Jonathan Miller said a little earlier. The consideration of disease in my discussion is because of the problem one has if you are interested in trying to identify what the role is of "hardware" — that is of brain structure — in a variety of behavioral states. You are very limited by the opportunities that you have to investigate this matter. Disease states in man represent one of the very few opportunities to really make a set of observations that will allow you to sort out what are the behavioral implications of damaging a particular piece of "hardware." That's the reason one turns to that so often. It's not what you really like to do, but it is one of the few sources for data on human brain function available to you.

# CHAPTER 37

# The Consequences of Consciousness: Emory University Discussion

Q: Where is consciousness going from here?

JAYNES: Yes, if consciousness changed this much in one hundred generations, how about a hundred generations from now? There are lots of ways I could try to reply, which I'll probably not — I go out on enough limbs. I of course think that consciousness in our time and what is happening to us is a very significant thing in history. Let's imagine the year 20,000 and people looking back at our own time. They are going to see the swiftness of change in media, communications, art, and every kind of thing. And what exactly it all means? I certainly can't express it. I tend to have a positive view. I'm hoping that consciousness can develop into perhaps better kinds of self-control, until, for example, those of us who want to give up smoking can just make a decision to do so, and that's all there is to it. I think we might be able to train consciousness so that we are suggestible to ourselves to a greater degree.

Incidentally, I might just repeat a story that the reporter who interviewed me for the article in tonight's journal told me about his attempt to give up smoking. He went to a hypnotist here in Atlanta to help him give up smoking — and it worked! It was fine — he gave up smoking. Then a month later, after being free of smoking and feeling just wonderful that he'd given up smoking, he saw a television show on which the same psychiatrist that had been his hypnotist casually said, "Well, yes it works sometimes, but sometimes it doesn't work at all." The next day he was smoking a pack and a half a day [laughs]. So you see how suggestible we are and how that suggestion can also be removed — you just pull it out and we can't seem to control that. Perhaps consciousness can be moved in such a way that we are not as vulnerable to external suggestion and we

Transcribed and edited from a question and answer session following Julian Jaynes's "The Consequences of Consciousness" lecture, presented at Emory University on May 23, 1978.

have greater control over our own lives. I honestly don't know. But I think you're pointing to a very interesting thing.

But as Robert Browning said, "Grow old with me, the best is yet to be." Because there are so many challenges around us — intellectual, emotional, ethical challenges — it's a great time to be alive.

Q: What type of responses have you received? Have the responses you've received been different from scientists as opposed to those working in the humanities?

JAYNES: Yes, I get all kinds of responses and I'm not sure that it's divided up into one thing and another. There are people in the sciences who say that what I'm doing is nonsense. I get things all the way from a behaviorist-type of response that trying to bring consciousness back is ridiculous — that we got rid of it and now it's coming back through the side door, through this analysis of history. But mostly I get a kind of skeptical interest: "That's interesting — what can we do with this particular aspect or how can we disprove it?" — which is a proper kind of response to my work. In the humanities I get a great deal of interest from people in English departments, because my emphasis on narratization and its importance in consciousness points to the importance of literature and the importance of standardized narratizations — which is what literature is. The importance of narratization to one's mental make-up points back to the importance of stories in one's childhood — so people in English departments seem to be very interested.

Q: How do we know that people didn't have consciousness before the bicameral period and then lost it?

JAYNES: You're making a very good point: I've gone back into the ancient literature and shown that, at least in the literature that I could see and understand, there wasn't consciousness, so why can't one go back just a few millennia before that and say, "Everybody was conscious back then and then they lost it and went through the bicameral period and then came back out?" Yes, one could say that. But there is a continuity of the artifacts that goes back to 9000 B.C. in terms of effigies — what I call idols — that seems to indicate that man had a similar kind of bicameral mind back then as I think one finds in the data that is pointed to by the *Iliad*. The *Iliad* of course is late and it's a revision and copy of something that goes back to bicameral times. But it's been changed in the process. But you're quite right, from some of the things that I've been saying — if you want to make a science of it — how can one prove that people don't have consciousness? It is indeed a problematic thing and I certainly recognize the problem.

Q: Do you get much response from people with an artistic background? We're a whole group of artists that came in from Athens [Georgia] to hear you. The artists are very interested in your theories and feel they are very applicable — the whole idea of the right brain being involved in art...

JAYNES: Thank you — that's very flattering. It's very interesting... I'd like everyone to remember the caution I mentioned last night of going too much into the simplicities of the right hemisphere being artistic and so on. We have to be cautious. But if you keep that caution in mind, I'll tell you a little story [laughs]. This is the case of a boy in New York who had epilepsy leading to *status epilepticus,* which involves persistent seizures that can become so severe that they can be fatal. In temporal lobe epilepsy, the excitation begins in the temporal lobe, then spreads and seems to magnify, and then jumps across to other hemisphere via the corpus callosum. This is why in some of these cases they perform what's called the split-brain procedure, where they cut the commissures between the two hemispheres so as to restrict the seizures to one side of the brain.

Well this boy — who wanted to be an artist — had this unfortunate kind of epilepsy. They had him make some drawings before they operated on him. And after he recovered — and it did help his epilepsy — they asked him to draw a man. With his right hand (which is controlled by the left hemisphere) he drew a stick figure, with all the fingers and toes put in and the head and eyes and everything else — all anatomically just right but without any sort of artistic element to it. And then they asked him to draw a man with his left hand (which is controlled by the right hemisphere), and there was all this sweeping movement, but not enough of this left hemisphere analysis to put it all together. So there you had two drawings — one done by the left hemisphere and one done by the right hemisphere, and then the previous work, done by both of them together. So in art, you need both hemispheres — it can't just be the right hemisphere. And if you'll notice I have not come out with any neurological theory of consciousness at all. I'm still working on that, but I certainly think it has something to do with the cooperation of the hemispheres in a slightly different way than in the bicameral mind.

Q: What caused the breakdown of the bicameral mind?

JAYNES: The reasons for the breakdown of the bicameral mind are several, as I mentioned last night. One of them is the spread of writing, because that is a visual way of perceiving information instead of the auditory hallucinations. Another important cause is the tremendous growth of populations and the complexity of civilizations. The bicameral mind isn't as functional with very large populations — it's like a house of cards that has to be kept together with all kind of ritual and people doing the same thing. You can see in the Maya and in many other places that it breaks down periodically. In the Near East, it broke down in the midst of these great cities that had their own economies churning on, so people there stayed in the situation and learned this new thing called consciousness, instead of going back to being tribes.

Q (CONT.): So you are saying that consciousness was a functional necessity rather than a structural change?

JAYNES: That is correct. And it is not genetic or biologically evolved. There is the possibility that I could make a case for a genetic component to the change because of the huge percentage of the population that died in the catastrophes that took place at the end of the second millennium B.C. But I think that is going too far. I place a tremendous importance on child development. It's fantastic what child development can do to the brain. It's almost as though the brain is learning to develop itself.

I like to use an example, and although it's not on the same point, it makes the point of just how much can happen in child development for the brain to organize itself until you have a normal, conscious human being such as ourselves. And this was just one case that was brought to light by a friend of mine, Burt Rosner at the University of Pennsylvania, a case of a man who died in an automobile accident or something — I've forgotten what — and so they performed an autopsy on him. They opened up his brain, and lo and behold, when they looked at the interior part of his brain, the limbic system, it was a twisted mass and half of it was missing.[1] There are three parts: the brain stem, the limbic system — which is involved in our emotional life — and then the cortex on top of it — so there is some sense of a "triune brain" as Paul MacLean talks about it.[2]

---

1. Burton S. Rosner, "Brain Functions," *Annual Review of Psychology*, 1970, *21*, 555–594.

2. Paul D. MacLean, *The Triune Concept of the Brain and Behavior* (Toronto: University of Toronto Press, 1974).

If you stimulate the limbic system with an electrode in an animal you might get aggression or sexual behavior or something like that — it's an emotional center in the brain. And here this man was missing half of it and you couldn't recognize the different parts of it. The people doing the autopsy said, "What kind of a monster has this man been? He must have been horrible." But when they looked at this life, they discovered he had led his class in school, he had been president of his class, he had been a good citizen, he had been a salesman for an insurance company, and lived a happy life with no problems at all.

The point of the story is that this was a congenital defect, probably early in fetal life, and what a mystery this is that somehow the brain learns to compensate to the extent that the man did not experience any behavioral problems at all. In spite of the damage, the brain develops itself so that in the end you have a normal conscious individual. This is the great mystery of the embryology of the nervous system that is so important.

Q: I'm interested in education and early childhood development. I wonder if there are methods or directions we could pursue that would be an improvement in helping the development of consciousness in children?

JAYNES: I don't know and I wish I did know. As you know there are many educational theories about how to help young children along. There are now some Piagetians that are trying to teach some of these conservation tasks at earlier ages, thinking that this will help the child progress more or faster. Then there are the Montessori methods that have very prescribed rules of concrete things that people have to do. Now there is a movement — going back to the right hemisphere education movement of the late nineteenth and early twentieth centuries — arguing that we have to educate the right hemisphere more. My friend Joe Bogen, the neurosurgeon who did the split-brain surgeries, feels very definitely that way — that we should have an educational system that caters more to the right hemisphere.

But I don't know exactly what that can mean. Sure, we can teach music and art, which are more right hemispheric. But I think I would prefer that education not use the newer things in modern neurology to do that. I feel we should instead have an ideal of a responsible, cultured individual that we should try to make our children into, that is a cultural norm — instead of, let's say, just trying to make a child more creative. I don't know what that means because I certainly don't want a neurosurgeon to be more creative, I don't want the policeman giving me a ticket to be more creative — in certain things we value responsibility and efficiency.

Q: I am very interested in the idea of shame — the importance of shame. Were you saying that shame was not present in preconscious people?

JAYNES: No, shame was present. I think shame is present in dogs. You can shame a dog, you can shame chimpanzees. This is a genetic built-in response to certain — particularly social — situations. It is guilt that is not there. And guilt is like fantasized shame … [Break in recording.]

Q: Your choice of the term "bicameral mind" to characterize preliterate societies — were you saying that they were better off not having modern consciousness? And your remarks about the future of education and about art education did not suggest that you have a very warm feeling about where education might take this up and perhaps go back and compensate for our over-education of the left hemisphere.

JAYNES: Let me answer your second part first. It's just that I feel we should use some caution in anything where we are being responsible toward other human beings, particularly the young. I feel a caution in education is most admirable, just as in medicine a caution is most admirable. It's almost too easy to pick up on a certain fashion and feel we're more helpful if "now we do this." I don't know enough about the changes in mathematics, but the "new math" as it was called — I'm not sure, I've just read the criticisms — but now we seem to be going back to the older method because it became too much of a fashion. That's one example. I wouldn't want people to think, "We've got to educate the right hemisphere more and then we're going to have happy people." And then we found people who couldn't write or express themselves properly and so then they couldn't get jobs later on, and so on. So that's the answer to your second question.

The answer to the first part of your question of whether or not consciousness is a good thing — what I tried to say is that ethics only comes in with consciousness and our feelings of right or wrong or better or worse are only conscious kinds of attributes. So it is wrong to call bicameral man good or bad or bicamerality good or bad, because these are conscious evaluative terms. We who are conscious can see ourselves before and after. So once you are conscious, then you have these evaluative systems. So, yes, I think that consciousness is good and hopeful. I think education is hopeful. It's just that I don't want us to lurch into something just because it seems so interesting, and this kind of responsibility towards children I think is so important.

Q: Do children go through a bicameral phase in their development? If not, are there different levels of consciousness between children and adults?

JAYNES: Yes, in children, consciousness develops between the ages of 4 and 6. We are trying to do experiments on this now. An experiment I've done is a study in children's dreams, in which you can show them going through some of the stages of dreams that I've described. The child in dreams is operating in a space that slowly grows beyond their bedroom and out into the world. We're trying to get at how this consciousness grows in children. Perhaps out of that will come something that may be useful in education. I would genuinely like to think so. Perhaps it will say something about right hemispheric input. But at the present time I don't feel that we know. The interview technique that we use with children is difficult because children have a variety of verbal formulae and you have to go through a lot of procedures beforehand, such as playing games, in order to develop the proper rapport.[3]

Q: What about the primitive societies of today, are they bicameral societies based on your interpretation?

JAYNES: The problem of the mentality of different tribes is a very interesting one. I think you can classify tribes in terms of their history: those that for instance are products of previous bicameral kingdoms — which I think many of the ones we've studied the ethnographies of were — plus those that have acquired semi-bicameral practices through diffusion. I don't think at the present time, with the possible exception of two tribes in the Amazon that can't be reached and are probably rapidly decreasing in numbers, that there is any tribe today that doesn't have a semblance of modern consciousness. There have been several movements through history: one is conquest, another is missionaries teaching a dualism (particularly Christian missionaries), another is anthropologists, who at the time they were studying ethnography were behavioristic, studying how grains were ground and spears were made, instead of studying thoughts. It's only now that we're getting around to appreciating some of the differences in

---

3. See David Foulkes, *Children's Dreaming and the Development of Consciousness* (Cambridge, MA: Harvard University Press, 2002). David Foulkes was a professor at Emory University at the time and attended this lecture. The influence of Jaynes's ideas can be seen in Foulkes's book. —*Ed.*

mentality and some of the data that a man named Lévy-Bruhl[4] back in the 1920s developed into a theory. It was shot down by American anthropologists like Margaret Mead and so on because it seemed racist to them, but it didn't really have to be.[5]

Let me give you an example of how hard it is to do anthropological research and to study tribes and get real data. A man — a friend of a friend of mine — was studying a tribe of Mayan Indians that seemed to be isolated in a northern part of Yucatán. He was very interested in their divination practices, which were extremely elaborate. He was studying them for one summer and every Saturday night all of the men disappeared — they all left camp. The women were left behind and he was left behind as well. And he was wondering, "What wonderful ritual was this that they were all leaving for?" And he just hoped, as an anthropologist would, that he could make friends with them and learn their language and so on until they would reveal to him what was going on at this time. Finally, towards the end of the summer, he was included in the group, and he was asked if he'd like to go to this event — they had some type of Mayan name for it — and he said that yes, he'd like to. So it came time to leave the settlement, they trotted through all these well worn paths, and other tribes came in from other places, and they all came together into a space about this size. Everyone was talking in an excited manner, and then they all sat down at a certain time. And up in front there was a large box-like structure with a black cloth over it. And at a certain signal they whipped off the black cloth and under it was a battery-powered television and they all watched *The Dick Van Dyke Show* dubbed into Spanish [laughs]. And here he had hopes that, "Here's my Ph.D. thesis, I've discovered this new ritual."

Q: I have a question on authorization — which you refer to in your book and you've referred to tonight — and perhaps to push it to the direction of what I call conviction. And whether or not there is some kind of [inaudible] in the conscious mind between that kind of narratizing, spatializing, and the analog 'I' that has the kind of grounding in certainty that is beyond or deeper than consciousness. [Inaudible] the kind of nostalgia I hear at the end of your book for a quality of authorization or conviction that consciousness seems to be bereft of. I'd like to hear you speculate on that or address that if you would.

---

4. See Lucien Lévy-Bruhl, *Primitive Mentality* (AMS Press, 1923/1975) and *How Natives Think* (Arno Press, 1926/1979).

5. See also note 3, page 291.

JAYNES: It's hard to me to give a proper answer and you seem to be most sensitive to what I was saying in the last third of my book. We do have a nostalgia for the certainties and the religious deities of the bicameral mind. That is a conscious thing and it is part of the territory. That is to say that if we were living back in that time, we wouldn't necessarily like it. So it's not a real nostalgia. It is that we have to seek our certainty in other things than simply hearing voices. And of course I do think and try to show that science is a part of this. And I do think that true science is not going to destroy art, for example, but should be an enhancement of it. There's no reason why science has to be a bitter, hard, cruel kind of thing.

One of the things we've been through in science and psychology is the idea of man as a machine and the use of the term "mechanist." That has such a bad tone to many people. But one of the most interesting things about that — and this is why I'm interested in the history of science is to trace that back — and where does it come from? It comes from the medical materialists back in the middle of the nineteenth century in Germany. And what were they trying to do? Help mankind — with medicine. They were cheered on, by the discovery of bacteria, for example, and all of these wonderful scientific discoveries. They believed they could get rid of poverty — they were all socialists and so on. It all comes from them, from the idea of doing good. Now by the time it gets to John B. Watson, I'm afraid the ethical motivation of it isn't there anymore. To a psychologist it is still okay, because we like to do experiments. But to a person outside of psychology who is looking at psychology — which is supposed to be a study of man's mind — it can seem to be a very crippling kind of doctrine. I think we're out of that now. And to return to your observation, yes we are still seeking authorization. And I try to say that perhaps we can seek this within ourselves in better ways than before. I can only end up with that statement — I hope that about myself. We all have our own problems and this is what I hope for myself — but who knows?

Q: Have you worked at all with the contemporary phenomenon of glossolalia and the relationship of that both to the understanding of the present, post-bicameral period, and also projecting back into the period of the bicameral mind?

JAYNES: I did indeed look at glossolalia which I was very interested in at one time. So far as I can see it begins in the Acts with Pentecost, particularly in the writings attributed to Paul. If you go back to some of the

Christian theologians they feel it happens in the Old Testament, when God pours out his spirit and some of these metaphors, but I don't really agree with that.

I'd like to refer you to a book by Felicitas Goodman, *Trance, Healing, and Hallucination* (1982), which has some of her own material in it and as well as material from her students. It is one of the best studies that I know in this area. She did a study in South America among people practicing the Umbanda religion, in this very volatile situation in Brazil where you have all these different types of people — everything from former African slaves, to Brazilian natives, to some Europeans — all mixing up together. There were a lot of dispossessed people that had some need for a religion stronger and more intimate than the Catholic religion. Most of them were Catholic, but at the same time they practiced this Umbanda religion, which is a possession religion. And as an offshoot of that they were practicing glossolalia in a remarkable way.

Of course it has become almost a fashion in this country. There are groups practicing it in New York and everywhere else. A friend of mine who is a Professor of Theology at Manhattan College did an investigation in which he went into Protestant groups that were practicing glossolalia and made tape recordings of them. He then played the tapes back to other members of the group and the recordings didn't mean anything to them. But I don't like to say too much on this subject because I feel that there are people who are helped by attaining a state of glossolalia, which means to them something about being unified with spiritual forces in the world that are very helpful to them. As long as it has that meaning to them and it results in goodness and kindness, that's a kind of proof or a kind of validity and I'd just like to leave it at that.

Q: What can you say on mystical religious conversion experiences?

JAYNES: I'm not sure what I can say about that. I think we are all susceptible to certain kinds of special authorization or being part of something — a relationship that can define us or give us meaning in our lives. If someone comes along and says just the right words to us, and we are in the position or state to be receptive to this, then this kind of leap can be made. And if this is helpful to someone, I think that's fine.[6]

---

6. See also note 7, page 340.

Q: I'm interested in this distinction between shame and guilt. Anthropologists have argued along the lines that shame societies are more concerned with the reaction of other people to them, whereas guilt societies like our own control our actions because of something internalized. Do you argue first of all that shame societies are not conscious? And secondly, how do you respond to the notion that shame supposes consciousness in the sense that to feel shame, one would have to put oneself in the place of others and see oneself from their perspective?

JAYNES: Let me reply to the first part of your question first. This is about the distinction between shame societies and guilt societies. This starts up in a few paragraphs in Ruth Benedicts's *The Chrysanthemum and the Sword*, in which she compares Japan and the United States and she calls Japan a shame society and the United States a guilt society. This has then been picked up by other people. You can find it in E. R. Dodds's *The Greeks and the Irrational*, where he is making a distinction between early Greece and later Greece in the same way that I am.

I would say that it is wrong to call Japan a shame culture, although the pattern seems to be there. It is most certainly a conscious society. But there is also some indication that the hemispheres may be connected in a slightly different way in the Japanese. There is some fascinating research coming out on that by Tsunoda, finding that the relationships between the hemispheres both in understanding language and writing language is not identical to what it is in our culture.[7]

But what I'm trying to say is that as I am using shame and guilt, I'm talking about the pure shame society — which is not a conscious society. I'm talking about the Homeric Greeks, the Greeks before Mycenae, and other bicameral civilizations.

Now the second part of your question was how can you be shamed by a group around you unless you are conscious of what they are doing? I would go back to what I described yesterday at the beginning about what consciousness is not. Consciousness is not being aware of another person. Awareness takes place non-consciously. Consciousness comes in later.

Just the way if you say, "No!" to a dog — whether the dog has done anything wrong or not — it will put its tail between its legs. At least an obedient dog will. It will try to hide or show you this shame posture. So

7. See Tadanobu Tsunoda, "Functional Differences Between Right- and Left-Cerebral Hemispheres Detected by the Key-Tapping Method," *Brain and Language*, 1975, *2* and "Difference in the Mechanism of Emotion in Japanese and Westerner," *Psychotherapy and Psychosomatics*, 1979, *31*.

you can say, "How can the dog feel that shame unless the dog is aware?" Certainly the dog is aware of that "no," but it isn't consciousness. It isn't introspective, reflective consciousness — a metaphorical mind built up, as I've tried to express in these two lectures, back at a certain time in history, in this agony of indecision, and in our own culture, in children between the ages of four and six, where we can still see it develop.

Thank you very much for being a very fine audience.

# CHAPTER 38

# The Consequences of Consciousness: Harvard University Discussion

Q: You noted that a number of the first religious leaders and philosophers all lived at about the same time: Lao Tzu, Confucius, Buddha, Socrates, Zarathustra. It always struck me, especially after I read your book, that something was happening at this time.

JAYNES: Yes — the question which you probably all heard, is why do we have this period where everything seems to be changing all over the world? I of course think it is due to consciousness. This is a hard thing to say sometimes. I've stressed Greece because the record is there. But if we find that in China the same thing was happening, how does it get over to China? They didn't have planes to fly over there — but there were trade routes. And all I can say is that indeed there was this diffusion of consciousness very quickly.[1]

It could be that Greece was not the first to develop consciousness. It's just the best record. Consciousness could have developed first in Egypt perhaps, with its long ancient history. But there was all this trade going back and forth, and I do think it is due to trade, and that it didn't happen completely independently in China and India.

So when you find Buddha coming just after 600 B.C., at the same time as Solon in Greece — he lived around 600 B.C. — why should that be happening all at once? This has been remarked on by many people and all I can say is that I think it is the diffusion of consciousness. And Buddhist teaching is very conscious.

---

Transcribed and edited from a question and answer session following Julian Jaynes's "The Consequences of Consciousness" lecture, presented at Harvard University on December 3, 1988 at a conference dedicated to discussing his theory.
1. For more on the transition from bicameralism to consciousness in China see Michael Carr, "The *Shi* 'Corpse/Personator' Ceremony in Early China," in Marcel Kuijsten (ed.), *Reflections on the Dawn of Consciousness* (Henderson, NV: Julian Jaynes Society, 2006). — *Ed.*

Q: You indicated there was not a physiological change to bring about the end of the bicameral mind? So what initiated it then? Why didn't it take place 2,000 years before that, or 10,000 years before that, or 10,000 years after that?

JAYNES: Well, first I don't think it was due to a biological change. But with every psychological change there is a biological change. Even right now, because you've been listening to me — whether you've been bored or interested — there is a change that has happened in your brain, even though it is very minute.

Now in the breakdown of the bicameral mind, I think that there were greater biological changes, in that whole areas of the cortex were being suppressed and inhibited. I think it is Wernicke's area on the right hemisphere. I think that it was inhibited in this chaos. This is something that is possible in neurology — areas can be inhibited. Then something indeed replaced that. So there were biological changes in that sense but I think that they were brought about culturally. I emphasize the malleability of the brain and how much it can change.

The second part of your question was "Why didn't it happen at an early time?" I think it is because of the progression of things that it happened when it did. Why didn't man evolve a million years earlier than he did? Those questions are very hard to answer — evolution had to go in certain gradual steps. You have to remember that the population of the world back at the time that this was beginning — let's say around 10,000 B.C. — I think it comprised no more than two million people. Then population develops, particularly when you have the bicameral mind coming in, that allows people to live in cities and allows the success of these agricultural communities. So the reason all this didn't happen before is you have to have human beings in a certain concentration for this to happen, and you have to have the right conditions for that. You could even look at climate. There is evidence that the climate around 10,000 B.C. was changing.

# Index

JULIAN JAYNES (1920–1997) is author of the popular, influential, and controversial *The Origin of Consciousness in the Breakdown of the Bicameral Mind*. He taught psychology at Princeton University from 1966 to 1990 and lectured widely on consciousness and related themes.

MARCEL KUIJSTEN is Founder and Executive Director of the Julian Jaynes Society. His other books are *Gods, Voices, and the Bicameral Mind: The Theories of Julian Jaynes* and *Reflections on the Dawn of Consciousness: Julian Jaynes's Bicameral Mind Theory Revisited*.